PHI DELTA KAPPA SYMPOSIUM ON EDUCATIONAL RESEARCH

HUMANISTIC EDUCATION
Visions and Realities

EDITED BY
Richard H. Weller
University of North Carolina, Greensboro

A Phi Delta Kappa Publication

distributed by

McCutchan Publishing Corporation
2526 Grove Street
Berkeley, California 94704

ISBN: 0-8211-2256-8
Library of Congress Catalog Card Number: 77-071196

© 1977 by McCutchan Publishing Corporation
All rights reserved

Printed in the United States of America

BOARD OF DIRECTORS OF PHI DELTA KAPPA, 1976-77

OFFICERS

Bill L. Turney
President

Gerald S. Leischuck
Vice-President

Rex K. Reckewey
Vice-President

William K. Poston
Vice-President

Ray Tobiason
Vice-President

DISTRICT REPRESENTATIVES

Gerald L. Berry
District I

Jerome G. Kopp
District II

J. Ed York
District III

Cecil K. Phillips
District IV

Don L. Park
District V

Phillip G. Meissner
District VI

Carrel M. Anderson
District VII

PROFESSIONAL STAFF

Lowell C. Rose
Executive Secretary

Stanley Elam
Editor

Wilmer K. Bugher
Associate Executive Secretary

William J. Gephart
*Director,
Center on Evaluation,
Development and Research*

Robert E. McDaniel
*Director of
Administrative Services*

PHI DELTA KAPPA SYMPOSIA ON EDUCATIONAL RESEARCH

First Annual Phi Delta Kappa Symposium on Educational Research, University of Virginia, 1959 (Out of print)

Research Design and Analysis, Second Symposium on Educational Research—University of Minnesota, 1960 (Out of print)

Dissemination and Implementation, Third Symposium on Educational Research—University of Oregon, 1961 (Out of print)

Simulation Models for Education, Fourth Symposium on Educational Research—Indiana University, 1962 (Out of print)

Education and the Structure of Knowledge, Fifth Symposium on Educational Research—University of Illinois, 1963 (Out of print)

The Training and Nurture of Educational Researchers, Sixth Symposium on Educational Research—Ohio State University, 1964 (Out of print)

Improving Experimental Design and Statistical Analysis, Seventh Symposium on Educational Research—University of Wisconsin, 1965 (Out of print)

Learning Research and School Subjects, Eighth Symposium on Educational Research—University of California, Berkeley, 1966 (Out of print)

Bayesian Statistics, Ninth Symposium on Educational Research—Syracuse University, 1967 (Published by F. E. Peacock)

Tenth Symposium on Educational Research—Salt Lake City, 1968 (Proceedings not published)

Educational Evaluation and Decision Making, Eleventh Symposium on Educational Research—Ohio State University, 1969 (Manuscript central to but not a report of the proceedings. Published by F. E. Peacock)

Leaderhip: The Science and the Art Today, Twelfth Symposium on Educational Research—Bloomington, Indiana, 1971 (Published by F. E. Peacock)

Accountability: A State, a Process, or a Product? Thirteenth Symposium on Educational Research—Bloomington, Indiana, 1973 (Published by Phi Delta Kappa)

Humanistic Education: Visions and Realities, Fourteenth Symposium on Educational Research—University of North Carolina, Greensboro, 1976 (Published by Phi Delta Kappa and distributed by McCutchan Publishing Corporation)

SCHEDULE
PHI DELTA KAPPA NATIONAL SYMPOSIUM
ON HUMANISTIC EDUCATION

University of North Carolina, Greensboro   January 26-28, 1976

January 26, 1976

9:00-9:20	Welcome and Introduction—**Robert B. Ingle,** University of Wisconsin, Milwaukee
9:20-9:50	Overview of the Symposium—**James B. Macdonald,** University of North Carolina, Greensboro
10:00-11:00	Paper 1: What Do Schools Teach? **Michael W. Apple** (presenter), University of Wisconsin, Madison, and **Nancy R. King,** Wheelock College
11:00-12:00	General Discussion of Paper 1
1:30-2:30	Paper 2: Social Action and Humanistic Education—**Fred M. Newmann,** University of Wisconsin, Madison
2:30-3:25	General Discussion of Paper 2
3:35-4:35	Paper 3: An Interpersonal Approach to Humanizing Education—**David N. Aspy,** Texas Woman's University (presented by Flora Nell Roebuck, Johns Hopkins University)
4:35-5:30	General Discussion of Paper 3

January 27, 1976

9:00-9:50	Discussion of the Proceedings of the First Day
10:00-11:00	Paper 4: Education for Human Development—**Ralph Mosher,** Boston University
11:00-12:00	General Discussion of Paper 4
1:30-2:30	Paper 5: The Odyssey of Organizational Theory and Implications for Humanizing Education—**Thomas J. Sergiovanni,** University of Illinois, Urbana-Champaign
2:30-3:25	General Discussion of Paper 5
3:35-4:35	Paper 6: A Critical Analysis of the Social and Economic Limits to the Humanizing of Education—**Walter Feinberg,** University of Illinois, Urbana-Champaign
4:35-5:30	General Discussion of Paper 6

January 28, 1976
9:00-10:00   Group Discussion: Cultural Consciousness and the Concern for Humanizing Education
10:10-11:10   General Discussion of All Papers
11:10-12:00   Summary Discussion and Wrap-up

This symposium was jointly sponsored and planned by Phi Delta Kappa and the Center for Educational Reform, University of North Carolina, Greensboro, and hosted by the School of Education at the university. Members of the Center for Educational Reform are: James B. Macdonald, Robert M. O'Kane, David E. Purpel, and Richard H. Weller.

Preface

The topic for this symposium on humanistic education was not selected because of a certainty that schooling is (or is becoming) more dehumanized. Rather, it was selected because of the debate wherein some assert that it is, others that it is not. Further, at the time the topic was selected a number of approaches to humanizing schooling were being presented to professional educators and to educational policy makers. Phi Delta Kappa's Research Advisory Committee agreed that this was a propitious time for a symposium on the topic and asked James Macdonald at the University of North Carolina, Greensboro, to arrange a planning session.

The planning team decided to ignore the debate and to focus, instead, on possible approaches to humanizing the formal educational experience. The major question is not whether education is a humanizing or a dehumanizing experience. Such thinking, although typical of the dichotomous logic too often found in problem-solving efforts, is not always helpful, especially insofar as the formal educational experience is simultaneously humanizing *and* dehumanizing. Formal education is an institution designed at least in part to help young people to develop pride in their work and gain feelings of self-worth; to learn to accept and get along with people who think, dress, and act differently; to develop good character and self-respect; to learn the responsibilities of citizenship. Learning to understand and accept oneself and learning concern for others and how to interact with them harmoniously and productively are humane goals that are not accomplished accidentally; nor do they occur naturally. If schools can develop greater skill in achieving these goals, society in general and individuals in particular can grow in their ability to create situations that allow humaneness to flourish.

At the same time the institution created to accomplish these humane ends remains a system. Like all systems, it has undergone progressive specialization of its parts, and the work to be accomplished by the parts has become standardized, making the part more specialized and more efficient in accomplishing the subtask. Systems standardized largely to achieve efficiency are not bastions of kindness or benevolence. Instead, they exert ever-increasing pressure for everyone to do the same thing in the same way at the same time, a movement that seems antithetical to humanistic goals.

Some argue that the solution to this dilemma is deschooling or treating every individual as a unique case. This is unacceptable for at least two reasons. First, it demands unlimited resources. Second, humanizing education seems to require something for the individual as well as something from the individual. One must learn that there are constraints as well as freedoms and learn how to live productively within both the freedoms and the constraints. A setting in which constraints are an integral part seems a more likely place for desired humanization to take place.

It is interesting that, just as a coin has a head and a tail, formal education is both humanizing and dehumanizing. Given this consideration and the fact that formal education is a dynamic system, humanizing education is a continuing challenge, and the planning team is to be saluted for not bogging down in the either-or debate.

In developing the program, the planning team by design built in some tensions. These included the questions: What are we really teaching? What is the hidden curriculum? Next it focused on apparently competitive approaches that might be undertaken in search of greater humanism in the education system, including curricular, psychological, sociological, and organizational ones. This volume contains the ideas of leading proponents of different approaches and discussions of those ideas. It is not presented as *the* answer. In fact, it discourages the effort to try to seek *the* answer. Neither the education system nor the humanity of mankind are stable entities. They are dynamic and ever changing. This volume does not even constitute the search for *an* answer; instead, it seeks direction. The participants, although partial to the directions they espouse, concur that the task of humanizing education is a difficult one and that there are no clear signposts.

The difficulty of the task is documented by the discussion sessions. Even the participants, all genuinely concerned about the way other people are treated, were unable to break out of some of our unwritten and inordinately inhumane rules for how one effectively participates in a symposium. Conversion from the spoken to the written word has masked much of this, but it was recorded in the tapes of the discussions. In transcribing those tapes I became acutely aware of the fact that many statements made by discussants started while someone else was talking. When a person wanted to participate, it would appear that he listened for a slight hesitation and then interrupted. It was also evident that the women who participated, in spite of repeated efforts, seldom got the floor.

These are not inconsiderate people. It was evident that they are deeply concerned about the humane treatment of all. It would seem that our system is deeply afflicted with operational patterns, patterns deeply ingrained in our day-to-day behaviors, that do *not* rest on humanistic principles. Further, the reward systems in our culture reinforce dehumanizing operational patterns. In the education system, as in other natural systems, internal modifications are directed at making it more effective and more efficient at doing what it is now doing. Continued examination and continued redirection are needed if we are even to see alternatives for humanizing the formal educational experience.

One critical ingredient seems to have been overlooked in the development of the symposium. The focus was on humanizing education. But, what would a humanized education look like, sound like, feel like? The planning team, having recognized "humanizing education" as a concept with a variety of meanings, considered two strategies. One called for a presentation that would define the concept and propose a single definition as the central thrust of the effort. The second was to leave definition to proponents of the various approaches. The second strategy was followed in the belief that it more nearly follows the state of our art today. A totally accepted, carefully articulated definition of the concept still does not exist. It was believed that any attempt to generate a single one that would serve as the central thrust for the symposium would either distort reality by creating the mirage that one exists or lock the symposium into the refutation of any projected definition.

A body of irrefutable research that supports this or that definition of "humanizing education" simply does not exist. We do not, individually or collectively, develop personal definitions of the term based on cold empirical data. Our values play the predominant role.

The meaning of the term, for each of us, evolves from the interactions of our values, our predispositions, and the hard data we encounter. That is why the planning team asked that definition be a facet of any approach proposed as a means of humanizing education in an effort to understand more clearly the value bases on which a given approach rests.

The symposium opened with a paper by Michael Apple and Nancy King that focused on "the hidden curriculum." What is it that is being done in the education system? The authors used an in-depth study of the early phases of a kindergarten class to establish the fact that the accomplishments of schooling are much broader than the stated curriculum. The observations led to the conclusion that, in the particular classroom being studied, the children were learning to distinguish between work and play and developing attitudes toward work. The authors, in the presentation and in the discussion, asserted that they were unable to answer the question, "What is *the* hidden curriculum?" They indicated, however, that what they observed was *a* hidden curriculum that had long-range cultural ramifications. They suggested that the question of educational purposes should be raised continually and that extensive investigative work is needed to determine the purposes that are being served in any given setting and to show the discrepancy between "should" and "are."

The presentations by Fred Newmann, Ralph Mosher, and David Aspy approached the humanizing of education by focusing on treatment of the individual. Newmann's premise was that competence and the search for it are universal psychological building blocks. He asserted that there is "a fundamental human need to affect one's social destiny that cannot be satisfied simply through economic affluence or exclusive preoccupation with private activity." He proposed a social action curriculum to build the individual student's competence to affect his or her environment.

Mosher built on an earlier essay that focused on individual and human development, and he urged a move toward developmental psychology as the basis for human development. While admitting that we are a long way from surety about the consecutive developmental tasks needed, he did express certainty that we need to order experiences to stimulate development and that we have the outline for gaining that surety. In light of those convictions, Mosher discussed the curriculum he would follow at present. It represents a

Preface   xiii

"best guess to date" as to how to stimulate human development and develop human rationality, character, social responsiveness, and action.

The third approach relies on an interpersonal skills focus. Aspy's presentation, given by Flora Roebuck, proposed that "the prime value of all human endeavors is facilitation to its fullest potential of the physical, intellectual, and emotional health of man—both individually and collectively." Aspy argued that all of us must develop and use our interpersonal skills at the highest possible level, and he based his work on research done through the National Consortium for Humanizing Education (NCHE). Aspy suggested that interpersonal skills training for all teachers be a guiding structure for the curriculum.

In the belief that institutions make a contribution to the degree of humanism in our world, the planning team asked Thomas Sergiovanni to speak to the question of organizational modifications that might contribute to the humanizing of education. Sergiovanni charted ". . . the evolution of organizational thought" and analyzed the impact of various schools of thought on the structure and operation of schools. With reference to humanistic values, he concluded that the evolution is "not so glorious." After making the point that the details of the "most effective" organizational structure depend upon the institution's mission, he used a matrix that displayed six subsystems of the school as an organization and stated the general nature of each as it related to the four organizational schools.

In the final presentation Walter Feinberg analyzed social and economic limits to the humanizing of education. He specified what to him was the essential relationship between schooling and society, how that relationship established both the goals and limits of education, and how the prominent theories of education still serve the relationship. His analysis suggests that schools are as humane as they can be within the society they serve and that an expansion of the humaneness of schools is unlikely without a similar change in society.

For me, the symposium seemed to indicate the following:
—There is a desire, verbalized by a growing number of people, to increase the humaneness of schooling in order simultaneously to treat individual learners more humanely and to assist them in being more humane with others.

- The satisfaction of that desire is complicated, in part owing to a lack of specificity and consensus as to what "humanized education" is and in part owing to the symbiotic relationship between society and its schools.
- Schooling, as it is conducted in different locations, is contributing to the values, habits, attitudes, expectations, and skills of the learner in subtle and pervasive ways that are not usually discussed.
- The search for ways to humanize schooling is paying off both in terms of programmatic approaches focused on the learner and of organizational modification.

This summary suggests two major directions. First, a definition of humanism is needed. One of the limiting factors in the symposium, it seemed to me, was the absence of an explicit, common definition of the concept being discussed. Despite the fact that humanism is a dynamic concept, communication about it and problem solving related to it could be improved if there were a systematic effort to define it. A definition or a composite set of definitions does not evolve by chance. Deliberate steps must be taken to develop, weigh, and gain consensus on a comprehensive definition of humanism. Richard Weller's introduction, although it was not presented at the symposium, has been included in this volume because it is a step in the needed direction. Second, the limiting aspects of the relationship between society and schooling demand attention. Schooling will not value the individual if society does not. Efforts to humanize education must be both intra- and extramural.

William J. Gephart, Director
Center on Evaluation, Development
and Research

Contributors

Michael W. Apple is a Professor in the Department of Curriculum and Instruction at the University of Wisconsin, Madison. He is the author of articles and monographs in curriculum theory and development on such topics as ideology and curriculum thought, the hidden curriculum, and students' rights. He has been particularly interested and active in the field of political and human rights for students and teachers. His most recent publications include *Educational Evaluation: Analysis and Responsibility* (McCutchan, 1974) and *Schooling and the Rights of Children,* with Vernon Haubrich (McCutchan, 1975). The guiding theme behind most of his work is the investigation of how schools function in the reproduction of an unequal social order.

David N. Aspy is presently Professor of Counselor Education on leave from Texas Woman's University in Denton, Texas. He was principal investigator for the National Consortium for Humanizing Education in which massive amounts of data from multi-ethnic settings consistently showed that the teacher's level of empathy most effectively predicts student and teacher performance in school. His major professional quest has been for a technology to humanize education, with special emphasis on classroom settings. Among his major publications are *Toward a Technology for Humanizing Education* (Research Press, 1972) and *Physical Health for Educators,* with June H. Buhler (North Texas State University Press, 1975).

Walter Feinberg is a Professor of Educational Policy Studies at the University of Illinois, Urbana-Champaign. His interest in educational theory and policy emerges from both his studies in social philosophy and his work in curriculum reform and program

xv

development for public school and university students. He is the editor of *Work, Technology and Education*, with Henry Rosemont (University of Illinois Press, 1975); the author of *Reason and Rhetoric: The Intellectual Foundations of Twentieth Century Educational Policy* (John Wiley and Sons, 1975), which was selected by *Choice* as one of the outstanding books published in education that year; and the editor of the forthcoming *Equality and Social Policy*.

Nancy R. King is an Assistant Professor on the faculty of Wheelock College, Boston, Massachusetts. King's research interests include the issues of methodology in educational inquiry, the hidden curriculum, the role of schooling in our society, and nondevelopment research of children's culture. She is currently involved in a study of the meanings of work and play in a wide variety of open-classroom settings. Active in preservice teacher education, the development of day-care centers, and scholarly research in curriculum history and theory, she has also published in *Educational Theory*.

James B. Macdonald is Distinguished Professor of Education at the University of North Carolina, Greensboro. A leading theorist and advocate of humanistic education for more than twenty years, Macdonald's initial interest in empirical educational research led him to a focus on humanistic educational reform and finally to his current emphasis on theoretical and theological perspectives on education. He has published widely in a variety of journals and texts, has been active in educational reform movements and program development for the public schools, and is currently at work on a book entitled *Theology of Education*.

Ralph Mosher is Professor and Chairman of the Department of Counselor Education at Boston University. From a beginning as a teacher, vice-principal, guidance counselor, and hockey coach in a small town in Nova Scotia, he went on to teach counseling psychology and curriculum at Harvard University. His major theoretical and developmental interests have been in the area of deliberate psychological education in the schools and in devising programs for emotional, intellectual, and moral development in the schools. He is the author of *Guidance: An Examination*, with Richard Carle and Chris Kehas (Harcourt, Brace and

Contributors

World, 1965), and *Supervision: The Reluctant Profession*, with David Purpel (Houghton-Mifflin, 1972), as well as numerous articles in professional journals.

Fred M. Newmann is Professor of Curriculum and Instruction at the University of Wisconsin, Madison. His main interest is education for community participation. With Donald Oliver at Harvard University, he developed a social science curriculum to teach students the analysis of public controversy, now widely used in secondary schools, and has lately been conceptualizing and advocating a curriculum that helps students to translate analysis into intelligent action. His most recent work, *Education for Citizen Action: Challenge for Secondary Schools* (McCutchan, 1975) is a rationale for the combination of reflection and action in secondary education, and it is currently being translated into a Citizenship Participation Curriculum Project at the University of Wisconsin, Madison.

Robert M. O'Kane is Professor of Administration at the University of North Carolina, Greensboro. A former teacher, principal, superintendent, director of combined Department of Defense Schools (Europe-Africa-Middle East), and Dean of the School of Education at the University of North Carolina, Greensboro, he is currently focusing his attention on moral dilemmas in decision making, value conflicts, and social and cultural change. A member of the Board of Directors of the Center for the Study of Man and His Values, O'Kane is in the process of writing a book on "man, his values, his dilemmas, and his decisions."

David E. Purpel is Professor of Education at the University of North Carolina, Greensboro. Previously he was Associate Professor and director of the Training of Teacher Trainers Program at Harvard University. A man of broad interests, he has recently written or edited books in supervision (*Supervision: The Reluctant Profession*, with Ralph Mosher [Houghton-Mifflin, 1972]), curriculum (*Curriculum and the Cultural Revolution*, with Maurice Belanger [McCutchan, 1972]), and moral education (*Moral Education: It Comes with the Territory*, with Kevin Ryan [McCutchan, 1967]). His current major interest lies in the area of moral education—moral dilemmas inherent in the process of schooling, human development, and the ethical and moral values transmitted by schools.

Flora Nell Roebuck's interest in humanizing education has led her to accept a position as Assistant Professor of Education Applied in Medicine at Johns Hopkins University School of Medicine, where she will be doing research in the quality of life both for patients and medical personnel and in the psychological bases of the facilitative interpersonal condition. Formerly she was Assistant Professor at Texas Woman's University. The author of numerous books, technical reports, and articles, her most recent book, *A Lever Long Enough,* coauthored with David N. Aspy (Taylor Publishing Co., in process) should appear this summer.

Thomas J. Sergiovanni is a Professor in the Department of Educational Administration and Supervision at the University of Illinois, Urbana-Champaign. A prolific theorist and author, he has written or edited six books in the last eight years in the areas of organizational and administrative theory, educational supervision, and organizational leadership. He has concentrated primarily on the attempt to conceptualize the tensions that exist between the political, administrative, and educational subsystems of schools as organizations. He is presently involved in developing more naturalistic alternatives to current teacher evaluation and supervision strategies.

Richard H. Weller is an Associate Professor at the University of North Carolina, Greensboro, and formerly Assistant Professor at Harvard. After careers as an oceanographic geophysicist and later as a science teacher in the public schools, he went on to work with the science curriculum and teacher education. His current interest is in the area of alternative theories of curriculum and supervision. He has been active in the design and support of alternative schools, particularly those focusing on the development of educative communities. He is the author of *Verbal Interaction in Instructional Supervision* (Teachers College Press, 1971) and is currently at work on a book on theories of instructional supervision.

Contents

Preface, by William J. Gephart   ix

Introduction, by Richard H. Weller
One Perspective on Humanistic Education   1

First Presentation, by Michael W. Apple and Nancy R. King
What Do Schools Teach?   27
Discussion   48

Second Presentation, by Fred M. Newmann
Social Action and Humanistic Education   65
Discussion   100

Third Presentation, by David N. Aspy
An Interpersonal Approach to Humanizing Education   121
Discussion   141

Fourth Presentation, by Ralph Mosher
Education for Human Development   159
Discussion   182

Fifth Presentation, by Thomas J. Sergiovanni
The Odyssey of Organizational Theory and Implications for Humanizing Education   197
Discussion   232

Sixth Presentation, by Walter Feinberg
A Critical Analysis of the Social and Economic Limits to the Humanizing of Education   247
Discussion   270

Reactions

Reactions and Reflections, by David E. Purpel   289
Humanistic Education from an HRD Viewpoint, by Flora Nell Roebuck   301
Humanism and the Politics of Educational Argumentation, by Michael W. Apple   315
The Fourth Face of Humanism, by Robert M. O'Kane   331

Epilogue, by James B. Macdonald
Toward a Platform for Humanistic Education   343

Notes   357

Introduction

Richard H. Weller

One Perspective on Humanistic Education

Any discussion of humanistic education raises difficult questions of definition and perspective. The concept has itself become so broad and complex that one could almost argue that all education is fundamentally humanistic in intent. No longer does the mention of humanistic education call to mind the classics, or man-centered versus God-centered education, or even a broadly conceived education in humanistic studies. Seemingly contradictory focuses now compete for recognition. There is little doubt that science as a value system and discipline of knowledge and technology as a tool for dealing with problems and improving man's lot have a rightful place in modern notions of humanistic education. Nor can one say that "affective education" is necessarily more humanistic than systematic reading instruction.

Many educators have turned their attention to processes deemed "humanistic" in one way or another. There is, however, little consensus among those who consider humanistic education to be a process. Most agree that personal invalidation of students and oppressive academic competition have little place in humanistic education. But are sensitivity, love, and indirect teaching sufficient where a definite sense of direction is lacking? And how does one determine what is a humane course of action toward any particular person? In some cases this might mean acceptance and encouragement; in others it might mean outright challenge, contradiction, or even presentation of appropriate content!

There are those who would argue that to define humanistic education is to destroy it, but most educators would probably accept a broad definition, for example, that it is "education designed to increase the dignity and quality of life for all people." Such a definition offers little in the way of clarification, however. One man's "dignity" might be another's intractable stubbornness, and who is to determine what "quality" means for another?

Implications of a Deficit Orientation

These conceptual and programmatic problems obviously derive from many sources, but there appear to be at least three salient factors behind the present uncertainty and disarray: a prevailing deficiency orientation, fragmented vision, and overemphasis on programmatic concerns. Like the "chicken and the egg," these factors are related, and it is difficult to decide "which came first." The deficiency orientation of education, because it appears to be the most basic, is the first to be considered here.

Most professions, it seems, reflect a broad and subtle deficit orientation, with a focus on deficiencies, ills, and problems. Stress is on the expert application of knowledge and skill to correct the ills of individuals and society, through processes of diagnosis and prescription. The intent is to cure a specific problem and to preserve and defend against further outside threat. One unintended consequence, a preoccupation with the ills themselves, blinds practitioners to the ultimate aim of their profession: the doctor preoccupied with disease and injury can lose sight of an integrated vision of "health"; the lawyer working to solve legal problems and protect his clients' rights may not retain a broader concept of justice; mental health workers may concentrate on mental illness to the exclusion of a vibrant notion of positive "being in the world."

Educators are not immune. Even the casual observer can see that public attention centers largely on students who are not being helped, rather than on those who are; that teaching frequently overreacts to the complaints of teachers in succeeding grades or to public pressure resulting from poor test results; that the difficulties of getting and holding a job preoccupy educators and students at all levels; that the tests themselves measure far better what students do not know than what they do.

In deficiency orientations, particularly in a "crisis atmosphere," there is a tendency to focus on an oversimplified part removed from the context of the whole, which is related to the second element in the current paralysis of humanistic education—fragmented vision. It is difficult to maintain a "sense of the whole," much less to communicate it, when under attack or pressure to solve specific problems. Indeed, one of the major ways of dealing with crisis in such an orientation is to develop narrow specializations where one can claim expertise and be held accountable only for the part, rather than the whole. This disconnectedness and fragmentation can alter perspective, confuse directions, and diffuse overall responsibility.

Given the specialization that arises from a deficiency orientation, it is natural for concern to focus on the success of particular individual operations—out of context, unrelated to preceding or succeeding operations, and blind to the student as a unique person in a particular life situation. The net effect is to define the person in terms of a particular program or process, and humanistic education becomes "problem solving" in a narrow programmatic and technical sense that does not help the individual deal with the continuing dilemmas associated with "being human."

This same deficit orientation characterizes much of public education: objectives, operations, evaluation, and even language (consider the critical distinctions between the term "responsibility" and the more recent favorite "accountability"). Language is both a vehicle for communicating ideas and the basis for a particular world view. It is extremely difficult to conceptualize something for which there is no readily accessible terminology. Thus, the shift to a deficiency-oriented language has repercussions far beyond the intended scope of operations. Language, as an all-enveloping medium, both implies and generates particular assumption systems that may be all but invisible to the user.

It is an initial assumption in this introduction that a pervasive deficit orientation toward education, reinforced by evident successes of technological approaches in other areas such as medicine, has helped to obscure a positive vision of humanness and a broad perspective on the education of whole persons. Subtly and inexorably man has come to be seen as the sum total of his deficiencies, ills, and problems. In effect, a person to be educated becomes equated with a problem to be solved.

A Transcendent Conception of Man's Humanness

A deficit orientation is not, however, the only alternative. There are also what could be called a consonant orientation (dealing with balance, harmony, and integration) and a transcendent orientation (dealing with ultimate possibility beyond what would be considered ordinary limits). The theoretical language of the professions, if not their practice, frequently operates on a consonant level, and the further one gets from the pressures of practice in a crisis atmosphere the more consonant or even transcendent the language can become. Practitioners argue that this is a luxury available only to those who do not have to "get on with it"; scholars argue that nothing is ultimately more "practical" than really good theory.

If one accepts an alternative orientation for humanistic education in contrast to the prevailing deficit one, this does not necessarily prevent fragmented vision or a narrow programmatic focus. It might, however, serve to place current practice into a clearer perspective. It might also help to counter some of the more destructive aspects of current educational practice, particularly the negative "self-fulfilling prophesy" and the effects of deficiency labeling and sorting.

In order to avoid the problem of overly romanticizing a transcendent view of man, consider a positive vision of man's basic humanness in the context of active life and relationship. If humanistic education were defined as education to produce "fully functioning human beings," what would this imply? Does anybody know a fully functioning human? Even so, it might be possible to catch infrequent glimpses or "snapshots" of such functioning, possibly in the characteristics of peak experiences described by Abraham Maslow[1] or in the attributes of children who have not yet been "shut down" by the accumulated distress and invalidation that are inevitably part of our world.

Most parents have remarked on the zest with which their youngsters first encounter the world—open questioning, probing, and active physical engagement. We remark how aware and curious children are, how boundless and exuberant their affections, how courageous their ventures into the unknown. At times, as adults, we may experience feelings, however brief, of childlike wonder, or love, or delight in accomplishment. Are these transcendent experiences and feelings merely aberrations, or primitive stages through which we must pass en route to "maturity"? Or are they, rather, clues to a more natural side of our humanity that has been overlooked or, even worse, deformed by the ceaseless pushing, probing, and shaping of our "educative world"?

What clues do these glimpses provide of the natural way for humans to be, given the chance? In the first place, fully functioning people take an active delight in challenge, investigation, solving problems, and exploring the possibilities of their world. A basic aspect of humanity appears to be the exercise of creative ingenuity, the development of competence, and the use of enormous intelligence in actively dealing with the surrounding world. Human beings seem naturally disposed toward processes of inquiry, the will to action, and delight in personal agency.

A second but qualitatively different aspect of fully functioning humans can only be called love, including both receiving and giving through understanding, communication, and genuine personal concern. Humans appear to have an innate capacity and desire to relate interpersonally, to participate in a vibrant sense of community, to be cooperative and morally responsible with one another. We are, in effect, one with our fellow humans in a transactional way. Each participant grows from both giving and receiving.

Yet a third aspect of fully functioning humanity is a zestful consciousness of life and an immediate presence and openness to all aspects of the world around us and to the actualization of the potential and uniqueness within us. This can be characterized as personal authenticity and as freedom from psychological and spiritual debilitation. All persons have at least the possibility of a joyous and transcendent awareness of wholeness, well-being, and vibrant "presence in the world."

It appears that most psychological analyses of human "needs" and, indeed, most spiritual and philosophical analyses of human "oughts" (for example, the golden rule) can be encompassed within these three distinct areas of positive human functioning. That they are infrequently expressed in most people may be primarily a function of the dehumanizing effects of society that distort or suppress their natural emergence.

I contend that a transcendent view of persons in active life and relationship can be developed from particular instances of peak human functioning and that it is precisely this interactive combination of effective and active use of power, love and mutual responsibility, and vibrant awareness that characterizes what is uniquely human. Thus, alternative views of human beings frequently expressed in the literature—the mechanistic view of man as an object to be shaped and determined from without; the social view of man as definable only through his interactions in a particular culture or community; the biological view of independent organisms genetically flowering, each in a unique direction—all are distorted and fragmented glimpses of the whole.

If an educator believes that the potential for full humanity is imminently present in each person and that it is possible for persons to grow and "heal" themselves with effective help in areas that are stuck or distorted, then the charge of humanistic education becomes clear. I would argue that each of the three areas of development is necessary for full humanity, that none is ultimately sufficient or even possible without the others, and that the charge of humanistic education is to promote their simultaneous development in each person.

It may indeed be argued that this analysis commits the "naturalistic fallacy" (confusing or combining fact and value, going from the "is" to the "ought"), but the basic charge of the educator remains: from an understanding of what is, to move toward an ideal of what should be. In a sense, it does "go with the territory." The question of values has always been paramount in education. There can be little doubt, like it or not, that the job of the educator is heavily value laden, and the essential task is a moral one: to develop the values, attitudes, knowledge, and skills of other human beings in particular valued directions. Neutrality is rarely possible or even desirable in the classroom.

I would argue that precisely what education needs in the present context is a strong statement of values with respect to a positive and holistic conception of humanity—however undefinable and unattainable this may appear to be. What better area in which to risk committing the "naturalistic fallacy" than in a transcendent vision of man's fullest humanity? I propose one such vision, involving a conception of three interrelated areas of transcendent human functioning: effective action, compassionate responsibility, and zestful awareness of life.

These appear to correspond to three major domains of human civilization: societal organization of the elements of technical production, distribution of power, and relationship to the external physical and political world; cultural systems of interpersonal value, shared meaning, and common heritage; and personal and spiritual domains of ego development, individual human potential, and spiritual relationship. Those who would pursue reform by focusing on any single area are misguided, be that area the reconstruction of society, the reformation of culture, or the actualization of individual human beings.

Relationship and Interdependence

It does not seem accidental that these also correspond historically to three of the most fundamental aims of education: technical competence, induction into cultural membership, and personal or spiritual growth and therapy. It is also evident that these are interrelated and interdependent. Significant educational reform must involve all three areas. If we recognize that development in any one area is not enough, that social action, community responsibility, and personal development are interdependent, then we can begin to understand the nature of the problem.

Indeed, it appears that what usually happens both in society and in schooling is an imbalance that can become dangerously distorted. For example, effective and creative action (where appropriate steps are taken on the basis of the reality of the total situation) requires perspective and support. A sense of community helps one to develop shared meanings, positive directions, and a moral context for action. Also, the communal relationship provides the personal security to "move out," the encouragement and even push to action, and the promise of support. How often have we charged our leaders to action and then abandoned them when the going got rough? Neglecting the communal context for action or power results in such distortions as industrial "progress" without consideration for the effects of human dislocation or blight and a technological mentality that encourages saturation bombing without respect for moral implications or effect on human beings, whether "enemy" or "innocent."

Similarly, communities remain innocent of the effective use of power at their peril. The economic, social, and political world exhibits trenchant inequality and unjust distribution and application of power. Love is not enough! Communities require protection from outside destruction. Indeed, some of the most striking instances of the emergence of man's basic sense of moral responsibility and manifestations of love occur when there is an active external threat to community, from persecution, war, or natural disaster. But protection alone is not enough. A broader notion of community requires that effective action be taken to liberate all persons, everywhere, from oppression of all kinds.

In another domain, effective action and the development of personal competence are directly related to a sense of self: openness to alternatives, flexibility of response, and the ability to avoid being incapacitated by emotional overload or stress. The major obstacles to what we are able to do frequently lie in the area of what we think or believe we can do, and enormous resources of human potential become mired in fear, self-doubt, and emotional distress. The negative self-fulfilling prophesy, whatever its roots (prejudice, invalidation, or feelings of powerlessness), may well be the major obstacle to human emergence.

But this is a two-way street. One's sense of self and personal identity are largely a function of what one is willing and able to do. Risking new challenge and actively operating on the world around us provide both a context and a push for growth. The most effective psychological liberation movements appear to combine personal reflection with commitment to action. In actively dealing with the world we learn about ourselves in new and powerful ways. How we feel about ourselves is directly related to how well we learn and our ability to cope and grow, but it is through new challenge and active coping that we enlarge the basic sense of self.

This emergence or self-actualization is also intimately related to community and love. Personal development cannot long exist in isolation from others. Much personal meaning comes from involvement with shared meanings and interpersonal responsibility, and the courage to grow requires support, encouragement, and perspective. We desperately need effective help from those who love us, both to let us see through the masks we create to hide our feelings of impotence and fear and to enable us to break through. A major problem with some recent psychological liberation movements has been their isolation from active involvement with community. Many have been hedonistic and self-centered, where individuals "do their own thing" without concern for their fellowman or where "self-expression and authenticity" are used to bludgeon and humiliate others. In other cases the psychologically or spiritually "saved" have withdrawn to peripheral warrens of noninvolvement.

Similarly, communities need liberated and authentic individuals to keep them honest and alive. Love and responsibility must coexist to prevent abuses of dependency, xenophobia, and elitism: mob rule and a sense of superiority have powered oppression in the face of minimum courageous opposition; a sense of "patriotism" has led to the vilification of conscientious objectors; moral fervor has allowed heretics to be burned and apostates to be shunned in the search for "salvation."

It would appear that genuine humanistic education must be involved with all three of the major areas of human functioning (effective action, compassionate responsibility, and personal growth), individually and in interaction. Indeed, virtually all statements of humanistic educational aims and rationales for practice involve this vision of youngsters actively growing in self-concept and self-respect, community responsibility and understanding, and personal environmental competence. Implied also, but rarely expressed, is the critical concept of interdependence: that challenge must be balanced by support, that personal growth implies concomitant responsibility, and that effectiveness is largely dependent on self-esteem.

Distortions in Practice

The difficulty for the humanistic educator lies primarily in maintaining balance when actively attempting to promote change. We must continually resolve the dilemmas associated with interdependence: any action produces repercussions on community and self; the course of personal growth frequently challenges accepted notions of appropriate behavior; a strong sense of community may produce both dependency and conformity.

These dilemmas are aggravated by the need for educators to establish priorities, to implement specific programs translating aims into practice, and to demonstrate their effectiveness. Educators frequently operate on their own priorities, which may be more a function of their needs (for power, relationship, or identity) than those of their students. Also, programmatic alternatives contain within themselves the seeds for generating their own ends. Not only is there a danger of ends justifying means, but it is also possible that means generate their own inappropriate ends.

Possibly the most difficult problem lies in the area of assessment and evaluation. It is far more difficult to assess what is really happening in the areas of community and personal development than in the area of effective action, and evaluation has become the classic example of the tail that wags the educational "dog." Conceptual difficulties and different time frames involved in consensual and personal modes of evaluation have been critical in upsetting the needed educational balance.

It would appear that each of the three areas of human functioning has become isolated in educational practice and reform. Each has led to a separate vision of "humanistic education" with its own disciples, world view, and modes of educational practice. In this process we have unraveled the individual strands of man's humanity and set them up in isolation, even in competition, in the schools. The time is already late to transform the accelerating warfare among these movements into a more holistic thrust toward mankind's fuller emergence.

It is possible here to see the effects of a deficit orientation "collapsing" an integrated view of man into fragmented elements. The deficit language has become so specialized and polarized that communication among groups has virtually broken down. This incipient conflict is quite real. In the cause of humanistic education, the "scientists," the "scholastics," and the "personalists" of education have developed competing ideologies so strong that communication is difficult and compromise is tantamount to heresy. Because of the focus on separate aspects of man's basic humanity, singularly distorted views of human nature are developing, each with its accompanying value system and assumptions about the aims and practices of humanistic education that represent nothing less than alternative world views. While these are only fractional views of man, they give the appearance of completeness and integration. A perspective on alternative views of humanistic education could provide a context for examining individual contributions to the symposium and for proposing possible areas of synthesis.

The Metaphoric Perspective

Rather than dealing with conventional categories, I propose using the framework of alternative metaphors for viewing the approaches to humanistic education. Metaphors are analogies to contexts that are well known and experientially vivid. They embody a wide range of emotional and cognitive associations, and frequently lead to an integrated understanding that is lost in more technical or theoretical analysis. Since I contend that each of these approaches to education embodies an integrated set of attitudes, values, and assumptions about the nature of man and his development—a set that erroneously implies a comprehensive vision of man—the metaphor seems appropriate as a vehicle for seeing and understanding. It is frequently used in education (for example, seeing the student as a jug to be filled with knowledge), but it is as often abused by being extended too far or too literally. Metaphors do, however, enable us to examine different models along a continuum of complexity or focus (such as the "family school," the "factory school," the "corporation school"[2]).

As a heuristic, what I would characterize as instrumental, tribal, and organic metaphors can be used to examine education. Each should be viewed along a continuum from deficit to consonant to transcendent orientations toward human functioning and development. At the intersections (a metaphor oriented in a given way) familiar models or perspectives on educational practice are visible.

An *instrumental* metaphor for education has an active, problematic focus. It implies that education has technical qualities operating on the basis of functional control and change. Scientific or pragmatic knowledge and technological operations with feedback control tend to predominate. Focus tends to be primarily on the nature of the "instrument" or methodology, and the effectiveness and efficiency of its use. In a *tribal* metaphor the image of the social and cultural group predominates. Here the critical variables include communication and relationships among people; shared meanings acquired through tradition, ritual, and participation in a common value system; and conceptions of duty, responsibility, and moral obligation. The educational metaphor of the tribe may encompass initiation to the family, church, and nation, as well as to the "community of scholars" and the "brotherhood of man." The *organic* metaphor focuses on the natural growth of an individual organism through biological processes of development, maturation, and differentiation. Considering the nature of the individual and the species, what environmental conditions hinder or facilitate growth? What unique potential lies in the individual's genes? What is the evolutionary history and potential of the species? In education the analogy to promoting individual growth is clear.

The following table shows how specific instructional and organizational patterns relate to the framework.

Orientation	Educational patterns, by metaphor		
	Instrumental	Tribal	Organic
Transcendent (reformulation and liberation)	Social reconstruction	Cultural reformation	Personal fulfillment
Consonant (accommodation and balance)	Social effectiveness	Communal involvement	Personal development
Deficit (preservation and correction)	Social utility	Cultural preservation	Self-discipline

Metaphoric Consideration of Educational Orientations

Instrumental Education

The instrumental metaphor implies an objective to be shaped or changed in particular ways, an instrument (be it tool, machine, or human being) used in appropriate fashion, and certain criteria for determining effective or efficient accomplishment. One must also consider at least the purpose, context, and broader implications of the change itself, the suitability and capabilities of the instrument, and the motives of the utilizer.

In the context of humanistic education the source of educational objectives in an instrumental metaphor is society itself[3] (or the educator's vision of a better society)—the needs of individuals to function well in a changing technological world and the demands of society for effective, useful members who will have a creative impact on its maintenance or development. One might say, with Jürgen Habermas,[4] that this metaphor operates within the human interest in control, through the empirical-analytical sciences and the normative social sciences. Focus is on understanding, control, and, ultimately, improvement of the external world through feedback-monitored action. The humanistic intent is to give man effective control over himself and the world around him.

In a *deficit* orientation, the instrumental metaphor finds expression in the remedying of societally defined deficiencies and the developing of useful skills and practical knowledge to fit students into society in appropriate ways. Stress is on the maintenance and preservation of society itself, and the shaping of the individual to fit societal needs. Examples in education include vocational and technical training, as well as more complex uses of programming and simulation. While the oppressive "factory school" may be a thing of the past, its close relatives persist in what I would call a "social utility" perspective.

The same metaphor in a *consonant* orientation focuses on the effective interaction of man with various aspects of society. While also stressing systematic knowledge and skill, the emphasis is on problem posing and problem solving, effective coping strategies, and the processes of career exploration and development. In educational practice we can see evidence of the comprehensive or "corporation school" with multiple levels and alternatives according to the student's ability and interest. One might call this a "social effectiveness" perspective.

Within a *transcendent* orientation the individual student becomes a primary change agent *on* society, applying knowledge and skill directly to the problems of creating a better political, economic, and social world. Concern is with the environmental, moral, and human impact of technology and social structures with a view toward shaping a better world in which to live. All transcendent orientations move the educator and the student out of the world of schools and preformulated curricula and into a broadly different realm of education—in this case the real social world in a "social reconstruction" perspective.

Tribal Education

Turning to the tribal metaphor, we find major stress on persons living, working, and relating to one another in the primary context of community, communication, and communion. It is within the "tribe" that one finds support, love, and personal relationship. In its fullest extension one can experience a vibrant sense of shared meaning in active life and tradition, mutual empathy and responsibility, and a living interpersonal morality based on positive concern and compassion. The focus on society changes to an emphasis on cultural understanding, a coherent system of values, and participation. This metaphor embodies strong cognitive and moral associations.

In the context of humanistic education the objectives may derive from the traditions, values, and understandings of a particular culture, frequently represented by time-honored disciplines that convey knowledge and meaning. This educational metaphor operates within the human interest in consensus—mutual understanding, group identity, pluralistic meanings—and has given rise to the hermeneutic-historic sciences. Rather than experimentation and empirical analysis, these sciences involve immersion in the entire contextual framework of life and relationship. The humanistic intent is to help people develop responsibility and meaning in communion with one another.

The *deficit* orientation of the metaphor provides the image of a tribe under siege or external pressure. Stress is on the preservation and restoration of the cultural heritage and on imbuing the student with this heritage and meaning system. There is strict adherence to cultural norms of behavior and belief, correction of social deviance, discipline, and conformity. Classic examples can be found in education—the parochial school, the yeshiva, the Latin grammar school, and others—testimony to the fact that this "cultural preservation" perspective has frequently provided the major rationale for schooling. Despite current emphasis on fundamental skills and preparation for the world of work, research on the hidden curriculum indicates that this orientation still permeates much of the covert functioning of the public schools.

In a *consonant* orientation there is an interactive effect, both between the person and his tribe and also among tribes. Active participation, cooperation, democratic citizenship, shared values, and responsibility are emphasized, and there is stress on improving human relationships and promoting multicultural understanding. The broad focus of liberal education, current curriculum developments emphasizing the structure and modes of inquiry of various disciplines (such as introduction to the "community of physicists") recent curricular concern for moral and values education, multiethnic programs —all come within the "communal involvement" purview.

Finally, but all too rarely, there is evidence that some educators operate within what I would call the "cultural reformation" perspective in the context of a tribal metaphor. If one considers the *transcendent* view of man's communal relationship and responsibility, the focus is on the creation of morally just and utopian communities of consent, the development of genuine cultural pluralism, and the active destruction of all forms of oppression, injustice, and inequality. This perspective is usually found outside the world of the "school" as commonly defined.

Organic Education

The final metaphor used in considering humanistic education is the organic one. Perhaps the best analogy to use is that of a flower growing and maturing in a supportive environment. Enormous potential is present within the seed, which needs only to be nurtured (watered and fertilized), protected from environmental damage or distortion, and possibly catalyzed or encouraged from without. Individuals are viewed as growing from within, fulfilling their unique destinies, and striving for inner goals: self-actualization, enlightenment, salvation. Each individual is considered to be unique, incomparable, and significant in and of himself, and the personal worth and boundless potential of each individual must be considered before all else.

Proponents of humanistic education within this metaphor see no knowledge or skills as indispensable. The objectives of education are found within each individual—the unique needs, interests, and potential of the person. With Habermas, one might say that this metaphor operates within the human interest in liberation—both *from* unnecessary external constraint and internal debilitation, and *toward* full human emergence, autonomy, and actualization.[5]

It is possible, however, to operate under a *deficit* orientation, even within this metaphor. Assume that it is a difficult world out there. In order to survive, either physically or spiritually, man needs to develop the self-discipline, strength, and fortitude to cope with and finally surmount the forces of either the world or the devil. In terms of education this means military school, survival training, corrective physical or psychological treatment, and various forms of spiritual asceticism and self-denial. This might be called the "self-discipline" perspective in education.

A more common recent orientation of humanistic educators within the organic metaphor is the *consonant* orientation, in which the "personal development" perspective is stressed. The child-centered aspect of progressive education and current support of open education are among the most obvious examples, and these have been reinforced most recently by "third force" psychologists and the genetic epistemology of Jean Piaget. The objective is to develop individual awareness, personal interests, and individually meaningful knowledge and skills by focusing on creative transactions between the child and his environment (human and physical) and the development of the whole person: happy, mentally healthy, adjusted, and with a sense of personal identity.

Finally, there are some educators who maintain a *transcendent* vision of fully actualized or emergent humans who recognize and delight in their emotional and spiritual lives, are zestfully aware of the reality of their existence, who are cooperative and loving in their relationships with others, and who are actively and responsibly taking charge of their own destinies. Although the ideal is found far more frequently in literature than in practice, particularly in the context of conventional schools, the "personal fulfillment" perspective remains a significant one for humanistic education.

Educational Practices Considered Metaphorically

Such sharp distinctions as those drawn above rarely exist in a pure state, at least in the public schools. This is particularly true where statements of educational intention are concerned. Attempts to set forth the broad purposes and aims of education, to develop rationales for curriculum, to establish theoretical patterns of school organization and governance, even to design new school buildings—all seem to reflect comprehensive and humanistic values and intentions. Rarely do those involved with the public schools try to fragment human functioning in such specific ways, and many would argue that any such attempt would prove to be extremely unfair and unrealistic.

The situation appears different, however, when we turn to actual school practice and observe concrete effects on students. Broad aims get "lost" through translation into behavioral terms; measurable objectives and standardized test scores are dominant concerns; flexible scheduling becomes a modular straitjacket; elitist and personally destructive grouping procedures become accentuated or else transformed into lonely patterns of individualization; maintenance of discipline preoccupies teacher and public alike. Most fundamental arguments in education arise over abuses and distortions that become visible only in the classroom, and the language of dissent frequently falls into the patterns discussed earlier.

There can be little doubt that the public schools generally operate under a broad deficit orientation, that there is a hidden curriculum of social utility and cultural preservation, that instrumental metaphors related to job training and career education hold sway, that children who are not self-disciplined or culturally conforming are invalidated and ultimately pushed out of the system, and that curricula focusing on democratic citizenship and personal development are destroyed in a generally autocratic and oppressive context. A vast gulf exists between expectations and reality.

The public cries out for reform in experientially familiar terms: "What was good enough for us should be good enough for our kids!" "If I didn't learn they'd paddle me good—why don't teachers just do their job?" In this way we transfer to children existing patterns of abuse and competition. Without effective demonstration of alternatives, such cries are hard to refute. The language of accountability falls all too easily into patterns of immediate, visible, and measurable production, and ignores the responsibility to communicate the complexity and wholeness of human development in educational contexts.

Educators must recognize and act on critical interdependencies when attempting educational reform. In reaction to abuses new curricula and alternative schools have been developed that show the same narrow conceptions of human functioning: communal models isolated from the problems of the broader social community contain their own pressures to conform; stress on "togetherness" lacks a sense of appropriate content or direction; emphasis on affective education and self-actualization neglects the development of a sense of responsibility and societal competence; values clarification is divorced from a perspective of genuine moral concern; the efficiency and accountability of "humane" training models overshadow the human context of the intent. In many cases educators have moved "further than they really intended to go," and they have dispensed with much that was genuinely solid and compelling in education.

Given the focus of this conference, humanistic education, I propose this analysis as a vehicle to explore humanistic reform movements. The main danger, of course, is that fragmented analysis could lead to the further fragmentation of thinking on human nature and humanistic education, but there is, on the other hand, the possibility that awareness of different domains of human functioning could lead to a more integrated and holistic vision of man's emergence through education. One possible use of such an analysis is to put current humanistic curriculum developments into perspective, both to avoid problems in implementation, particularly where evaluation is concerned, and to uncover areas of needed development and integration.

Consider the science curriculum, a traditional academic area. Following the launching of the first *Sputnik*, science education clearly reflected abuses in traditional curricula that parallel the three educational metaphors: mechanical learning of dysfunctional knowledge and skills; content that does not reflect the structure, modes of inquiry, or patterns of value and belief that characterize the "community of science"; and oppressive methodologies that have frightened students away from or deadened their interest in the beauty and actualizing potential present in the natural world. The curricula that have resulted (particularly the unique elementary alternatives: *Science: A Process Approach*,[6] *Science Curriculum Improvement Study*,[7] and *Elementary Science Study*[8]) epitomize the instrumental, tribal, and organic metaphors in striking ways. There has, however, been defensiveness and even hostility among developers and users of these newer approaches, and curriculum developers have produced little in the way of a synthesis. The packaging is new, but the children are still being shortchanged. At the same time, the newer approaches do underscore the need for interaction and synthesis. The real potential of such alternatives lies in building on their strengths and integrating them into a more powerful and harmonious whole.

In a nonacademic curriculum area there are similar examples in what is termed "movement education." This focus has developed in reaction to abuses in the deficit orientation of conventional physical education programs: mass calisthenics and routinized skill development; tribal competition, elitism, and distorted ritual; self-denial and self-discipline, often destructive in terms of individual development.

Newer curricula respond to more consonant and transcendent orientations within these same metaphors: development of grace, competence and flexibility in full-body movement; stress on relationship and communication in traditional dance and the development of cooperative and responsible games through group consensus; modern dance and creative movement, with attendant emotional and aesthetic development.

It is important to recognize that, while there are fundamental differences among these metaphors that must be preserved with integrity, there is also a basic interdependence. None can really stand alone in the fullest development of human potential in movement. Unless the public can be educated concerning the basic differences and the need for alternative evaluation criteria, it may prove difficult to implement such programs with integrity. Their potential impact on humanizing the schools, given the opportunity, is, however, enormous.

Perhaps a fitting final consideration is of the concept of "individualization." This is another area that has developed largely because of patterned abuses in traditional instruction, but the term has become almost meaningless because of apparent metaphorical differences. "Ability grouping" fits a basic instrumental metaphor, and individualization, commonly conceived, appears to be an efficient and nondestructive alternative. In the tribal metaphor, however, the concept of the group becomes primary, and its composition and internal dynamics are paramount. The notion of "individualization at all costs" becomes meaningless and destructive. In the organic metaphor, individualization is no longer a means to an end, but, as frequently termed "personalization," it becomes an end in itself. Rather than "controlling for individual differences," as in a mechanical treatment, the very aim of education becomes a celebration of those differences.

This same analytic framework can be used to explore the implications of alternative schools, particularly by examining the potential within a given metaphor. Educators have long agreed that the translation of aims into practice without distortion is exceedingly difficult in preexisting contexts where function frequently follows form. Large comprehensive schools satisfy nobody in their organizational attempts to please everybody. One consequence is a growing emphasis on alternative schools or learning environments that are smaller, more flexible, and more consistent in structure and operation with basic aims.

As in previous examples, the alternatives generally arise from dissatisfaction within a limited metaphorical domain (too much *or* too little skill development, religious enculturation, social control, self-discipline, freedom of expression). Alternatives, from fundamentals schools through various ethnic and religious "cultural" schools and finally "open" schools, show similarly limited perspective. It is instructive to consider the implications of taking a "pure" metaphorical perspective. What are the possibilities in such schools if any one metaphor were to be developed to its fullest? Where would the problems arise?

A major advantage of such consistent implementation lies in protection from the destructive effects of the careless mixed metaphor, a condition extremely common in the public schools. How often have teachers proclaimed organic objectives, but implemented them through archaic tribal means and then proceeded to evaluate through inappropriate instrumental tests? How often are tribal objectives and aims distorted by the rigid instrumental organization of schools? At the very least, within a given metaphor it is possible to have "internal integrity" in the process of agreeing upon, implementing, and evaluating basic aims. Like-minded groups of educational reformers, freed from external constraints and conventions, can often create alternative learning environments quickly and effectively.

A major disadvantage does, however, lie on the opposite side of this same coin. Just as the distorted mixed metaphor is the bane of educational practice, so is the creative mixed metaphor the necessary and ultimate extension of this whole view of humanistic education. Humans simply do not function in narrow metaphorical ways! Humanistic development requires that the three threads of fully functioning humanity be developed and interwoven progressively and continually, both in the school and in the larger social community.

Take, for example, the instrumental metaphor. Highly sophisticated examples have been developed. The prime case might be systematic training of astronauts through developmental skill hierarchies and simulation. Discovery learning and democratic processes would be inefficient and very hard on astronauts! Although simulation training is appropriate in similar areas of limited scope, including some technical and vocational training, the implications become quite different as one progresses from deficit through consonant and transcendent orientations. The problem of divorce from tribal and organic considerations becomes paramount as the scope of the action, the amount of potential power, and the complexity of the situation increase. Deliver us all from psychologically arrested and morally neutral "change agents"! We even now face overdevelopment of instrumental technology applied to schooling and social issues without attendant tribal and organic checks and balances.

The situation with organic schools is similar. Given this society's love affair with technology, genuine organic alternatives require careful protection and nurturance. Most schools deal with organic concerns in instrumental ways: behavior modification, "adjustment counseling," and corrective therapy. Open schools, storefront schools, and romantic "free" schools seek to foster the free and spontaneous growth of unique individuals in the face of, and in competition with, environmental shaping toward predetermined ends.

As alternatives, particularly for children who have already been severely damaged by society, organic schools are necessary and important. They almost never, however, exist in a pure state. The communal definition of "school" logically precludes this. Even A. S. Neill's dictum for Summerhill ("Freedom—not license"[9]) implies that organic growth is inseparable from tribal responsibility. The few relatively pure models generally center on a guru, prophet, or artist whose charismatic power can catalyze unique growth in others. In such cases, however, many have recognized the significant danger of abandoning basic human compassion and withdrawing from active involvement in political and social affairs.

Most alternative schools in a tribal metaphor are examples of a cultural preservation perspective (elite private schools, parochial schools, or ethnic heritage schools). A major advantage has been protection from the destructive mixed metaphor, permitting the transmission of cultural heritage and values in a technically insensitive world. Co-option by instrumental mixed metaphors has been common, as when many "black heritage" schools were transformed into fundamentals schools in order to promote the skills needed to "make it in the system." There is also a destructive impact of organic concerns. More individualistic values and personal concerns have led to withdrawal and alienation from community.

The Need for a New Educational "Tribalism"

Despite the evident problems associated with alternatives in a tribal metaphor (exclusiveness, noninvolvement, defensiveness), the more consonant and transcendent orientations appear to provide a necessary "center" for the development of other realms of human functioning. It is here, I would argue, that major initiatives for humanistic education should be developed—not, as so frequently happens, where the "tribe" or community becomes an end in itself, but rather where the tribe becomes a context or vehicle to accomplish instrumental, organic, and tribal ends at a higher level of relationship.

Fundamentally, both school and society have lost their tribal core, that is, the patterns of relationship and shared value that give direction and meaning to life. The school as a primary functional community has experienced severe shocks in recent years from such factors as school consolidation efforts, crosstown busing, and extensive bureaucratization. Not only has the school's relationship to the surrounding community frequently suffered, but there has also been a breakdown within individual schools and classrooms of a "sense of community"—the system of interrelationships, shared meanings, participation, and mutual concern that characterizes an active and responsible "tribe."

Most recent reform movements and curricular theorizing appear to have concentrated primarily on the relationship of schools or individuals to society (for example, the social reconstruction perspective) or on human development and individuation. These two powerful but frequently opposing positions, strikingly evident in the educational literature, retain their prominence throughout this volume. There is a significant need for corresponding development of tribal reforms and curriculum theorizing.

It is important for educators to ask: How does one facilitate the integration of these areas of human functioning? What is the potential and the role of human dialogue in the educative process?[10] How can a language of affirmation and affiliation be generated for educational communication? What potential is there in the field of hermeneutics, especially in participant hermeneutics, for educational understanding?[11] In what ways is education necessarily a moral enterprise? How can relatively nondistorted human communication take place within educational settings? How can educational research and evaluation come to grips with a broader conceptualization of human functioning? What steps can be taken to reestablish supportive and progressive "tribal" orientations within schools?

If schools are ever to become truly humanistic institutions, and particularly if they are ever to have a humanizing impact on society itself, this tribal core must be reestablished in new and compelling ways. The critical difference might be a tribal conception that focuses outside of itself—on dealing with the external world in creative and powerful ways, on working with the individual to catalyze personal growth, and on opening itself up to more consonant and transcendent functioning.

This shift in tribal or community focus outside of itself is a difficult and somewhat foreign notion, particularly where institutions are concerned. Organizations most commonly do the reverse, using tribal procedures in a manipulative way to maintain their own equilibrium (as when schools focus on "team spirit" and ritualistic loyalty). There is some evidence, however, of powerful ways in which a tribe can serve as a vehicle, support mechanism, and necessary temporary refuge to enable individuals to accomplish other ends if the tribe does not become an end in itself.

Take, for example, some uses of a "tribe" for purposes of rehabilitation. In Alcoholics Anonymous the tribal community serves as primary support and encouragement for curing an addiction; in Synanon, an outgrowth of Alcoholics Anonymous that helps drug abusers, the "tribe" has grown to serve wider functions of curing, personal growth, and dealing more effectively with the external world; and at Delancey Street, an even broader extension that helps former convicts and former addicts, the tribal commitment has extended into the areas of politics, education, and social reform to become a powerful communal-based social movement.[12] The integration of personal development, social action, and tribal responsibility is particularly striking in the last example.

There are similar examples where the school or class community serves as a temporary vehicle for multiple ends—as when a class or group commitment, such as establishing a drug-action center in the community or a cross-age tutoring program, leads to genuine social involvement and some measure of social change, an enhanced sense of social responsibility and relationship, and a heightened competence and self-concept on the part of the students involved. Indeed, it may be that "temporary tribal vehicles" are essential elements of integrated humanistic education in an age when more traditional community and family structures are undergoing dramatic changes.

It is unfortunate that such cases rarely receive much attention in either the public or the educational press, either because they are considered "outside the real business of schooling" or because they get lost in a preoccupation with the piecemeal and specialized aspects of problem solving. One must admit that they are complex, idiosyncratic, and frequently oversensitive to outside interference. It is much easier to define and implement narrow programs with dramatic deficit orientations than to become involved with the complexities and richness of an entire educational experience. Also, current modes of research and evaluation appear unable to deal with the necessary interdependencies. Not only are researchers frequently obsessed with proving a point rather than searching for interactional effects, but they also tend to be wary of nonempirical data. Only rarely are case studies and historical or experiential research efforts recognized for their ability to deal with the subtleties of positive human growth and interaction over time.

But the evidence is beginning to accumulate. It is becoming more evident that growth in different areas of human functioning *is* interrelated, and that programmatic efforts to achieve change in one domain not only require balance from the others but also result in corresponding growth in related areas.[13] The time may indeed be near when an adequately comprehensive perspective on human development and functioning may be related to a growing technology capable of bringing this about. A major hope must be that this will lead to a fuller liberation of that which is most transcendently human in all persons, rather than a more effective means of maintaining current inequalities in both society and the schools.

First
   Presentation

Michael W. Apple
Nancy R. King

What Do Schools Teach?

Schooling and Cultural Capital

One of the least attractive complaints about schools in recent years has been that they are relatively unexciting, boring, or what have you because of mindlessness.[1] The basis of this argument is that schools covertly teach all those things that humanistic critics of schools like to write and talk about—among them, behavioral consensus, institutional rather than personal goals and norms, alienation from one's products—because teachers, administrators, and other educators do not really know what they are doing. Such a perspective is misleading at best. In the first place, it is thoroughly ahistorical. It ignores the fact that schools were in part designed to teach exactly these things. The hidden curriculum, the tacit teaching of social and economic norms and expectations to students in schools, was not as hidden or "mindless" as many educators believe. Such a perspective also ignores the critical task that schools, as the fundamental set of institutions in advanced industrial societies, do perform in order to certify adult competence, and it pulls schools out of their setting within the larger and much more powerful nexus of economic and political institutions that give schools their meaning. That is, schools seem to do what they are in fact supposed to do, by and large, at least in terms of roughly providing dispositions and propensities that are quite functional to one's later life in a complex and stratified social and economic order.

While there is no doubt that mindlessness does exist outside Charles Silberman's mind, neither it, nor venality, nor indifference are adequate descriptive devices in explaining why schools are so resistant to change or why schools teach what they do.[2] Nor is it an appropriate conceptual tool for use in ferreting out what exact kinds of things are taught in schools or why certain social meanings and not others are used to organize school life. Yet it is not just the critics of schools who tend to oversimplify their analysis of the social and economic meaning of schools.

All too often the social meaning of school experience has been accepted as unproblematic by sociologists of education or as merely engineering problems by curriculum specialists and other programmatically inclined educators. The curriculum field especially, among other educational areas, has been dominated by a perspective that might best be called "technological" in that the major interest guiding its work has involved finding the one best set of means to reach prechosen educational ends.[3] Against this relatively ameliorative and uncritical background, a number of sociologists and curriculum scholars, influenced strongly by the sociology of knowledge in both its Marxist or "Neo-Marxist" and phenomenological variants, have begun to raise serious questions about this lack of attention to the relationship of school knowledge to extraschool phenomena. A fundamental basis for these investigations has been best articulated by Michael F. D. Young. He notes that there is a "dialectical relationship between access to power and the opportunity to legitimize certain dominant categories, and the process by which the availability of such categories to some group enables them to assert power and control over others."[4] In essence, just as there is a relatively unequal distribution of economic capital in society, so, too, is there a similar system of distribution surrounding cultural capital.[5] In advanced industrial societies, schools become particularly important as distributors of this cultural capital and play a critical role in giving legitimacy to certain categories and forms of knowledge. The very fact that certain traditions and normative "content" are construed as school knowledge is prima facie evidence of perceived legitimacy.

The argument in this presentation is that the *problem* of educational knowledge, of what is taught in schools, has to be considered a form of the larger distribution of goods and services in a society. It is not merely an analytic problem (What shall be construed as knowledge?), nor exclusively a technical consideration (How do we organize and store knowledge so that children have access to it and can "master" it?), nor solely a psychological concern (How do we get students to learn X?). Rather, the study of educational knowledge is a study in ideology, the investigation of what is considered legitimate knowledge (be it knowledge of the logical type of "that," "how," or "to") by specific social groups and classes, in specific institutions, at specific historical moments. It is, further, a critically oriented form of investigation in that it chooses to focus on how this knowledge, as distributed in schools, can contribute to cognitive and dispositional development that strengthens or reinforces existing and often problematic institutional arrangements in society. In clearer terms, the overt and covert knowledge found within school settings and the principles of selection, organization, and evaluation of this knowledge are valuative selections from a much larger universe of possible knowledge and collection principles. As valuative selections, they must not be accepted as given, but must be made problematic—bracketed, if you will—so that the social and economic ideologies and the institutionally patterned meanings that stand behind them can be scrutinized. It is the latent meaning, the configuration that lies behind the commonsense acceptability of a position, that may be its most important attribute. And these hidden institutional meanings and relations[6] are almost never uncovered if we are guided only by amelioration. As Daniel Kallos has noted recently, there are both manifest and latent "functions" of any educational system. These functions need to be characterized not only in educational (learning) terms but, more importantly, in politico-economic terms. In short, discussions about the quality of educational life are relatively meaningless if the "specific functions of the educational system are unrecognized."[7] If much of the literature on what schools tacitly teach is accurate, then the specific functions may be more economic than "intellectual."

The focus here is on certain aspects of the problem of schooling and social and economic meaning. Schools are viewed as institutions that embody collective traditions and human intentions that are the products of identifiable social and economic ideologies. The starting point might best be phrased as a question: *Whose* meanings are collected and distributed through the overt and hidden curricula in schools? That is, as Marx was fond of saying, reality does not stalk around with a label. The curriculum in schools responds to and represents ideological and cultural resources that come from somewhere. Not all groups' visions are represented and not all groups' meanings are responded to. How, then, do schools act to distribute this cultural capital? Whose reality "stalks" in the corridors and classrooms of American schools? The concern here is, first, to describe the historical process through which certain social meanings became particularly *school* meanings, and thus now have the weight of decades of acceptance behind them. Second, we shall offer empirical evidence of a study of kindergarten experience to document the potency and staying power of these particular social meanings. Finally, we shall raise the question of whether piecemeal reforms, be they humanistically oriented or other, can succeed.

The task of dealing with sets of meanings in schools has traditionally fallen to the curriculum specialist. Historically, however, this concern for meaning in schools by curriculum specialists has been linked to varied notions of social control. This should not be surprising. It should be obvious, though it usually is not, that questions about meanings in social institutions tend to become questions of control.[8] Forms of knowledge—both overt and covert—found within school settings imply relations of power and economic resources and control. The very choice of school knowledge, that is, the act of designing school environments, consciously or unconsciously reflects ideological and economic presuppositions that provide the commonsense rules for educators' thoughts and actions. Perhaps the link between meaning and control in schools can be made clearer by a relatively brief account of curricular history.

Meaning and Control in Curricular History

Bill Williamson, a British sociologist, argues that men and women "have to contend with the institutional and ideological forms of earlier times as the basic constraints on what they can achieve."[9] If one takes this notion seriously in looking at education, what is both provided and taught in schools must be understood historically. Speaking specifically about schools, Williamson notes: "Earlier educational attitudes of dominant groups in society still carry historical weight and are exemplified even in the bricks and mortar of the school buildings themselves."[10]

If we are to be honest with ourselves, the curriculum field itself has its roots in the soil of social control. From its beginnings early in the twentieth century, when its intellectual paradigm took shape and became an identifiable set of procedures for selecting and organizing school knowledge, a set that should be taught to teachers and other educators, the fundamental consideration of the formative members of the curriculum field was that of social control. Part of this concern for social control is understandable. Many historically important figures who influenced the curriculum field (such as Charles C. Peters, Ross Finney, and, especially, David Snedden) had interests that spanned both the field of educational sociology and the more general problem of what should concretely happen in school. Given the growing importance of the idea of social control in the American Sociological Society at the time, an idea that seemed to capture the imagination and energy of so many of the nation's intelligentsia, as well as powerful segments of the business community, it is not difficult to see how it also attracted those people interested in both sociology and curriculum.[11]

Interest in schooling as a mechanism for exerting social control did not have merely sociological origins. Individuals who first called themselves curriculists (men like Franklin Bobbitt and W. W. Charters) were vitally concerned with social control for ideological reasons as well. Influenced strongly by the scientific management movement and the work of social measurement specialists[12] and guided by beliefs that found the popular eugenics movement a "progressive" social force, these men brought social control into the very heart of the field that was concerned with developing criteria to guide selection of those meanings students would encounter in educational institutions.

This is not to say that social control in and of itself is always negative, of course. In fact, it is nearly impossible to envision social life without some element of control, if only because institutions, as such, tend to respond to the *regularities* of human interaction. What strongly influenced early curriculum workers was a historically specific set of assumptions, commonsense rules, about school meanings and control that incorporated not merely the idea that organized society must maintain itself through the preservation of some of its valued forms of interaction and meaning, which implied a quite general and wholly understandable "weak" sense of social control. Deeply embedded in their ideological perspective was a "strong" sense of control wherein education in general and the everyday meanings of the curriculum in particular were seen as essential to the preservation of the existing social privilege, interests, and knowledge of one element of the population at the expense of less powerful groups.[13] Most often this took the form of attempting to guarantee expert and scientific control in society, to eliminate or "socialize" unwanted racial or ethnic groups or characteristics, or to produce an economically efficient group of citizens in order to, as C. C. Peters put it, reduce the maladjustment of workers from their jobs. It is this latter interest, the economic substratum of everyday school life, that will become of particular importance when we look at what schools teach about work and play in a later section of this presentation.

Of course, neither the idea of nor an interest in social control emerged newborn through the early curriculum movement's attempts to use school knowledge for rather conservative social ends. Social control had been the implied aim of a substantial number of ameliorative social and political programs carried out during the nineteenth century by both state and private agencies so that order and stability, and the imperative of industrial growth, might be maintained in the face of a variety of social and economic changes.[14] Walter Feinberg's analysis of the ideological roots of liberal educational policy demonstrates even in this century many of the proposed "reforms" in schools and elsewhere latently serve the conservative social interests of stability and social stratification.[15]

The argument presented so far is not meant to belittle the efforts of educators and social reformers. Instead, it is an attempt to place the current arguments over the "lack of humaneness in schools," the tacit teaching of social norms and values, and similar considerations within a larger historical context. Without such a context, it is impossible to understand fully the relationship between what schools actually do and an advanced industrial economy. The best example of this context can be found in the changing ideological functions of schooling in general and curricular meanings in particular. Behind much of the argumentation about the role of formal education during the nineteenth century in the United States were concerns about the standardization of educational environments, the teaching through day-to-day school interaction of moral, normative, and dispositional values, and economic functionalism. Today these concerns have been termed the "hidden curriculum" by Philip Jackson[16] and others. But it is the very question of its hiddenness that may help us uncover the historical relationship between what is taught in schools and the larger context of institutions that surround them.

We should be aware that historically the hidden curriculum was not hidden at all; instead, it was the overt function of schools during much of their existence as an institution. During the nineteenth century, the increasing diversity of political, social, and cultural attributes and structures "pushed educators to resume with renewed vigor the language of social control and homogenization that had dominated educational rhetoric from the earliest colonial period."[17] As the century progressed, the rhetoric of reform, of justifying one ideological position against that of other interest groups, did not focus merely on the critical need for social homogeneity. The use of schools to inculcate values, to create an "American community," was no longer sufficient. The growing pressures of modernization and industrialization also created certain expectations of efficiency and functionalism among certain classes and an industrial elite in society as well. As Elizabeth Vallance puts it, "to assertive socialization was added a focus on organizational efficiency." Thus, the reforms having the greatest effect on school organization and ultimately the procedures and principles governing life in classrooms were dominated by the language of and an interest in production, well-adjusted economic functioning, and bureaucratic skills. In this process the underlying reasons for reform in a modern industrial society slowly changed from active concern for valuative consensus to a recognized need for economic functionalism.[18] But this could only occur if the prior period, with its search for a standardized national character built in large part through the characteristics of schools, had been both perceived and accepted as successful. Thus it was that the institutional outlines of schools, the relatively standardized day-to-day forms of interaction, provided the mechanisms by which a normative consensus could be "taught." And within these broad outlines, these behavioral regularities of the institution if you will, an ideological set of commonsense rules for curriculum selection and organizing school experience based on efficiency, economic functionalism, and bureaucratic exigencies took hold. The valuative consensus became the deep structure, the first hidden curriculum, which encased the normative economic one. Once the hidden curriculum became hidden, when a uniform and standardized learning context became established and when social selection and control were taken as given in schooling, only then could attention be paid to the needs of the individual or other more "ethereal" concerns.[19]

Thus it was that a core of commonsense meanings combining normative consensus and economic adjustment was built into the very structure of formal education. This is not to say that there have been no significant educational movements toward, say, education for self-development. Rather, it would appear that behind preferential choices about individual needs there is a more powerful set of expectations surrounding schooling that provides the constitutive structure of school experience. As a number of economists have recently noted, the most economically important "latent function" of school life seems to be the selection and generation of personality attributes and normative meanings that enable one to have a supposed chance at economic rewards.[20] Since the school is the only major institution that stands between the family and the labor market, it is not odd that, both historically and currently, certain social meanings that have differential benefits are distributed in schools. But what are these particular social meanings? How are they organized and displayed in everyday school life? It is these questions to which we shall now turn.

Ideology and the Curriculum in Use

The larger concerns with the relationship between ideology and school knowledge, between meaning and control, of the prior section tend to be altogether too vague unless they can be seen as active forces in the activity of school people and students as they go about their particular lives in the classroom. As investigators of the hidden curriculum and others have noted, the concrete modes by which knowledge is distributed in classrooms and the commonsense practices of teachers and students can illuminate the connection between school life and the structures of ideology, power, and economic resources, of which schools are a part.[21]

Just as there is a social distribution of cultural capital in society, so, too, is there a social distribution of knowledge within classrooms. For example, different "kinds" of students get different kinds of knowledge, as Nell Keddie so well documents in her study of the knowledge teachers have of their students and the curricular knowledge then made available to the students.[22] While the differential distribution of classroom knowledge does exist and is intimately linked to the process of social labeling that occurs in schools,[23] it is less important to this analysis than what might be called the "deep structure" of school experience. What underlying meanings are negotiated and transmitted in schools behind the actual formal "stuff" of curriculum content? What happens when knowledge is filtered through teachers? Through what categories of normality and deviance is knowledge filtered? What is the *basic and organizing framework* of normative and conceptual knowledge that students actually get? In short, what is the curriculum in use? Only by seeing the deeper structure does it become obvious that social norms, institutions, and ideological rules are ongoingly sustained by the day-to-day interaction of commonsense actors as they go about their normal practices.[24] This is especially true in classrooms. Social definitions about school knowledge, definitions that are both dialectically related to and rest within the larger context of the surrounding social and economic institutions, are maintained and re-created by the commonsense practices of teaching and evaluation in classrooms.[25]

We shall focus on kindergarten here because it occupies a critical moment in the process by which students become competent in the rules, norms, values, and dispositions "necessary" to function within institutional life as it now exists. Learning the role of student is a complex activity, one that takes time and requires continual interaction with institutional expectations. By focusing on both how this occurs and the content of the dispositions that are both overtly and covertly part of kindergarten knowledge, it is possible to illuminate the background knowledge children use as organizing principles for much of the rest of their school career.

In short, the social definitions internalized during initial school life provide the constitutive rules for later life in classrooms. Thus, what is construed as work or play, "school knowledge" or merely "my knowledge," normality or deviance are the elements that require observation. As we shall see, the use of praise, rules governing access to materials, control of both time and emotion—all make significant contributions to teaching social meanings in school. But as we shall also see it is the meanings attached to the category of work that most clearly illuminate the possible place of schools in the complex nexus of economic and social institutions that surround us all.

Kindergarten experience serves as a foundation for the years of schooling to follow. Children who have attended kindergarten tend to demonstrate a general superiority in achievement in the elementary grades over children who have not attended kindergarten. Attempts to determine exactly which teaching techniques and learning experiences contribute most directly to the "intellectual and emotional growth" of kindergarten children have, however, produced inconclusive results. Kindergarten training appears to exert its most powerful and lasting influence on the attitudes and the behavior of children by acclimating them to a classroom environment. The children are introduced to their roles as elementary school pupils, and it is the understanding and mastery of this *role* that makes for the greater success of kindergarten-trained children in elementary school.

Socialization in kindergarten classrooms includes the learning of norms and definitions of social interactions. It is the continuous development of a working definition of the situation by the participants. In order to function adequately in a social situation, those involved must reach a common understanding of the meanings, limitations, and potential the setting affords for their interaction. During the first few weeks of the school year, the children and the teacher forge a common definition of the situation out of repeated interaction in the classroom. When one common set of social meanings is accepted, classroom activities proceed smoothly. Most often these common meanings remain relatively stable unless the flow of events in the setting ceases to be orderly.

Socialization is not, however, a one-way process.[26] To some extent, the children in a classroom socialize the teacher as well as becoming socialized themselves, but children and teacher do not have an equal influence in determining the working definition of the situation. On the first day of school in a kindergarten classroom, the teacher has a more highly organized set of commonsense rules than the children do. Since the teacher also holds most of the power to control events and resources in the classroom, it is his or her set of meanings that is dominant. This does not mean that teachers are free to define the classroom situation in any way they choose. As we saw earlier in this presentation, the school is a well-established institution, and it may be that neither the teacher nor the children can perceive more than marginal ways to deviate to any significant degree from the commonsense rules and expectations that set the school apart from any other institution.

The negotiation of meanings in a kindergarten classroom is a critical phase in the socialization of the children. The meanings of classroom objects and events are not intrinsic to them, but are formed through social interaction. As with other aspects of the definition of the situation, these meanings may shift initially. At some point, however, they become stable, and they are not likely to be renegotiated unless the orderly flow of events in the classroom is disrupted.

The meanings of objects and events become clear to the children as they participate in the social setting. The *use* of materials, the nature of authority, the quality of personal relationships, the spontaneous remarks, as well as other aspects of daily classroom life, contribute to the children's growing awareness of their roles in the classroom and their understanding of the social setting. Therefore, to understand the social reality of schooling, it is necessary to study it in actual classroom settings. Each concept, role, and object is a social creation bound to the situation in which it is produced. The meanings of classroom interaction cannot be assumed; they must be discovered. The abstraction of these meanings and the generalizations and insights drawn from them may apply to other contexts, but the researcher's initial descriptions, understandings, and interpretations require that social phenomena be encountered where they are produced, that is, in the classroom.[27]

By observing and interviewing the participants in one particular public school kindergarten classroom it was established that the social meanings of events and materials became fixed remarkably early in the school year.[28] As with most classroom settings, the socialization of the children took overt priority during the opening weeks of school. The four most important skills the teacher expected the children to learn during those opening weeks were to share, to listen, to put things away, and to follow the classroom routine. It was her statement of her goals for the children's early school experiences that constituted the definition of socialized behavior in the classroom.

The children had no part in organizing the classroom materials and had little effect on the course of daily events. The teacher made no special effort to make the children comfortable in the room or to reduce their uncertainty about the schedule of activities. Rather than mediating intrusive aspects of the environment, she chose to require that the children accommodate themselves to the materials as presented. When the noise from another class in the hallway distracted the children, for example, the teacher called for their attention, but she did not close the door. Similarly, the individual cubbies where the children kept their crayons, smocks, and tennis shoes were not labeled although the children had considerable difficulty remembering which cubby was theirs. Despite the many instances of lost crayons and crying children, the teacher refused to permit the student teacher to label the cubbies. She told the student teacher that the children must learn to remember their assigned cubbies because "that is their job." When one girl forgot where her cubby was on the day after they had been assigned, the teacher pointed her out to the class as an example of a "girl who was not listening yesterday."

The objects in the classroom were attractively displayed in an apparent invitation to the class to interact with them. Most of the materials were placed on the floor or on shelves within easy reach of the children. Opportunities to interact with materials in the classroom were, however, severely circumscribed. The teacher's organization of time in the classroom contradicted the apparent availability of materials in the physical setting. During most of the kindergarten session, the children were not permitted to handle objects. The materials, then, were organized so that the children learned restraint; they learned to handle things within easy reach only when permitted to do so by the teacher. The children were "punished" for touching things when the time was not right and praised for the moments when they were capable of restraint. For example, the teacher praised the children for prompt obedience when they quickly stopped bouncing basketballs after being told to do so in the gym, but made no mention of their ball-handling skills.

The teacher made it clear to the children that good kindergartners were quiet and cooperative. One morning a child brought two large stuffed dolls to school and put them in her assigned seat. During the first period of large group instruction, the teacher referred to them saying, "Raggedy Ann and Raggedy Andy are such good helpers! They haven't said a thing all morning."

As part of learning to exhibit socialized behavior, the children learned to tolerate ambiguity and discomfort in the classroom and to accept a considerable degree of arbitrariness in their school activities. They were required to adjust their emotional responses to conform to those considered appropriate by the teacher. They learned to respond to her personally and to the manner in which she organized the classroom environment.

After some two weeks of kindergarten experience, the children had established a category system for defining and organizing their social reality in the classroom, but interview responses indicated that the activities in the classroom did not have intrinsic meanings. The children assigned meanings depending upon the context in which each was carried on. The teacher presented the classroom materials either as a part of instruction, or, more overtly, she discussed and demonstrated their uses to the class. This is a critical point. The use of a particular object, that is, the manner in which we are predisposed to act toward it, constitutes its meaning for us. In defining the meanings of the things in the classroom, then, a teacher defines the nature of the relationships between the children and the materials with contextual meanings bound to the classroom environment.

When asked about classroom objects, the children responded with remarkable agreement and uniformity. The children divided the materials into two categories: things to work with and things to play with. No child organized any material in violation to what seemed to be their guiding principle. Those materials which the children used at the direction of the teacher were work materials. They included books, paper, paste, crayons, glue, and other materials traditionally associated with school tasks. No child chose to use these materials during "play" time early in the school year. The materials which the children chose during free time were labeled play materials or toys. They included, among other things, games, small manipulatives, the playhouse, dolls, and the wagon. The meaning of classroom materials, then, is derived from the nature of the activity in which they are used, and the separate categories for work and play emerge as powerful organizers of classroom reality early in the school year.

Both the teacher and the children considered work activities more important than play activities. Information which the children said they learned in school was what the teacher had told them during activities they considered "work." Play activities were permitted only if time allowed and the child had finished the assigned work activities. Observation data revealed that the category of work had several well-defined parameters that sharply separated it from the category of play. First, work includes any and all teacher-directed activities; only free time activities were called "play" activities by the children. Activities such as coloring, drawing, waiting in line, listening to stories, watching movies, cleaning up, and singing were called "work." To work, then, is to do what one is *told* to do, no matter what the nature of the activity involved. Second, all work activities, and only work activities, were compulsory. For example, children were required to draw pictures about specific topics on numerous occasions. During singing the teacher often interrupted to encourage and exhort the children who were not singing or who were singing too softly. Any choices permitted during work periods were circumscribed to fit the limits of accepted uniform procedure.

During an Indian dance, for example, the kindergarten teacher allowed the "sleeping" children to snore if they wanted. After a trip to the fire station all of the children were required to draw a picture, but each child was permitted to choose whatever part of the tour he liked best as the subject of his picture. (Of course it is also true that each child was required to illustrate his favorite part of the trip.) When introducing another art project, the teacher said, "Today you will make a cowboy horse. You can make your horse any color you want, black or gray or brown." At another time she announced with great emphasis that the children could choose three colors for the flowers they were making from cupcake liners. The children gasped with excitement and applauded. These choices did not change the fact that the children were required to use the same materials in the same manner during work periods. If anything, the nature of the choices emphasizes the general principle. Not only was every work activity required, but every child had to start at the designated time. The entire class worked on all assigned tasks simultaneously. Further, all of the children were required to complete the assigned tasks during the designated work period. In a typical incident that occurred on the second day of school, many children complained that they either could not or did not want to finish a lengthy art project. The teacher said that everyone must finish. One child asked if she could finish "next time," but the teacher replied, "You must finish now."

In addition to requiring that all the children do the same thing at

What Do Schools Teach?

the same time, work activities also involved the children with the same materials. During work periods the same materials were presented to the entire class simultaneously. All of the children were expected to use work materials in the same way. Even seemingly inconsequential procedures had to be followed by every child. For example, after large-group instruction on the second day of school, the teacher told the children, "Get a piece of paper and your crayons, and go back to your seats." One child, who got her crayons first, was reminded to get her paper first.

The products or skills which the children exhibited at the completion of a period of work were also supposed to be similar or identical. The teacher demonstrated most art projects to the entire class before the children got their materials. The children then tried to produce a product as similar to the one the teacher had made as possible. Only those pieces of art work that most closely resembled the product the teacher used for demonstration were saved and displayed in the classroom.

Work periods, as defined by the children, then, involved every child simultaneously in the same directed activity with the same materials to the same ends. The point of work activities was to *do* them, not necessarily to do them well. By the second day of school, many children hastily finished their assigned tasks in order to join their friends playing with toys. During music, for example, the teacher exhorted the children to sing loudly. Neither tunefulness, rhythm, nor purity of tone and mood were mentioned to the children, or expected of them. It was enthusiastic and lusty participation that was required. Similarly, the teacher accepted any child's art project upon which sufficient time had been spent. The assigned tasks were compulsory and identical, and, in accepting all finished products, the teacher often accepted poor or shoddy work. The acceptance of such work nullified the notion of excellence as an evaluative category. Diligence, perseverence, obedience, and participation—behaviors of the children, not characteristics of their work—were rewarded. In this way the notion of excellence became separated from the concept of successful or acceptable work and was replaced by the criteria of adequate participation.

The children interviewed in September, and again in October, used the categories of work and play to create and describe their social reality. Their responses indicated that the first few weeks of school were an important time for learning about the nature of work in the classroom. In September no child said "work" when asked what children do in kindergarten. In October half of those interviewed responded with the word "work." All of the children talked more about working and less about playing in October than they had in September. The teacher was pleased with the progress of the class during the first weeks of school and repeatedly referred to the children as "my good workers."

The teacher often justified her presentation of work activities in the classroom in terms of the preparation of the children for elementary school and for adulthood. For example, she believed that work activities should be compulsory because the children needed practice following directions without exercising options as preparation for the reality of adult work. The children were expected to view kindergarten as a year of preparation for the first grade. In stressing the importance of coloring neatly or putting pictures in the proper sequence, the teacher spoke of the necessity of having these skills in first grade and how difficult it would be the following year for children who were inattentive in kindergarten. The children were relatively powerless to influence the flow of daily events, and obedience was valued more highly than ingenuity. Again, this atmosphere was seen as an important bridge between home and future work situations. The teacher expected the children to adjust to the classroom setting and to tolerate whatever level of discomfort that adjustment included.

Thus, as part of initiation into the kindergarten community, young children also receive their first initiation into the social dimension of the world of work. The content of specific lessons is relatively less important than the experience of being a worker. Personal attributes of obedience, enthusiasm, adaptability, and perseverence are more highly valued than academic competence. Unquestioning acceptance of authority and the vicissitudes of life in institutional settings are among the first lessons learned in kindergarten. It is in the progressive acceptance as natural, as the world "tout court," of meanings of important and unimportant knowledge, of work and play, of normality and deviance, that these lessons reside.

Beyond a Rhetorical Humanism

As the late Italian social theorist Antonio Gramsci argued, the control of the knowledge-preserving and producing sectors of a society becomes a critical factor in enhancing the ideological dominance of one group of people or class over less powerful groups of people or classes.[29] If this is so, the role of the school in selecting, preserving, and passing on conceptions of competence, ideological norms and values, and often only certain social groups' "knowledge"—all of which are embedded within both the overt and hidden curricula in schools—is of no small moment.

At least two aspects of school life serve rather interesting distributive social and economic functions. As the growing literature on the hidden curriculum and the historical and empirical evidence provided here seek to demonstrate, the forms of interaction in school life may serve as mechanisms for communicating normative and dispositional meanings to students. Yet, the body of school knowledge itself— what is included and excluded, what is important and what is unimportant—also often serves an ideological purpose.

As one of this paper's authors has demonstrated in an earlier analysis, much of the formal content of curricular knowledge is dominated by a consensus ideology. Conflict, either intellectual or normative, is seen as a negative attribute in social life.[30] Thus, there is a peculiar kind of redundancy in school knowledge. Both the everyday experience and the curricular knowledge itself display messages of normative and cognitive consensus. The deep structure of school life, the basic and organizing framework of commonsense rules that is negotiated, internalized, and ultimately seems to give meaning to our experiences in educational institutions, appears to be closely linked to the normative and communicative structures of industrial life.[31] How could it be otherwise?

Perhaps we can expect little more from school experience than what has been portrayed here, given the distribution of resources in the United States and given the wishes of a major segment of the citizenry. Nor can one dismiss the hypothesis that schools actually do work. In an odd way they may succeed in reproducing a population that is roughly equivalent to the economic and social stratification in society. Thus, when one asks of schools, "Where is their humaneness?" perhaps the answers may be more difficult to grapple with than the questioner expects.

For example, one could interpret this presentation as being a statement against a particular community's commitment to education or as a negative statement about particular kinds of teachers who are "less able than they might be." This would, however, be inaccurate.

The city in question is educationally oriented. It spends a sizable proportion of its resources on schooling and feels that it deserves its reputation as having one of the best school systems in the area, if not the nation.

Just as important, we should be careful not to view this kind of teacher as poorly trained, unsuccessful, or uncaring. Exactly the opposite is often the case. The classroom teacher who was observed is, in fact, perceived as a competent teacher by administrators, colleagues, and parents. Given this, the teacher's activities must be understood not merely in terms of the patterns of social interaction that dominate classrooms, but in terms of the wider patterning of social and economic relationships in the social structure of which he or she and the school itself are a part.[32]

When teachers distribute normative interpretations of, say, work and play like the ones we have documented historically and currently here, one must ask, "to what problems are these viable solutions for the teacher?"[33] "What is the commonsense interpretive framework of teachers and to what set of ideological presuppositions does it respond?" In this way we can situate classroom knowledge and activity within the larger framework of structural relationships which, either through teacher and parent expectations, the classroom material environment, the focus of important problems, or the relationship between schools and, say, the economic sector of a society, often determine what goes on in classrooms.

This work alone will not confirm the fact that schools seem to act latently to enhance an already unequal and stratified social order. It does, however, confirm a number of recent analyses that point out how schools, through their distribution of a number of social and ideological categories, contribute to the promotion of a rather static framework of institutions.[34] Thus, our argument should not be seen as a statement against an individual school or any particular group of teachers. Rather, it suggests that educators need to see teachers as "encapsulated" within a social and economic context that by necessity often produces the problems teachers are confronted with and the material limitations on their responses. This very "external" context provides substantial legitimation for the allocation of teachers' time and energies[35] and for the kinds of cultural capital embodied in the school itself.

If this is the case, as we strongly suggest it is, the questions asked should go beyond the humanistic level (without losing their humanistic and emancipatory intent) to a more relational approach. While educators continue to ask what is wrong in schools and what can be done (Can our problems be "solved" with more humanistic teachers, more openness, better content, and so on?), it is of immense importance that we begin to take seriously these questions: "In whose interest do schools often function today?" "What is the relation between the distribution of cultural capital and economic capital?" "Can we deal with the political and economic realities of creating institutions that enhance meaning and lessen control?"

Rachel Sharp and Anthony Green summarize this concern about a rhetorical humanism rather well:

... [We] want to stress that a humanist concern for the child necessitates a greater awareness of the limits within which teacher autonomy can operate, and to pose the questions, "What interests do schools serve, those of the parents and children, or those of the teachers and headmaster?" and "What wider interests are served by the school?", and, possibly more importantly, "How do we conceptualize 'interests' in social reality?" Therefore instead of seeing the classroom as a social system and as such insulated from wider structural processes, we suggest that the teacher who has developed an understanding of his [or her] location in the wider process may well be in a better position to understand where and how it is possible to alter that situation. The educator who is of necessity a moralist must preoccupy himself with the social and [economic] preconditions for the achievement of his ideals. Rather than affirming the separation of politics and education, as is done within commonsense liberal assumptions, the authors assume all education to be in its implications a political process.[36]

Thus, to isolate school experience from the complex totality of which it is a constitutive part is to be a bit too limited in one's analysis. In fact, the study of the relationship between ideology and school knowledge is especially important for understanding the larger social collectivity of which we are all a part. It enables us to begin to see how a society reproduces itself, how it perpetuates its conditions of existence through the selection and transmission of certain kinds of cultural capital upon which a complex yet unequal industrial society depends, and how it maintains cohesion among its classes and individuals by propagating ideologies that ultimately sanction existing institutional arrangements that can cause unnecessary stratification and inequality in the first place.[37] Can we afford not to understand these things?

Discussion

Participants (in order of speaking): *James B. Macdonald, Michael W. Apple, Walter Feinberg, Nancy R. King, David E. Purpel, Ralph Mosher, Fred M. Newmann, Thomas J. Sergiovanni,* and *Flora Nell Roebuck*

Macdonald: Would you elaborate a little? I gather that, although you are not totally pessimistic, you are doubtful that what we usually call humanistic reform actually deals with more latent structures. Is this one of your major messages?

Apple: Right. It might be that there would be no significant difference in the economic substrata in day-to-day life in schools or in the passivist positions that are taught if you had a more or less humane teacher or if formal content were changed or not changed.

Feinberg: The teacher in the example given is obviously as much a victim as the student.

Apple: Exactly!

Feinberg: The hidden curriculum that the teacher articulates is probably latent within the person. Isn't the school also a victim-spectator? That is, these are all functions of society and forces larger than the school itself. It's a self-sealing cycle. How does one break in? Obviously teacher education institutions have little to do with how teachers behave in classrooms. Children have learned how schools operate even before they enter kindergarten—through playing with other children who have been there.

King: I think one breaks in everywhere at once. It *is* a task for educators. As people concerned with the quality of life and, more specifically, the quality of life for young children, we are duty bound to break in even though the task may seem to be beyond us. In fact, raising ideas of this sort to a level of awareness in educators may be the first step.

Purpel: I want to raise a question of ideology, or the lack of it, among educators. I'm confused about whether or not humanism equals individualism. Is that what we mean by humanistic? There is a second and related question: Is the concept of "meaning" antithetical to control?

Apple: As it is normally used in this society, humanism tends to be couched in a language of individual growth and development. That tends to be a specific historical form; in other countries it is not talked about in that way. As far as the distinction between meaning and control, I see forms of control embodied in forms of meaning. It is difficult to ferret out what forms of meaning are forms of control. Perhaps the more accurate distinction is between necessary and unnecessary control, given a vision of social justice. But the basic argument is that we have to look at *whose* social meanings get into the schools. Which groups do they support? One can then articulate a relationship between what happens in schools, in terms of distribution of meaning, and what children do later.

Mosher: I feel that adolescents, at least young adults, must have rules and social orders and norms and institutional structures to react to developmentally. It is a critical developmental prerequisite in cognitive, moral, and social terms. Indeed, they must attend institutions such as schools. If you examine the definitions of conventional moral reasoning or conventional ego development in psychological terms, it is obvious that there is a critical progression developmentally. Much of the purpose of secondary schooling and experience is in fact to move individuals into a greater correspondence, an ideological sympathy and ability to operate within the norms of ever-larger social units. My reading of developmental psychology says that people *must* move into that structure of thought, consolidate it, and become comfortable with it before they can appropriate it, understand it, and function in it as adults. Certainly this is necessary before they can begin to move to postconventional structures of thinking or action. It could be that people may need considerable experience with what you are describing before they can develop further. In my opinion the critical issue is whether they then move on to the reformulation of those institutions.

Apple: But it's the *content* of those meanings that is critical. I'm not advocating at all that open education is best for every child or that one should have totally free choice. It is not a question of either oppression or nothing; it's a question of the content of those social norms and values that are distributed. It is becoming increasingly important to look at the differential benefits of schooling. The hidden curriculum has to be viewed in two ways. One consideration is what every youngster gets in school, regardless of race, sex, social class, or any other quality, or, what is the social meaning behind schools being schools? A more important consideration, however, is identifying the differential curricula. What different kinds of schooling (content and process) do youngsters get, and does this depend on their future probable positions on the economic ladder? You have to begin to think about what forms of knowledge go to what kinds of youngsters. You can only learn by observing, by seeing the day-to-day forms of interaction, because the curricular content looks exactly the same everywhere. Even achievement scores may also look the same.

Newmann: I'd like to focus on one of the first points made in the presentation: the attempt to uncover the ideology behind curricula or institutions. I'm trying to uncover the ideology behind this presentation. If you are going to implore other people to be frank about their ideologies, I think you have to set an example. On the one hand, I get the message that you are opposed to institutional norms, but not really. You say that such norms are necessary. I get the message that you are not really opposed to institutional norms as such, but, rather, to particular ones that were manifested in some of the examples. Are you against any form of institutionalized role expectations, or are there just particular kinds of roles you find antihumanistic or immoral? Another weakness that relates to "making explicit your ideology," is that you implore *us* to ask the questions: Whose interests are being served by the way the roles are defined and the way knowledge is being distributed? What is the nature of the distribution of the cultural capital? As students, and presumably experts in hidden curriculum, you should *tell* us whose interests are being served. You should tell us how it is being distributed differentially among groups rather than teasing us to ask the question. These are admittedly important questions, but we need some answers, too.

Apple: Let me respond to the second point first. I don't think we know enough to say unequivocally whose interests are being served. This is not a question that has been asked about curriculum, apart from the ideological debates of the 1930's and the early 1940's.

Newmann: If, after intensive study of one classroom, you cannot even begin to suggest whose interests are served in this classroom, who is ever going to be able to help us with that question?

Apple: Let me give you an example that might tie this discussion to your first concern. Much of the rhetoric of schooling is couched in the language of equality of educational opportunity. That is, the schools are there to teach you so that you can get a job. If you look at schools, you find out that those students who succeed have cultural capital when they enter; they come from the social class that has certain expectations built in. The schools accept that and go further. Children who do not have that cultural capital don't make it. That is what compensatory education is about. What I'd like to argue very strongly is that schools were initially designed with certain quite obvious social interests in mind. They were initially intended to socialize the work force. The question, now, is whether that is what we want schools to do. That vaguely humanistic question has been being asked for a number of years. A more important question, to me, goes a step further and asks what social class then reaps the fruits of that labor. We are now verging on Marxism.

Newmann: We've already had that analysis! What I want to know is how this presentation on hidden curriculum advances us in that direction.

Apple: What we can now see is the documentation of the mechanisms by which it occurs in the schools.

Newmann: In that sense I think it was enlightening. From the presentation I can get data establishing that certain kinds of roles are reinforced in the classroom and that children look at work and play in different ways—that's very convincing. This still doesn't answer the question that you raise in the chapter regarding whose interests these roles are serving. Is this milieu differentially distributing the knowledge capital among different groups of children? Does the presentation answer that? You've shown that there are indeed roles and that certain children are rewarded for certain kinds of behavior and others are not. If I tried to answer your question, I'd say that the children who conform to the role expectations get rewards and those who do not are not rewarded. That is, however, simplistic; it doesn't help my class analysis of anything. Am I supposed to conclude that upper-class children are more likely to conform? Or are lower-class children more likely to do so?

Macdonald: It seems to me that we could profitably put this discussion into a broader perspective. My question arises from the social data that are available, data provided by Coleman, Moynihan, Jencks, and Bowles and Gintis, claiming that the school more closely resembles a greased skid. One interpretation of available data is that the quality of what comes out only equals what went in. If this is so, what do schools really do? It seems to me that this is a crucial question, and yours is at least partial and penetrating insight into it. In the case of interactive participation, there simply isn't much documentation. Instead, we talk about schools as agencies that are supposed to facilitate meaning for people, but there is little documentation of what we could actually do in schools to facilitate the outcome of the education system that we know exists. All that has been established is that there are unique interactive mechanisms in the schools that do facilitate the outcome, but only when we have the necessary descriptive material or the necessary insight can we even hope to humanize the schools.

Purpel: The question that seems to me more basic and constitutes a challenge to all of us is whether we are disagreeing with existing institutional norms or disagreeing with a larger social framework. You talked about 25 percent poverty. Would you prefer that it be reduced to 10 percent and nothing else changed? You mentioned in one example that somebody valued obedience over ingenuity. Does that mean that you value ingenuity over obedience? Do you value achievement over meeting standards? It seems to me that what is missing, not only in the presentation but in other works devoted to education, is the question of ideology. Should educators work within an ideological framework? Are the questions being raised here simply technical? Is the objective in improving the school merely to reduce or eliminate poverty? Is the major goal of education to work for different kinds of social and cultural institutions? Are the values in the schools changing?

Apple: I don't think it is a choice that educators have. Whether tacit or overt, schools tend to be political and economic institutions, just by their functioning.

Purpel: I'm asking for your personal opinion! I ask the same questions of myself. What would *you* like to do? Should educators work for an ideology within the institutional framework, or should educators simply point out the gaps, problems, and discrepancies and say: "How terrible!"

Apple: The tradition of humanistic talk has been in the latter direction, and it hasn't been very helpful. I think the only way one changes institutions in a lasting way is to commit oneself to larger social programs. This requires that activities in schools be tactical as well as educational. My commitment to the students' rights movement, for example, becomes more and more tactical than educational. We have talked about the ideological question before. It requires a sense of what outcomes were initially envisioned for schooling (there is an implied social criticism—that the data can, to date, be merely descriptive). If Horace Mann took money from factory owners to build public schools, this would imply that the model would tend to evolve into a strongly socialized institution. Once that is established, one is able to say, "That's good," or "That's bad." The fact that the model is still with us yet remains to be documented; it is not merely a historical consideration. The data fit together in a very interesting way. Schools, it would appear, do things that many of us find uncomfortable, but they do it differently to different classes of children. When you put that together, it presents a difficult choice. Where do you commit yourself? What is your choice? I'm at the point of committing myself to action that is not just educational, but is economic and political. This is a difficult choice because more overt activity can be unpopular, even personally threatening.

Newmann: Without making it seem too personal, I would think that the choice you are talking about in terms of your own work is a more formal choice in your intellectual framework: shifting from a heavily analytical tradition that has real potential for ethical relativism to a more prescriptive intellectual tradition.

Apple: Definitely! That brings up the question of whether school people should engage in overt political and economic criticism and action. We have lost the tradition of that debate. It was a major source of controversy in progressive education, and it is one reason why the Progressive Education Association split. Most of us here are not familiar with that debate or with that tradition. These dominant issues have confronted earlier educators and curriculum reformers. We are not alone in exclaiming: "My God! Look at what the schools are doing in terms of differential rewards!" We tend to hide our heads by saying that educators must be neutral. I don't believe neutrality is possible. One must try to be objective, certainly, but that is not neutrality.

Macdonald: It seems to me that the choice of the framework of analysis is itself a statement of the intentions of your ideology. Just the fact that you choose to talk about ideology says something, for it is not the traditional direction of someone intent on preserving the status quo.

Newmann: That's what I was assuming initially when I said that I sensed a certain ideology, a certain preference for values in the chapter. I expected a statement concerning a notion of equality, the distribution of wealth in this country, or changes in political structure.

Apple: There are certain policies that I tend to support: massive income redistribution and other practices that tend to accompany a socialist program. Whether they actually fit under that label, or whether I want to be labeled at all, is a different matter. Since we live primarily in a knowledge-based economy, one has to talk very seriously about the role of cultural capital in a way that is not traditional with economistic Marxism. It is more fruitful to link myself with the cultural Marxists, such as Gramsci. That is less a concern in the social policies I advocate than finding a framework in which to organize my commitments.

King: And, while all of that is being worked out, it is still appropriate to proceed with the critical analysis of schools.

Mosher: In my presentation ("Education for Human Development") I question whether I am developing a powerful curricular technology for an idea that is no longer relevant, that is, the Deweyan conception that the aim of education is the stimulation of human development conceived in very broad terms. I am haunted as to whether my efforts over a long period of time may begin to produce a practical technology to stimulate cognition and character development in human beings, but that education for human actualization has no powerful social lobby. To answer the question of ideology, we absolutely do need philosophical ideology related to psychological theory and to application. The need is even greater because those of us who are concerned about human beings and their development in schools have been vague or ambiguous, uncertain or politically afraid to assert those ideologies. I think that is part of our weakness. Another part of it is due to the fact that we have not really had the knowledge or the technology to achieve desired goals. I think that it is a fair charge for all of us to take a stand on the issue of what knowledge is of most worth, what should be the end of education, and to act consistently with our position. It is no surprise that our actions would go in diverse ways. Apple and King are clearly arguing for action that would take place largely outside the schools.

Apple: I would like to ask you a question related to this. Isn't it odd that educators look for age-stage kinds of theories and that such theories look like existing school structures? When we had the beginnings of the elementary school and junior and senior high school, the culture recapitulation theory legitimated what was done in the schools, and it resembled some ideas of the progressive education movement of the 1920's. Are these things really helpful, or do they simply confirm preexisting structures?

Mosher: That is fascinating! It seems to me that if I really make a critical analysis of conventional stages of human or individual development, as Piaget, Kohlberg, and Loevinger talk about them, that they must happen, they cannot be ignored; that they are relatively predictable; and that they give rise to a great deal of discussion about the characteristics of the stages (intellectual functioning, social perspective, moral point of view). Kohlberg's Stage 2 is a gorgeous metaphor for preadolescence; Stage 3, for adolescence. There *are* institutional parallels. There is no question that high schools are full of people at Stage 3—both students and teachers. I am unaware, however, of educational means by which one can circumvent the stages of development. Further, I am not surprised at some of the correspondence between educational institutions and the stages. Thinking is organized by interaction with one's environment. The more interesting issue here, to me, is how we get more postconventional people. I think you are arguing for the development of postconventional stages of moral reasoning and for the application of more formal operations in people's lives and for Loevinger's notions of higher stages of ego integration. Even more fascinating questions are: What kinds of educational and psychological interventions can we create to stimulate postconventional thinking and action? What kind of institutional and social consequences will result from providing experiences that will permit more people to move to postconventional stages of thought, moral point of view, and personal and social orientation? Developmental education and developmental psychology only begin to deal with this area, and this is our challenge, as I perceive it. Are we as serious about moving people to postconventional stages and action as about stimulating transition from preconventional to conventional stages?

Feinberg: I was just thinking that one of the things that interests me in the literature on moral education is the research program that guides it. It is very individualistic, as I see it. You tend to find out "what person conforms to what stage," instead of "what it is about our institutional structures that stimulates people at whatever stage you are talking about." This is, I think, a different order of analytic questioning. It shifts the spotlight to a different set of concerns.

Apple: A concrete example of that might be, let's say, teaching to read. Our tendency is to say, "We need massive funding to get better textual materials and other materials in schools." And we couch it in a psychological way. There is nothing wrong with that. But by that approach we do not illuminate the institutional regularities and the economic and political commitments that go with that. For instance, right now we have all the technical expertise around this table we need to design a program that doesn't need reading to have access to knowledge. We've actually got most of the equipment in here, too. There is no technical problem in that at all. However, the problem is very much an economic one: Who makes money from what kind of curricular storing devices, and so forth? That's a different order of question. What is it about schools that prevents asking this question?

Purpel: I don't think we ought to say that we teach reading because somebody makes money from teaching reading.

Apple: That's not my point! What I'm questioning is the social and political use of teaching reading. Take normative behavior, which all of us agree on: teaching children to read. Some children just are not going to do that. There is just too much evidence to deny this. Whether or not they can learn to read, we insist on putting them through the program, and they fail. Or, if they succeed, we renorm the test. By definition you *must* create 50 percent deviance! Having established this pattern (every time any social group tends to succeed you renorm the test), you can make some interesting observations regarding reading behavior that tend to illuminate the social activity that supports it. This is not to say that you don't want to teach children to read; rather, it's to illuminate the latent outcome of always defining our problem in psychological, rather than economic and political, terms.

Purpel: Let me push this position a little beyond the question of whether we should teach children to read. Do we want to *judge* them on how well they can read? Beyond that, do we want to judge people on anything? You have made judgments about being more ingenious, more inventive, more responsive. I would like to get to the value question. Are we going to talk about achievement as a norm, or are we going to talk about making judgments about people? Are we going to discriminate among people, not just in terms of reading but in terms of all kinds of phenomena? Now, if somebody says, "Let's not judge people on reading," I also want him to say, "Let's not judge people on how imaginative or sensitive they are."

Mosher: Speaking as a developmental psychologist, I've got to have blueprints as to characteristic differences in cognitive functioning along the human life cycle. At least I *feel* I have to have them in order to understand the human person developing and growing in front of me. I don't need to categorize Stage 3 as morally superior to Stage 2, but I do need empirical categorization to understand the difference between unique people at various stages. There are social and human consequences for people who are denied development. Now that's drawing a fine line relative to the issue of judgment. My purpose is not really to judge, but to be able to see human difference in a psychological sense. I need the best psychological understanding of those differences that I can get in order not to commit the naturalistic fallacy and in order to find educational conditions that produce more of the higher stages of development. I readily agree that it is easy to interpret that as judgment.

Feinberg: What is more important is how you are going to use those judgments. They can be used in a diagnostic way to expand an individual's opportunity and potential, or they can be used in a repressive way that denies certain individual rights.

Mosher: Right! We already know a great deal about cognitive development and how to stimulate it. The stimulation of formal operations in human beings is, I suppose, the ultimate gift you can give people. That knowledge and technology in the hands of people who are interested in social control can also, however, be frightening.

Apple: But it can operate apart from social interest! Take as an example the work of Rachel Sharp and Anthony Green. They analyzed progressive primary schools in Great Britain—the British Infant Schools. They wanted to see whether labeling goes on. That is, they wanted to see what happens when you break the labeling processes of traditional schools and try to stimulate children's creativity. What they found was that, independent of the interests of everybody in that institution, certain unequal social outcomes occurred. In the British Infant Schools you are now expanding the amount of legitimate school knowledge. It is not just the academic disciplines or work-related skills. It's now affect—a range of feelings, cooperation, and many different kinds of things—so you have a much wider distribution of social categories. The school, then, performs a much better function with a soft notion of control than it did with a hard notion of control because schooling becomes fun. And that is independent of the wishes of either students or teacher.

Mosher: You're saying that the Coleman findings still hold: children leave with essentially what they entered with in terms of cultural capital. Is that right?

Apple: No, I'm saying that there is a massive distribution that reinforces existing cultural capital coming from childrens' homes, and some that does not. You have to pinpoint what kinds of children get what and discover the range of "getting." Is it simply subject matter? Or is it much more? As we begin to break down and get into less formal settings, we find that children work on their own as they pursue projects in the world. And then we discover that, because of that, other things are happening. The labels are then distributed over a much wider range, and this gives teachers and schools more of an area in which to do the sorting. The same students that were sorted out the other way get sorted out this way, but more effectively.

Feinberg: What do you do about exploited people who don't realize that there is, or who do not even want, an increased range of options? A lower-income parent in an urban area may not want open education, for it increases the realms of meaning that his child can explore in school. This same parent may not want the "humane classroom," which provides many options for students. Such parents often want their children to learn how to read and to perform practical mathematics functions—that's all! They may also want their children to know the difference between work and play. What do we do in that situation?

Apple: They also want discipline. These things are always situational. There are no general principles.

Feinberg: Do you believe that education should be better for such children and that their parents are wrong? I feel that these kinds of questions are pushing this analysis into a mold that is reducing its power. I may have an idea of what education ought to be. It may be fairly well thought out. Perhaps I do not see it as elitist, but I could see where a group of parents might think otherwise. I begin to wonder, then, what it is that those parents are seeing for their children and what makes them want that kind of education. I then take this as an indication that one should look beyond the school to discover what the parents are expecting from the schools and why they are expecting it. This gets us back to the business of the relationships between schooling and work structures. When you are confronted with this kind of situation, one tendency is to try to convince the parents that they ought to at least consider something else. You also want to make them aware of why they want what they want. That is, you want to bring them to an awareness of political and economic structures and how those might be otherwise. That's what the question should be pointing to, rather than feelings.

Sergiovanni: It seems to me that there is a better way than confronting the person with the prospect that they change their point of view to match yours. Maybe, by making the hidden curriculum public and understanding it better, the person has a wider choice. It seems to me that the value of this approach is not to confront somebody with the hidden curriculum and say, "See, it's bad! Now, you change." Rather, you are saying, "See, this is what it really is. Now, does this agree with what you want?" And, if it does not, then maybe you [the educator] put your hat on and walk away, and just assume that, for others, it might not be the answer.

Roebuck: For us just to say, "Here it is. Is this what you want or shall we change it?" does not seem to me to be adequate. We also have to work with the parents to make explicit their goals and possible goals for the quality of life their children can expect. We are responsible for developing programs, specific programs and a specific curricula that are not hidden, making them clear and precise in an effort to achieve those goals.

Sergiovanni: Well, one alternative strikes me, but I don't know how viable it is. Perhaps the hidden curriculum could be made part of the public curriculum and be taught. For example, let's take the question of competition in the classroom. I'm thinking about my own child, who simply could not get through the competitive five-minute multiplication tests for each of the times tables. The teacher used stars on a chart to record the progress of each student as he mastered the tests. Each glance at the chart showed him how "stupid" he was compared with other students. When I talked to the teacher about this, the teacher told me: "Competition is good! That's the real life. Youngsters are going to have to live in a world where they'll have to know what their limitations are. They're going to have to struggle." Well, that's an example of the hidden curriculum. Maybe an alternative is to say, "An alternative future is a competitive society. What would a competitive society be like? Can we simulate that for the children?" As we teach mathematics or anything else, we could give them work to do or problems to solve in a very competitive way and analyze it.

Purpel: Another alternative is for the schools to work toward a less competitive society.

Sergiovanni: The alternative is not to prescribe at all, but to teach the alternatives.

Feinberg: You can push that too far! Sure, there's merit in not imposing or prescribing for somebody else. But, we often take that to mean that you can't give good reasons for preferring one kind of alternative over another kind, and that's wrong. If you have good reasons, I don't see why you shouldn't bring them to the surface and confront others who feel that they have equally good reasons. To remain on the level of description or analysis is probably not sufficient. We should and do have preferences, and those deserve a hearing also.

Apple: That's exactly right. And shouldn't students also have preferences?

King: Suppose one teacher decides to teach the children to be competitive, and they are given tasks that create a competitive atmosphere in the classroom. Then another teacher decides to teach the children to be cooperative and assigns tasks that create a spirit of cooperation in the classroom. I would argue that the place of the child has not changed—that the political structure in the classroom itself is still one in which children do what they are told to do. I am not sure that the difference in the model creates a great difference in the world of the child in the classroom.

Purpel: Now, the issue to me is whether it is more important to teach the children to deal with the value of competition or noncompetition, and who controls this. It is not clear to me whether you are talking about the level of the value to be taught or who is going to choose the value.

Apple: The social definition of what is important and unimportant becomes critical here because there must be a reason why, within a five-minute span, the same action described as cheating in a test situation is considered to be cooperation before the test. The fundamental economic function of schools is to do something that is not just teaching; it is to provide a rough distribution of people. It stands to reason that much of the activity must be predominantly individualistic, no matter what the overt content, simply because of this fundamental notion of what schooling is about. In China tests are taken in groups. Why? Because there the notion is that human ability is much more a collective issue than an individual issue. In the United States one does not get group diplomas. One does not even get group grades. One gets individual diplomas and individual grades and certain kinds of students get this diploma and these grades; other students get that diploma and those grades, and this seems to be related to larger structural conditions to which schools respond.

Macdonald: Now I'm wondering if those of us who have been trying to reform schools have been doing a service. I've spent a lot of years trying to open up schools, to get them to put in alternatives and provide more options. There may be some good things in that and maybe not. But, what bothers me is that it now has become the major way of avoiding any value judgments, the major way of not confronting the issue of schooling on its level of values. You just say, "Okay! You can have that school, and your child can choose to go there or not to go there. If you parents want traditional education, we'll give you that." I'm just now reaching a stage where I'm confused in my own reform efforts. Perhaps that is because I've stayed within the school rather than gotten out—I've analyzed what's outside, but I've acted primarily within the system. It seems to me, once again, that we are failing to face up to fundamental conflict.

Mosher: It would appear that there is no way around the political process and a program of adult education intended to convince parents. I think we clearly have to persuade parents and society. I'm ideologically sympathetic with what seems to me to bear some resemblance to the democratic process. But, relative to working in the area of moral education, I am for open covenants, openly arrived at. I sweat whenever I go before the Brookline School Committee for two hours to argue the case for moral education. But in a sense I very much want to share that ideology—as to how we define morality and what our educational intervention would be and what the theory behind it is—with parents, teachers, and the students themselves. That's really essential.

Apple: I just don't think that focusing totally on the schools is going to make much of a difference. Let me go back to the reading example. This is a good area because it is so often focused on. In the data on the relationship of reading to economics we find that there is a strong correlation—once people reach a certain income level, then their children start to read better. What policy implications can we possibly draw from that? This may be difficult to accept, but it may be that the question we need to ask is not school related. It is more related to how equitably we distribute money in the United States because in the past that is what has helped. This may be a more fruitful way of looking at the issue, but it takes the problem out of my hands as an educator. It is a paradox.

Purpel: I still see that as a technical response. You're saying we go and work in the schools for X or we will have to go and work outside the schools for X. I still haven't seen the X.

Apple: Okay. One is income distribution. A second is local control of as many institutions as possible. It also means the sharing of significant power in our institutions with children, which is a school-related thing.

Mosher: That's a curriculum in the school—democracy of education.

Apple: Not necessarily! Because once one begins to confront the fact that children have few or no rights in schools and tries to put those rights into schools, you find all hell breaks loose. And it isn't so much from teachers or administrators as from the ordinary citizen.

Mosher: As an educator I would in a very simple-minded way work very hard to try to make the experiences of children in educational institutions more just. I would try to give them much more participation in the democratic management of those institutions, classrooms, or school units. That's a lifetime of work for a large number of us.

Feinberg: There are certain booby traps in the idea of developing more participation in the classrooms or student rights. That's fine, but the booby trap is that it is dysfunctional, because people in their work place don't have participation and lots of people in their work place have limited rights, and parents know that. So the booby trap is that the parents often rebel. The rebellion of the parents will be reflected in chaos in the classroom.

Mosher: That's speculative and antithetical to action.

Feinberg: No, it's not speculative at all. The implication is that what happens in school is itself a reflection of what happens elsewhere. You can't just work on schools.

Sergiovanni: What Feinberg may be saying is that if students don't see society or any of its institutions as credible—because they are hungry or they suffer from some other injustice—they're not likely to see the schools or other institutions in society as credible either, regardless of the power equalization strategies that you want to implement. Often you find that administrators with the best of intentions try to distribute power throughout an organization—then the whole thing disintegrates. It's a mess!

Mosher: I certainly argue a holistic conception of human development and educational response to human development. I think we have seen enough of the single-variable approach to multivariable problems in education, and I'm not arguing that giving students significant participation in school governance is a total educational or psychological answer. I think I can plot some of the consequences for the moral and social development of those children, and they would probably be significant in developing the potential for making moral judgments, for taking social action, and for improving social skills. That's not a whole answer, but it's a possible one.

Sergiovanni: It's a booby trap!

Mosher: Sure it's a booby trap, but I'm prepared to face some booby traps. That's one of the issues we're facing around this table. Are we prepared to confront some social, parental, and institutional booby traps? If not, then let's go home!

*Second
     Presentation*

                              Fred M. Newmann

Social Action and Humanistic Education

How do you go about humanizing education? Do you give the educators training in human relations to increase their sensitivity and respect for human needs? Do you change the organizational structure within schools to decrease bureaucratic hierarchy and increase student and staff participation in governance? Do you reduce certain societal demands on the student such as competitive pressure to earn high grades as vehicles to further education or success in the job market? Do you modify the curriculum to include, for example, more electives responsive to diverse student interests, more attention to humanistic fields, a change in the student role from passive dependency to active responsibility? While all of these approaches may be tried, here we concentrate on curriculum reform and, within that category, the particular topic of social action curriculum.[1]

Of course, people become educated not simply through school curriculum, but also through a complex fabric of expectations and messages from a variety of institutions—family, marketplace, job, mass media, peer group, church, and others. Any successful attempt to humanize education, therefore, requires a more comprehensive examination of social structures and systems of meaning. Thoughtful critiques offered elsewhere call for fundamentally changing the economic system in order to redistribute wealth, minimizing the obsession with technology, limiting the growth of centralized bureaucracy, and strengthening the local community to become the primary social unit. Once the case for fundamental social change has been argued, however, and even if some of the changes were actually made, a critical question remains: What should the school curriculum be?

Community Involvement—An Emerging National Movement

Recently several reports on secondary education have stressed the need for student involvement in community life, for action learning, for volunteer service, for adolescent participation in responsible roles with adults.[2] Schools are urged to place students in an active, rather than passive, learning role; to emphasize participation in specific, concrete tasks with observable effects in personal life in contrast to the heavy dose of abstract verbal analysis that dominates the curriculum; to involve students in the affairs of the community beyond the school. The phrases "community involvement," "action learning," "youth participation," "social action," strike responsive chords for educational critics and reformers. "Community" bespeaks a desire to build a sense of collective interdependence, to break down walls that isolate individual students from each other, and to end the isolation of formal instruction from life in the world at large. It conveys a sense of unity and relatedness, a holistic vision as an antidote to the fragmentation, specialization, and individual competition that make it difficult for humans in this society to relate to each other on a "human" level. Involvement suggests that education ought to help students become engaged and excited through personal investment in the intrinsic value of learning, rather than forcing them to play the game of school, apathetically going through the motions in a detached, alienated manner. "Action" represents assertiveness as opposed to passivity; a tendency to influence rather than accept reality; a desire to take some responsibility for, rather than be controlled by, events; a propensity for "doing" rather than only thinking or talking.

These phrases carry symbolic power for those who seek to make education more "relevant" to the needs of students and their society, but we must not adopt them too quickly as panaceas for the ills of education. Educators who work toward a more "relevant" curriculum may feel a sense of community in their mutual struggle to change curriculum, but even those who claim to be working toward community involvement, youth participation, and social action may not seek common goals. Slogans can obscure distinct and sometimes contradictory philosophies of education.

A first step in identifying commonalities and differences among approaches is to make the distinction between educational activities and the objectives that the activity is intended to serve. A given educational activity can presumably serve several, possibly competing, objectives. In visiting a home for the elderly, for example, teacher and students might have as their objective any of the following:
- A. Providing a community service by giving companionship to senior citizens.
- B. Conducting a study of elderly people as a vehicle to learning in the disciplines of psychology, sociology, or history.
- C. Exploring student interest in a particular career choice, such as professional care of the elderly.
- D. Gathering information to be used in a social campaign to persuade public officials to allocate more financial resources to care for the elderly.
- E. Improving students' abilities to communicate with persons different from themselves.
- F. Having a learning experience in the "real" world, that is, outside of the school where learning tends to be excessively verbal and abstract.

Some of these objectives may complement each other (A and C), but others may not (B and D). Before passing judgment on the educational value of any activity, it can be helpful to articulate which objectives it is intended to serve. If multiple objectives seem possible, priorities must be established and compatibility determined.

Community involvement activities can serve a whole range of objectives.

1. For the academician the activities could be pedagogical devices for illustrating theory, findings, insights that have been contributed by a number of disciplines in the humanities, or in the physical or social sciences. For the inquiry teacher, community involvement could assist in the formation of hypotheses or in the collection and analysis of data (for example, students making observations about human behavior or probing public and private records).

2. The vocational educator might see community involvement and social action as orientation for careers and vocations through internships with practicing social workers, journalists, programmers, lawyers, mechanics, politicians, and police.

3. The humanitarian or good Samaritan may see such activity as providing manpower for needed public services (environmental cleanup, day care, consumer education, tutoring) that are not currently provided by existing institutions.

4. The experiential educator could favor such activities as a means of ensuring that learning is rooted in the "reality" of the learner rather than in the often abstract, formal, excessively verbal nature of the conventional curriculum.

5. For a political conservative, community involvement and social action might be a means of demonstrating the basic legitimacy of existing political institutions. As students become deeply involved in social problems, perhaps they will conclude that existing institutions operate as fairly and as efficiently as can reasonably be expected and that lack of solutions is due more to the complexity of the problems than the nature of the political system. Through direct participation in decision-making processes, students may well learn that the existing structure, though not perfect, is the lesser of evils. By involving students with persons in government, business, and the professions who have this orientation and can point to apparent progress in several areas, the view might be persuasively communicated.

6. The political revolutionary, on the other hand, could see community involvement and social action as a means of exposing basic contradictions and injustice in the system, thereby demonstrating the need for radical restructuring of institutions. Involving students with certain groups (racial minorities, the poor) who have suffered and been exploited and whose grievances have not been redressed through "legitimate" channels would strengthen this view.

7. For the advocate of group awareness and group development, community involvement and social action could signify a desire to break down the isolation and alienation of persons from themselves and from each other, thus enabling a more "human" or "caring" community to develop. One example would be the formation of intimate groups of students who work together on a project of their choice, in or out of school.

8. Placing students in roles that require caring for others and tak-

ing responsibility for one's actions in the "real world" beyond school may, for the developmental psychologist, constitute a vehicle to promote growth in cognitive complexity, moral reasoning, or the accumulation of ego-strength.

9. An advocate of community control or the use of paraprofessionals in schools might want to increase local input and urge the use of local resources to improve the teaching of the conventional curriculum.

If objectives as diverse as these were all included in a school's community involvement and social action programs, the program could conceivably support activities in or outside of school; it might involve few or many adults; it could include conventional didactic as well as unstructured experiential learning; students could be relatively unsupervised or strictly supervised by professional educators; students might be involved in various combinations of study and research, volunteer service, apprenticeships, or political advocacy—working in groups or individually. The tremendous diversity of objectives could generate a plethora of activities that would confuse students, teachers, and adults in the community. Because community involvement and social action activities can be offered in pursuit of such diverse and potentially conflicting educational objectives, educators should specify the objectives sought and then determine whether particular forms of community involvement and social action might assist in their achievement.

The contention here is that competence in social action is a justifiable educational objective, worthy of far more support than it has received. To achieve this competence, students must participate in attempts to exert influence in public affairs. To endorse unconditionally all such attempts, however, would be inappropriate, for it could involve us in supporting social action experiences that are uneducational, immoral, or nonhumanistic. To help ensure that social action education be directed in humanistic ways, criteria should be established that promote experiences consistent with humanistic education. The teaching of social action competence and the insistence that it be guided by certain criteria have important implications regarding new curriculum development, the general instructional climate of schools, and the school's alleged position of "political neutrality," each of which will be discussed.

Defining and Justifying Social Action

Definition

We propose that social action be defined as intentional behavior to exert influence in public affairs.[3] Public affairs are those issues of concern to groups of people to which, it is generally agreed, institutions of government should respond—through legislation, administrative action, judicial opinion, and other activities. Sometimes it is difficult to distinguish between private and public affairs. A student may feel that a parent has unjustly restricted use of the family car. What apparently is a private dispute can escalate into a public issue if the student attempts to challenge the constitutionality of regulations that deny certain rights to minors and that give parents powers to restrict the liberty of children without due process of law. Rather than classifying issues categorically as either private or public, it is more helpful to view them on a continuum. A problem can be regarded as "public" when increasing numbers of people become concerned with how it is resolved and feel that it falls within the realm of governmental interest. To the extent that a problem is viewed as idiosyncratic to individuals, rather than groups, and to the extent that it is not deemed to fall within governmental interest, it should be considered private.[4]

There may be a tendency to identify public affairs as being only those issues of widespread significance usually depicted in the mass media (wars, elections, inflation, pollution, and other societal "crises"). The definition used here expands the conception to include countless additional issues, more local in nature and less likely to receive media coverage. Cyclists may wish to establish and assist in the regulation of bike trails. Volunteer workers may wish to change some regulations in a mental hospital. Housing organizers may seek more frequent trash collection or more frequent inspection for code violations. Students may advocate an increased budget for women's athletics at the high school. A center for runaways may attempt to influence policies in a police department or a juvenile court. A black student union may have to work for official recognition by the school. According to the broader definition, these are all attempts to exert influence in public affairs.

Social action might imply only militant kinds of behavior such as protests through marches, demonstrations, and boycotts, but this also would be too restrictive. The behaviors would include telephone

Social Action

conversations, letter writing, participation in meetings, research and study, testifying before public bodies, door-to-door canvassing, fund raising, media production, bargaining and negotiation, and also publicly visible activity associated with the more militant forms. Social action can take place in or out of school and, if out of school, not necessarily on the streets, but in homes, offices, and workplaces. It might involve movement among several locations or concentration at one.

Student participation in such activities should not alone be considered evidence of social action. They might conduct a survey of attitudes toward the police only to assess the level of public support. They might distribute leaflets door to door, not to advocate a position but to provide impartial information to help the citizenry make an informed decision. While these are examples of citizen participation from which much can be learned, they do not qualify as social action unless they are part of a strategy to affect public policy in a particular direction. Before labeling behavior as social action, therefore, it is necessary to know something about the intentions of the actors.

Justification

Any given example of social action might be criticized from a number of points of view: ethics, legality, efficiency, accuracy of factual assumptions, or logic. Social action, then, as a general class of behaviors, is not inherently good, valid, or justifiable. Each instance must be justified as to its merit. Further, no inherently "humanistic" qualities are claimed for social action, but it can be argued that the *ability* to engage in social action is by its very nature a good, positive, valid, or humanistic educational goal. The distinction between the ability to exert intentional influence in public affairs and the act of trying to exert influence is important. The ability to exert influence is desirable because it helps to meet a critical psychological human need (a sense of competence); it contributes to individual identity as a moral agent; and it is required to operate a democratic political system based on the principle of consent of the governed.

Psychological Development

Robert White, who reviewed a wide range of research in the psychoanalytic tradition, empirical studies of animal and human behavior, and cognitive psychological theory, has identified a persistent human tendency, beginning in early childhood, to explore, manipulate, and influence one's environment.[5] White explains how findings of numerous studies suggest that this behavior cannot be construed merely as a form of coping with more basic instinctual drives (sex, food, aggression, and others). Instead, this seems to constitute a bundle of independent ego energies which he labels effectance. To try to act upon the environment and to derive satisfaction therefrom is a basic element in human nature that is also apparent in other animals. In humans, this form of satisfaction can be called a feeling of efficacy:

> My thesis is that the feeling of efficacy is a primitive biological endowment as basic as the satisfactions that accompany feeding or sexual gratification, though not nearly as intense. We feel efficacious when we throw the ball over the plate, swim to the raft, or mend the broken household appliance. But the feeling does not have to be connected with the achievement of a particular intended result. With exploratory behavior, where results cannot be anticipated, it seems a better guess to say that feelings of efficacy accompany the whole process of producing effects. The activity is satisfying in itself, not for specific consequences.[6]

White claims no originality in recognizing effectance as a psychic phenomenon, and he acknowledges many other investigators who have been intrigued with its manifestations. White's contribution is his insistence that action or manipulative and exploratory behavior be regarded not simply as the playful use of superfluous energy or an expression of idle curiosity in one's surroundings, but as a "major aspect of the adaptive process and a vital theme in the growth of personality." Effectance, especially in young children, is not consciously purposeful or instrumental. Their early actions upon the world are undertaken unintentionally, not in order to learn useful skills or to prepare for future contingencies but because there is something inherently satisfying about the actions.

At the same time, noninstrumental behavior involving assertive, exploratory interaction with the environment stimulates cognitive development and also produces substantive knowledge, however "accidentally." White's work is thus consistent with cognitive developmental theory, particularly the research of Piaget[7] and others on the growth of cognitive complexity in children. A child's earliest conception of causality, for example, emerges not through passive observation and reflection, but from feelings associated with specific actions on concrete phenomena in the environment. Similarly, Dewey, in his explanation of cognitive growth, argues that reconstruction of experience occurs only through the person's active intervention or interaction with people and objects in the environment.[8] Whether we look at growth through Piaget's notion of cognitive complexity, through Dewey's "reconstruction of experience," or through Kohlberg's stages in the development of moral reasoning,[9] there is wide agreement that development is generated, in large part, through perception of dissonance, inconsistency, mystery, or some other manifestation of intellectual inadequacy and that the personal sense of such inadequacy arises from our attempts to influence and confront reality external to self. Our effectance needs apparently have evolutionary value. White reminds us that, while the pursuit of effectance is intrinsically satisfying, the concomitant learning it brings about can make the difference between life and death for an organism or species.

As the individual grows, it is hoped that the exercise of effectance and feelings of efficacy will be directed toward specific kinds of mastery so that competence and a sense of competence are developed. These are, respectively, the actual ability to bring about specific results in one's environment and the sense that one can bring about such results consistently. Though many of White's illustrations deal with the physical world, he emphasizes the equal significance of social or interpersonal efficacy—the ability to act toward persons in such a way that elicits human responses in accord with one's intentions. In a further modification of psychoanalytic theory, White explains how children's attempts to identify with adults can be seen not merely as incorporating the person of the adult into oneself, but copying the competence of others in order to improve one's own competence. Competence also constitutes the foundation of self-esteem based on self-respect, in contrast, for example, to self-love, as particular standards for mastery in the environment become internalized criteria for one's self-esteem. Finally, White indicates how an accumulated sense of competence is a useful way of referring to what others may call ego-strength—the ability to overcome anxiety associated with perceived "dangers" or "threats" because of the accrued confidence that one can act upon, rather than be a victim of, the environment.

The psychological significance of environmental competence is evident in many other works, although, until now, these two specific words have not been joined. Edrita Fried, on the basis of her clinical practice in psychotherapy and scholarly inquiries, posits the need for "activeness" as the "crucial psychological dimension."[10] She argues that the major dynamic in human personality is not tension reduction or the pursuit of hedonistic pleasure in a passive sense, but a vital and active desire to affect reality. Passivity occurs essentially as a defensive reaction to the blocking of or failure to nurture the active need. Smith, drawing from biological, psychological, and sociological studies, contributes a major synthesis in the study of competence. He recommends that the concept of a competent self should orient our thinking about socialization from youth to adulthood. The core of the competent self is the ability to act in one's environment:

> The self is perceived as causally important, as effective in the world—which is to a major extent a world of other people—as likely to be able to bring about desired effects, and as accepting responsibility when effects do not correspond to desire.[11]

Coleman's finding that a sense of control over one's environment and future seems to have a stronger relationship to school achievement than all other "school" factors (for example, dollars per pupil, education of teachers) together[12] further demonstrates the significance of this need.

A concern for the psychological potency of environmental competence is present in Erikson's conception of identity formation.[13] His stages of autonomy, initiative, industry, identity, intimacy, generativity, and integrity all presume a person who acts upon reality, rather than passively observing or merely understanding it. Maslow's ideal of self-actualization[14] also implies the ability of an individual to affect reality in accord with intentions. In short, most of our conceptions of psychological health, mental health, or functional personality development, expressed in professional or lay language, rely upon this notion.

There are, of course, many ways in which an individual might gain a sense of competence through making an impact in the environment: arts, crafts, sports, interpersonal relations, agriculture, interior decorating, occupational or professional competence from salesmanship to surgery. Is it really necessary that our need for efficacy reach to the realm of public issues and community affairs? Do private, individualistic forms of efficacy fill this psychological need? In my opinion they are inadequate. It is virtually impossible to escape the constant flow of information on public affairs, either local or across the planet. We are bombarded with messages that evoke strong feelings of injustice.

In spite of a sense of powerlessness, these messages cannot be entirely blocked out, and many people hold strong views on selected social problems. Commitment to private individual endeavors may offer temporary relief, but for most people, including adolescents, this does not resolve an underlying frustration. Rawls speaks to this problem when he claims that those deprived of positions of power in society would rightfully feel unjustly treated even though they were to gain great benefits from the efforts of a privileged few.[15] They would be justified in their complaint not only because they were excluded from external rewards of wealth and privilege, "but because they were debarred from experiencing the realization of self which comes from a skillful and devoted exercise of social duties. They would be deprived of one of the main forms of human good." We concur in recognizing a fundamental human need to affect one's social destiny that cannot be satisfied simply through economic affluence or exclusive preoccupation with private activity.

Moral Identity

In addition to meeting a basic psychological need, the ability to exert influence in public affairs is required for moral identity. The less ability one has to exert intentional impact in the environment, the more difficult it becomes to consider oneself a moral agent. A moral agent is defined as someone who deliberates upon what he or she ought to do in situations that involve possible conflicts between self-interests and the interests of others, or between the rights of parties in conflict. Some philosophers may require that a person deliberate only upon what ought to be done, but not necessarily upon what one, as an individual, ought to do. Unless our deliberations focus upon our own personal rights, duties, responsibilities, obligations—that is, what we ought to do—such deliberation is empty, academic, unrelated to the realities of our existence. We stipulate, therefore, that our moral nature derives from the existential necessity of deciding what we ought to do. Deliberating upon what ought to be done in a general sense and upon what others ought to do is important, but, unless this is supplemented by a concern for what I as an individual ought to do, I cannot properly be considered a moral agent.[16]

The less we are able to influence reality, the less we are able to deliberate about what we ought to do. Suppose that, while walking upon a deserted beach, I come upon a swimmer fifteen yards from shore who is calling for help. Nearby are a canoe and paddle, several loose strands of rope, and an automobile with keys in the ignition. I recognize as a general moral principle or prima facie duty that one should save a human life if this is at all possible. Suppose, however, that I do not know how to swim, manage a canoe, tie knots, or drive an auto. Nor do I have knowledge of where I might find the nearest person or telephone. Because of such overwhelming incompetence, it is meaningless to ask what I ought to do. Because I can do nothing to influence the situation, what I ought to do is not a genuine question.[17] If my incompetence prevents me from asking this question, it has in a sense deprived me of the essence of my nature as a moral agent.

By way of contrast, suppose that I was highly skilled in lifesaving, canoeing, knot tying, and driving, and that I knew how to summon help at this place. Thanks to these varied competencies to exert influence, I could choose to act in any of these ways, or not to act at all. Such competencies, having created a choice among actions, have thereby given birth to the important question: What should I do? Endowed with the ability to influence the environment, I am now capable of asking what I ought to do and therefore it is possible, albeit perhaps more stressful, to consider myself a moral agent. Such competencies are important not only because they help to make the important question "askable," but also because they make it possible for a person to act in accord with ethical duties.

The claim that ability to exert influence is critical to our existence as moral agents should be interpreted with care. This does not require an individual to harbor specific intentions, make specific judgments, or act in specific ways that philosophers might consider morally correct. An extremely competent person in the above situation could conceivably choose *not* to help the drowning person for a variety of reasons—some, perhaps, selfish and immoral; others, ethically justifiable. Or, a totally incompetent person might make heroic attempts to save the swimmer, yet both could die in the process.

Whether an individual wishes to attempt a rescue, actually attempts a rescue, or succeeds in rescuing the swimmer is not central to this argument, although such matters may be significant in making moral judgments of other types. We claim only that a critical and defining (perhaps necessary but not sufficient) feature of a moral agent is one's ability to deliberate about what one as an individual ought to do. The point of the swimmer analogy is to demonstrate that, to the extent that we lack the ability to influence the environment, we are also deprived of the chance to inquire about what we ought to do.[18]

The ethical importance of environmental competence is particularly evident in public issues. Imagine a student who, while studying reformatories and other institutions for "youthful offenders," concludes that reforms are needed and that she ought to be active in working toward certain policy changes. She writes a letter to a prison official and one to her congressman, requesting that they take the necessary steps to implement her proposals, among them more licensed foster homes for offenders and runaways. Both letters are answered noncommittally: "Thank you for your interest. I will certainly consider your suggestions." The student concludes that nothing more can be done to advance her cause. She is unaware of other actions she might take, including, for example, finding and working with groups that have advocated similar policies, developing a new organization, working for the election of candidates who support her views. Her lack of knowledge of such approaches renders her powerless to act on what she considers to be her moral obligation.[19]

Events as varied as the knifing of Kitty Genovese in New York, the My Lai massacre, Watergate, or the advertised sale of term papers on college campuses seem to have triggered a widespread sense of moral outrage and a renewed interest in "moral education." To cure the moral pathology allegedly plaguing our civilization, different educational prescriptions are offered for youth: more effective inculcation of certain substantive values, such as honesty, respect for life, constitutional rights; direct analysis of students' confusion over personal values and help in identifying the values to which they are genuinely committed;[20] cultivation of better structures within which to carry on moral deliberation, advancing, for example, from hedonistic orientation and conventional obedience to law to principled reasoning based on a philosophically adequate conception of justice.[21] It is possible, however, that even the more sophisticated attempts to clarify the nature of moral discourse appropriate for schools have missed the mark, for they do not give adequate attention to the ethical implications of student incompetence to exert influence in their environment.

Consider the kinds of ethical issues often presented in values-oriented curricula. One case (used in Kohlberg's research) tells of a man who, in order to save his wife from a fatal disease, must steal a wonder drug because he cannot afford to pay for it. Then there is the classic lifeboat situation in which the lives of some people must apparently be sacrificed if anyone is to survive. When studying matters of public policy, students may be asked to evaluate the morality of Truman's decision to use the atomic bomb or to discuss whether a soldier who killed innocent civilians under orders from a superior officer should be morally condemned. While each of these situations raises fundamental ethical issues of universal significance and while each may assist students in arriving at clearer and more consistent statements of the abstract principles on which to base ethical choices, these subjects of moral discourse are inadequate as a basis for moral education. In each situation the individual whose actions are being evaluated *does* have the ability to act in ways that exert important influence in the environment. The decision maker's problem lies not in the attainment of the ability to exert influence, but in choosing how one's rather considerable power ought to be used. Because the decision maker is assumed to have enough environmental competence to make a dramatic difference, discourse restricted to "what should be done" can neglect the basic point that "real" moral dilemmas exist only when a person has the specific ability to affect reality.

This is particularly important when we consider the actual or perceived inability of young people to exert influence in their own lives. They may have a sense of injustice with regard to many topics: environmental decay, economic exploitation of certain groups, violations of constitutional rights, or international violence. Because they do not consider themselves capable of action to remedy such injustices, they, in effect, face no actual moral dilemmas. The challenge for moral education is not simply to improve the process of reasoned verification of ethical choices, but also to build competence to affect the environment so that ethical choices actually present themselves to students. Moral education on how to reason about ethical choices

Social Action

would then become even more appropriate, for students would be able to see themselves as moral agents.

Consent of the Governed

The United States operates, presumably, on the assumption that the fairest methods for arriving at public policy are those defined by representative democracy, with an active system of consent of the governed and protections to guarantee equal liberty to each individual. We assume that the political mission of public education is to support that vision of a representative democratic system. While there may be some dispute about the defining characteristics of a democratic system, the principle of consent of the governed is a central requirement, and there is little doubt that this is well established as an *ideal* in American culture. Numerous legal provisions reinforce each citizen's right to influence the course of public affairs: universal suffrage; periodic election of officials for relatively short terms; electoral districts drawn presumably to give each person equal proportional representation; the use of majority rule to resolve public disagreement; protection of freedom of political expression and the right of assembly; opportunity for citizen-initiated petitions, referenda, and recall; public access to government meetings and records. The attention paid to many surveys of public opinion (not required by law) endows the "will of the people" with further dignity. If these various mechanisms are to have meaning, however, citizens must possess the competence to formulate their views and express them influentially within the political-legal system.

This is not to say that the consent ideal has been sufficiently realized;[22] it has not, and education is, in part, responsible for this failure. In spite of evidence that many citizens do not actually participate extensively or effectively in their government, we must recognize, nevertheless, an emotionally powerful consensus that they ought to have this right. So much of the rhetoric in public discourse extols the virtue of the consent ideal that few would dare to attack it.

On the other hand, few can explain why the consent principle ought to be upheld. Without discussing numerous complications in political philosophy or delineating the sophisticated contributions of seminal thinkers on this subject, two powerful routes of justification can be summarized. From an ethical point of view, the consent principle is a mechanism for the realization of a central value in theories of morality and justice: the value of equality. We assume that the general moral significance of equality has been adequately demonstrated.[23] The concern here is to see the consent principle as a device for institutionalizing equality in political matters.[24]

A basic moral premise is that every human being, because of one's humanity, is entitled to respect and dignity. That dignity is possible only if the claims and interests of each person are treated impartially, that is, given equal consideration. It is a social fact, however, that some persons who might gain power over others might also subjugate or deny equal rights to the powerless. To guard against this possibility, it would be helpful to organize society through a political principle that disperses and distributes power itself as equally as possible. Consent of the governed serves this purpose, for it requires that each citizen should have equal opportunity to affect the use of power, both through periodic selection of leaders and through direct participation to affect the outcome of specific issues. By emphasizing equal access to power, the consent principle minimizes the likelihood that equal rights, the cornerstone of morality and justice, can be violated. Consent of the governed, therefore, has an ethical foundation.

The second justification is that an open consent process serves to ferret out the "truth," and compensate for errors in judgment. Others have developed this argument more carefully.[25] For many questions of public policy, there is often genuine dispute that cannot be attributed to political bias alone, for even the most impartial experts will disagree. Thus, solutions objectively verified beyond doubt can rarely be found. We also learn through hindsight that in science and in public affairs men have often held up as sacred truths claims later proved wrong. Realizing our inability to find eternally valid answers to questions on public affairs (or scientific matters), we must guard against becoming victimized by adherence to mistaken orthodoxies. One safeguard is to provide equal opportunity for all citizens continuously to advocate solutions as they see fit. If the power to influence policy is widely dispersed among the citizenry, there is more likely to be a "sifting and winnowing" of ideas, an experimentation with alternative proposals, an openness and constructive struggle for the "right" answers. Such a process would not be possible if power were restricted to a special group. In this sense the justification for consent of the governed is similar to arguments for academic freedom and freedom of speech: it tries to maximize our opportunity to arrive at the "truest" or "wisest" decision, however temporary it may prove to be.[26]

Though we have defined and justified the ability to engage in social action, we have not discussed a number of objections raised to the prospect of public schools sponsoring and awarding academic credit for student involvement in political controversy.[27] One of the major questions is whether the school should automatically endorse a project or give a student carte blanche to undertake any project he or she chooses. Should the curriculum help students to exert influence in public affairs by offering instruction on techniques of terrorism and guerilla warfare? The example shows that certain forms of social action may not have a humanizing influence, and should not, therefore, be supported by public education. The challenge, then, is to distinguish between humanistic and nonhumanistic forms of social action.

Criteria for Humanistic Social Action

A scholarly treatise on the definition of humanism is not necessary, but the concept seems to imply at least three critical dimensions. The first is an ethical premise emphasizing the universal right of every individual to equal respect and the universal obligation of every individual not to violate that inalienable right for other individuals. The second is respect for uniqueness in human culture as manifested in diversity among individuals and groups with regard to values, life styles, modes of expression, and institutional structures. This dimension, seen as an extension of the equality principle, translated or operationalized into the principle of equal liberty of individuals and groups to pursue unique goals and purposes. It is the "fulfillment" aspect of humanism. Finally, humanism takes form in the cultivation of the arts, history, philosophy, literature, and other fields that offer commentary on the human search for truth, beauty, and goodness. This places value on individual attempts to stand back from their own experience, to analyze, to interpret, to find meaning in their existence. This is the reflective dimension of humanism. Recent so-called "humanistic" critiques of formal education have argued that forces such as scientism, technology, or specific political-social ideologies have influenced educational institutions in ways that violate one or more of these general dimensions.

If instruction for competence in social action is to help humanize education, it should be consistent with the ethical, the unique fulfillment, and the reflective dimension of humanism itself. Three educational criteria appear to parallel these meanings, although in a different order. First, social action must occur in a context of rational reflection (reflective dimension). Second, the ends and means of social action must be justified by the students with reference to principles of justice (ethical dimension). Third, the social action experience of students must contribute to their sense of personal competence (fulfillment dimension). To phrase it negatively, mindless social action that is not ethically justified and that does not assist in developing personal competence should not be supported by schools and cannot be considered to "humanize" education. There may be other criteria, but these seem required as a minimum.

Rational Reflection

One special quality of our humaneness is, presumably, the capacity to analyze our own existence, our capacity to construct meaning systems and to reflect upon them. To humanize education is, in part, to inspire and make use of this reflective potential. In the realm of social action, rational reflection is demonstrated by several intellectual operations, most importantly the offering of reasons for one's views when asked: Why? Rather than simply reaffirming intuitive or emotionally pleasing preferences, "reasons" should include reliable evidence to back up factual claims, useful definitions of ambiguous key terms, propositions that are logically consistent, value judgments sufficiently qualified so as not to entail unsupportable implications. Rational reflection takes seriously the merits of various views, regardless of their source. It encourages mutual inquiry into problem solving rather than trickery, belligerence, or deception to win an argument. It stresses the development of unique personal positions rather than dogmatic consensus. Recognizing the impossibility of "pure" objectivity and the inevitability of nonrational influences on personal views, a rational approach attempts to ferret out the rational and nonrational aspects of any given point of view. In other words, as students engage in social action to enhance their ability to exert influence in public affairs, they should learn how to justify and explain their goals and actions within a rational, reflective framework.

I have discussed the reasons for requiring rationality elsewhere.[28] Rational reflection has an ethical justification in that it promotes in subtle ways two important values: liberty and equality. The expectation that we must be open to diverse possible solutions to public problems rather being irrationally doctrinaire tends to expand horizons and to broaden the range of choice, thereby enhancing freedom. The expectation that all claims, regardless of their source, deserve evaluation on their merits and that logical inconsistencies must be avoided tends to apply the concept of equal treatment. From an epistemological point of view, the requirements of rational method and verification are considered to be protections against falling victim to mistaken conclusions, assuming that the truth, however tentative and subject to change, is more likely to be discerned through rational discourse than through its abuse. From a socio-linguistic point of view, the ground rules for rational reflection seem to supply a common language system, without which we simply could not communicate about questions of verification or justification. That is, rationality provides a symbolic means of pursuing disagreements. Finally, rationality can have practical political value, for we predict that, all other things being equal, the individual able to reflect rationally on personal social action is more likely to succeed than someone who has no such ability.

The case for rationality is made here with full realization that public policy is often made through a process that many would characterize as irrational. Public agencies often make glaring mistakes that reflect inadequate knowledge. And vested interests often override the quest for objective truth. The most obvious reason that these points should not deter the quest for rational social action is evident in the criticism itself: the implication that public policy ought to be informed and based as often as possible on "objective" data reflects a commitment to rationality. There is obviously more to humanism than tough-minded rationality. Aesthetic experience, nonverbal manipulation of artifacts, developing body movement, or nonlogical expressions of affect certainly all contribute to a humanistic education. Here, however, attention must be directed to the particular problem of arriving at community-wide public policies, and these must be justified, so far as possible, through a reflective rational process.

Justice

It would be irresponsible to give students, or any citizen, the unconditional right to exert influence. As persons should be challenged to justify their actions rationally, those rationales should be grounded in principles of justice. The most fundamental, underlying ethical principle, as previously mentioned, is that equal respect be given to every person. At the very least this requires that each person have equal opportunity to participate in the consent process through which public policy is made, that individuals be guaranteed equal liberty to specific rights that even a democratically chosen majority cannot take away (such as freedom of speech and religion or voluntary association), and that every individual who comes in conflict with the state be accorded due process of law. This concept of justice views persons as ends in themselves, not as instrumental means. It also presumes a universality in moral deliberation. That is, deciding what is just requires general universally applicable conclusions in which like cases are treated alike.[29]

As persons engage in social action they have a responsibility to justify their efforts with reference to principles of justice, but the principles alone are often not sufficient to resolve controversy or to bring consensus on specific policy questions. They do, at times, lead to a virtually unanimous conclusion that certain actions are just and others unjust, but many actions cannot be judged indisputably right or wrong by applying the principles. This means that the ethical framework must be seen as inconclusive or indeterminate in many cases. Indeterminacy can be traced to lack of factual knowledge about the future effects of given actions (Will a guaranteed minimum income actually destroy the will to work?), to definitional controversy (Does equal opportunity include the right to use preferential hiring to redress past inequities?), to weighing good and harm in the short and long term, among different individuals, and within an individual (Which, among many charitable organizations working for principles of justice, is most "deserving" of my support?), and to possible conflicts among the "highest" principles themselves (Does respect for the sanctity of life compel us to prevent a person from committing suicide if that choice was made voluntarily?). The value of this ethical cornerstone rests not, therefore, in its prescriptive power to *solve* all moral controversies, but in providing ethically defensible and philosophically consistent principles through which to deliberate about human conflict.

The instructional task is not to indoctrinate blind allegiance to the principles, but to help students develop and articulate ethical justifications for their actions that can meet the challenge of rational debate. This must include an honest examination of the confusion over defining the principles, of positions that challenge the desirability or validity of the principles themselves, and of the admittedly discouraging historical evidence that the principles actually do influence life.

This concept of justice legitimates the right of school authorities to refuse support for student projects that can be shown to be immoral. In cases where the morality of a proposed action is disputed among thoughtful observers who operate from this ethical frame, however, both students and school authorities must accept some ambiguity, along with the possibility that some projects will be rejected and others accepted in the absence of conclusive ethical justification. It is possible authorities, under the guise of "moral" objections, will prohibit student projects for other reasons, including the desire to maintain adult control or the attempt to avoid inconveniences within a bureaucracy. Suppression of the opportunity of students to learn to exert influence in public affairs for such reasons alone, however, is unjustifiable. The school has every right to insist that students' social action be ethically justifiable, based on the principles discussed, but the school has no right to censor student participation unless the case for suppression is grounded in that same ethical framework.

Sense of Competence

The difference between a program of social action (for example, a plan to improve counseling services for runaways) and a program of *education* for social action is critical. The purpose of action is to achieve a policy result. The purpose of an educational program is to enhance personal competence to act (an example would be teaching a student how to testify before a public agency). Personal growth through the development of competence is the third humanistic criterion for social action in education. Development of competence is consistent with the humanistic notion of helping each individual reach "full potential." It is quite possible, however, for people to engage in social action, even to meet the criteria of rational reflection based on principles of justice, without increasing personal competence. Students working in an election campaign may have thought carefully about the merits of their candidate and may have ethically justified their candidate's case and their campaign techniques. Yet, if they spend virtually all of their time addressing envelopes, they are unlikely to increase their skills in such areas as research, negotiation strategies, or fund-raising techniques.[30] If, at the end of the election, they are left with no sense of increased competence, their social action experience would not have been sufficiently humanizing.

An important challenge for curriculum is the articulation of the kinds of competencies that seem to enhance the general ability to exert influence in public affairs. I have elsewhere suggested seven areas: moral deliberation, social policy research, knowledge of political-legal process, advocacy skills, group process skills, organization-management techniques, and resolution of "psycho-philosophic" concerns.[31] Once a conception of skills is developed, curriculum can be planned. That effort, however, must guard against those applications of competency-based models which themselves can violate humanistic principles. By focusing exclusively on *individual* competence, for example, schools may in subtle ways, through the "hidden" curriculum, promote socially irresponsible autonomy rather than collective cooperation. If self-worth is assessed only in terms of how successfully an individual can impose one's will on others, this would contradict the notion of equal respect and run counter to the need for human interdependence. Competence to exercise influence should not be seen as a one-way process that terminates when the actor convinces the "audience." Instead, the ability to exert influence should be construed within an interactive or synergetic process in which actors and "audiences" affect each other in many ways, depend upon each other for personal development, and cooperate mutually for the survival of the species. In other words, a sense of individual competence must be built within a sense of community.

To structure social action experiences so that they enhance student competence is an enormous challenge, especially because of vast individual differences and the unpredictable nature of experience in the community. Dewey explained long ago that experiences will be educational only to the extent that they follow the principles of continuity (connecting the present with past and future experiences in a way that "arouses curiosity, strengthens initiative and sets up desires and purposes") and interaction (matching appropriate external conditions with internal states of mind in the learner).[32] Developmentalists (Piaget, Kohlberg, and others) further elaborate on the problem of selecting those experiences that trigger in the learner the attempt to make sense out of the environment. We do not know what kinds of social action experience generally will contribute to growth of particular kinds of competence, but, if social action education is to be humanistic, the experiences should perhaps be designed for individual learners with this issue prominently in mind. In addition to these challenges in instructional design, we face a significant problem in evaluation: What criteria should be used to assess competence or the ability to exert influence in public affairs? This notion of competence suggests, perhaps, a new set of human proficiencies, undoubtedly more complicated to measure than familiar skills in reading, mathematics, or other conventional school subjects.

Program Implications

A humanistic approach to social action education will admittedly present problems for school programs. A new curriculum that focuses on social action competence rather than conventional subject matter must be developed. It must be taught within a humanistic climate in the school at large, and schools must be willing to sponsor students' active participation in social controversy.

New Curriculum

If schools were to take seriously the objective of enhancing student ability to exert influence in public affairs, what would the curriculum look like? We need some indication of the kinds of knowledge, skills, and attitudes to be addressed. The figure below illustrates a possible framework. Prior to exerting influence or trying to implement a position, a person must learn to clarify and justify the particular policies, candidates, and actions that he or she supports (or opposes). These become one's goals or desired outcomes in public affairs. They should be formulated not on the basis of impulse, whim, or duress, but upon moral deliberation and rational social research. That is, prescriptive claims involving possible value conflicts (We ought to legalize abortion.) should be justified through a principled, ethical framework, and controversial empirical, definitional, or legal claims (The parents of unwanted children and the children themselves lead a difficult life.) should be supported with as much evidence as possible.

Having formulated goals (for example, repeal of an antiabortion

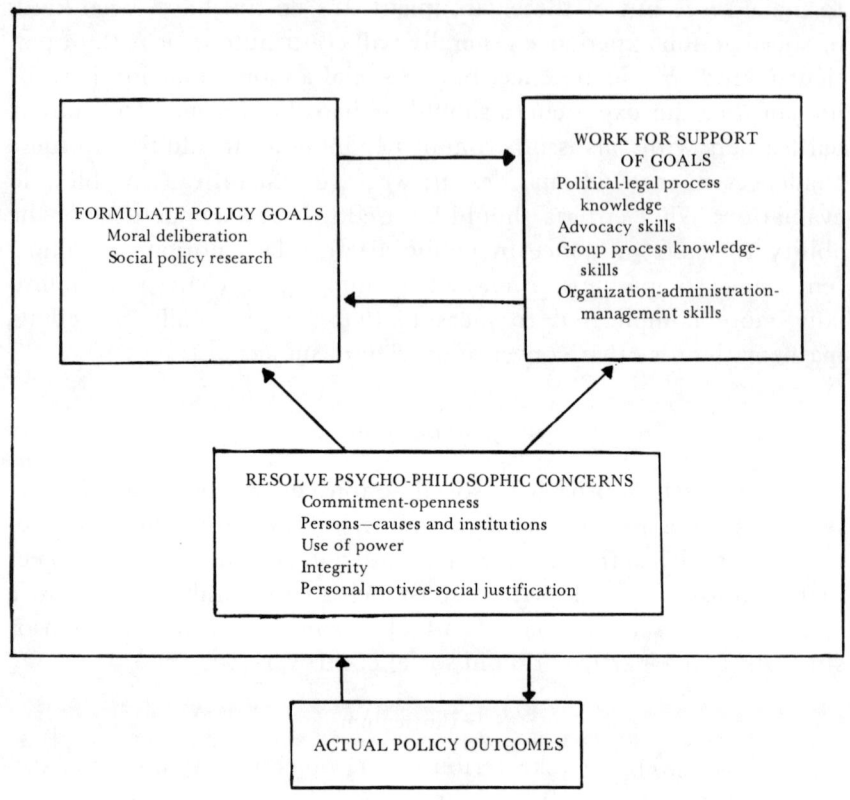

FIGURE 2.1
Areas of competence required to exert influence
in public affairs

law, starting an abortion counseling service, or electing an official who would press on these matters), the citizen works to muster support after determining whose support is required to implement the goal. Accurate information is required on how power is distributed and how decisions are made within institutions relevant to the goal. This can be summarized as knowledge of the realities of political-legal process. To communicate and justify the goal to appropriate individuals, agencies, or publics, advocacy skills in writing, speaking, and the use of various media are needed. Assistance from different groups, also critical in mobilizing support, makes knowledge of group behavior and skills in group dynamics a third component. Finally, effective campaign management requires record keeping, planning and scheduling of meetings, fund raising, negotiation tactics, and other practical competencies summarized as skills in organization-administration-management.

In formulating goals and in trying to win support, a number of concerns or "psycho-philosophic dilemmas" are likely to confront the activist. Suppose one person is so ambivalent that he cannot act with conviction on any public issue. Another feels so omnipotent that she often sets goals impossible to achieve. Some citizens may be reluctant to act because they see public controversy mainly as a form of interpersonal warfare, and they shy away from "hurting people." Others may have difficulty trying to decide how much they can compromise without losing their personal integrity. Some may participate, but they feel guilty when personal motives for acting do not seem to match the ostensible social justification of the cause. Because stress and anxiety roused by these concerns may interfere with productive action, a citizen action curriculum should make an attempt to help people resolve such difficulties.

The model may seem overly idealized or formalized. Certainly all the activities of effective citizens cannot be neatly charted according to these components. Nor should the components be viewed as being isolated from one another or as being organized in linear sequence. The process of winning support may actually assist in clarifying goals. Involvement in advocacy and persuasion may lead to deeper moral deliberation or further policy research. Psycho-philosophic concerns may either encourage certain action strategies or result from them. In other words, the parts of the model continually interact in patterns idiosyncratic to the nature of each person's involvement in a given issue. The components are outlined here only to focus attention on specific and theoretically distinct aspects in a conception of ability to exert influence in public affairs. Analytic dissection makes it easier to see whether or how well the existing curriculum covers various facets involved in the exercise of influence. The secondary curriculum may already deal with some of the components indirectly, but in general the model offers a totally new agenda for instruction.

Recent reports of national commissions and a number of curriculum projects emphasize points consistent in spirit with this curriculum model. As urged by the Panel on Youth, such a curriculum would place youth in contact with the nonschool adult world and involve them in collective endeavors.[33] As recommended by the Kettering Commissions,[34] such curriculum would stress community involvement, could provide an "alternative path" to high school completion, would encourage "credit for experience," and would emphasize "action learning," a theme recently advocated by the National Association of Secondary School Principals.[35] It is consistent with the thrust toward community involvement encouraged by the National Commission on Resources for Youth[36] and the expanding efforts of many schools to help students offer volunteer service to community agencies.

Curriculum innovations in the areas of moral development,[37] law-related education,[38] and analysis of public controversy[39] can all be relevant to the proposed model. Unfortunately, however, these disparate efforts have not been synthesized into a comprehensive approach to enhance competence in social action. Curriculum in moral development, for example, may focus excessively on ethical dilemmas more in the realm of private, interpersonal relations than public policy, and it seems oriented almost exclusively toward developing a cognitive position rather than also learning to act consistently with it. In contrast, volunteer service programs emphasize action and community involvement, but may devote little systematic attention to the reflective, cognitive dimensions, and some tend to shy away from assertive, change-oriented projects. Efforts in law-related education expose students to specific laws and general concepts to help them understand the legal system, but possibly neglect realities of informal legal-political process that an effective activist must know. A major curriculum challenge is to bring these diverse efforts into a systematic focus on social action and to convince schools that such curriculum deserves a significant place in their program.

Instructional Climate

Even if an adequate curriculum were developed, it alone is unlikely to humanize education unless it affects the pervasive instructional climate in which it is taught. Will students view citizen action courses simply as another arena for gamesmanship in making it through their term in the school "prison"? Will they view such courses as novel ways for adults to foist upon children notions of the

Social Action

"right" preparation required to become a productive citizen? Will the courses, in spite of rhetoric about helping them exert influence, actually inhibit their use of power? Although the curriculum may officially stress the importance of collective cooperation in the exercise of influence, does the process of instruction encourage destructive individual competition? We must alert ourselves to ways in which various program structures can suppress or nurture the essential spirit of a social action curriculum. At least three particular aspects of "climate" must be confronted.

Paternalism versus self-assertion. In several ways a school can convey the idea that prepackaged education has been prepared by adults who know what is best and that the student role is to receive and absorb it, passively accepting what is given. This message is manifested, however unintentionally, when the teacher plans in advance, without student input, everything that a student will do in a course (readings, assignments, exercises, games, exams, field trips); when the school provides for the student all the resources needed for learning; when the school establishes for students a system of governance that allows them no responsibility for the making or enforcing of policy and insists that they obey policies set by adults; when particular policies actually *prohibit* students from exerting influence in their school environment (no decoration of the walls, no student participation in school landscaping, no use of school facilities for conducting political campaigns). For social action curriculum to be consistent with its own justification, it must avoid these practices.

Social action courses should place students in roles where they assume meaningful responsibility for asserting themselves. Instead of being engaged in learning that has only private consequences, students working toward adoption or repeal of actual policies should be publicly accountable for some of their actions. This can be particularly important in the school environment where students should have a voice, though not a unilateral one, in determining their own citizen action curriculum. Students should have to act assertively to acquire resources, apart from minimal ones (especially telephones), that must be supplied at the outset. In action projects students should be involved in the formulation of their own learning objectives. Within a single course and operating within the larger school structure, students may, in concert with the teacher, establish policies on attendance, evaluation, requirements for "products," methods for access to facilities. More extensive opportunities for governance could be provided by a "sabbatical" model, a one-year, full-time curriculum in which students earn major credits toward graduation. Under this program students would have only minimal obligations to other courses within the school, and they could, therefore, participate in authentic governance of their own separate program.[40]

In general, the exercise of influence as a central purpose of curriculum stands opposed to paternalistic climates and to apathetic or fatalistic orientations. (Accept the world as it is, for there is nothing we can do to change it.) Instead, self-assertion to affect the environment is valued. When students encounter obstacles to self-assertion in the school itself (a rule against painting the walls, or lack of student representation on the school board), they must be encouraged to investigate the justifications behind apparent obstacles. They must not be penalized for mounting campaigns against them. A citizen action curriculum will be ineffective unless the general school climate supports assertive behavior to make an impact in the immediate environment as well as in the community beyond the school.

Individualism versus collective cooperation. The ensuing critique of individualism is offered not to diminish but to reaffirm the ethical obligation to respect the dignity of each individual human. To secure individual rights in public affairs, it becomes necessary for the individual to work within collectives of persons with mutual interests. Many facets of school, through overwhelming attention to the individual, however, communicate a conspicuous lack of recognition of the significance of collective effort and responsibility. While we often complain that instruction in the schools is not individualized enough, a preoccupation with the individual to the exclusion of the collective is illustrated in many practices.

Programs of instruction are selected for students through individualized counseling and career planning, giving students the impression that the entire purpose of education is to enhance one's individual mobility or opportunity in life. Learning materials are assigned to individual students (checking out of library books or equipment), and locker space is also allocated on an individual basis. Discipline is oriented toward finding the individual responsible for breaking the rules. Work assignments within courses are the responsibility of individual students. Cooperation with others in the completion of work is often punished as "cheating." Finally, the grading system assigns marks to individuals and encourages competitive individual comparison by bestowing status upon high rank in class. Awards to valedictorians and special privileges for other high academic achievers further reinforces individual competition.

This is not to say that all such practices should be abolished, for instructional programs must recognize individual needs and must also hold individuals responsible for their actions. Social action curriculum, however, faces a special challenge in conveying to students the significance and legitimacy of collective action and cooperation. Because of a dominant emphasis on individualism in society, the collective mentality may be difficult to establish, but some practices can assist in this effort. Individual students should not be encouraged to go off and do their individual "thing," for their ability to exert influence in public policy will not be enhanced unless they learn to work within groups. Student work should be organized into group activities, and various members involved in a project should all have responsibilities that assist in reaching a common goal. The evaluation of student performance can also be oriented toward accomplishments and shortcomings of the group rather than the comparative achievements of individuals. All individual evaluation should not, however, be abandoned. Individuals within groups should evaluate each other as to the extent of their contribution to the group effort and how that contribution might be enhanced in the future. Responsibility for equipment and for obedience to institutional policy can also be assigned to a project group, with the group as a whole being responsible for losses or infractions. Internally, the group could distribute blame or punishment as it deemed just. The point of modifying instructional climate in such ways is not to stamp out individualism, but to prevent its excesses from inhibiting the collective effort required in the exercise of influence.

Intrinsic versus extrinsic value. Much activity in school, if valued at all by students, is valued only for its extrinsic or instrumental worth. Studying [X] is good because it leads to something else, such as a diploma, a college education, or money. The instrumental value of learning can infect instructional climate, as teachers candidly inform students that they may not enjoy [X], but it is necessary if they wish to move ahead in life. Many educators cannot justify, either to themselves or to students, certain aspects of the curriculum except that they are required by some other institution.

The fragmentation of time in scheduling reflects in part the primacy of extrinsic over intrinsic values. If, in a student's eyes, a subject is worthy of study in its own right, there is no reason why the ringing of a bell or the requirement that one must also complete work in other subjects simultaneously should prevent the student from pursuing it. A busy schedule can make it virtually impossible to become absorbed in something intrinsically satisfying, and students have little choice but to roam through the curriculum touching many subjects superficially.

Citizen action courses must take care not to communicate to students the idea that instruction in this area is merely a vehicle to some other value (good citizenship or personal power). Avoiding this message may be difficult, for we admittedly see social action in an instrumental sense, that is, as one means toward the end of exerting influence. At the same time, if students are led to construe their work *only* as means, lacking intrinsic value, they are unlikely to become seriously engaged. An instructional climate might emphasize the intrinsic worth of an activity if students are allowed to pursue it in a sustained fashion, uninterrupted by other obligations; if staff members show enthusiasm for its intrinsic value and can rationally justify its value in other than instrumental terms; and if formal institutional rewards and punishments for engaging in the activity or for one's level of performance are kept to a minimum. These recommendations on instructional climate would be appropriate for humanizing education in general, but the first two, assertion and collective cooperation, seem especially crucial for the teaching of competence in social action.

Political Neutrality of the School

Curriculum for citizen action might escalate the school's entanglement in political controversy. If students are to learn to exert influence in public affairs, the school must provide an appropriate "laboratory" experience, namely, authentic participation in social action projects. For those who view school as a neutral, impartial citadel of wisdom standing above the biases and passions of political-economic life, the prospect of school-sponsored student involvement in public affairs can be frightening, indeed. The fear is that groups with special political interests will begin to dominate the curriculum, thereby violating the professional integrity which, presumably, educators alone bring to subject matter. If commitment to social causes were to replace dispassionate inquiry as a goal of education, could this not infringe on academic freedom and freedom of speech? Any response to this point depends upon one's conception of the alleged "political neutrality" of state-supported schools.

Granted, in a certain sense, the school ought to be as "politically neutral" as possible. That is, it should be a model of pluralism in which students are free to learn about a variety of political philosophies and cultural styles. Inquiry should not be restricted by the temporary objectives of specific political, economic, or ethnic groups. The academic justification for this notion of neutrality is that "truth" itself cannot be ascertained without uncensored investigation of a wide range of pluralistic "answers" to the important "questions" of life. There is also a political justification for academic freedom. The principles of justice and representative democracy require the state to ensure that all groups have a reasonably equal chance to express themselves in order that they have a reasonably equal chance to govern themselves. In this sense the insistence on political neutrality in specific matters stems from a more general ethical-political vision, and the school cannot, therefore, be neutral with regard to this ideal. As a vehicle of a democratic state, the school must work to fulfill the political principles of consent of the governed and equal liberty. It should not therefore, be considered "politically neutral" in an absolute sense.

Thus, for both academic and political reasons the school should design programs that cultivate in every student the ability to exert influence, whether one holds a minority or a majority point of view, whether one belongs to a group that has negligible or awesome power. Student action projects should be able to confront and oppose each other. Some may work for increases in welfare payments; others for decreases. Some may lobby for more parks; others for more parking lots. Opposing candidates for public office might each have students working in their organizations. To the extent that a school is committed to pluralism of this sort, it can stimulate free inquiry, which could keep it from becoming a "tool" of special interests. In this sense it remains "neutral," even when its students are politically active.

A school might encourage action projects considered "constructive" (for example, volunteer programs for the elderly), but prohibit others (for example, a campaign to expose financial investments of school officials). To the extent that projects become censored, not for moral or legal reasons, but to maintain the power of a particular regime, the school is no longer neutral. It is possible to conclude that schools have never been or can never be neutral, for their very existence depends upon the political and economic support of constituencies with specific biases. Where this interpretation prevails, citizen action projects may help students exert influence in public affairs, but only in narrow directions acceptable to the establishment. To the extent that schools restrict the range of action that students may undertake, they no doubt violate the pluralistic philosophy. Indoctrination, partisanship, or one-sidedness arising from group attempts to maintain power, however, are problems that pervade *all* curricula; they are not unique to citizen action. If schools by their nature are inevitably and exclusively involved in power maintenance, then the question is not whether schools should support student action projects, but whether schools will tolerate *any* learning that might pose a threat to the values and policies of existing regimes. It is possible, of course, that many schools will sincerely endorse the neutrality and pluralism advocated here, if only because such openness would increase student support for school authorities.

We advise, on the one hand, that schools support student involvement in a wide range of controversial community issues. On the other hand, we affirm the responsibility of school authorities to see that student involvement is ethically justifiable. Mechanisms must be established through which the "legitimacy" of various forms of student involvement is openly considered. This might involve a committee of students, teachers, parents, and administrators who review student proposals and offer students (and their teachers) the opportunity to plead their case when ethical questions are raised.

Social action and community involvement activities vary widely in their potential benefit to students and society. They should not, therefore, be unconditionally endorsed as methods for humanizing education. However, the educational goal of enhancing student *competence* in social action (that is, increasing their ability to exert influence in public affairs) is justified and significant, for it contributes to individual psychological identity, establishes identity as moral agents, and fulfills the democratic political principle of consent of the governed. To educate for increased competence in social action, schools must provide laboratory experience in action projects. If these projects are to qualify as humanistic, they must involve students in rational reflection and in ethical justification grounded in principles of justice, and they must actually contribute to increased student competence. To implement this general approach, schools should develop new curricula based on an analysis of action competencies. Changes in the general instructional climate should also occur, including more emphasis on assertion and collective responsibility. The school will have to take a politically neutral stance in allowing student participation in a plurality of causes.

Discussion

Participants (in order of speaking): *David E. Purpel, Fred M. Newmann, Ralph Mosher, James B. Macdonald, Walter Feinberg, Michael W. Apple, Thomas J. Sergiovanni, Flora Nell Roebuck, Nancy R. King, Bill Wesley Brown,* and *Robert M. O'Kane*

Purpel: Would you go so far as to say that it's inherently good for people to be socially active, that it's not just a technique? I think you often claim that for adults, but you seem to have reservations when it comes to youngsters.

Newmann: If you take Rawls seriously, along with some Aristotelian principles, you must say that it is inherently good for people—adults as well as youngsters—to be involved in the affairs of the community. On the other hand, I cannot endorse unconditionally all forms of community involvement. First, there is an ethical problem. I can envision Hitler and a lot of his friends involved in the affairs of their community, and this should illustrate that involvement per se, whether for kids or adults, is not necessarily good. Involvement is not good if it aims toward violation of fundamental rights. Second, and this is most relevant to involvement of school children, all forms of involvement are not inherently educational. To be educationally justified, involvement must bring increased personal competence.

Purpel: Well, I think you left something out of the presentation then. It sounds to me like you are now saying that if you get involved and do good things, social action is okay; if you get involved and do bad things, however, it is not okay.

Newmann: No. My claim is only that, if you get involved, you have an obligation to justify your actions with regard to a certain ethical framework. The framework cannot indisputably solve all ethical questions, and people will continue to disagree as to whether a given "justification" is adequate; for example, one person might be acting to legalize abortion, another working to prohibit it, but both could be reasoning from the ethical framework based on equal respect for life.

Purpel: You want them to be involved in a certain way, then I'm not just involved for the sake of being involved, but involved along the lines you suggest, including rational discussion and other manifestations of social activity.

Newmann: Right.

Purpel: I have one more concern. Most people are indifferent. They have no desire to participate. How are we to view them?

Newmann: Lack of interest could be due to a variety of factors. As educators, however, we should try to focus on one in particular: overcoming the lack of interest, or sense of alienation or powerlessness that derives from lack of personal competence. I assume that most inactive citizens fail to participate—in part at least—because they are incompetent. There is virtually no evidence to indicate that they are in fact competent, but have chosen to drop out for other reasons. The real choice as to whether to become involved can come only after a person has developed some competence to participate. This, of course, introduces another problem: Should all students be required to take a program in citizen action? Perhaps this should be mandated in order to ensure that one's interest or lack of interest in community affairs cannot be attributed to incompetence. At the moment, I have no grounds for insisting that all students take such a program, primarily because I cannot demonstrate that it is actually possible to teach the necessary competencies.

Mosher: And if you could?

Newmann: Requiring a course amounts to a restriction on liberty, because it denies people the opportunity to do other things during school time, like, for example, learning to play the cello. We should think carefully about whether forcing people to develop skills in civic action is an ethically justifiable restriction on their liberty.

Macdonald: I think that, if anything is going to be required, it ought to be this. In order to have a participatory democracy, which is a given since that is the way we choose to live together, it is critical to develop participatory skills. It doesn't make a bit of difference to me whether you play the cello or not. I have to live with you and your participatory skills. If you're not competent, somebody can manipulate you, possibly to exploit me. To make participatory democracy work, all of us must be competent to participate intelligently. I depend on your skill as well as my own in social action.

Newmann: I would agree with that. If anything is going to be required, it should be instruction in civic action, assuming, of course, that we could deliver what we promise. So, you would argue that this would be a more fundamental reason for restricting individual liberty than any other?

Macdonald: Yes, I bought your basic assumption—I want us to live together in a community that is a participatory democracy. That's just a value. Here I stand. After that I have no trouble at all imposing certain requirements on people.

Feinberg: Why do you speak as if you were restricting liberty? It seems to me that, in order for liberty to exist, certain things need to be. If you require a person to learn to read, are you restricting his liberty or increasing the prospects that individual liberty will work?

Newmann: Well, that's a sensible justification. You do force someone to do something that he otherwise might not do, but you justify it on the grounds that it will enhance choice. A short-run restriction of liberty is, in the long-run, consistent with that principle. I think you could make a similar argument for requiring citizen action curriculum, assuming that you guarantee effective instruction.

Mosher: One of your original arguments, as I heard it, was that you would require a social action curriculum, because it would mean, assuming it was effective, that individual development would not be permanently retarded or fixed.

Newmann: Right. I referred to this as the personal competence or "fulfillment" criterion for humanistic education.

Apple: What is the criterion of success? Is it necessary that children actually accomplish what they set out to do? Or is it possible that failure and the realization that you may be unable to change what you tried could be an important lesson?

Newmann: Winning actual social struggles cannot be the criterion for educational success. It is logically impossible to have a social system in which there is controversy and still have everyone skillful enough to implement all their views. To measure educational success, we must step back from the criterion of success in actual social struggles and look at what might be considered more discrete skills and competencies.

Apple: But what do you do? Do you establish tests to show students how good they are at political canvassing, running meetings, speaking clearly to public audiences? Can you establish a logical connection between these competencies and success with the students' social objectives (for example, legalizing marijuana)?

Newmann: We already have workable conceptions of mathematical ability and reading ability, but I'm dealing with a new conception, the notion of ability to exert influence in public affairs. I see this as a frontier problem for educational measurement. You're right that it may be impossible to establish a logical connection, but complete success in the social struggles is not necessarily the ultimate educational goal, and we cannot rely on this type of success as an exclusive criterion for personal competence. If you're a Republican and I'm a Democrat it is impossible for both of us to succeed in winning a particular election, but it does seem possible that, win or lose, during the campaign each of us could gain competence in exerting influence. The measurement challenge is to identify other ways in which our competence can be recognized.

Feinberg: The context of your presentation basically assumes what I would take to be acceptable avenues of political participation, organization, criticism, and . . .

Newmann: Not necessarily. What do you mean by "acceptable"?

Feinberg: Well, borderline acceptability would be things like boycotts and strikes, sit-ins at principals' offices, and so forth. Beyond the borderline would be things like destruction of property, beating up students, or . . .

Newmann: Can you think of situations in which beating up students would be ethically justifiable from the principles that I have enumerated?

Feinberg: No.

Newmann: How about sit-ins?

Mosher: Yes, probably.

Newmann: The only thing I ask is that you apply the criteria of rational justification with reference to principles of justice. I can think of many situations in which thoughtful reasoners, using these principles, can offer persuasive justifications for the use of violence or breaking the law, and equally thoughtful people, using the same criteria, will disagree. As I noted in my presentation, many ethical controversies, because of factual and definitional uncertainty, are simply unresolvable. School administrations may censor certain student actions for reasons of regime preservation or administrative convenience, but my curriculum position argues that all tactics should be allowed unless they can be proven ethically unjustifiable.

Apple: It just seems like a strangely disembodied, apolitical approach. Are you arguing that schools should be neutral?

Newmann: No. Schools should take a vigorous stand in defense of representative democracy. That's not politically neutral.

Apple: Okay, neutrality of a different sort. That is, one that does not favor any position, and regards all positions as equally good.

Newmann: No. You miss the ethical qualification. Schools must not be neutral with regard to the principles of justice on which representative democracy is based. This requires, for example, that schools take a stand in favor of a defendant's right to due process or against genocide.

Feinberg: But on the abortion question, for example—if group A is interested in having the laws more strongly enforced and group B wants the same laws eliminated or changed, both groups could operate within the social science department of the high school.

Newmann: Yes.

Feinberg: In that sense it's politically neutral.

Newmann: Yes. The school must remain neutral on questions of specific policy and on partisan issues that do not entail clear violations of the principles of justice and equality.

Apple: Given the distribution of power in most communities, I think you would have a high probability of certain kinds of action prevailing and certain kinds of action not being found at all. What's your view about that?

Newmann: It would be wrong for schools to censor or constrain student action on criteria other than those I have suggested. It is common to claim that schools exist primarily to bolster existing political-economic structures, and particular regimes, and that they would, therefore, never condone actions that threaten the status quo. The point may be well-taken, but note that it negates the value of virtually all school-based instruction. For according to this view, *everything* that is taught (from reading to music) must be seen only as a device by which a ruling elite keeps others in submission. If the interpretation is true, then I suppose education could never be improved until some radical societal upheaval altered the underlying relationship between schools and society. However, I think the interpretation is debatable, and, to the extent that it is open to question, we have no reason to refrain from developing vigorous citizen action curricula.

Macdonald: Do you see the social action curriculum as being connected with any substantive areas already in the school curriculum? For example, youngsters get involved with a "problem of living" theme such as pollution through a study of problems evident in the environment. Is social action curriculum going to emerge from that, as well as such broader issues as abortion?

Newmann: Sure. It could come out of anything. For many reasons I would not recommend a national curriculum; but one drawing largely on local concerns.

Macdonald: Maybe some of the difficulties broached in the presentation by Apple and King could be resolved if there were substantive connections as well as local concern.

Newmann: I don't think so. If a school really exists to maintain the power of certain groups in society, it's going to perform in a way to do that, whether through adopting an English reader or introducing this curriculum.

Apple: I know that you're in the process of trying to work with schools on this. If it were instituted, however, it would probably resemble many programs from the past. Because the basic regularities of the school experience remain fairly traditional, any social action program would be conservative. In my mind that carries a negative connotation.

Newmann: When schools have allowed students to venture into the community, you're right—projects have tended to be what you call "conservative." Why? Many factors could be responsible. Did the administration prevent radical students from acting? Do few students have radical ideas? I don't have a complete explanation, but I would not assume that forces in the school administration are primarily responsible. Yet, what does it matter whether students, after they have enhanced their competence to act, choose to act in conservative ways? The point of education for citizen action is not to promote liberal causes, but to enliven democratic participation.

Mosher: Precisely! One reason the programs may be characterized as conservative is that adolescence, from a developmental perspective, is clearly a rehearsing and practicing of conventional roles, attributes, thinking, functioning. It is a time of preparation to fill the role of conventional adult. So that does not surprise me. Real tests should be concerned, rather, with the kinds of competencies the students should acquire, the impact of the experience on their moral reasoning, and their social perspective.

Newmann: If we find a prevailing conservative or conventional social perspective, let us not blame the schools alone. We cannot ignore the pervasive cultural messages communicated through the media, parenting, peer culture, and so on. I would agree that cultural blindness and obsession with convention is in one sense "negative," but it is no reason to avoid trying to teach a more assertive citizenship.

Feinberg: There are actually two questions involved here. The first is concerned with what we should do if the direction of a social action effort is other than what we would desire. I guess your answer to that would be to see if it fit the broad rubric of the kind of competency to be developed and did not violate broad ethical norms. Then you wouldn't disagree with the particular program.

Newmann: Right.

Feinberg: The second concern, which is to me somewhat more interesting, calls for an explanation of why such programs usually follow conservative lines. I tend to reject the developmental explanation. Even if children at a certain age rehearse adult roles, you must ask whether that stage, namely adolescence, is itself a peculiarity of a certain culture rather than a universal psychological happening. Another question comes to mind: Why do social roles reflect a basically conservative trend? Let's not throw out the developmental consideration as an ingredient in the explanation, but it should also call attention to other societal phenomena.

Mosher: When you confront young people with societal norms, rules, ways of thinking, and roles, there's no way of avoiding the psychological factor that strengthens conventional thought. There is massive reinforcement from adults, institutions, the cultural norms around them, as well as from the courts. For me, the answer is to look at what we know about the kinds of experiences—educational, psychological, social—that permit people to develop post-conventional perspectives.

Newmann: That is helpful. Some of the political participation literature has shown that, as a group, conservatives are more active politically than liberals in this society.

Macdonald: They are more competent in the terms you mentioned before, and they also win more often.

Newmann: Compare a person who sees himself as outside the institutions all the time and wanting to change them (call him the "radical") versus a person who feels that the institutions really work for him so that he wants to reinforce them (he's the conservative). Isn't it psychologically more comfortable to be on the inside trying to improve something, than on the outside trying to attack or replace it? This may explain why conservatives tend to become more involved, and alienated radicals shy away from it. Social action curriculum has a special obligation to help those who feel on the outside deal with the stress and anxiety inherent in the role of "outsider."

Purpel: I want to pursue the psycho-philosophic point and the need for support—not so much in relation to radical young people but in relation to the mass of young people who don't care. It seems to me that this model is missing some concept of compassion, of caring, and that this is a problem both young people and adults have. Where does compassion enter the discussion? Call it motivation, if you prefer psychological terms, but it seems to me that it should spring from some deeply felt concern. I've been thinking about the kinds of projects you're talking about. I can see students going through a series of social action projects where the focus is on a swimming pool, a better water purification system, electing a competent member to the school board. Meanwhile, there is world hunger, abject poverty, armed conflict, social injustice. Would the orientation you propose be a way of denying the reality of basic social injustice and other serious problems? Would local experience overshadow them?

Newmann: I agree that concern for local problems should not be pursued in ways that neglect more global dimensions. However, I think even the so-called apathetic people do care. People have a profound sense of injustice over what they see in the world. The reason they are not more deeply involved is not because they don't care, but because they see no way to act productively on the compassionate instincts that are roused. I think the feeling is there, but that something like a social action curriculum is needed to give it a constructive outlet. Maybe in my book (*Education for Citizen Action*) I overemphasized local problems. I did this to help counteract the common response, "Kids can't really do anything about national or global problems." In focusing on local problems as ways to develop competence, however, I did not intend to neglect more pervasive injustices. In the section called "use of power," I discussed the problem of balance between different levels of participation. Whether to use one's competence to gain a local swimming pool for a low-income neighborhood or in an attempt to change federal tax laws to redistribute the wealth is a genuine dilemma for any person who wants to act on the problem of economic inequality. There is no universal solution that indicates how one should direct his energy. We have to accept choices like these as real sources of stress for the thoughtful activist, and the curriculum should help students anticipate and reflect on the dilemmas.

Sergiovanni: Are these all individual student decisions, or is the social action curriculum part of the broader context of general instruction? I assume that there must be some clarification of values, and the process of making the actual decision could assume varied forms—all of which could serve to highlight potential projects.

Newmann: That's right.

Sergiovanni: It would appear, then, that whoever facilitates the decision-making process could help to alleviate some of the above criticisms by making sure, in the stage where values are clarified, that issues are developed and examined from many perspectives before a decision is made. And it might also be feasible, after several projects were implemented, to study the character of the decisions and look at the more traditional biases. I don't see social action as just being out there, set apart from the school.

Newmann: Certainly.

Roebuck: I hear a value principle in all you've been saying: that equal liberty for all is the ultimate goal for social action.

Newmann: That's what I would call a central principle of justice.

Roebuck: Okay. Then, if your curriculum explicitly states this, it becomes a criterion to which the students, when putting these things into practice, come back repeatedly. This is the responsibility of the facilitator of that curriculum. It seems that, with these principles explicitly stated as part of the curriculum, you have a means of gaining consideration, even in the conservative community, for radical, different, new, or nonconservative programs.

Newmann: Yes. But I want to point out two common misinterpretations of our emphasis on equal liberty. One is the assumption that equal liberty means that any student should be free to undertake any project he or she wants, without trying to justify it to others in terms of that principle. I've indicated, I hope, that the principle requires that projects be defended with regard to the principle itself. Second, people tend to assume that we would teach the principle moralistically, or through some form of arbitrary indoctrination. This approach to teaching is unjustifiable, because it is inefficient pedagogy, and because it violates the principle itself. Instead, the principle should be "taught" by having students confront and reason about social conflict, and by encouraging them to define for themselves the most defensible ethical principles. This open examination of ethical norms may reach a point where the student says, "I don't give a damn about equal liberty. What I want is something for me. It's survival of the fittest that counts in this society and that's what I'm going to do. I'm going to rip somebody off because that's going to give me more power." At that point your moral obligation may be to stop the student from acting, but your *instructional* responsibility is to help the student clarify those principles that can be best defended from an ethical and philosophical point of view.

Roebuck: Didn't you refer to the ultimate value of justice, of equal liberty for all, as one of the criteria by which a program would be judged?

Newmann: It is, but it is dysfunctional if it is presented as an arbitrary virtue or commandment. Students must be encouraged to study and question the principles in such a way that they can develop their own, rationally based commitment to them.

Roebuck: Then we're saying the same thing. I'm saying that, if the person responsible for facilitating is aware of these kinds of goals, then you're not so likely to get into the narrower kinds of social action.

Apple: I'm not so sure. You have to look at this as a language of justification, too—not just philosophical justification but how it actually will work in schools. It is quite possible to interpret schools as dysfunctional places for black children in the inner city, as unhelpful institutions, as places that divide students. These points are as significant as the one stating: "some of them get to read." We also know that, because of the behavioral regularities of the institution, when something new is introduced it tends to become much like what preceded it. Do you see any problems with people looking at what you are proposing and saying, "Look, we already have social action curriculum in the schools—and some students really enjoy it"? Can't this be used to justify a school program which in general is often harmful to many students? Would you speak to the politics and the economics of introducing social action into the curriculum so that it doesn't simply add to the rhetoric of justification for what goes on. ("We've got a little social action; it keeps the kids cool; and we can go right on doing our job with no fundamental changes in the institution.")

Newmann: I spend most of my intellectual energy trying to conceptualize curriculum, not analyzing the underlying politics that may affect the use of language. I would be delighted if schools really did implement a curriculum similar to what I propose, and if they then "used" this to justify their general operation, then I might have to agree with them. Perhaps the conference could devote some time to dealing with your question on redesigning the whole institution. In short, however, I do not believe we should oppose good programs on the grounds that they tend to make bad institutions look better.

Apple: Let me restate the second part of my question. It is possible to view American history as a participatory democracy, a pluralistic democracy in which competing pressure groups, all fighting for their interests, have produced solutions to social problems. Unfortunately, the facts show that people without power have never had their problems solved through this process. The same groups tend to stay powerless generation after generation. While income levels may go up, power is not redistributed equally. Won't social action curriculum give people a false sense of confidence that basic changes can be made, when in fact they may be impossible without structural alterations? Of course you could say that social action curriculum has never really been tried, and, once it is, these fundamental problems would be solved through people's increased competence.

Newmann: I agree that we find enormous disparities in power, considerable injustice, but there are many possible explanations for this. One is that the nature of this society's political-economic system thrives on such disparities and will forever maintain them. Another is that problems in the modern world are so complex as to overwhelm human intelligence—we are incapable of handling all the information needed to eliminate inequalities. A third is that a certain amount of inequality or injustice could be rectified through increased personal competence in social affairs. As educators it seems to me we should do all we can to eliminate personal incompetence as one of the causes of social injustice. For a moment, entertain the fantasy that our proposed curriculum were tremendously successful nation-wide and that every student's competence to participate in public affairs were increased to the highest degree possible. What would you predict? Would there be "solutions" to any major social problems?

Apple: You'd have another Italy.

Roebuck: Yes, a separate political party for every citizen.

Newmann: But how would public policy change, what would our social blueprint look like? Would we have massive citizen participation? Redistribution of wealth? A national health insurance program? Voluntary school attendance? I must admit I have no notion of how substantive policy would change or what would happen to the distribution of wealth. The question is whether you as an educator have a more specific vision of what the blueprint should look like. If, for example, your goal is redistribution of wealth, perhaps the worst thing you could do is increase everyone's competence to participate, for then perhaps the propertied interests would gain more power than they now have. Perhaps the best way to bring in your social vision is to train an elite corps of revolutionaries to seize power and redistribute wealth before anyone has a chance to protest.

Apple: As you know, some countries have turned to that answer.

Newmann: There is a crucial difference between educating for a neo-Marxist social structure and educating to improve democratic political process. The social blueprint I have in mind is grounded in a conception of people participating equally to affect affairs in their own communities. This may or may not result in radical redistribution of wealth. While I am personally in favor of that, I don't believe it is logically required; nor can I think of specific policies to bring it about that are so indisputably valid to warrant teaching them as the foundation of a curriculum. Instead, it makes more sense to help people participate in the process so *they* can determine whether the neo-Marxist plan is what they want.

Feinberg: What if everyone maximizes their competence, but the result is greater disparity in the amount of liberty different groups have in the society?

Newmann: If we believe in the principle of consent of the governed, that is a risk we must take. According to my position, however, it is not much of a risk, for if people do what I say they ought, that is, justify their actions with regard to the principles of justice or equal liberty, it is unlikely that gross violations of the principles would be tolerated.

Feinberg: Suppose we have a competence scale that is like an IQ scale, but a real measure of competence to participate. If we create a program to develop everybody's competence to the maximum, we would expect variation at the end, for some people have more potential than others. In developing their potential, people become capable of using their competence to serve their own ends even better than they are serving those ends right now.

Newmann: Right, but they would pursue exclusively selfish ends only if they ignored the ethical commitment to equal liberty.

Feinberg: It seems that you're willing to allow students to undertake any project they wish if it is in pursuit of their liberty, but it's conceivable that the net result would be a reduction in liberty with people being less equal than they are now.

Newmann: I don't see how that follows if you maintain the commitment to the ethical framework based on equal liberty. Though I will not dictate which policies students work toward, I would insist that all projects be justified with regard to that basic principle.

King: It may be that children's opportunities to participate are diminished by their early school experiences. You indicated in your presentation that certain competencies are required before one can come to grips with moral dilemmas. I don't see any place in Figure 2.1 for these skills. The diagram seems to jump to the level of moral deliberation. What skills and competencies would a child have to bring to a problem before moral deliberation would be possible? Could it be that the early school years do not provide children with an equal chance to face problems of participation? If so, this would mean that early school experiences may limit a person's potential for becoming socially competent.

Newmann: That's a good point. But I think you could take this model and apply it anywhere in the curriculum. That is, you could say, "In order to get moral deliberation skills by the eleventh grade, we need to be working on certain other prerequisites before then." Any of the other skill areas might be approached in the same way.

Brown: Let's say that in your social action curriculum you had a problem of agreement about the issue of busing—whether it is either good or bad—and the students decided to take a stand and work for change. One student wrote a letter to the editor; one student tried to get a school board member defeated and another elected; one student dropped out of school in his frustration; other students participated in other ways. Are all responses equally good in your judgment?

Newmann: Good in what sense?

Brown: That's what I'm trying to determine.

Newmann: Suppose a student were to come to me and say he wanted to defeat busing in the community. According to the model, the first question would be: Why do you want to do that? We must first help the student examine whether he can justify what he wants to do from an empirical point of view, an ethical point of view, and so forth. Then, assuming that the general goal can be justified, the next concern is how to go about accomplishing it. If the student says he is going to write a letter to the school board to solve the problem and this is discussed among students, they might feel that such an effort is dumb in that it would be wasted. Such a tactic alone would be "bad" in the sense that it would not succeed in exerting any influence. If another student suggests bombing the home of the president of the school board, students might say this was "bad" for two reasons: it would be unethical, and it would not achieve the desired effect. In examining the rationale for any action, a number of good or bad judgments can be made at different levels.

Apple: I'm still not clear as to the short-term motivation. Most of the social action projects would, of necessity, last only for a short period of time. It takes much longer to influence public affairs. How do you evaluate them? It is difficult to establish a logical connection between having knowledge and having a disposition to do something. In the course of evaluation you might find a student who knows how to do all of the things you are suggesting. He feels competent, but he is never going to *do* anything. Can you deal with that?

Newmann: I agree that there's a logical gap between having competence and actually using it to exert influence in a long-term sense. Within the time period of a program, however, we can look at what students actually accomplish, the specific competencies they demonstrate regardless of success, and also their attitudes toward participation. It is an empirical question as to whether positive results on these measures would be associated with their behavior beyond the program.

Roebuck: One of the things we sometimes use to measure the success of the teaching of reading in the public schools is to ask the public librarian to keep a count of the number of books children check out. Maybe you can measure the tendency to participate by seeing what they voluntarily begin to do and measuring that unobtrusively.

Newmann: The main goal isn't necessarily to get them all to participate frequently. I'd be curious about this, but that isn't the basic goal.

Sergiovanni: What would our society be like after twenty-five years of enthusiastic acceptance of your program? There may be some very positive futures, but there may also be very negative ones, some of which have already been suggested. Certainly the analogy to governance in Italy cannot be completely dismissed. One thing that might happen is that conflict could be legitimized by being taught and accentuated. That raises a couple of questions. How much ambiguity and uncertainty can a community or school or classroom take? And, assuming that there are winners and losers for each of the issues at stake and that people make decisions based on factors beyond the control of educators (for example, home influences), would society be any different than it is now? Or, would it be more competitive? We might have the same elements, but perhaps they would be more accentuated, more exaggerated, more volatile, more personal. I'm not suggesting this as the likely outcome, but, rather, as a possible outcome after years of successful programming.

Newmann: It interests me that a number of these comments reflect the same fears that I have heard expressed by other adults and school people. They are afraid of what would happen if everybody's ability to participate in their community were increased. There's much rhetoric about how wonderful it is to live in a democracy and to govern ourselves, but we're really not sure that we want the people to have the power to govern themselves because they might do it wrong!

Sergiovanni: I don't think that's what I was suggesting.

Newmann: I hear Apple and Feinberg and you suggesting that. Are you sure you're not? Aren't you showing concern for the undesirable consequences of a more active citizenry?

Sergiovanni: There could indeed be undesirable consequences, but I don't think that people's social action tendencies ought to be repressed. As long as perspectives are being shared, opinions are being expressed, the critical process is working. Fifteen percent participating in the society can express the same views as if there were 75-percent participation, but the negative consequences of the latter should be considered. For you've now formalized and exaggerated latent social conflicts. The very conflicts that we encounter around this table could bring things to a halt if everyone were involved in more social action: writing letters, rousing support, and other activities. Again, I'm not saying that this is going to happen or that it's likely, but it certainly is an alternative future that one has to consider as a possible negative consequence.

Newmann: I would agree that the dangers you foresee are unlikely even if our program were successful, but that is really not the point. I'm trying to show that, to be consistent with the values of consent and equal liberty, you have to take that risk. Not to take it means that you are denying people the ability to participate.

Mosher: Precisely!

Roebuck: I'm not sure of the basic assumption that the goal of education in this country is participatory democracy. Is that what we're trying to attain?

Newmann: There's a lot of evidence that suggests that this country is not really trying to do that. You certainly don't see any evidence that we're trying to do it in the school curriculum and never have, although it is true that the rhetoric is all about that goal.

Mosher: You (Newmann) argue that you look for the effects of education through the enhancement of human rationality, ethical and moral sensibility, and the capacity for responsible social and political action. And you are prepared to take the risk. The outcome is uncertain as to whether that kind of enhancement of human rationality and character and social responsiveness will lead in positive directions. We don't know the outcome of that. *I'm* also prepared to take that risk personally. I don't have much time left. I think we might be able to generate some curriculum to do that in the next ten to fifteen years.

Feinberg: I'm not sure that it's so much of a risk for the established element of society. I think we know the kinds of tendencies in the society right now. We pretty well know how this kind of program will come out. People—children, adolescents, or whatever—have a tendency to be conservative. I don't think we really have to worry about it. We're all concerned about some kind of social order. It will be an interesting and, incidentally, I think worthwhile, ameliorative instrument. I'd be willing to see the program built on the value of equal liberty. But if equal liberty really became the goal of the program, it should work through some kind of ideology that would be reasonably compatible with that goal. If you just give everybody opportunities for social participation, I think that's good, too. But, I don't think it's complete. I think that the risk is minimal, and the outcome would probably be pretty conservative.

Macdonald: Let's say that we had had this program in the late 1950's or the early 1960's. People become radicalized at different times in their lives. You've had young people who developed competencies and social action skills, and they've been cleaning up the environment; it's all conservative stuff. Then you have a Vietnam, and the students become angry, *and* suppose they were competent. It could have been much different if the students had been competent in the early 1960's.

Mosher: If more adults had had competencies, there would have been a different outcome.

Feinberg: It's the evaluating of policy in accord with some norm that undercuts the jingoism of the Department of State and the Department of Defense. The participation needs to take place in the context of some kind of intelligent, ethical action, not just participation for its own sake.

Newmann: I agree—the point of participation is to serve the principles of justice.

Purpel: You could help your model by elaborating the concept of justice. Bread, for example, is part of justice. There are minimum sufficient conditions of livelihood required for human dignity. If we stop simply at procedural rights, we may have overlooked something else. For instance, a person has a procedural right to starve to death, but that doesn't fill me with awe! The point is: What constitutes an ethic of justice? What constitutes maintaining a person's dignity?

Mosher: Certainly, keeping them alive.

Purpel: Keeping them alive, yes, but what beyond that? I agree that part of your model is lacking in that it doesn't pay sufficient attention to other conditions for justice and dignity, conditions other than procedural guarantees.

Mosher: There is an important distinction. Newmann said earlier that, as an educator, he's concerned about youngsters having extensive experience in governance and participatory democracy because they will learn certain critical skills. That will also, from my point of view, have profound, nonreversible, developmental consequences in terms of their moral and social development. He also said, however, that what one does as a citizen to ameliorate social ills in the society is separate from what one proposes as a philosophy of education. You can't ban his educational program as I perceive it by saying that there are manifest social injustices in the larger society.

Purpel: But the model ought to deal with the question of where he got that definition of justice.

Mosher: Okay. I hate to simplify it, but his answer to pervasive social injustices is really to produce a more moral and more socially responsible individual, and large numbers of them, as the result of an incremental educational process.

Feinberg: I think we're being hung up by a confusion in the presentation. The confusion is the principle by which a school person judges whether a project is worth undertaking on the one hand, and the kind of student that ought to come out of this process on the other hand. That is to say, in your program, projects ought to be judged by their contributions to, or consistency with, the principle of equal liberty. But when it comes to saying what kind of person ought to come out, you are saying that you leave that open. Okay?

Newmann: No! That is central. Moral deliberation is part of the definition of personal competence. Moral deliberation is absolutely required in order to be consistent with the principles of equal liberty.

Apple: Okay. That's what I've been trying to determine.

Feinberg: I see, you want a person to come out of this not only with competencies but also with commitment to humanity and equal liberty.

Newmann: Yes. I'm sorry that didn't get across, because that's one of the first elements in the model. It's fundamental.

Mosher: It's a very small point, but I predict that some adolescents would have highly extrinsic reasons for participating in the social action program, and we should expect that. They go on a twenty-five-mile walkathon to help famine victims because their peers are going—that's the real reason—but it also touches a wellspring of concern for starving children in Africa. And that is related to a gradual emergence of a sense of empathy and social perspective. I would capitalize on that rather than denigrate it.

O'Kane: If you see humanistic education as the antecedent to social action and concern, what are the antecedents to humanistic education? Some people here have said, "Avoid it! You can't fool with the term." If you don't "fool with it," however, there's a danger. Harvey Kirk's *On Humanism* is very pragmatic and real; Tillich says humanism is based on a religious experience, and he is really concerned about a humanistic personality. In terms of curriculum, do you take something out and call it "humanistic education" and concentrate on it prior to getting students involved in social action? A second point: social action sounds like an "explosion" kind of thing, and humanistic education is more an "implosion" that brings us back to essentials of the human condition, character, and personality. These are not contradictions; perhaps they work for each other. A third point: another term I've heard frequently is "moral agent." I don't hear about the "moral client" because we become both. We don't just remain the agent; we frequently become the client. I'm also concerned, if we're going to push the moral and get young people involved, do they need surrogates? Other questions are: Are we getting involved in things that are nonethical? Is there a significant difference between what is ethical and what is moral? If we accept things as moral when the general culture agrees with them, such as social security . . .

Newmann: You've raised so many issues. My impression of humanistic education *in practice* is that it is unlikely to lead to citizen participation. It's too inward, too individualistic, too navel gazing. By focusing only on getting in touch with oneself, learning to express oneself and to fulfill oneself, it can be overindividualistic and ignore the community.

Purpel: Aren't you doing the same thing in this? What I heard you saying was that, as long as you follow certain procedures, you go off on your own. You want to work with the group, but I haven't heard you use the word community; nor have I heard anything about a common ethic except for procedures.

Newmann: Because I have chosen a competency framework, attention is directed toward the individual, and I can see, therefore, that the concept of community appears to be neglected. I believe, however, that individuals can find fulfillment only through meaningful community association. If we were to discuss more of the specifics of what to include in a social action curriculum, you would see that I put major emphasis on teaching kids to work within a collective framework in order to achieve action goals. The emphasis on moral deliberation also assumes a community context, based on the notion of respect for others.

Mosher: On that point, you do describe a climate of collective cooperation as one criterion for humanistic education.

Third
    Presentation

                                  David N. Aspy

An Interpersonal Approach to Humanizing Education

It seems appropriate to take a closer look at interpersonal relationships as an aspect of humanizing education since this concern may well be the heart of that process. If it were, the prime value of all human endeavors would be facilitation to the fullest potential of the physical, intellectual, and emotional health of man—both individually and collectively. Fulfillment of this constructive potential requires that each individual acquire the interpersonal skills necessary for facilitating self and others in the three dimensions of physical, intellectual, and emotional growth and that he utilize those skills at his highest level of capability. The ultimate goal of this process is a society designed to reinforce the delivery of helping skills to all members. That is, society would be so organized that its rewards would be given to those individuals and groups which facilitate the well-being of others rather than to those who exploit others.

Although some educators may wonder if schools should be involved in such personal concerns, the justification for this effort has some powerful support data. Mental health statistics describe a plethora of deficiencies in interpersonal functioning. Dropout rates and academic underachievement data indicate that personal failure regularly occurs within the school's interpersonal context. Expanding the view to national and international proportions confirms the same rather dismal picture found within individuals and in smaller groups. Apparently most of us have difficulty getting along with ourselves and with other people.

These interpersonal problems are vital concerns at both ends of the destruct-construct continuum. At one extreme there is the possibility that angry, isolated people could destroy the world through an atomic holocaust, while, at the other extreme, individuals and groups become bogged down in a morass of nonfacilitative interpersonal behavior that retards growth. Certainly interpersonal problems are not the only difficulties impeding progress, but it is pleasant to conjecture just how effective people could be if interpersonal friction were either eliminated or substantially reduced. The cynic will say that these problems are man's Achilles' heel, while the optimist will fantasize about the interpersonal millennium. Fortunately, there is a third option. Interpersonal problems can be studied and reduced systematically through continued efforts directed toward them. I contend that interpersonal difficulties are subject to the same types of strategies that have ameliorated some of mankind's other maladies. Man has it within his grasp to lessen his interpersonal problems. The question lies not in the inevitability of the difficulties but rather in the priority rating they receive in the consignment of human resources. *Interpersonal functioning is as subject to change as man's other behaviors.* Thus, it can be improved through learning, and it is a fit subject for those concerned with the improvement of education.

A second aspect of this issue makes current deliberation timely. Specifically, interpersonal training procedures are being researched and developed for the express purpose of applying them to large numbers of people at differing developmental levels. These efforts have at worst created a climate in which interpersonal relationships can be discussed, and at best they are effective. What is perhaps more important, these efforts have softened the interface between technology and the mysticism frequently associated with human feelings. For example, it is now possible to speak of a humane technology without appearing to be proposing an impossibility. This makes it feasible to introduce computer technology and sophisticated statistical analyses into settings previously closed to them, making possible tremendous advances in understanding and quantifying educational problems and finding solutions in interpersonal areas.

In a broader perspective it would appear that the current zeitgeist offers a splendid opportunity for applying powerful technologies to the toughest human problems. It may be that we are at the stage where Lake Erie found itself recently. It could be saved, but only if massive efforts were directed toward that end. Without meaning to sound alarmist, it is important to add that all of our constructive efforts may well exist in a time frame determined by the race between dehumanized people's destructive uses of atomic energy and the humanizing application of interpersonal skills development programs. If this seems rather remote, just ponder whether the United States would use nuclear bombs rather than be captured by a foreign power. Well, many nations with expansionist desires and the ability to construct nuclear bombs now coexist.

We live in a world of tensions, and it can be destroyed. Interpersonal skills seem critical as a deterrent to our destruct capacity, which, in this sense, puts those skills beyond being a frill or a luxury. They are essential for survival as well as growth.

A Model for Interpersonal Relationships

The term "interpersonal relationships" connotes a wide variety of meanings, so it is necessary to explain the one employed here. This orientation is based upon the theoretical work of Carl Rogers[1] and the empirical verification of his constructs by Robert Carkhuff.[2]

It is assumed that each of us has an emotional response to nearly every event in our lives. These may range from highly positive to highly negative or from intense to apathetic, but they are a real part of the "lived" experience. Some people assign various words to these emotional responses, and, though they are not the experience itself, they communicate something about it that may have meaning for others who understand the words. Others use movements of the body to describe emotional states. Most people employ both means of expressing or symbolizing their feelings, and of course, a few do not use either. This means that most people are constantly communicating their feelings to others. One aspect of interpersonal relationships is response to expressed feelings.

A second facet of interpersonal relationships is concerned with substantive content. For example a person might say, "I'm hungry," and we could respond with, "You're really hurting." This responds to the feeling but not the content. A more complete response would be, "You're hurting because you're hungry." This responds to both the feeling and the person's reason for that feeling.

A third aspect of interpersonal relationships focuses upon doing things effectively. In a way this is the productive phase of life. When it is effective, people can select goals and devise and execute courses of action to achieve them consistently. To return to an earlier example, we could say that, after we have responded to another person's feelings and the reasons for them, we would plan a way to get them some food. Thus, we began with experience and culminated with activity.

In the following model of interpersonal relationships,[3] we see that the first two phases provide the base that permits the third to proceed effectively. It can be repeated cyclically because the third phase leads to experiences and feelings that set the stage for further courses of action. This, then, is a model for both long- and short-term interpersonal relationships.

$$\boxed{\text{Model 1: Feeling + Content} \rightarrow \text{Action}}$$

Through this conceptual model, interpersonal relationships can be divided into: (1) response to feelings, (2) response to content, and (3) formulating and executing courses of action. These are shown in the second of the models, which provides the basis for investigating

$$\boxed{\begin{array}{c} \text{Model 2: Feelings} + \text{Content} \rightarrow \text{Action} \\ \uparrow \qquad\qquad \uparrow \qquad\qquad \uparrow \\ \text{Response} + \text{Response} \rightarrow \text{Programs} \end{array}}$$

each component. The prime interpersonal questions for assessing an individual's level of skills then become:

1. Do you know how the other person feels?
2. Do you know what makes the other person feel as he does?

3. Do you know how to plan courses of action for or with other people?

If the answers are affirmative, then the person has a high order of interpersonal skills. Of course, the opposite is also true.

Implementation of the Model

If interpersonal relationships can be assessed by the model proposed above, then the question "How?" emerges. Considerable exploration of procedures necessary for this task have been conducted, and some feasible logistics have been developed.

I contend that the primary need in the area of humanizing interpersonal relationships in schools is the translation of humane models into viable programs that humanize daily procedures within schools. I was involved in a project that allowed the implementation of humanizing activities in the work-a-day world of the school, and, at the risk of sounding immodest, I would like to share with you an experience in the area of education and interpersonal relationships that such eminent workers as Carl Rogers, Robert Carkhuff, and George Gazda have described as pathfinding.

The project, called the National Consortium for Humanizing Education (NCHE), focused attention for ten years upon interpersonal relationships in classrooms.[4] The activities included both research and training, and both phenomenological and scientific procedures were employed. Through a range of approaches, the NCHE examined relationships between interpersonal behaviors and a variety of factors such as attitudes (self, school, others), discipline problems, physical health, attendance, IQ changes, and cognitive growth. These investigations involved elementary, secondary, and college populations from forty-two states and seven foreign countries (Germany, Israel, Gaza, the Virgin Islands, Canada, Mexico, and England), and I outline the logistics of some of this work as an example of what *can* be accomplished.

The NCHE assumed that the best evidence of what occurred in a classroom would be a precise record of classroom behaviors that could be investigated repeatedly from many points of view. As usual, one practical concern was that the financial cost of such data had to be relatively low, but not so low that this would destroy the integrity of the data. After repeated investigations it was decided that audiotapes would provide a valid source of information about interpersonal behaviors in a classroom.[5] Such recordings are inexpensive, and intrusion into the normal classroom setting is minimal. The NCHE then used the tapes to conduct a series of studies intended to examine interpersonal behaviors in classrooms according to the conceptual model developed earlier.

The most difficult component in the study was managing the people who observed the events. This difficulty was reduced considerably by taking the recordings to a central location where trained observers assessed them. The observers were experienced technicians whose observational reliability could be assessed systematically through interrater and intrarater studies. Both indexes routinely exceeded .90.

Early work by the NCHE indicated that most classroom teachers were not concerned deeply about maintaining facilitative interpersonal behaviors in their classroom as an end in itself. They were, rather, interested in those things that affect students' immediate schooling behaviors, that is, learning, discipline, and attendance. Thus, the NCHE adopted a general attitude of closing the gap between researchers and practitioners.

The NCHE's search for procedures that would make the investigations meaningful to teachers encouraged efforts to depict the relationship between facilitative interpersonal behaviors and outcomes valued by teachers. This effort was directed toward demonstrating to teachers that they could enhance achievement of their academic goals by improving their interpersonal behaviors. While this may seem like an obvious point, it may well be the major gap between the human relations specialist and the classroom teacher, and delineating that gap assumes importance. The human relations specialist tends to view interpersonal behavior as preeminent and substantive content as secondary, while the classroom teacher views substantive content as primary and human relations as secondary.

Studies showed that the teacher was the most important interpersonal factor in the classroom and that it was essential to present interpersonal behavior training as an adjunct to effective instruction. Training was, therefore, introduced by indicating that certain types of teacher behaviors were related to increased student learning. In this way the interpersonal model was related to an appropriate learning model with which the teachers could identify. (See Model 3.)

Interpersonal Approach

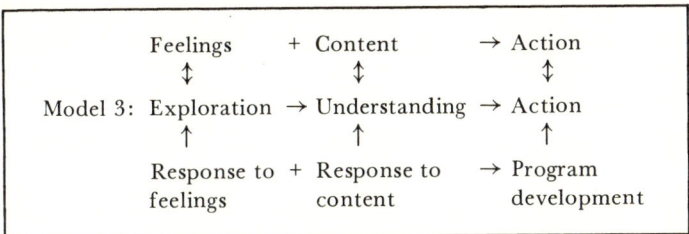

In order to explore the interpersonal events, the NCHE employed Flander's Interaction Analysis[6] because it was couched in "teacher's language" and seemed to communicate to teachers that their behavior has some relationship to that of students. At a broader level the teacher discovered how long he talked in contrast to how long his students talked in class. This simple component of interpersonal relationships was a significant learning experience for most classroom teachers who found that about 80 percent of classroom time was taken up by the teacher talking, 10 percent by all students talking, and 10 percent by silence or confusion. Many teachers, surprised at this finding, began to seek ways to decrease the amount of time they talked while increasing the amount of time their students talked.

The NCHE recently completed a companion study of teaching in colleges of education at ten universities throughout the country. In most classrooms, the amount of time the students talked was the largest component in verbal interaction, but it was not spontaneous, conversational talk. It was students reporting on some assigned topic. It seems that in colleges of education professors have decided that students should talk more in class, but they simply delegate the responsibility for conducting a monologue to someone else. Teacher educators apparently do not know how to engage students in conversational dialogue. This suggests that human relations in most classrooms tend to be formal and rigid because there are no functional behaviors to relax them. At least the evidence suggests that teachers do not use such behaviors in their classrooms.

The results of the investigations of interpersonal behaviors and their relationship to cognitive behaviors were quite interesting. Both student and teacher behavior were assessed according to Bloom's Taxonomy of Educational Objectives,[7] which contains six categories. Such a large percentage of behavior occurred in the first category (memory) that it was difficult to find behaviors that could be called thinking or problem solving. The typical classroom in the samples studied employed the lowest order of cognitive behavior (memory) almost exclusively. This result was surprising to most teachers who thought they were eliciting higher orders of cognitive behavior from their students. They were even more disturbed when they discovered that they themselves rarely used higher-order cognitive behavior in the classroom. That is, they neither served as a model nor did they request thinking from their students. In one sample involving 692 hours of teaching at the secondary level by a total of ninety teachers, the total amount of time devoted to thinking behavior by the teacher was one hour and three minutes.

Without stretching the data too far, it seems logical to infer from the foregoing that teachers do not have much intellectual respect for their students. This conclusion seems warranted by the fact that they rarely ask them to think in class. It may be that most teachers do not know how to elicit thinking behavior from students, and, thus, cannot do so. This rests upon the notion that teaching behavior is a function of response repertoire.

These studies were successful in that they led to a broad confirmation of the position that positive interpersonal relationships facilitate learning. The totality of the findings also led to some broad understandings. There was, for example, a general misconception that teachers have well-developed human relations skills. The broad-based data of the NCHE supports the contention that teachers (principals and supervisors, too) have a very low order of interpersonal skills and need rudimentary training in how to respond to other people. (See Table 3.1.)

By way of illustration, one study found that some teachers cannot maintain eye contact with another person for more than a fleeting moment and that some students never receive eye contact from a teacher unless they are being disruptive. As a result of these findings eye contact became one school's humanizing goal for an academic year, and classroom attendance increased significantly. This is the kind of basic skill that seems to be the proper starting point for interpersonal training programs for educators.

In order to give the research and training programs meaning for teachers, the NCHE adopted a feedback procedure so that those participating in the studies could benefit from the data obtained from

TABLE 3.1
Teacher means by geographic groups of naturally occurring (before training) levels of interpersonal functioning

Location	Number	Mean
Florida	400	2.3
Kansas	120	2.0
Kentucky	36	2.3
Louisiana	60	2.1
Massachusetts	20	2.2
North Carolina	40	2.1
Texas	600	2.2

their classroom teaching. The procedure was to (1) *rate* the audio recording according to Flander's Interaction Analysis, Bloom's Taxonomy of Educational Objectives, and Aspy's Scales for Interpersonal Processes, (2) *feed* the results into a computer that would provide a printout summary of the results from each scale, and (3) *send* the printout to the teacher. Prior to receiving the computer printout, each teacher was taught the general concept and procedures of each scale. Finally, each teacher had access to a consultant if there was need to discuss the results.

As the teachers received feedback, they formulated goals, and they were given systematic training in a chosen area. Some wanted to improve their ability to ask questions, others wanted to be more responsive to students' feelings, others wanted to accept the ideas of students more readily, and there were other goals. Each area was approached through a systematic training program that had clear-cut procedures to reach the goals. The alternation of training and feedback helped teachers both in determining goals and in assessing their attainment.

During the training-feedback period, the NCHE staff considered other outcomes of the teacher's work, such as achievement tests, IQ, attendance, and so forth, so that they could see the long-range benefits of daily shifts in classroom processes. At a higher level, an entire school could see changes in its behavior in relation to its levels of interpersonal skills. In one instance this feature stood out clearly. When the school's interpersonal functioning fell to a low level, there was a student revolt, a student rape, and the principal was attacked.

Different levels of interpersonal functioning clearly preceded and were associated with the dire events.

All of the data collection, analysis, and feedback was completed in such a way that the identity of the participants remained anonymous. A code system permitted computerization of the results for both feedback and research. The computer could also tell those same teachers about their students' performances on a variety of indexes they normally would not have been able to follow because of time and personal constraints. This would seem to indicate that a humane technology is both a conceptual and a logistical possibility.

The report on the training programs indicated that it was effective in increasing teachers' interpersonal skills and in enhancing student performance. (See Table 3.2.) This seemed to portend the emergence of a wide range of humane technologies that use systematic procedures to accomplish humane ends.

TABLE 3.2

Chi-square statistics for number of means associated with expected direction of treatment benefits for teachers at all grade levels (1-12)

Sample	Number of means		Calculated χ^2
	Experimental (training)	Control (no training)	
Year 1	14	11	0.36
Year 2	25	0	25.00[b]
Year 3	19	5	7.89[a]
Total (all three years)	58	16	12.00[b]

[a] Significant at .005; $\chi^2 .005, 1 = 7.88$.
[b] Significant at .001; $\chi^2 .001, 1 = 10.8$.

As stated earlier, the work of the NCHE began with a direct approach to the levels of response to human feelings expressed in the classroom. That led to investigations of training programs directed toward elevating levels of interpersonal functioning in classrooms. These evolved into explorations of the interrelationships between interpersonal and cognitive indexes, which are the major concerns of the educational community. (See Table 3.3.)

TABLE 3.3
Relationship between teacher levels of interpersonal functioning and student levels of cognitive functioning

Interpersonal variable	Group I[a] (level 1) $\bar{X}_O$	Group II[a] (level 2-6) $\bar{X}_I$	Total $\bar{X}.$	Teachers $S_{x.}$	Biserial coefficient $r_{bis.}$
Empathy	2.56	2.83	2.695	.5315	.3223
Congruence	2.57	2.81	2.687	.5679	.2626
Positive regard	2.58	3.35	2.965	.5950	.8213[b]

[a] Groups differentiated according to levels of cognitive functioning (on Bloom's taxonomy) attained by students.
[b] Significant at point .001.

The area of interrelationships expanded into indexes such as discipline, attendance, and attitudes. Thus, as the results of the investigations accumulated, it was possible to conclude that, in general, positive human relations are related to positive human behaviors. That was not startling, but the findings that teachers could be trained to higher levels of interpersonal functioning in relatively short periods of time was more unusual, and it opened a new series of investigations.

As expected, teachers responded differently to interpersonal skills training. Some experienced rapid growth; others did not improve at all, a few even regressed. Upon examining the results of the training programs, it was discovered that improvement in interpersonal skills is a function of the teacher's initial level of interpersonal functioning and level of physical fitness as assessed by a variety of tests. Both relationships were positive.

Several investigations of the physical fitness dimension supported the early ones, so it appears that fatigue, poor nutrition, and lack of physical exercise are deterrents to positive interpersonal relationships. The data from subsequent work suggests strongly that physical fitness is necessary for sustaining constructive interpersonal relationships across long periods of time.[8] It seems that all teachers who understand constructive human relationships can be humane for a short period of time, but levels of physical fitness determine the durability of interpersonal facilitation.

One point must, however, be made clear. Physical fitness is not the only factor in constructive interpersonal behavior. A person may be

TABLE 3.4
Prediction of training gain from entering levels of teacher functioning (N = 150; S.I. = Student Involvement Process scale)

Classroom process	MCR^2	Significance level $p <$	Predictors (in order)
Teacher accepts ideas	.28	.05	Respect, fitness
Teacher lectures	.34	.05	Respect, S.I., fitness
Teacher criticizes	.31	.01	Fitness, S.I., congruence
Teacher recalls facts	.27	.05	Respect, fitness
Teacher asks questions	.41	.01	Respect, fitness
Student responds	.21	.05	Empathy, fitness
Student initiates	.12	.10	Fitness, empathy

quite fit physically and still be inept interpersonally. And not all teachers who provide good interpersonal facilitation are physically fit. What can be said is that levels of physical fitness do determine the length of time highest interpersonal skills can be employed. If the skills are limited, high levels of physical fitness can do nothing to enhance them. *Physical fitness, therefore, seems to be a necessary but not a sufficient condition for sustaining high levels of interpersonal functioning.*

The findings about physical fitness and interpersonal functioning are so compatible with common sense as to be obvious and hardly worth mentioning except for the fact that investigation indicated that, as a group, teachers are unfit physically, and their knowledge of physical health is quite low. Many school practices do not encourage physical fitness for either students or teachers. For instance, few schools provide exercise facilities for teachers. Lunch periods are often very short and associated with stressful conditions of noise, responsibility for student behavior, and isolation. In light of the data relating physical fitness and interpersonal functioning, there is little wonder that teachers often provide low levels of interpersonal facilitation.

If we were to summarize the bits and pieces of this work so far, it would go something like this: physical fitness seems to be the foundation out of which interpersonal skills can develop, and they, in turn, lay the basis for intellectual growth. This is not a new set of formulations. It is a reaffirmation of things that have been undersupported for a long time in schools.

NCHE as a Model

The NCHE has made a prototypical effort to humanize interpersonal relationships in education by introducing a model that seems appropriate for humanistic intervention at this time. There are three major steps in the approach:
1. adoption of a theoretical model of humanistic interpersonal relationships,
2. formulation of logistics to gather information about that theoretical model in the "real" school settings, and
3. dissemination of the obtained information to the profession.

To state this somewhat differently, the NCHE made the first effort to take a fairly precise stand on what humanistic interpersonal relationships were, to explore that position in a range of studies, and to inform professional educators about the results. This is the type of integration of theory and practice that must be done in the future if educators are to be taken seriously by the larger community.

It is important to recognize that the NCHE chose *one* model of humanistic interpersonal relationships for its work. That choice was necessary because there are many options for a theoretical stance under the broad rubric of humanistic orientations to interpersonal relationships. This is perhaps the crux of the humanistic dilemma. The broad tolerance limits for differing positions is both a strength and a weakness. When one tries to communicate with those unfamiliar with a particular setting, questions relating to the implementation of humanistic interpersonal relationships appear to go unanswered because it is first necessary to find a mutually acceptable definition of "humanistic" education before one can begin to look for answers.

This is not peculiar to the NCHE. Most groups encounter the difficulty of definition. There are many possible answers to the question, "How does a democrat behave in his political role?" It is not until specific issues arise and the leader indicates how he will behave and gives evidence to support his position that he occupies anything but neutral ground that can be termed "wishy-washy" or, more euphemistically, "flexible."

A clear-cut stance at a point in time does not militate against flexibility. We should consider seriously Gordon Allport's notion that we need "openly committed" people. We should know where we are headed at a particular moment and yet remain open to changing our position as more information becomes available. It seems that our desire to remain open and tolerant has nearly obliterated the need for enough closure to be functional in the daily routines of schools. In order to avoid this crippling circumstance, there should be longitudinal investigation of a variety of interpersonal relationship models, and answers to such questions as: What is "it"? What happens when you try "it"? Even a loyal humanist like Carl Rogers says that people often need some structure as they begin to change. It is not enough to tell educators to try a humanistic model and "see what happens." They need to know that, within at least some limits, certain models will help them achieve certain goals that they perceive as being legitimate goals for schools to try to attain.

Recognizing the need for specificity, the NCHE selected interpersonal relationships as a model because it could be delineated rather precisely. The terms could be quantified and pursued with some degree of rigor while, at the same time, there was room to consider that intangible aspect of interpersonal behavior called "feelings" or "emotions." This, then, was an integrative stance that moved from phenomenological data toward precise measures. When a verbal interaction was observed, it was possible to assess rather clearly whether there was a response to the expressed feelings, a response to the content, and a course of action was possible.

There was no "hard" data to prove that the responses were accurate. Measurement rested upon the statistical reliability of observation by judges. The predictive validity of those observations was, however, demonstrated in a variety of settings. Unbiased, trained raters expressed high levels of agreement (.90+) about the accuracy of responses to feelings, and their ratings correlated significantly with differential performances by students on a variety of behavioral indexes: IQ changes, achievement test gains, behavioral difficulties, absences, cognitive process, self-concept, and self-disclosure. All of these relationships were in the expected directions and at statistically significant levels of magnitude. And they were "meaningful" in the real world. (See Tables 3.5 to 3.7.)

In working with this same model, the NCHE developed training procedures that enhanced teacher levels of functioning in these skills. It is important to stress the word *skill* in interpersonal relationships since it assumes significance in the model employed. Interpersonal skills, defined somewhat narrowly, were stepping stones in the

TABLE 3.5
Results of ANOVA on differences in absenteeism of students of high- and low-functioning teachers

Humane level of teacher functioning	Average number of days absent per student each year	Significance level
High	5	$p < .005$
Low	9	

TABLE 3.6
Mean differences (experimental and control) in adjusted gain

	Achievement		
Grade level	Reading	Mathematics	English
1-3	10.88[a, e]	No test	No test
4-6	3.66[b, e]	15.44[a, e]	18.66[a, e]
7-9	2.96[b, e]	4.10[b, e]	11.75[a, e]
10-12	1.56[a, e]	1.94[c, e]	0.96[d, e]

[a] $p < .001$.
[b] $p < .01$.
[c] $p < .05$.
[d] Not significant.
[e] In favor of experimental (training) group.

process of delineating the critical variables of interpersonal relationships. A skill was defined as a replicable act available to the person. (We can do it whenever we want to do it.) The objective of interpersonal skills programs becomes that of training for the skills that theory suggests and research supports as being significantly related to effective interpersonal functioning.

In teacher-training programs, the NCHE increased its effectiveness when it used well-defined interpersonal skills and systematic retraining programs. It seemed that teachers learned more effectively when they understood the skills and could evaluate whether or not they were acquiring them. Fear of interpersonal training seemed to yield to a systematic approach in which each interpersonal skill became as tangible as all other human behaviors. In short, the teacher-training programs worked.

TABLE 3.7
Results of comparisons of adjusted treatment means from
How I See Myself (HISM) test scores (NS = Not significant)

	Grades 3-6			Grades 7-12		
HISM factor	Experimental $\bar{X}$	Control $\bar{X}$	Significance level $p <$	Experimental $\bar{X}$	Control $\bar{X}$	Significance level $p <$
Teacher-school	2.56	1.61	.05	1.52	0.53	NS
Physical appearance	1.45	−0.96	.01	1.81	0.01	.05
Interpersonal adequacy	2.87	2.20	.05	1.99	−0.28	.01
Autonomy	0.96	−1.89	.01	2.19	0.89	.01
Academic adequacy	1.25	0.02	.05	0.86	0.30	.05
Total	8.61	1.08	.001	6.85	0.92	.001

Impediments

Evidence supporting the development of humanistic interpersonal relationships usually leads to questions about why they receive so little emphasis in schools. The answers are nearly as varied as the thousands of school systems. It is fortunate that there are common threads in the many varied situations.

One is that the exploration of the influence of interpersonal relationships in a normal school setting is complicated frequently by the "researcher effect." This occurs when a researcher tries to get data to support a particular position, and it seems to flourish in a pluralistic society where few curricular decisions are based upon rigorous investigations of a particular question. Thus, there is data to support differing positions—often antagonistic ones—and most of them are highly vulnerable to attacks on the investigative procedures used. The result is that the area of interpersonal relationships remains an unclarified but important concern.

Another tendency is for researcher-educators to dichotomize "interpersonal skills" and "on-the-job success." This spirit is depicted by the phrase, "It's nice to be nice but you gotta teach them something." It seems that most of us have not yet integrated our responsive interpersonal dimension with our assertiveness dimension. The effect of this polarization is that teachers often choose between being tender or tough. Those who select tenderness often find that they also chose nonpromotion; those who opt for toughness discover that isolation and loneliness accompany it.

Schools also often operate in terms of immediacy rather than of long-range needs. This is enhanced when resources are limited, as in a time of economic recession. In this context, interpersonal relations receive emphasis in proportion to the crisis levels in a given school. Entry onto the scene of operations is often limited to crisis intervention and remedial functions. If so, the growth and prevention dimensions of interpersonal skills tend to be neglected in many school settings.

Then, an interpersonal skills-training program often focuses upon horizontal and downward relationships. This helps educators relate more effectively to colleagues and students but not to administrators, parents, board members, and others. The outcome is that teachers tend to form mutually reinforcing support groups that do not benefit from wider acquaintance. Mutual support groups are necessary, but they are incomplete; some important interfaces remain untouched.

And, as alluded to earlier, human relations specialists tend to be somewhat overzealous for interpersonal relationships and neglectful of the school's substantive responsibility. This happens when the human relations specialist fails to employ his own skills for entering the teacher's frame of reference. Such instances produce a kind of struggle between teachers and the interpersonal programs.

The last of the common tendencies considered here is that interpersonal skills programs frequently are not based on individual readiness levels. That is why many of them fail to bring success to trainees.

It would appear that interpersonal skills training in education works; that, when teachers use higher levels of interpersonal skills with their students, the quality of life in the classroom is changed; that classroom changes are consistent with society's expressed goals for the education of its young people; and that a technology exists for implementing such training on a wide basis. I now return to the two basic premises of this paper: humanistic education is pluralistic in nature, and the NCHE has provided a model for integrating theory and practice from differing orientations. Each attempt at humanizing education must be considered not only on the basis of its own consistency but on its evidenced ability to operate in the *real* arena—the schools of our nation.

Perhaps the most important statement made here is that the technology exists to bring each model to trial. The question remains, "Will society devote enough of its resources to the improvement of the quality of interpersonal relations (including the physical, the intellectual, and the emotional well-being of each person) to allow the building of a constructive system powerful enough and soon enough to withstand or defeat destructive systems already in existence?"

Discussion

Participants (in order of speaking): *Ralph Mosher, Flora Nell Roebuck, Fred M. Newmann, James B. Macdonald, Thomas J. Sergiovanni, David E. Purpel, Nancy R. King, Michael W. Apple,* and *Walter Feinberg*

Mosher: I would say initially that this is a very comprehensive study, and it's most impressive. I do have some questions, one of which is: What guarantee do we have that these skills will hold up over any significant period of time? I raise it as a "friend of the court" because it's likely to be a question that will be directed toward this research.

Roebuck: David Aspy and I are looking at that now. We have some reason to assume that they will hold up. We have tested the same control teachers across a two- or three-year period during which they received no training. Although there is a cyclical variation of skills across the school years, the teacher who entered the first school year in September with a 3.31 rating probably entered at 3.3 the second year. There are also individual variations. Something may have happened in the home environment: the person may have been sick; skill levels may drop because of lack of energy—that sort of thing. The level at which a person operates, however, seems to remain relatively unchanged. The assumption is that, if you teach them to operate on higher levels, and, if they in fact translate those levels into action and receive positive feedback from the translation, they tend to continue operating at the higher level. That is as yet an assumption, and we are testing it now.

Mosher: I do think there is evidence from the Carkhuff studies that that is *not* what happens. Regardless of what the finding is, unless people go on using the skills and are supported by principals or continued in-service training, they are likely to lose the skills.

Roebuck: That's why we have trained entire faculties instead of individual teachers. There is a feedback factor operating. We also have peer trainers—persons trained to our level who are placed in the school system for maintenance of skills.

Newmann: Have there been comparisons between teachers working in self-contained classrooms and teachers that are family-grouped, or organized in some other way?

Roebuck: We have not made those comparisons because we were taking entire schools and sometimes an entire school district. Whatever variations there were already existed within the school district.

Macdonald: What would an optimum score be?

Roebuck: Five. I have never seen a "five" teacher. The highest I've seen is a 4.5.

Newmann: Getting at this score, I need a quick rundown on the dependent variable. What are the categories you are using for detecting high levels versus low levels?

Roebuck: Four are from Flanders' categories, and there are process scales that I assume you are familiar with from Rogers and Bloom. The process scales we are using are: understanding of meaning, genuineness of emotion, student involvement, and positive regard. Meaning, genuineness, and respect are derived from Rogers' constructs of empathy, congruence, and positive regard. We think of them in terms of questions such as: Does the teacher know who the student is? Can the teacher respond to the student as a person? Does the teacher know herself? Does she respond to the student on a personal level or as if she were playing a role? Does she communicate regard or respect for the student? Then success promotion is: Does the teacher promote the success of the student's individual goals in the classroom? Student involvement is the measure of how involved in and excited about learning activities the student becomes.

Newmann: Then there is a merger of these items to a score, the highest of which is five?

Roebuck: We get a score on each item based on a scale of 1 to 5.

Newmann: Now, you obviously can't apply all of the items to people who aren't teaching, such as a principal or a trainer?

Roebuck: For the principal we use the same items except, for example, when it comes to success promotion. A principal or trainer does not promote goals of the individual student; rather, he promotes goals of the person or persons with whom he is interacting.

Newmann: Do you omit items related to success promotion for principals and trainers?

Roebuck: No, we still use them. But, we change the relationship. In other words, you can see that in Flanders' category two the focus is on praise or encouragement. It doesn't matter who provides that.

You can identify a statement of praise or encouragement regardless of the context in which it is being made.

Newmann: How about Bloom's categories?

Roebuck: The same applies. You can almost always identify whether a person is using recalling or thinking behaviors. It does become a little difficult in some of the interactions, for example, between a principal and one child or a principal and one teacher. For those we just put down a "no response" label and don't count that data.

Newmann: That's interesting. I'm trying to imagine a principal who submits a tape of running a faculty meeting or a conference he is having with a teacher or with an individual student. The role of the individual in these different contexts really varies. I think it might be straining things a bit to apply categories originally designed for classroom instruction to other human roles.

Roebuck: What we are saying is that these are descriptive indexes. We've made no evaluative judgments.

Newmann: I'm sorry! I thought these all added up to scores on how well one functions interpersonally.

Roebuck: No. When I refer to high levels of interpersonal functioning, it is in specific reference to the process scale.

Mosher: On that point I remember Carl Rogers at Harvard, whose opening remark was: "The first thing that I want to say is that I am not a Rogerian." But, *I* am a reconstructed Rogerian. Client-centered therapy was an important part of my own training program in counseling some twelve or fifteen years ago. I think that I've always had misgivings about the generalization of Rogers' ideas about what contributes to effectiveness in therapist and client interaction. Nor, incidentally, am I persuaded that Traux's data, which is *the* classical documentation for the effectiveness of these conditions, is particularly convincing.

Roebuck: Carkhuff has gone beyond this personal documentation.

Mosher: My point is that I'm not prepared to generalize those "facilitative conditions" to apply to all conditions of interpersonal relationships. When you do that, you have to be prepared to defend your position.

Roebuck: Well, we are saying that within the educational context we have data that shows predictive validity. That is, within the educational context, which is where our work has remained, we can make these predictions in a replicative fashion. They work wherever we've tried them. For the variable labeled "student involvement," we are saying that, "if we know how much Flanders' 9 there is in a classroom, and how much cognitive 7, then we can predict to some degree what student involvement will be." We can also predict in the opposite direction, from student involvement to Flanders' 9. And now we are in the process of developing the same kind of response surfaces for achievement, IQ, and similar data.

Newmann: Flora, you say, "we can predict." Let's look at that more carefully. Take student involvement and your multiple correlation squared. You are telling me you can predict a little less than 50 percent of the variance if you know those two things.

Roebuck: That's pretty high in educational terms.

Newmann: Okay. In your other relationships what order of magnitude are you getting? Is that the best you have gotten?

Roebuck: No! We are saying interpersonal relationships take place within a context. We took into account other things—student IQ, prior learning, or pretest scores—that affect what goes on in that classroom besides the teacher's interpersonal skills, but we still think that interpersonal skill is a major factor and one that is amenable to change. If you make a regression or a prediction equation that includes a student's IQ scores, his pretest scores as a measure of prior learning, and the teacher's interpersonal skills, we can predict as much as 70 percent or 80 percent of the variance.

Mosher: How much of the variance is attributable to the teacher's interpersonal skills?

Roebuck: I don't know offhand; I don't have that data with me. But the data presented here were all done without IQ and other factors, and the correlations squared (R^2) run .71, .84, .38, .42, and .54.

Newmann: Predict 70 percent to 80 percent of the variance in what? What's the dependent variable?

Roebuck: That's a good question. It depends upon the particular test that we are using and the grade level. It varies quite a bit.

Newmann: Are we talking about academic achievement?

Roebuck: It could be academic achievement; it could be the number of days absent. The correlations I just quoted were for absentee data and levels of interpersonal skills with the lower correlations at the upper grade levels. When I said 70 percent or 80 percent earlier, I was thinking about reading scores, which is a particular area that interests me. You asked for high scores, and those are some of the highest we've gotten. The variance prediction for absence rate is also extremely high. I think the highest was around 80 percent of variance. Let me say another thing: through the use of control group data we can compare the achievement of teachers who use a high level of interpersonal skill and those who do not.

Sergiovanni: There is a contradiction between some of the opening statements in your paper and our discussion of achievement. Why is achievement the important dependent variable? Is that why you were engaging in interpersonal training?

Roebuck: No, we chose achievement as a dependent variable because we are more welcome in a school when we say, "Look, we know that interpersonal training can make a difference in achievement," than if we were to say, "Look, we can teach your people how to be nicer to each other." That's getting into their frame of reference.

Sergiovanni: Yes, but the impact you want to make is weakened because you are simply reinforcing their frame of reference.

Purpel: What would happen if the data showed no particular correlation? What if the data were inconclusive and achievement weren't particularly related? What would you say then?

Roebuck: For me that doesn't make any difference because what I'm after is improving the quality of life in classrooms. I would just say "It may not make a difference here in achievement, but it does elsewhere." My experience has been that, when we can show that what we want to do will also further the goals of the person with whom we are working, we get much better cooperation, much higher interest, and it does not seem to retard their adoption or use of the skills. As a matter of fact, we find that once a teacher who is primarily concerned with cognitive growth has had experience in using these skills with children in the classroom, and has accepted her own experiential data showing what happened to the children and to her, and to their relationship with her, we don't hear questions about achievement and cognitive gains anymore.

Sergiovanni: Could you get away from the data and answer this more intuitively for a moment? What would you guess would be the differences in the quality and the climate of the classrooms of two teachers who enthusiastically accepted these prescriptions: one because they were a means by which the youngster could achieve traditional academic objectives, and the other because she believed children deserve to be heard and ought to have a say in what is going on? What differences might you expect in these classes?

Roebuck: First, I don't accept your assumption that the teacher who tries these will *remain* interested in cognitive indexes. But, if we buy that assumption, then I would say that you probably would find no differences in the peak values of the skills, provided they both had been taught to equal levels. What you could find would be a difference in the sustaining of those skills across a period of time.

Macdonald: I'm interested in one of the problems that ties in with the Apple and King presentation. It seems to me that there is a "bracket" on your interpersonal skills. That is, if you look at your data, you have found tremendous regularity in the behaviors of teachers. Then you train them and you again get tremendous regularity once they become adept at interpersonal skills. It's all in role relationships with unequal power. The whole thing is bracketed by the fact that you are talking about interpersonal relationships in a role where there is unequal power between the teacher and the students. My question is: is that *all* there is to interpersonal relationships in a role where there is unequal power? Is there nothing else legitimate in and of itself? Are you really talking about interpersonal relationships? Or, are you talking about a very special role relationship and improving the "good" feeling about each other in that special role relationship?

Roebuck: No! There is, if you look at our model, a movement in which you go from exploration to understanding to action. In the latter two stages of the role relationship there should be shifts in power. For one thing, the student's goals should become more of a deciding factor in what goes on in the classroom.

Newmann: Do you have data as to whether the goals of the teacher shift or the power configuration shifts?

Roebuck: We didn't take power into account. But we do have data to show that success promotion (which we did not teach, by the way, but it is something we measured) does shift as the teacher moves up into the other levels, and so does the teacher's response to student's goals.

Macdonald: These are all skills that depend on your engaging the other person in an active fashion. But can't you be with people and have interpersonal skills where you are not engaging in a manipulative, interaction situation but in which you are disengaging? I mean, perhaps a good teacher is one who doesn't do things instead of one who does do things.

Roebuck: I would respond to that by saying that, if you have high levels of skills, this is one of the things you know when to do and when not to do.

King: I wanted to ask if you thought the training programs were appropriate to be used directly with the children?

Roebuck: Yes; well, not this exact training program, but the model works with students. As a matter of fact, we have trained college students to use it in their classrooms. Ordinarily I begin my college teaching by going through the model, particularly with Flanders. Then, on a given day I walk in and say, "For today we'll have a 9−3." Sometimes a student will ask, "Can we have a 9−3?"

Mosher: In my situation we got into the business of personal education and psychological education by training high school adolescents as counselors. I have real problems with this social learning theory technology of teaching about human communication, teaching empathy, teaching how to listen to another person, and teaching how to identify ideas and feelings and respond to them. I think there's a generic issue that will be important to focus on at some point in this conference: To what extent do these social learning technologies and applications (which are anathema to humanists), contribute to humanizing, or are they just mechanical vehicles? There are two questions that need to be dealt with. First, won't these techniques, this technology, be applied mechanistically in a way that is uncaring, a way that fails to attend to anything but surface problems? They are already part of our educational means of giving certain kinds of human skills to other people. My other question concerns whether these experiences have their greatest potential for stimulating the development—social, empathetic, and moral—of preadolescents, adolescents, and young adults. Shouldn't these experiences be part of the general education of large numbers of people?

King: Are you asking: What is the result of giving these techniques to a teacher who does not have a genuine caring for the child?

Mosher: I'm concerned about several other things, too. This kind of experience, perhaps freed from or run through this technology of training, has been demonstrated to have significant nonreversible developmental consequences for preadolescents, adolescents, and young adults. It is a powerful human experience to have to learn to attend to another human being's thinking and feeling and respond to it.

Apple: There's a question that has been raised at every session so I'll raise it again. Let's use a metaphor that this is something like a skin rash—which is seen not as a problem but a symptom. In most major institutions, be they welfare institutions, schools, etc., certain symptoms seem to emerge—people don't pay attention to each other; they don't give a damn, and so on. As with the skin rash, you put salve on, and it stops itching even though the disease is still present. There are two concerns: (1) *Why* is there such poor interpersonal functioning in so many institutions, and how can we deal with the problem? (2) Of more immediate concern, there are evident patterns from family to school to labor market. School settings tend to be familial in kindergarten, and there's a much higher level of interpersonal responsiveness there. As a student progresses up the age-grade ladder, there's a corresponding decrease in interpersonal responsiveness the closer you get to the labor market or employment. How do you feel about that? What are the possible social and economic roots of your concerns and strategies?

Roebuck: Let me tackle the "serious strategy" problem first. When one knows how it feels to be "there," it's very difficult not to care about another person's feelings and not to do something about it. This seems to be a built-in response for the person who is open and willing to give it a chance. So we find that the person who is using the skills, through the process of using them, becomes more sensitized to the other person and to his needs and problems as well. A confidence factor is built into our model. It is not enough just to get into the other person's frame of reference and then go back to your own thing. If you do use these skills, you are more likely to use them all the way to developing a program and doing something about society's ills. So I'd say that, although initially it would resemble putting medicine on a rash, it should eventually lead to a serious attack on the disease itself. The second thing you asked about was why this happens in our institutions. We have some data to show that throughout America, not just in schools but in every situation, the level of interpersonal response and sensitivity to other people is low. We form groups—parents, ministers, counselors, lay people, educated people entering training of various kinds—and in all of these situations no one functions above 3.0. Rarely do individuals function at levels higher than 2.3 or 2.5. Elementary teachers function at higher levels than the general populace, and they score highest in the education groups. They consider their students more frequently than other people do. Beyond the elementary level there is a general lack of a sense of being *with* other people throughout the entire population.

There is another thing that is related to what we talked about previously—legitimacy of goals. A person who is in a bureaucracy finds that to care about other people may frequently be antagonistic to the goals of that bureaucracy. One of the things we're saying is that if you increase caring you've also got to give people a way to do something about it within the limitations of their environment or show them how to change the limitations of that environment. You can't just teach caring unless you also teach how to do something about what's there. In schools we can do that. I don't know if it is possible in other bureaucracies.

Newmann: I think that the model of interpersonal relations is consistent with the points suggested by Apple. It urges us to say, "If I begin caring about another individual, according to the model, I first have to get in touch with their feelings. Then I've got to try to understand why that person is feeling that way." Once you get into that "why," there is every opportunity for the broadest kind of institutional analysis. Dialogue concerning "why" you are feeling a certain way could include the statement, "We've got a political-economic system that simply couldn't function if you were to feel any differently." In other words, the political-economic system couldn't continue if people really were to care and have different kinds of feelings.

Now, the model also says: "Once we understand why you are feeling that way, we have to figure out a way to do something about it." Dialogue about what we are going to do need not restrict itself to putting a little salve on the rash. The dialogue could encompass a much broader, even macrorevolutionary, kind of solution. Thus, the model makes it possible for children to develop fundamental institutional analyses of the sources of their feelings of alienation, but it won't *necessarily* lead to that. It all depends on what goes on in that classroom when people start checking out why they're alienated or why they're feeling a particular way.

Purpel: And that's a criticism of *both* your models. They may or may not deal with a set of agenda items that many people consider basic and urgent. Again, it seems to me that these two models reflect a problem that is basic to the whole humanistic notion, that is, a tremendous amount of responsibility must be put on the individual. In a sense it says to children in your model, "If you want to deal with the swimming pool problem, okay." You're saying, "If you want to deal with the problem of being oppressed in the high school by coping with it and by dealing with bureaucracy, that's okay." I see enormous similarity between the two. There is great emphasis on process, and it rests with individuals and groups to set their own agenda.

Roebuck: I think our model goes a little beyond this, because we say, "It's not okay. It must become a part. It must!"

Purpel: What must become a part?

Roebuck: In the third step it's not enough to figure out what's okay. It's not enough to figure why the child is feeling that way. If you don't take a third step and help him plan a course of action to do something about the problem, then you have not completed the model.

Purpel: Let me press this as an example. We have one urgent, desperate problem that the whole world faces—hunger. All right? And, one could say that, no matter what we do in our schools, every person in school, every person in our culture, must confront the appalling fact that many people in the world are hungry. Is there anything in either of your models which would say that everybody in the school is going to make an effort to deal with that problem?

Roebuck: No.

Newmann: No, and I'd argue vigorously that there shouldn't be anything in the model that says that the central problem that everybody should deal with is hunger, or the central problem that everyone should deal with is the economic-political system, or the central problem is anything else. The best minds in the world would argue forever as to what the central problem is that everybody ought to be addressing. I'll be damned if I'm going to force an agenda upon people that can't be defended very conclusively and persuasively.

Purpel: And the consequence of that is that it's left to whom?

Newmann: It's left to conflict, to people's conflicting agendas.

Macdonald: But let's look at it not as a problem to study but in terms of the data we are considering here, which show that teachers who aren't well nourished don't have these skills. Well what's good for the goose is good for the gander. Obviously, if you've got children who are malnourished, they can't operate in either of your programs. Nourishment becomes a fundamental necessity if anybody is to improve interpersonal skills or social action competencies.

King: But also, the focus of your interpersonal skills programs links to one of your impediments—the focus is to work with an underling. I think that until you use the model to teach an *underling*, whether it be the child to work with the teacher, or the teacher to work with the administrator, or the administrator to work with the city council, the use of your interpersonal skills program will not achieve broader aims. Such goals cannot be realized within your present format.

Roebuck: This is true. We realize this, and in our later training program this is what we do. We teach a teacher: "This is the way you work with children and here is how you work with the principal." When working with a principal we say: "Here is the way the skills are applied when you are working with your teachers." Or, "These are the ways to use the skills when dealing with the board of education or with parents or with other groups." So you're right! That is a very good point and we haven't carried it far enough yet.

King: The most radical of all would be, "Here, kindergartner, is how you develop your interpersonal skills to deal with adults."

Roebuck: We've done it with junior high school students and with college students dealing with their teachers. But that's as far as we have taken it. Yours is the next exciting step.

Mosher: Two quick points. First, I think there *is* evidence to support your very persuasive statement, your very personal response to Apple's first question. In fact, one can, through this experience, enhance human capacity and capability for empathy and for the understanding of another's feelings and ideas. That to me is central to moral development and moral responsiveness. My second point is that, as a developmental psychologist, to assist individuals to de-center, to assist them to be able to go into the intellectual and emotional framework of another human being, to begin to understand the claims of that person, the rights of that person, and one's obligations to that person are fundamental developmental shifts. In fact, it is the essence of the movement from preconventional to conventional development, regardless of whether modern psychology defines that as moral or social development. I think a prerequisite to systematic social action or social service is recognition of a wider set of human claims on the individual than simply his own.

Apple: It's possible to argue that many of the symptoms that you see are the result of a strong current of individualism and our lack of collective responsibility. That is one of the points in Newmann's presentation. I don't mean this merely as a chicken-and-egg kind of thing. I think where one starts is very important. It's not merely a tactical decision. It may be true that many of the symptoms we see are the result both of the psychologies that dominate what we do and of the very individualistic kinds of use-value relationships that we have. Therefore, it is possible that by dealing with individualistic problems one can't get hold of the real basis of our widespread problems. You are caught in a tautological relationship.

Newmann: That's why my program doesn't focus on an individualistic problem.

Apple: Yes, I wasn't making that as a comment on your model. The other issue that I think we have to focus on is the one that Purpel brought up—do you cop out? And, I don't mean that as a negative thing but as a very pressing problem. One has a range of social actions or a range of processes one can try to do. We leave it up to the individual to make that decision. Unfortunately, all too often we know, given what we see from day-to-day life throughout the United States, what that decision will be. We know that prediction!

Roebuck: Are you asking why I'm so concerned with these individuals and think it will make a difference? The answer is this: One of the things we are pretty certain about is that, as long as I'm thirsty, I'm only going to concentrate on getting some water; as long as I'm hungry, I'm only going to concentrate on getting some food; as long as I'm emotionally unsatisfied in my personal life so that I feel unhappy, downtrodden, and depressed, the only thing

I'm going to concentrate on is resolving the problems. I have no energy left to devote to anything else. It is only after I am assured that I have enough food, enough water, enough shelter, enough feelings of competence, enough feelings of security, that there is enough excess energy to solve another person's problems. For me, therefore, the place to start is interpersonal relations. It helps the individual build what I call a reservoir of caring which he can then use with other people, and it's a place where *I* can do something. Does that answer your question as to why? Now, what we find in schools with teachers is that a major reason why they concentrate on the cognitive area is that this is something they know they can do, something they can handle. We can teach them other ways. But we can't do that by merely talking about utopias or exhorting them to change. What we have to do is to build programs and skills. Now I'm not saying we don't also deal with the big things, but I think it has to be a two-level attack. On the individual level you provide more people a reservoir of caring, energy that they can devote to caring for others. At the same time those people who already have reservoirs of caring must begin to do things on the larger-group level.

Apple: I'm just wondering whether it's not a failure of nerve. We mandate procedural approaches such as: "Everyone will have human relations training!" Boom! It's mandated! Yet one might also argue about particular social problems. Let's take the Gallo strike as an example. There are "oppressed" people. Should everyone be taught about objective conditions with some strategies for changing that?

Newmann: Sure, why not?

Mosher: I think the answer is yes to both.

Sergiovanni: Isn't there a basic ideological difference here though? One is to attempt to seek accommodation to humanistic values within the existing social order; the other is to seek accommodation to humanistic values by reconstructing that social order. It seems obvious that people make choices. You take a look at both of the alternatives and you tend to reject one and to stick with the other. I think that's sort of the hidden agenda around this table. It seems to me that Apple tends to see the alternative of pursuing humanistic values within the existing social order as being very compromising. I think others may very well feel that the other alternative, reconstructing the social order, is not very pragmatic, given social conditions right now. Now, one way in which you can build readiness to reconstruct the social order is by concentrating on accommodation within it until the possibilities and chances for reconstruction increase.

Feinberg: I want to make a few remarks because this has very personal meaning. But, I want to preface them by saying that I don't deny that there is value to what you are doing. There are a few dilemmas, though, and I'll just mention a personal experience to show why I moved away from this kind of approach in my earlier years. I was involved in some human relations training for a couple of years. One of the dilemmas occurred during the Vietnam War protests. I saw university administrators who were very much involved in perpetuating research that was feeding the War Department, trying to use those same skills to elicit empathy from me and from others involved in their projects. They were really masterful at eye contact, talking about "we," and this kind of business. I saw in that setting what I would call a sort of perversion of the interpersonal skills, perversion because people were using them without thinking about the end product they were being used for. I am *not* opposed at all to these kinds of things, but you've got to *think* to use them appropriately.

There is another dilemma that I found as well. When I was involved in human relations training as a graduate student, I had occasion to work with a group of school administrators in a certain school district. One weekend the group—superintendent of schools, principals, assistant superintendents, and so on—sat around a table like this. Initially the trainer said something about what he was going to do, and there was silence. Then the superintendent, who couldn't stand the silence, got up and asked what we wanted to do that weekend. He started going around the room, pointing his finger at each person to get a response. When he came to us, we broke the pattern. By the time the weekend was over we did have, I think, a very good fluid group relationship. The superintendent and the others had begun to understand a lot about what we were trying to teach them. After the group returned to school, we ran periodic sessions once every two weeks. What happened was obvious from the very first session. The relationships had crystallized again, and there was no way to break them. We tried repeatedly, but nothing worked. They were back in their power and influence setting where salary increases, promotions, things over which people have real power to do something were deciding factors. I must say I was still impressed enough to use a lot of the techniques in my teaching, but not impressed enough to view this as coming to grips with some of the really basic problems.

Roebuck: Let me respond to a couple of items. I would like to distinguish very clearly between human relations training and interpersonal skills training. They are quite frequently mistaken for one another. We feel that interpersonal skills training is a step beyond human relations training in a couple of ways. Human relations training tends to come out of a theory of management organization in which the training is manipulatory toward management's goals. It is done to make the worker obedient to the manager. You smile at him so he does his job and doesn't complain. Interpersonal skills training is the exact opposite. It's designed to make the manager sensitive to the worker so that the manager will voluntarily yield some of his power to the worker because he understands where the worker is and, incidentally, feels he can trust the worker.

Sergiovanni: Personally, I don't see that as a very significant change. By the way in which you stated it the techniques still become policies of appeasement, so that the person is more pliable and performs to regulations.

Roebuck: No! When you appease, you calm the other person to achieve your own goals.

Sergiovanni: But you appease his social needs and his need to feel he is involved so that you can manipulate him more artfully.

Roebuck: No! When we say "give power," we are talking about developing real programs in schools to solve the problems that are there, not to keep the children subservient to the teacher. When you finally get the new programs down to the classroom, you find that the youngsters are doing most of the decision making about learning goals. They have more power than the teacher. There is a second, basic consideration. Our model is not completed—the task is not finished—until it is translated into some kind of action. It is not just responding to feelings and understanding where the person is and then walking off. Part of the programs should include shifts of authority relationships within the classroom. And this happens for one very important reason: In all other relationships the teacher has the answer, she is the person who judges right or wrong. But the person who applies our model must, whenever she makes an interchangeable response, submit her judgment and her sense of accuracy to the student's judgment of how accurate she was. In other words, her response is not judged accurate until it is accepted as accurate by the student. That in itself is a very basic change in terms of where the power in the classroom lies.

Newmann: I want to take off on Sergiovanni's dichotomy, the hidden agenda here of reconstructing the social order or working within it. I think we can assume that all of us here see injustice in the social order. You ask: "What is the response to injustice?" One response would be, "We have some positive scenarios as to how the social order, if changed, would remedy the injustice." Now, assuming that we could all agree on certain injustices, what needs to be changed in the social order? Around this table we're going to find tremendous disagreement as to what needs to be changed, what particular programs, structures, or processes in the society need to be changed so that we no longer have the feeling of injustice. We can agree that there should be some reconstruction, but it would be very difficult to agree to the way in which that reconstruction ought to occur. That to me indicates a lack of "knowledge." We don't have knowledge in the sense of any consensus based on evidence among very thoughtful people as to what needs to be changed and in what direction first. In the absence of that knowledge as intellectuals, or scholars, or others, we're unjustified in proposing a nation-wide or world-wide agenda for social reconstruction. I'm not saying that nobody has any ideas or that nobody can defend their ideas, but there are many ideas and programs, all of which seem persuasive and defensible. We must recognize this lack of conclusive knowledge or answers as to what direction the reconstruction ought to proceed and say: "All right, with agreement on injustice and some vague sense of reconstruction, we have to allow people, thinking people, the opportunity to play out, defend, and fight about what those directions ought to be." We have to allow people to move, to think, and to compete for the various agendas: Marxist, anti-Marxist, or whatever. Everyone has their own idea as to how it ought to be reconstructed. So, you can take a phrase like "working within the existing social order" and create educational programs that allow people to try to alleviate their sense of injustice. And some of the people within those educational programs will work very hard toward a fundamental reconstruction of the social order. Some people within the program will work toward maintaining a lot of things in the social order that they like, and that they can tolerate. There's going to be that conflict. I don't see any way out of it. If you accept my first premise, that there is genuine and responsible disagreement as to the ways in which society ought to be reconstructed, then you can't say there is a national or a societal direction that we ought to take.

Sergiovanni: Is this a moral or a pragmatic question?

Newmann: I'm going to defend the process.

Purpel: Without knowing the consequences?

Newmann: That's right, because you can't agree.

Apple: Would you also say, given that conflict, that one can also predict that certain people will have much more power to determine what we shall fight about? That is, we do not start with an equal distribution of power or resources; nor is there an equal distribution of who shall determine what that agenda will be. [*Everyone talking.*]

Feinberg: There is an agenda of priorities in society right now.

Newmann: That's right. But, by enhancing peoples' ability to exert influence, you enhance the opportunity for changing priorities.

Feinberg: Maybe, unless people are already much influenced by the priorities and don't see alternatives. But, analysis is *not* necessarily imposing an agenda on society. [*Interruption.*] Let me continue. If there is an analysis of what is going on and the analysis looks at variables in a new way, you don't have to see that as an agenda. You can see that as data that is intended to inform what has to be public decision making. You don't have to see that as an elitist point of view. It only becomes elitist if somebody keeps it to themselves and refuses to divulge it so that others can make judgments about it. What I hear you and others saying is that anybody who puts forth a new analysis, an analysis that somehow challenges the way we think about our common everyday experience, is somehow also putting forth an agenda that says where we ought to go and how we ought to get there—and that just isn't true.

Newmann: Okay. I apologize if I'm unfair in the characterization of your view. What I'm saying is that the questions you raise do suggest there's another agenda, but we haven't come out with it. I've been asking, "What is that agenda?" If you could come up with a program that could be justified, I could go along with it by definition. Your request for a "more fundamental analysis of the thing" are fine. I'm trying to say, "Okay, now, where does that lead?" If it leads to dialogue like this, that's one thing; if it leads to elitism of any sort, that's something entirely different.

Macdonald: I think "hidden agenda" is an unfortunate phrase because it is not actually hidden. We're caught fundamentally in the major intellectual problem of the twentieth century: Freud versus Marx, if you wish.

Mosher: I would substitute another European psychologist and some American psychologists for Freud—take Piaget!

Macdonald: Well, I think that the Freudian tradition is the basic intellectual movement for individual psychological analysis and solving problems by getting rid of neuroses and improving interpersonal skills, and what have you. But it seems to me that that's with us, and it's an important thing to dig at. It's not hidden; that's all I would say.

Fourth Presentation

Ralph Mosher

Education for Human Development

Six years ago Norman Sprinthall and I published an article entitled "Psychological Education in Secondary Schools: A Program to Promote Individual and Human Development."[1] The response to that article was quite extraordinary. For one thing, we received thousands of letters of inquiry. A progress report to educators is now in order. First, let me summarize briefly what we said in that original article.

Our initial argument was that personal development should be a central focus of education, after which we presented a sketchy outline of what education for personal development might be like. In retrospect our rationale was more persuasive-passionate than the alternate curriculum designed to stimulate personal development. Essentially, we wrote as counseling psychologists, humanists, and teachers frustrated by the gap between what we taught and offered adolescents and what we knew our students' lives and concerns to be. And we were writing at a time (the end of the 1960's) of marked turmoil, which the universities and young people experienced with particular intensity. We said then, and I still believe: "youth (both white and black) experience and are more deeply affected by such problems because they live, psychologically, in a more exposed and vulnerable position." Adolescence, in the best of times, is not something one would choose for his children; exacerbated by the divisions over Vietnam, racism, drugs, the "generation gap," and other problems, it seemed the worst of times to come of age. Perhaps we "catastrophized." Self-appointed tribunes of the young have been known to do this. But we also remembered John Kennedy and Martin Luther King and how they had represented to the young what seemed best about America. The evidence that "going along" has now replaced student militancy in suburbia; that a generation of poor adolescents, both black and white, will get, at best, an inferior education because of the short-term disaster that is urban school desegregation; and that alcohol rather than barbiturates is the current teenage drug of choice is cold comfort for anyone who continues to care about humanizing education.

Similarly, the "school is dead" theology or pessimism for the sake of pessimism had nothing to do with a second point made in the article. We believed that public schools were in trouble—clearly apparent in the city, more subtle in the suburbs. Confronted by a peculiarly confused and anguished group of young people, the schools lacked appropriate programs. "Schools, either city, suburban, or rural, have tended to define their role as the transmitters of academic ideas and skills. Recent efforts at reform have been directed toward revitalizing the existing academic curriculum and its teaching. Very little intellectual energy or funding has been directed toward reformulating education—that is, developing essentially new curricula and new forms of educating adolescents. In most schools and in most eras the personal side of education has had a lower priority than the academic. The school has always had extensive rhetoric about individual growth, but de facto personal or psychological development has been largely the result of random (and often inimical) forces in the school."

In short, we argued that psychology and education have no choice but to help adolescents and young adults as people who are trying to mature against unusual vicissitudes. We also said that new forms of education focusing on personal and moral development were needed. Neither the little white clinic nor the little red schoolhouse—with all they connoted—would get us there. Our argument, then, had little explicit philosophical rationale; its psychology was a humanistic-counseling hybrid. The real imperative was that many adolescents and young adults were profoundly disturbed by Vietnam, drugs, racism, and the feeling that schools, as well as other institutions, were not terribly responsive. And we had the predictable arrogance of young Harvard professors.

So what have we learned in the six years since that first article on psychological education? Apart from how to survive west of the Charles River and how to sustain our work in developmental education, along with a more mature sense of its premises, proportions, and promise, at least four things: John Dewey's conception that human development is the proper aim of education has been reformulated. Second, developmental psychology—for example, the research of Jean Piaget on cognitive development, Lawrence Kohlberg on moral development, and Jane Loevinger on ego formation—offers profound new understanding of how and why people develop intellectually, morally, and personally and serves as the basis for substantial educational application. It is also becoming apparent that the development, behavior, and education of each human being has to be conceived and provided for in holistic terms. The fourth and most original contribution is an awareness that education to stimulate human development *is* practicable.

Old Progressives Never Die; They Become Developmental Educators

R. D. Archambault,[2] in his preface to *John Dewey on Education*, has said, "It is a commonplace that everyone talks about Dewey and no one reads him." Twenty years ago I found Dewey the only philosopher of education worth reading. Recently, I reread Dewey and I find his argument that "the aim of education is development of individuals to the utmost of their potentialities" is still the clearest philosophical rationale for the education we are creating. Since I suspect that Dewey's writings have been perused less recently than my own, let me draw attention to a clear, succinct essay published originally in 1934 and entitled "The Need for a Philosophy of Education."[3] Were space available, I would be tempted to include the entire essay here and say: "Okay, that, with some emendations, is my educational creed." Let me compromise by selecting certain excerpts from this extraordinarily prescient man's essay and comment on them.

"What then is education when we find actual satisfactory specimens of it in existence? In the first place it is a process of development, of growth. And it is the process and not merely the result that is important . . . an educated person is the person who has the power to go on and get more education." Dewey then makes the point that Rousseau's notion of natural development (that is, human beings, analogous to seeds, have latent capacities which, if only they are left to themselves, will ultimately flower and bear fruit) has at least two fallacies. The first is that people are vastly more complex in their development and potential than plants; the second is that development is a matter of the kind of interaction that occurs between the organism and its environment. Nature and nurture, in interaction, produce development. And Dewey argued that development (or education) starts with the pupil. "Every mind, even of the youngest, is naturally or inherently seeking for those modes of active operation that are within the limits of its capacity. . . . The problem, a difficult and delicate one, is to discover what tendencies are especially seeking expression at a particular time and just what materials and methods will serve to evoke and direct a truly educative development." What Dewey did not and could not know was what indeed characterizes development, whether it be intellectual, moral, or social, at a particular stage of time in the person's life. A generation of research in genetic epistemology and developmental psychology, by such people as Piaget, Kohlberg, and Loevinger, now offers educators relatively clear blueprints of what people are like at various stages in their lives and what it is that stimulates their intellectual, moral, and personal-social growth. This information, available to us and not to Dewey, says much, in developmental "fact," about that remarkably prophetic phrase "the tendencies especially seeking expression at a particular time." What developmental psychology does not concern itself with, but developmental education does, is "just what materials and methods will serve to evoke and direct a truly educative development." But of that, which is the genuinely original thing we are learning about or contributing to, more later.

I devote little time here to Dewey's critique of traditional education—the external and authoritative imposition of subject matter and skills which he compared quaintly to "inscribing records upon a passive phonographic disc to result in giving back what has been inscribed when the proper button is pressed in recitation or examination." That system (and its more contemporary critique) is still too much with us, and criticism of it, in the final analysis, is cheap. Constructive reformulation of alternative educational practices is much harder work. But the critique of the schools adolescents attend that

Education for Human Development

Sprinthall and I formulated in our article is absolutely fundamental to understanding the continuing odyssey in developmental education.

Dewey's more important point for progressive education was *not* to stop short with the recognition of the importance of giving free scope to native capacities and interests. This is really another statement of the "don't fall into the Rousseau trap, or all you have to do is get out of the child's way." One has the impression that much of the criticism of progressivism as a "country-club existentialism" or "directionless activity" may have resulted from progressive educators and critics who genuinely misunderstood how much more Dewey was saying, both about the intricate characteristics of development in children and how they have to be seen as potentialities—processes that are not enduring or end points but which, with experience and time, will themselves evolve profoundly.

The special obligation of the educator to understand, profoundly, the psychology of cognitive, moral, and social development is part of the charge that Dewey was anticipating. The other part has to do with the core task of developmental education: the devising and testing of curricula, that is, systematic educational experiences, that permit the person continually to grow from experience. And Dewey anticipated something else we are learning: that we have to pay more, not less, attention to the subject matter and pedagogy of developmental education. Devising and validating those experiences that actually affect development is far more complex than rewriting a curriculum in American history or literature. There are just far more knowns, precedents, and criteria for doing the latter. Again, I run ahead of myself. Let's first hear Dewey on this dual task of the educator:

The great problems of the adult who has to deal with the young is to see, and to feel deeply as well as merely to see intellectually, the forces that are moving in the young; but it is to see them as possibilities, as signs and promises; to interpret them, in short, in the light of what they may come to be. Nor does the task end there. It is bound up with the further problem of judging and devising the conditions, the materials, both physical, such as tools of work, and moral and social, which will, once more, so *interact* with existing powers and preferences as to bring about transformation in the desired direction.

It would be nearly a generation before the first part of this metaphor, "to see intellectually the forces that are moving in the young," would be translated into comprehensive empirical psychological data or knowledge. I will talk about that knowledge of development shortly. And it is really only in the past five years that the educational work of translating the second part of the metaphor ("devising the conditions ... which will ... so interact with existing powers ... to bring about transformation") into concrete curriculum with developmental effects has begun. How rigorously that must be done was also anticipated by Dewey: "If we do not go on and go far in the positive direction of providing a body of subject matter much richer, more varied and flexible, and also in truth more definite ... than traditional education supplied, we shall tend to leave an educational vacuum in which anything can happen." My supposition is that this is what the progressive educators could not bring off. "Why" is a complex story, part of which Lawrence Cremin tells in *The Transformation of the School.* In my view some of it had to do with the fact that the psychological knowledge of the stages, characteristics, and experiences contributing to human development available to them was grossly inadequate. In any event, the project method is a pretty lightweight translation of what Dewey was suggesting. Maybe current or subsequent critics of developmental education will similarly damn our efforts with faint praise. The charge remains, however, as does the consequence of ineptitude. "The young live in some environment whether we intend it or not and this environment is constantly interacting with what children bring to it, and the result is the shaping of their interests—minds and character— either educatively or miseducatively. If the professed educator abdicates his responsibility for judging and selecting the kind of environment that his best understanding leads him to think will be conducive to growth, then the young are left at the mercy of all the unorganized and casual forces of the modern social environment that inevitably play upon them as long as they live."

Dewey makes two additional points in this essay that have profound meaning for contemporary developmental education. He says development is a continuous process, which means that the experiences or action that stimulate development will have a quality of consecutiveness, of planned order. He warns that "it is comparatively easy to improvise, to try a little of this today and this week and then something else tomorrow and next week ... without care and thought [this] results all too readily in a detached multiplicity of isolated short-time activities or projects and the continuity necessary for growth is lost." An honest appraisal of the curriculum that Sprinthall and I outlined in 1970 would see it as vulnerable to this charge; the curricula discussed in the last part of this presentation are less so. We are still some distance, however, from curricula or knowledge by which to order experiences to stimulate consecutive development. We perceive the need and the outline of how to get there, but much development and testing remains to be done. This is the essential raison d'être of developmental education.

Dewey finally argues that the central environment in which we grow is social and that the ultimate purpose of our life is improving the common life of all:

As the material of genuine development is that of human contacts and associations, so the end, the value that is the criterion and directing guide of educational work, is social. . . . Perhaps the greatest need for a philosophy of education . . . is the urgent need that exists for making clear in idea and effective in practice that its end is social, and that the criterion to be applied in estimating the value of the practices that exist in schools is also social. It is true that the aim of education is development of individuals to the utmost of their potentialities. But this statement in isolation leaves unanswered the question as to what is the measure of the development. A society of free individuals in which all, through their own work, contribute to the liberation and enrichment of the lives of others, is the only environment in which any individual can really grow normally to his full stature. An environment in which some are practically enslaved, degraded, limited, will always react to create conditions that prevent the full development even of those who fancy they enjoy complete freedom for unhindered growth.

So we end with the social aim of education as the central article in Dewey's creed. It is crass to suggest that, if Dewey had not already existed, we would have had to invent him. I have noted that *Democracy and Education* was the required text in my philosophy of education course at the bachelor's level twenty years ago. And Lawrence Cremin has said that the field of guidance is the most characteristic child of the progressive education movement. Perhaps it has taken that long—that much experience in education—to reconstruct or understand the ideas that Dewey advanced. Certainly our intuitive educational practice and development over the past six years fits philosophically with, and elaborates further, Dewey's ideas about education.

This may be another illustration of zeitgeist.[4] But I think we are doing more than warming over John Dewey or rediscovering that he has already done our philosophical homework. There is in Dewey, for example, the American ideal of individualism, human and social mutability, development or progress, responsible citizenship and democracy. The progressive education movement never established, in fact, that education could enhance human development; those ideals remained articles of educational faith. Much contemporary experience and thought would argue that they are naive, anachronistic views of human reality and potential. Six years of applied research persuades me that a progressive development of human rationality, character, and social responsiveness and action *is* possible through education. And I see no higher purpose for education than in helping people grow in wisdom, character, and personal integration. Thus, Dewey's faith in human beings and their potential begins to be borne out and made practicable by contemporary educational research. And that, if true, is important affirmation of Dewey, of our reformulations of him, and, most important, of the ability of human beings to go on growing and learning—and of the many social, political, and institutional structures created on that premise.

Developmental Psychology as a Basis for Developmental Education

Reformulating John Dewey has not been the only consequence of our work. In the six years since "Psychological Education in Secondary Schools" appeared in *American Psychologist*, we have also moved toward recognizing developmental psychology as being the best psychological basis for educational work. Kohlberg's constructive critique of an American Psychological Association presentation in 1970[5] has been influential in this shift, along with my own efforts. If you are going to commit the naturalistic fallacy, you might as well do so on the basis of the best knowledge of how human nature is constituted in the concrete. And we now know a great deal about how and why people develop cognitively, morally, and in the personal-social domain that was not known to Dewey or leaders of the progressive education movement. Let me illustrate by reference to that holiest of holies in the mission of the high school: teaching children to think. Harvard University awarded Piaget an honorary doctorate in 1936 (to speak again of zeitgeist just two years after the publication of Dewey's essay). But only in the last five or ten years have the seismic implications of accumulated knowledge about how and under what conditions human beings develop cognitively begun to register on schoolmen (or persons) in this country. As an example, take early adolescence, when change in thinking corresponds roughly to the change that occurs when a child acquires language. Anyone who has observed the earlier change knows how profoundly learning to talk alters a child's relationship with the world. I refer, of course, to the shift from what Piaget calls concrete operations, or thinking that is anchored in and limited by reality as the child experiences it, to "formal operations" or abstract thinking, to thinking that builds on thinking. Let me illustrate the problems of communication between people living in these different cognitive worlds. The channel selection dial on our family TV set broke recently. I rather cleverly solved the problem by substituting the UHF dial for the regular one. This did mean, however, the channel selection depended either on being able to substitute, mentally, low numbers for high numbers or a "seek and ye shall find" procedure. My eight-year-old daughter was watching *ZOOM* (which in my area appears on Channel 2). At the end of the program I asked her to turn the dial to Channel 4 so I might watch the evening news. Note my unexpressed solution: two turns to the left. Pammy made several abortive attempts to find the channel by turning the dial. Note her problem: What and where is Channel 4? Observing her inability to find the channel, I said, probably somewhat impatiently, "Pammy, where is Channel 4?" Immediately she picked up the broken channel dial, carried it to where I was sitting, pointed to the number 4 on it, and said, conclusively, "Here it is, daddy."

The intellectual capacity to deal with abstract hypotheses, relationships, theories, symbols, ideals, problems and reasoning—things that never were and never will be concrete—is critically essential to success in much of the secondary school program. Yet, until recently, we have not been aware of, or sensitive to, this development in adolescence. (One of the many unfortunate educational consequences of IQ testing has been the idea that a student's intellectual ability was a constant; either he was bright or dull, and that was that. The concept of mental age, which was closer to the "reality" of cognitive development as now understood, never received the attention it should have.) We have created and taught curricula that flew in the face of the fact that many kids (like Pammy) are simply unable or unready to deal with an implicit intellectual demand. Several of the innovative and imaginative curricula of the 1960's may have foundered here. Nor have we attempted to establish whether our ways of educating adolescents in fact contribute anything to this critical increment in human intelligence. Indeed, I suspect a careful comparative study of Piagetian developmental measures and traditional subject areas in the high school in terms of success in teaching students to think would produce explosive findings. My hunch is that we teach teenagers new content but not new ways of thinking. This corresponds to teaching them answers, albeit conventional, sophisticated, or useful, rather than teaching them to think about and act on problems. The essential point is that developmental psychology calls into question the cognitive fit of much of our present curricular material and pedagogy as this relates to adolescents, while at the same time establishing that this is a prime time for education. The issues in this paradox are: When does the individual adolescent make the transition to rational and abstract thought? What kinds of intellectual and educational experiences contribute to this development? What are the implications for present or alternate education programs if the bottle for any given class of adolescents can be both half-full and half-empty cognitively? Dulit[6] estimates that only one-third to one-half of American adolescents and adults achieve full capacity for formal thought.

A further indication that current developmental knowledge of children and adolescents and how they grow has profound implications for their education is to be found in Kohlberg's research on moral development. Most people who write about adolescents, for example, refer to the idealism of this age group. Adolescents have to make difficult personal decisions as to what is right and what is wrong. Their moral concern and sensibility may be easily subverted into rigid political ideology, into new and exotic moralities or religions, or into despair. Underlying all of this is a concern to make moral and ethical sense of their world. Ritual disagreements with authorities (for example, parents or teachers) and an idolatry of unconventional flora (for example, grass) and fauna (What adult can dig Elton John's costumes?) mask a profound adolescent movement toward the social and moral conventions of family, church, and state. Indeed, if adolescence goes according to the developmental script, it is a rehearsal and perfecting of the lines, roles, norms, and rules of being adult. In a social sense, adolescence means giving up an exclusive selfishness, a hedonism, and an instrumental use of others. The perspective which replaces this "Me Firstism" is a gradually enlarging recognition of the rights and feelings of other people—typically friends and family—that can also encompass a genuine concern, too, for others in the family of man. How else explain the idealism of twenty-five-mile walkathons for victims of muscular dystrophy or fasts for African famine relief?

Because of Kohlberg's[7] major theoretical contributions, we have a relatively clear blueprint for this aspect of human development: the characteristics of moral reasoning in childhood and adolescence, its progression, and some, at least, of the experiences critical to its stimulation. A précis of Kohlberg's Stage 2 moral reasoning or that of Stage 3 would be gratuitous to most readers. Yet these stages are powerful characterization-metaphors for preadolescence and adolescence. The knowledge that systematic discussion of moral dilemmas, learning to understand the thinking and feeling of other people, action on behalf of social and moral goals, and experiences in democratic rule making and in creating fairer institutions can stimulate development from Stage 2 to Stage 3 is both less gratuitous to the reader and what we should expect from developmental education. Indeed, knowledge specific enough to order these experiences and others to stimulate consecutive development is an aim and criterion of developmental education. I return to this challenge later. The general point is that developmental psychology, in Kohlberg's work, has established with considerable validity and exactness "what [moral] tendencies are especially seeking expression at a particular time." While the major educational and curricular applications of Kohlberg's theory as yet remain to be done, I believe that the theoretical understanding of moral development now available allows that practical work to go forward with dispatch and promise. The evidence of developmental psychology also is that the child, and especially the adolescent, is less likely to develop any more sophisticated ethical position as an adult if his natural efforts to create a personal moral philosophy are unsupported by systematic moral education. So adolescence is established by developmental psychology as a prime time for values or ethical education of a nonindoctrinative character—something eschewed by American public schools for forty years.

In summary, then, our work made clear to us, at least, that educators now have available an extraordinary amount of knowledge about human development. Morris Cogan used to say that the problem with educational psychology was not how little we knew about the learner and the processes of teaching or learning but how little *use* was made of what we knew when teaching. A central conclusion of our work is how far this steadily increasing body of psychological knowledge about the stage, sequence, and causes of human development, tied to Dewey's philosophical case for development as the aim of education, can lead if it is used to renew emphasis and substance for developmental education in this country.

Educating the Whole Child

A third thing we have learned from six years of work is that it is critical that we concern ourselves, conceptually and increasingly at the applied level, with the development and the education of the whole child or person. The logic and even the cliché governing the development and education of the individual whole comes from John Dewey, who talked about stimulating rationality and character and social responsibility. Developmental psychology as a field studies cognitive, moral, social, and ego development. But psychological education, with an explicit concern for personal or ego development, and moral education, with a preoccupation for the development of moral judgment, are ultimately too narrow. They clearly specialize in creating education to stimulate two broad strands of human development: ego and morality. But it seems to me that developmental education, by definition, must conceive of and potentially be able to stimulate all of the interrelated dimensions of human development: cognitive, moral, social, ego, emotional, aesthetic, vocational, physical. The basic idea is that education should discern and provide those systematic experiences that give the individual the greatest opportunity to develop or grow in interaction with the environment. And both the individual's development and education must be conceived holistically.

Why hold to a special mandate or objective of seeing the education and development of the whole child? The psychology of development is still incomplete. (For example, what theory of emotional or aesthetic development is adequate to the developmental educator?)

Education for Human Development

Measures of development are limited, and economy of available theory, personnel, and other resources could easily and sensibly dictate specialized research and development on those aspects of human growth best understood now. I see the need for a holistic conception of human development and education based on several arguments.

The first of the arguments is made powerfully, if metaphorically, by the song on tradition from *Fiddler On the Roof.* Education has always arrogated to itself the stimulation of intellect, of teaching people to think. The degree of success, as noted earlier, is another matter. While the personal development of students has been honored more by pious commencement rhetoric than by actual schooling, it has been at least a secondary concern behind some curricula in English and social studies, or it reflects the private guilt of committed teachers and counselors. It is one reason for many alternative schools. It is ridiculous to suggest that concern for complete human development is a heritage of the progressive education movement alone, but Dewey did give this idea vitality and respectability in American education, even if it was ultimately to be misapplied or ridiculed as containing "so little for the mind." Certainly to argue it is hardly to argue something new or radical although it may be misinterpreted as arguing something permissive or soft. Willie Loman in *Death of a Salesman* is asked by a son if he didn't get lonely during all his years on the road. He replies: "Lonely? Loneliness goes with the territory." In an analogous sense educators profoundly, if unintentionally, affect the identities, the values, the personal esteem of students through the hidden curriculum of schools. Affecting the whole human being inexorably goes with the territory of formal education. Further, it is perfectly obvious that people grow and live in three dimensions. Children do not come to school, or live outside it, simply from the neck up. To conceive of education on one dimension only—mind (or affect, or character)—is myopic, neglecting the way people grow and live. It is arguing the obvious to say we have to put mind-body and mind-other dualisms aside.

Finally, and by definition, people whose development and education is whole will be socially more responsible and competent. While it may be committing the naturalistic fallacy, any careful analysis of the "higher" stages of ego, moral, or social development indicates that an enlarged social perspective and responsibility, acceptance of social convention and law, an effort to consider other's rights and to be fair, and individuation responsive to principle are at the heart of individual development.

A holistic conception of education for human development, then, guards against idolatry of intellect, joy, the sensate, morality, political action, or any singular conception of what about human beings is of most worth. Educational dualisms, whether they be mind-body, mind-affect, or another, become pointless. The answer to each aspect of growth is yes. Morally, how can educators deny each individual the right to maximum growth? Clearly the position commits the naturalistic fallacy; let us hope it gets away from it. What *is* in the process of human development—an interrelated progression along major dimensions of human thinking and behavior—should be reflected in a comprehensive set of educational experiences to support and stimulate cognition, morality, emotions, ego, social life, career, the aesthetic, and the physical. Seeing human development in its whole potential and sequence guards against educational support for unbridled individualism—the "do your own thing" or Stage 4½ ethic, the bourgeois liberalism against which Chairman Mao and others of us who care about *this* society inveigh. ("The method of correction is primarily to strengthen education so as to rectify individualism ideologically.... In our educational work we must explain that in its social origin individualism is a reflection within the Party of petit-bourgeois and bourgeois ideas."[8]) It may also guard against the other half of that dualism: educating people solely to be conventional.

Developmental Education

So we come, finally, to the genuinely original thing we have learned in six years of curriculum research: "[Some of] what materials and methods will serve to evoke and direct a truly educative development." The most important point in support of the theoretical argument for developmental education is that it is practicable. Reasonable evidence now supports the fact that it is feasible, through education, to stimulate human development as modern psychology understands it. No one group of developmental educators can do it all, but the creation and testing of educational prototypes *is* feasible.

What is the evidence? Let me refer first to studies that document discrete effects on aspects of development—primarily moral and ego development. These studies include those initiated at Harvard by

Mosher and Sprinthall and by their students: Atkins, Dowell, Griffin, Katz, Mager, and Greenspan;[9] the research of Kohlberg and his associates: Blatt, Hickey, and Scharf;[10] Mosher and his students at Boston University: Grimes, Lorish, Mackie, Felton, Sullivan, Paolitto, and Stanley;[11] Sprinthall and his students at Minnesota: Erickson, Rustad, Schaffer, Hurt, and Brock;[12] and Beck and Sullivan at Toronto. The list goes on, and the number of studies in progress is extensive.[13]

The estimates or measures of development used have included the Kohlberg moral dilemmas; the Loevinger Ego Development Test; the Rest Defining Issues Test; the Harvey, Hunt, and Schroeder C.S.T.; William Perry's Measure of Intellectual Development; interviews with students; Thematic and Structural Analysis of Journals; and classroom climate inventories. On these measures of development the studies provide significant evidence of the effect of education on moral reasoning and ego development in children, adolescents, and young adults.

And there is replication of what has been found. For example, Dowell, Erickson, Rustad, and Sullivan all found significant effects on both moral reasoning and ego development when high school students took various courses in psychological and moral education. Dowell, Griffin, Sprinthall, and Felton taught adolescents to counsel and found that the experience had a significant effect on their development. Blatt, Grimes, and Paolitto established that it is practicable to stimulate the moral reasoning of elementary and junior high school students. Somewhat less extensive curriculum development has been accomplished with young adults. Hurst found significant increases in moral reasoning among juniors and seniors in college. Kohlberg and Gilligan reported similar effects with Harvard College undergraduates.[14] Brock's study of junior college students, by contrast, produced no change in the Kohlberg or Loevinger measures. Further studies now underway include Whiteley's research at the University of California (Irvine) on the effects of living and participating in a university residence community and Santa Luca's study of junior college women in Boston.

Research on developmental education with mature adults is quite limited. In part this is because of the absence of an adequate developmental psychology of adulthood and the general pessimism of existing developmental literature as to the possibility of genuine stage change in adulthood. Grimes, for example, found it practicable and advantageous to children to train their mothers in the psychology of moral development and as moral educators. But none of the mothers in the Grimes study increased their own moral reasoning scores as a result of learning how to conduct moral discussions with their children. Stanley[15] found change on a number of nondevelopmental measures (for example, a reduction in parents' authoritarian attitudes toward childrearing, with fathers changing more than mothers; an increase in parents' egalitarianism when making family decisions; greater democracy in making rules and resolving family conflicts) as a result of an experimental course focused on the "justice structure" of the family and its modification. Parents in Felton's study were the most proficient group in learning counseling skills, again a nondevelopmental measure.

A number of studies in this field have been directed at both men and women in prison. Arrested development is more difficult to affect than normal growth. But Hickey, Scharf, and Lorish report significant effects on the prisoners' moral reasoning, communication skills, and ability to make vocational decisions. The accumulating data of Kohlberg's research in the Niantic, Connecticut, Correctional Institutes in establishing prison units governed just by inmates is further documentation.

One can summarize the progress of developmental education as follows: For one thing, the volume of research on the developmental effects of various curricula is expanding quickly. The research, far from complete or definitive, is overly dependent on doctoral dissertations, and it is heuristic. Of the several strands of human development, we know most about how to educate for moral and ego development in preadolescence, adolescence, and young adults since stimulation of these two basic strands of development is practicable. The Biological Sciences Curriculum Study Project, "The Human Sciences, A Developmental Approach to Adolescent Education," may yield data on whether that three-year curriculum can at least stimulate movement from concrete to formal operations at the junior high school level. The variety of studies of moral education using the Kohlberg instrument, which is a cognitive developmental measure, are the only present indicators that it may be possible to "teach" people to think in more complex ways. It is my feeling that this will be the acid test of developmental education.[16] (I hasten to reiterate an earlier point: claims that the existing curriculum is teaching children to think are equally vulnerable and questionable.) Groundbreaking research in the area of education for aesthetic, vocational, and physical development remains to be done. In some instances the requisite developmental theory is lacking, and the need for hard thinking and hard educational development is quite apparent.

The further development of children, adolescents, and young adults is "easiest" (no "pure" development is easy) to affect by education when it is time for that development to occur normally. Grimes's study, in which all sixth-grade children in the experimental class moved from preconventional to conventional moral reasoning as a result of a course in moral education shared by their mothers is an illustration. From age eleven to age thirteen is the normal time for this transitional stage to occur. Grimes's research (so, too, Felton's and Stanley's) also underscores the importance of giving knowledge of human development, and how to support it by education, to parents, who are, obviously, the primary educators of their children. By contrast, education is most difficult and requires the most intensive interaction with people whose development has been arrested (see Paolitto, Hickey, Lorish, Scharf). But this is hardly surprising given the literature of therapy, corrections, and remedial education.

What we are able to learn about stimulating people's development by education is limited, in part, by what we can measure—by a paucity of valid measures of development (that is, instruments that can register the emergence of more complex ways of thinking about logical propositions or one's moral obligations, about who one is or an enlarging social conscience). The complexity and cost of administering some of the available measures is a further handicap. Other outcomes of the variety of curricula being tested are clearly significant: for example, adolescents can learn to counsel or teach as well as many professionals and, in the process, mature morally and socially, or, analogously, adolescents can create genuine student self-government, become skillful in conducting and participating in democratic groups, and acquire higher-stage moral reasoning in so doing.

It is especially important that we are learning what educational experiences are particularly appropriate to produce decalage or consolidation in development at a given period in an individual's life and to ensure transition to higher stages of moral reasoning or ego development. We also are beginning to understand the necessity that these experiences be consecutive. For example, we know that moral development is caused by several factors: being exposed to and interacting intellectually with higher-stage arguments; learning to understand the thinking and feeling of other people, having increased empathy for others, and enlarging social perspective and concern; and action on behalf of chosen moral and social goals. What educational experiences, then, may be expected to stimulate moral development? An initial category involves the discussion of moral dilemmas, of which current curriculum examples include written dilemmas (studies by Blatt, Speicher, and Colby and by Lockwood),[17] filmstrips (such as *First Things First,* prepared by Guidance Associates), and films (*Searching for Values: A Film Anthology,* prepared by Learning Corporation of America). A second kind of generic educational experience involves what Mead called role taking.[18] Curriculum experiences providing this include learning to counsel (studies by Dowell, Lorish, Felton, and Rustad), adolescents as moral educators (studies by Sullivan and Alexander), and Paolitto's role-taking curriculum for the junior high school. A third group of experiences in social service and social action stems from the study of the justice structure of institutions. The school, the family, the courts and government, and experiences in rule making, in creating fairer institutions, in democratic participation also contribute to moral development. Experimental curricula providing these kinds of experience include Sullivan's project, where adolescents taught moral education classes to younger children and formed a high school disciplinary appeals board; BSCS's *Human Sciences'* units on "Rules" and "What's Happening to Me?"; Newmann's curricula in social and political action; democratic high school experiments in Cambridge and Brookline, Massachusetts, and in Pittsburgh, Pennsylvania; Stanley's focus on the justice structure of the family as a focus for parent and adolescent education.[19]

It is now possible, on the basis of this growing body of research, to suggest what educational experiences are most appropriate to the person's stage of moral development and how they may be sequenced for progressive growth. For example, to stimulate development from preconventional to conventional moral reasoning in the fifth and sixth grades, Grimes's data suggest the discussion of moral dilemmas, creating original dilemmas and role playing, and training the children's mothers as moral educators. Paolitto used a variety of imaginative role-taking experiences to the same end with junior high students. Both Dowell, and the many others who taught adolescents to counsel, and Lorish, who trained prisoners to be peer counselors for other inmates, argue that teaching people to counsel others may be the single most powerful educational experience presently available to stimulate conventional moral thinking, empathy, and role taking.

To consolidate conventional moral reasoning, the discussion of dilemmas, the study of law, the reading of constitutions, the investigation of the governance and fairness of institutions, and involvement in social service and social-political action are "stage appropriate" educational experiences. To stimulate development toward principled moral reasoning, two kinds of educational experience have been demonstrated to be critical. The first is systematic experience in rule making and the democratic governance of classrooms, alternative high schools, or undergraduate residences. A second is participation in moral discussion (Kohlberg and Gilligan) through the study of normative philosophy or topics in ethics and moral philosophy with high school seniors (Beck and Sullivan).

So the picture of what we know is a mixed one. More extensive curricula are now being researched. In particular, I refer to the "just community," or democracy as education experiments at the high school level in Cambridge and Brookline, Massachusetts, in Pittsburgh, Pennsylvania, and at the University of California. Teachers and counselors are being trained in developmental psychology and in the creating and teaching of developmental curricula in Brookline, Cambridge, Pittsburgh, Minneapolis, and Tacoma. In Brookline, this teacher education is being extended from the elementary school level through adult education in moral development.[20] In Tacoma, it will involve, over three years, the development and testing of a moral education curriculum for the elementary school through senior high, the training of many teachers, and the dissemination of such programs to other school districts in the state of Washington.

Substantial educational development is underway. It is incomplete, fractionated, promising, and as vital a movement as currently exists anywhere in American public education. In the context of this conference, the case I am making is that we should "humanize" education by having it serve the process and end of human growth or development. This is a different objective than incorporating into the curriculum the classics of human thought, values, literature, arts (that is, the humanities) as models of emulation and inspiration for young people—a cultural heritage to be transmitted to animate schooling and inspire students. In my view, the humanities are educational means (albeit important and powerful) to human development; they are not ends in themselves. But I welcome a common cause with the humanities. In Brookline we are already developing prototype curricula to teach American history or English, maintaining the integrity of those disciplines but concurrently attempting to affect moral reasoning or ego development. In this respect the emerging curricula of developmental education will be both familiar (for example, in the area of moral education, role playing the constitutional debates in Philadelphia, arguing the case for and against assumption of the debts of the Continental Congress, discussing the need for a Bill of Rights, and so forth) and less familiar (adolescents studying Piaget's and Kohlberg's theories of moral development and teaching moral education classes to younger children, participating in genuine democratic government of their own classrooms or school). The critical test of any curriculum in developmental education is: How does a course, an experience, a discipline, a program of social service or action contribute to cognitive, moral, social, or ego development, and, ultimately, the whole development, of the individual?

It is true that this puts a greater burden on our theory or measures of development than they currently can bear. Anything as profound as human intellectual, moral, and personal development should not be expected to yield simple or immediate formulation, measurement, or stimulation. And the correlates of development in individual behavior and social outcomes have to be clarified. I believe, incidentally, that developmental education will contribute to our psychological understanding of the stages and characteristics of the human life cycle. But our most important contribution is that we are discovering the "how to" in terms of developing educational "technology" for human development. Further elaboration and validation of that technology is my primary concern, and I believe that it will require, at minimum, a decade of work. There is, of course, no guarantee that essential constituencies—teachers committed to their disciplines, school boards concerned with "zero growth" budgets, parents or other policy-making groups—will agree that human develoment is the proper aim of education. Indeed, there is probably less social support for this idea than was available to Dewey and the progressives. Are

Education for Human Development

we, then, arguing an idea whose time has passed and whose technology has arrived? I do not presume to know. Nor am I persuaded that open education programs (which I see as analogous in many ways at the elementary level to the work reported here), humanistic education, professors talking to one another at conferences, and a few foundation dollars a movement make. A common cause rather than doctrinal dispute is essential if we are serious about the franchise. Building an influential constituency for human development as the aim of education or for humanizing education is a crucial task. Education for human actualization has no lobby; dyslexia or learning disability, ironically enough, does. But I am optimistic that education to enhance human rationality and character is practicable and imminent, for it represents a way to move beyond Descartes's dictum to doubt everything.

Discussion

Participants (in order of speaking): *David E. Purpel, Ralph Mosher, James B. Macdonald, Michael W. Apple, Thomas J. Sergiovanni, Nancy R. King, Flora Nell Roebuck,* and *Walter Feinberg*

Purpel: Let me start off with a question. Can and should the schools somehow teach, promote, coach, encourage (whatever term you want to use) people to "give a *good* damn," to care a lot, to have some passion about their commitment in a real sense?

Mosher: We have not measured that, but I think there is all kinds of unobtrusive evidence that those students who are participating in the moral education programs in elementary or high schools and who are participating in the democratic governance of their own classrooms or of alternative schools care a great deal. Interestingly enough, it's *hard* to get students to participate in the democratic governance of their own classroom or school. I think there are lots of reasons: the tradition of student government, the developmental stage of the students, the press of the institution because many teachers and administrators fear such changes. But I think those students who do participate *care*.

Purpel: Is that unintended or intended?

Mosher: Oh, it's intended, of course! It has everything to do with being moral agents. I am not satisfied with a theory or with an educational program that simply stimulates moral judgment. That is one of the major Achilles' heels in this theory, incidentally—that it is a theory of moral judgment and not one of moral action. You recognize that. For me, caring *is* an intended consequence of any such program.

I would like to move a little further on an issue that was being debated at the end of an earlier discussion. I'm not sure how much more the schools *can* do in this regard. My own view is that, educationally and psychologically, we are at the point of beginning to know how to enhance human intellect—or thinking. We are also at the point of beginning to know how to stimulate a morality as this theory defines it. Also, we are at a point of knowing how to help people move to a more mature sense of meaning about their personal lives—ego integration. Given the white blood corpuscles and the time and the intelligence and the will that I have left, I don't think I can marshall the resources to do much more than validate those kinds of outcomes. And I can accept that. If I can, in fact, validate that it is possible to enhance a human intellect and character in that way, then I believe that education is making a profound social contribution. We shall be able to empower individuals by education. I'm also aware of all the antithetical forces in institutions and society that militate against that.

Macdonald: I have a question about the videotapes you showed of teachers using moral education techniques with children. The techniques tend to reject certain kinds of action and to categorize children's answers in certain ways. What level or moral stage is that technique reflecting, and is that consonant with what you are trying to develop in the children?

Mosher: Well, you're referring to the overt and the tacit curriculum, and that's a fair question. I would not reify the pedagogy you saw at all. My own preference is for a more free-flowing exchange of opinions on issues. All this particular technique has to recommend it is that teachers can comprehend it and begin to use it. It's important to move beyond that. My answer is to have a variety of ways for individuals to confront and debate moral questions and to participate in social service through teaching, working with older people in nursing homes, and tutoring or coaching younger people. We are also attempting to incorporate a variety of programs to encourage social action. For more than three years we have been trying to involve youngsters in the whole process of learning democratic participation, how to lead a group—in class and in school. The techniques you just saw are a small part of the total educational experience we are offering. Some other people, Ted Fenton, for example, might make the pragmatic case that there are limits to what you can incorporate into the instructional repertoire of large groups of teachers—that you have got to make it rather simplistic. I hope that is not true.

Apple: I want to raise a question, not about the pedagogy, but about "Kohlbergian Theory," as both an intellectual and a social construct. Two questions: What gives Stage 6 more legitimacy than Stage 5? Obviously Kohlberg has been confronted with that, but I'd like your view.

Mosher: I'm sure you've read his justification for Stage 6.

Apple: Yes, and I want your sense about it. My second question, which is just as important, concerns the basic regularities of the way institutions now exist. Is there a strong possibility that what developmental psychology does is give one more set of categories for social labeling?

Mosher: Social labeling, that's a Jerry Kagan argument that any category system will automatically be turned into a means of labeling people. To answer that one first, interestingly enough this does not seem to be a problem in the use of our theory with children. It is to some degree more of a problem when using our theory with teachers. I have not seen it used abusively in the way that IQ data have been.

Apple: I would be interested in exactly this issue as it relates to the moral reasoning that went on in two comparative videotapes: Brookline and Harlem. You might just find a predominance of the second level in Harlem.

Mosher: In the children you mean?

Apple: Yes. And you would probably say, "That is bad reasoning."

Mosher: No, I wouldn't.

Apple: That's interesting!

Mosher: What I mean is that it is moral reasoning. It is less complex reasoning in a cognitive sense—and less principled, but it is a moral point of view with integrity and the best reasoning the children are capable of. Let me answer the original question before I go to the first, however. The children do not use this as a category system to rank one another up or down. They are intrigued by the theory. In the same way I have found that, when you teach children about counseling and show them the film, *Three Approaches to Psychotherapy,* they rip into Carl Rogers, they rip into Fritz Perls, and they rip into Albert Ellis. They don't ask themselves: "Can I do as well as Carl Rogers, or would Fritz Perls approve of the way I just said that?" But they are intrigued by the theory. It is teachers who have used the stages as labels. I remember my first experience in a small high school in Nova Scotia as a guidance counselor. I did as guidance counselors were wont to do at that time: I administered group intelligence tests to the children and gave the scores to the teachers. One teacher proceeded to read the scores to her children! So that problem has been with us for a while. I agree that teachers may make more *Pygmalion in the Classroom* use of the stages, but I honestly have not found that they use them to categorize children and downgrade them. My impression is that a stage theory of moral reasoning is helpful to teachers in another way: to understand that, because Adam is thinking at one level and Blaire is thinking at a less comprehensive one, this does not mean that Blaire is dumb, immoral, obtuse, or out of it. Teachers seem helped by the notion of a developmental sequence in thinking that is characterized by increasing cognitive complexity and the application of more moral principles rather than less. It is helpful to them in understanding children's answers.

Art Linkletter has made a fortune amusing adults with the funny things that children say. And developmental psychologists offer us explanations as to why the things that we laugh at uproariously are quite predictable, understandable, evolutionary, and have integrity as the best organization of the child's experience and neural capacities at that point. That's part of the answer to the other question.

Sergiovanni: I'd like to push this in another direction just for a second. Let's suppose that you knew nothing else about the groups that were involved except that a dilemma has been resolved with decision A based on second-level reasoning and with decision B based on sixth-level reasoning. Given that information, which would you think is the better decision? Play the game the way that the teacher is playing it.

Mosher: I'll answer two ways. First, the second-level answer has its own integrity. It is a moral position—a moral point of view. It incorporates, incidentally, a conception of justice and of moral principle. It is simply a truncated conception of principle. From a cognitive or intellectual point of view, it is a less comprehensive answer. It takes into account fewer issues. That is another difference. I would prefer the sixth-stage answer because I would presume that it carries with it a consideration of a number of critical and perhaps universal moral principles, including justice, majority will, majority interest, a fundamental respect for the integrity of individual personality, rights, and concerns. If you wanted to parse it simply from an intellectual or a cognitive point of view, it undoubtedly would take into account more issues, and, incidentally, speak to the resolution of more problems than the second-stage answer. Clearly it would take into account much more elaborate criteria, and the rules would be more complex.

King: I would like to use this example and suggest that Stage 2 reasoning occurred in the Harlem School.

Mosher: It's in our prisons, too.

King: On both sides of the bars. You said at one time that you were fully aware of the elements mitigating against the adoption of this program in our schools.

Mosher: Not fully. That would be pretentious. I could show you my scars relative to attempting this.

King: What elements, in the Harlem school, for example, might prevent the children in this fictitious class from advancing beyond Stage 2 reasoning?

Mosher: That's almost rhetorical, isn't it? I mean, don't we probably share a sense of what those elements are?

King: I was wondering what elements in the school culture and the culture surrounding it you would stress as most important. The next question is: What can we do about it?

Mosher: Well, the first issue would obviously be where to begin. You've probably seen the film *High School*. The moral atmosphere of such institutions is probably not higher than Stage 2. Those institutions are involved in rather manipulative and exploitive trade-offs between adults and kids and between kids and kids.

King: In a sense, they teach a truncated morality.

Mosher: They live and represent a truncated preconventional stage of moral interaction and responsibility. Their rhetoric often reaches Stage 3 or Stage 4, just as it does in prisons. You are right, prisons are full of Stage 1 and Stage 2 people on both sides of the bars. There are also critical small masses of concerned, anguished teachers and administrators in such schools who have at least reached conventional stages. But the mass of them: Good Lord, Hyde Park High School in Boston has a hundred police officers in it! Social control is massive! The response to any kind of deviance is immediate manhandling. There is no discussion. And when it isn't force, or flat-out power, it's rather cynical deals between administrators and teachers, and between teachers and kids. All of those elements are there.

Your second question is: What do you do about that? What do I do about that? I'm not going to be glib. My answer is at least twofold. I am going to work very hard with whatever wit, energy, and commitment I have to conceptualize, explore, try out, and validate a variety of educational means and experiences to stimulate human beings along these dimensions of rationality, character, caring, and personal integration. That's a larger educational task, as I said earlier, than I have energy or intelligence left to complete. It's an extraordinarily important task, and I do work in those institutions. Sometimes the chaos is such that those involved will grasp at almost any kind of intervention. We ran training programs in moral education for school teachers in the public schools of Boston last spring, which was idiotic, given the fact that those schools were on fire. We have succeeded in gaining acceptance of some of the kinds of things that I've been talking about. We had Hyde Park students teaching moral education in elementary schools in Boston. My approach is a gradualist one; I fully recognize that the alteration of the moral atmosphere of institutions, certainly of more than one or two of them, is not something that I can accomplish in my professional lifetime.

Larry Kohlberg works in two prisons in Connecticut, correctional institutes for men and women. He's getting some dramatic data that prisoners can take substantial responsibility for making decisions about their own lives. What happens when you give them a "just community" (a pretentious phrase for management of a significant part of their own lives—as much as is possible in prison) is that most of the people at Stage 1 and Stage 2 predictably create a larger sorority or fraternity or extended family. The prisoners began to care for one another, to take responsibility for one another, and to think and decide in conjunction with one another. This means that they began to move toward Stage 3 in terms of moral development, that is, they began to show increments toward conventionality. To go back to a point that I've been reiterating— You've got to be conventional before you can be postconventional! At least if I read all of the evidence of developmental psychology, you can't leapfrog past that.

I don't know if this constitutes an answer to the question. I'm aware of the moral atmospheres of the schools and how those militate against what I'm trying to accomplish. But my basic purpose is to clarify, conceptually, how to educate for human development and, in practice, to validate, test for, and to get data. If you do these things, if you offer these kinds of experiences in consecutive ways (and I talk a lot about consecutiveness in ordering these experiences, something the progressives were never able to bring off), then you can expect these kinds of increments in human potential.

Sergiovanni: Must our explanations always be psychological? Aren't there other kinds—cultural, anthropological?

Mosher: Yes, but I'm a psychologist.

Sergiovanni: You say you are sure that the stages exist, that there's no way to leapfrog them, and that everybody must go through them?

Mosher: Yes.

Sergiovanni: Are there express cultural studies, for example?

Mosher: Yes there are.

Sergiovanni: Do they confirm this?

Mosher: Yes, but I'm also aware that five years ago developmental psychologists were saying that these stages were probably stable and not subject to change through systematic education. They argued that change resulted from more or less random interactions between what the individual has within his head and his environment. People clearly have unequal access to that kind of stimulation.

Sergiovanni: But psychology is always confounded by culture.

Mosher: That is so, but all I'm saying is that we've destabilized some of the assumptions of developmental psychology about the mutability of these stages of moral reasoning and of cognition. Incidentally, I think that the hardest one of all for us in developmental education to effect is the movement from concrete thought to formal operations. If we could find systematic educational means to increase the proportion of people capable of formal operations (abstract thinking), I would go to my grave content that I had made a profound educational contribution. Whether these structures, these ways of thinking, these capacities are more mutable than we have seen is an issue that's much debated now in developmental psychology. I have had colleagues who have said, "Hell, I could do this in a weekend." My experience over six or seven years of intensive work is that anything as profound as human cognition, morality, and social responsiveness is not subject to such easy development. We are going to need more powerful experiences. I think, as we now understand the relationships of such experiences and can organize them consecutively, that the potential for human beings to develop is still much underestimated. The role of *other* means of effecting changes in these capacities (for example, having youngsters live in different cultures) calls for work that is beyond my ability.

Macdonald: Let's stick for a time with the cultural question. You said that if you're going to commit the "naturalistic fallacy" you're going to do it in the developmental framework and on the best evidence of "what is" that you can get. I tend to go along with that—if you're going to do it, that's where I would do it, too. But there is one question I'm confused about. I don't quite see the analogy between *your* developmental framework and that of Piaget that I thought existed. As I understand Piaget, the development occurs through formative processes, and you can use it in a number of different substances. But, I don't see the formative process in yours. You have to deal with a substantive set of problems, whereas the cognitive development of Piaget isn't limited to any given set of cognitive problems. It makes me wonder whether the analogy is holding up . . . .

Mosher: Fair enough. Apparently I'm not representing a position well. I'm saying that the slow evolution and reconstruction of intelligence or cognition is content free. There are many means to achieve epistemological development; they are certainly not limited to five sacred subjects! Relative to moral development, at the moment we are limited only by what the theory tells us is related to stimulating moral development—debate, intellectual disagreement, and the dissonance that's created. There's also social service, social action in helping others (which relates to stimulating empathy), and the experience of moral choice. It also appears to have to do with participation in organizations where social perspectives are required. We can probably infer appropriate, analogous, or parallel educational experiences from that. There clearly may be other factors that contribute to moral development in other educational experiences. I think, hypothetically, that anything and everything could be the content of moral education and moral development. We are limited at the moment only by what we know from the theory and only by what we have been able to test.

Roebuck: I still am not clear in what way moral development as a closed field is different from cognition as a closed field. What I have seen so far is a cognitive analysis of another kind of problem solving, with the content being moral action. I don't know the difference, then, between moral development and cognitive development.

Mosher: A very good question! Kohlberg's theory is one of moral judgments, of thinking about a particular cluster or constellation of moral and ethical problems. It is, thus, a theory of rationality. It is also a developmental theory in that human thought relative to moral and ethical questions does go through a predictable sequence of increasing cognitive complexity. It also contains a sort of hidden factor when it moves toward the application of principles. But there are clear redundancies between Piagetian thought and Kohlberg's theory. Kohlberg really took a metaphor from Piaget's work. He then expanded it, elaborated it conceptually and philosophically, and validated it empirically in this culture and across cultures.

In relation to part of an earlier point made by Apple, I said I'm not satisfied with merely teaching more sophisticated and more principled moral judgment, although something is better than nothing. If I can help people think more clearly and comprehensively and in a more principled way about the moral issues that confront them, I have made some contribution. But I am also interested in studying the relationship between moral thought and moral action and, incidentally, the inverse relationship between moral action or experience and its effect on moral thought. One of the unresolved dilemmas in American psychology is whether you think yourself into new ways of behaving or behave yourself into new ways of thinking. My own view is that the answer is yes to both. That type of work is just now beginning in the area of moral development and moral education.

Newmann said that he disagreed "with Kohlberg and you guys on arguing about moral agency." I think it is evident that we are interested in having children, adolescents, and young adults be *more* than moral philosophers. We are interested in having them act on moral choice and in studying the effect of those actions, and that speaks to Purpel's point. With the exception of teaching moral education in the community, we have not really moved into a study of what happens if they take moral action on a wide range of social problems outside the purview of their own institution. Certainly moral education has already moved much beyond the definition of morality or judgment or reason.

Feinberg: Probably this is a cautionary note, but it does pick up on what Apple and some other people have said. I can think of situations where it might be problematic to teach people how to think and behave in a Stage 6, or postconventional, manner. The kind of thinking about moral affairs which individuals have, given the kind of environment they are in, may be the only functional way there is to think about these things.

Mosher: But it may be very dysfunctional to them.

Feinberg: No. It may be the *only* functional way to think.

Roebuck: It's like teaching a child to use proper English; then he uses it on the street and is beaten up by the gang.

Feinberg: That would be a good analogy. Or how do you teach a child to think about other people's feelings when he's in the kind of environment where nobody can possibly deal with *his* feelings? That brings me to a dimension of the studies that hasn't been examined: the relationship between somebody's responses and their social-class, ethnic, or some other situation.

Mosher: Do you mean the correlates or the consequences?

Feinberg: Both. Take a migrant farm worker. It may be that he's not incapable of thinking in terms of principles; he may know how to do it. We need to make a distinction between knowing how to do it and being able, in a given situation, to do it. I really do suspect that I could teach many people the techniques of incorporating other moral views into the way they answer questions about moral affairs, but that isn't what you're after, and it isn't what I'm after.

Mosher: It's only half a loaf.

Feinberg: Right, they may know how to do it. It may just be that they decided somewhere along the line that in this life they are not going to be able to do it.

Mosher: Well, I have several responses. The first will seem glib. All of us have access to lower stages of moral thinking. I think, if we are perfectly candid, we know when we use Stage 2 thinking. There are times when, as a department chairman, situations drive me to a Stage 2 kind of calculus. I don't mean to be anecdotal, but that creates a very real kind of anguish and tension for me as an individual. I am struggling, as I understand Stage 5, to operate a department that is democratic, that treats people fairly, and that accords people a kind of justice as individuals in terms of access to resources. Having to resort to Stage 2 reasoning creates anguish. There is another kind of tension and anxiety that people who are at postconventional stages feel in this culture. I think it has been expressed around this table in the last several days. Institutions that employ Stage 4 rhetoric, while their behavior toward teachers and children would be more consistently classified as Stage 2, have got to trouble perceptive educators. It seems to me that this is the essence of the cry for humanizing educational institutions.

My own answer to your basic question is: if I have available an educational means, a set of experiences that can move people to majority will, majority interest, and principled behavior, do I have the moral right as an educator to withhold that from people? Is this culture better off, or worse off, because Martin Luther King lived in it and affected it? If you want to read Stage 5 and Stage 6 statements, read King's speeches.

That question: "What right do you have . . ." comes up repeatedly and in fascinating ways. The radical critique goes: "I won't believe you guys about stimulating human development. You just really want to get everybody conventional, and stop it there, which is obviously dangerous. You've got a new kind of social control—a better technology to make people conventional." In essence, the radical critique is, "I don't believe that you guys are *really* for human development until you demonstrate that you can move significant proportions of people to postconventional moral and political positions. Then there are the people who come to us and say, "Maybe you've got the answer to the problem of lawlessness and violence in the schools. Make these kids conventional."

My own philosophical position as an educator is that, if I possess that technology, I have no right to create conditions of unequal access or opportunity to those experiences. I trust people. The alternative is to withhold the technology in order to keep people conventional. Such an alternative seems, however, to be a denial of the fundamental ethical premise of justice in according equal respect, integrity in operation, and opportunity to different personalities.

Apple: Another anecdote—in my early teaching, I used a lot of role playing by asking people to put themselves in other people's shoes and so forth. I found that the students who had the most difficulty doing this, who really put up a wall, were those who were the most deprived, and I would get angry and think: "Damn it.

I'm going to shake them to get into the other person's shoes," or similar thoughts. Then I began to understand that to put themselves in the shoes of the other person is potentially destructive.

Mosher: I agree. It's poignant. Peter Mackey, one of my doctoral candidates who taught counseling to high school students in vocational programs for whom high school was the end, tells a poignant story about going to a boy in the body shop and asking him to come to the class. The boy said, "Why should I come to that class? Nobody listens to my problems. I got problems that nobody will listen to. Why should I be empathetic and try to help another human being?" But if I know a way to enlarge that person's ability by taking the perspective of another person, whether it is a girlfriend, a father, a mother, or eventually one's own child, or to have some more enhanced moral sense of that other person's rights and their reciprocity as human beings, I can't withhold that, morally or philosophically.

Apple: Let me lay out a social scenario based on what you are saying. One of the problems of too radical a position is that it sees an overt conspiracy all over the place. It assumes that there is a group of people, an elite mass of twelve people, who sit in the boardroom and say, "We've got them now!" It's obviously not that simple, but I want to argue that the roots of this are conveyed and are re-created by the commonsense helping practices that people engage in. That is, as long as we continue amelioration, we can do no more than re-create what has gone on in the past. Now let me try and lay that out. I don't mean just to say, "Unless you shake up the institution, you are not going to do anything." The commonsense helping practices that we engage in also *create* the problems that we encounter. There is a dialectical relationship between what we do to help—not the repressive kinds of things, but the helping kinds of things—and the social problems we struggle with. As an example, no one in their right mind gives tests to children to hurt them. You ask them why they give tests, and they claim that they are trying to find out if they are doing a good job or that they are trying to help the students, or they give some other apparently valid reason. Here's the scenario I see from this. Existing rationality in the US is at least in part controlled and distributed by Educational Testing Service. In order to have large-scale educational innovation, to do what you want to do in every school system throughout the US, you have to develop a test of moral reasoning.

Mosher: We have one.

Apple: Right. And it would have to be administered and prepackaged in a formal way that would go through ETS. There has *never* been a test put out by ETS that hasn't latently served to create more social barriers than there were before, that hasn't served as a social control mechanism and a social sorting mechanism. Obviously, this is quite complex and is tied to the problem of cultural and economic reproduction, but I think we have to face that as a real issue. I am not saying, "Stop doing what you are doing," but I want to raise a question: What mechanisms can we build in now so that we don't re-create the past? We know what's going to happen. It's not as if this were a great cloudy area. What are we going to *do* with this in some way that can deal with those kinds of issues, since no matter what we try with schools they tend to work exactly the same way they always used to?

Mosher: Well, that is obviously not a problem that's exclusively mine to answer. I'm not, however, insensitive to it. Some of the remarks I make at the end of the presentation are somewhat pessimistic. I do perceive one answer and the very hazy outlines of another answer that confront all of us. The answer for me, as a developmental educator, is to work very hard to create experiences that produce more people in formal operations who are at least Stage 5 in terms of moral development. Parenthetically, one of the clearest predictors of the absence of racial and ethnic prejudice is the presence of postconventional moral thinking. So, one of my obligations as an educator is to worry about moving people to postconventional thought, morality, and personal integration—I think we can do that. I might say that the American Constitution is a Stage 5 document. I don't think it is hard to understand why we have not as yet passed an Equal Rights Amendment in this country. The data indicate that only about 20 percent of the American people at this point are able, philosophically, to comprehend the fundamental principles of the constitution. I have one educational answer that is not pie in the sky. We already have some significant ways to teach people participatory democracy and to stimulate a sense of justice and empathy. But the larger issue, which faces everyone of us but has no clear outline, is to make common cause! This field is riven with doctrinal disputes between humanistic educators, confluent educators, developmental educators, and human relations people. We are such a small critical mass, such a small red line, that we just haven't got time to be at each others' throats over the rather sophistic issues that we debate! My own view is that what Cremin talks about in *The Transformation of the School* is extraordinarily informative as to what has to *happen* in terms of alliances with social forces. There were people from the union movement, populists, and others who were heavily involved with progressive education. If we want the franchise, we've got to create a constituency. And it's at that point that even I sometimes lose my nerve. I know what I can do with the time I have left. I can produce the educational technology that will, at least when times are more propitious, contribute to human development. On that point I end this discussion.

Fifth
  Presentation

Thomas J. Sergiovanni

The Odyssey of Organizational Theory and Implications for Humanizing Education

Perhaps the title of this presentation might more accurately have read: "The Not So Glorious Evolution of Organizational Theory in Education, or, for the Humanist, Going from Bad to Worst." Organizational theory has never been a popular topic in education, and even yet it commands only a small following among scholars and practitioners. One reason for this neglect and, among some quarters, disdain for organizational theory can be traced to the general fragmentation and task specialization that seemingly run rampant throughout the academic community in education. For indications of fragmentation and overspecialization in education in a task sense, one need only review the array of departments and units in typical colleges of education and the assortment of professional certificates awarded by state departments of education.

Our amorous relationship with task specialization in education often results in reducing problems and issues into simple, presumably manageable, parts for inquiry within the rubrics of a given specialty. Thus, problems such as classroom organization, child development, objectives and evaluation, discipline, community conflict, change and innovation, organizational structure and climate, teacher motivation and commitment, collective bargaining, and curriculum improvement are typically treated separately. When integration does exist, it is likely to occur in predictable groupings, such as educational, management, and political, with little regard for relating issues across groupings.

When organizational theorists in education feel a sense of benign neglect or perhaps disdain from their brethren within the educational community, they may well be getting deserved treatment. Their work typically reflects a scant knowledge of, sensitivity to, and interest in the work of curriculum specialists, evaluation experts, those interested in classroom organization and instruction, and those who seek clarification of the value structure of education. This apparent separation of organizational and management concerns from educational concerns has resulted in a fragmented and often contradictory assault on educational problems, and I believe it has seriously retarded the intellectual development and advancement of practice within each area of concern.

The Organization as a System

Following Talcott Parsons,[1] I view the school as an organization concerned with three identifiably distinct levels of responsibility and control—technical, managerial, and institutional. The technical level, which is the professional subsystem of the school, is concerned operationally with the actual provision of classroom and other instructional opportunities to students. This level includes concern for intents and objectives, curriculum materials, teacher and student roles, classroom organization, instructional strategies, clinical supervision, and other aspects of the school's educational program.

At the managerial level Parsons refers to the servicing, facilitating, and procuring functions that sustain, control, and administer the technical level. I view this level broadly as the school's organizational subsystem, and it includes manifestations of structure such as the school's emphasis or lack of emphasis on formalization, specialization, reliability, centralization, integration, adaptiveness, efficiency, and productivity. The school's organizational climate is reflected in management assumptions, leadership processes, the distribution of power and authority, decision-making systems, and communications patterns.

The school, with its organizational and professional subsystems, is also part of a broader social system that Parsons refers to as the institutional level. It is this broader social system that legitimizes the school and provides it with support. State and local regulatory agencies, community pressure groups, and competing community organizations are examples of forces comprising the institutional level. In exchange for legitimization and support, the broader system makes demands upon the school's organizational and professional subsystems.

The Parsons distinction of organizational levels becomes important as one views patterns of interaction and interdependence that exist between and among levels. Further, the extent to which an organization such as a school is considered a relatively open system characterized by uncertainty or a closed system characterized by rationality, if viewed in juxtaposition with the Parsons conceptualization, can provide a useful analytical device for viewing differences and similarities among schools of thought in organizational theory.

As a Closed, Rational System

If an educational organization is viewed as a closed system, then the institutional level is viewed as providing a steady state of support to the school and as making fairly predictable and reliable demands in the form of expectations. These norms of rationality are characterized by a minimum of environmental uncertainty, and they permit the organizational level to devote attention to interface with the school's professional subsystem.

In such an environment the system is closed in the sense that uncertainty, not being an issue, is ignored and attention is turned to norms of rationality.[2] By norms of rationality I mean the ability of the organization to operate in an environment of certainty or a determinate system.[3] This permits the identification of clearly operational objectives and the development of plans, strategies, roles, and mechanisms that permit the maximizing of those objectives. Since the identification of objectives and the development of strategies are typically seen as management functions, the technical core of the organization (or, in the case of schools, the professional subsystem) is clearly subordinate to, and programmed by, the organizational subsystem. Classical management theorists are perhaps best represented by the writings of Frederick Taylor, Luther Gulick and L. Urwick, James Mooney and Allen Reilly, Henri Fayol, and Max Weber, who tend to view organizations as closed systems.[4]

As an Open, Uncertain System

At the other extreme is an open-system view of organization characterized by a frequent but uncertain and unpredictable flow of interaction and press between the organization and its broader social system—the institutional level. This openness introduces rapidly changing and often conflicting demands and expectations into the system. Further, the sheer volume of unpredictable input introduces more variables than can be handled by conventional rational strategies. There is no certainty when fixing goals and objectives, and planning is seen as unrealistic. The organizational elites in open, uncertain systems concede not only that rationality is beyond man and organization but also that attempts at approximating rationality are not possible.

In open-system thinking the organization is seen as constantly seeking a level of accommodation with its external environment. This accommodation requires adjustment both at the institutional level and within the organizational and technical subsystems. The Parsonian three-level conceptualization and its accompanying dynamics apply not just to the organization as a whole but to the suborganizations. Thus an academic department in a high school or college and, to a lesser extent, a family-grouped teaching team in an elementary school can be viewed as having a technical core and an organizational subsystem, each responding to an institutional level. In the case of a department, organizational-level regulatory agencies such as executive committees or curriculum councils, competing departments, and a core of organizational-level administrative elites comprise the institutional level.

Organizations attempt to insulate their technologies from institutional-level forces by erecting buffers.[5] The extent to which they are successful in this effort depends upon the strength of the technical core in question and upon the ability of organizational elites to articulate this technology persuasively. In medical organizations, for example, the technical core interacts either directly or through the organizational subsystem with the institutional level as an equal or superior partner. In elementary and secondary education the technical core seems by comparison weak. It is typically misunderstood or poorly articulated by the organizational elites, which leaves the technical core more vulnerable to forces at other levels.

As the organizational subsystem tries to mediate this institutional-technical core tension, the limits on rationality[6] are such that compromise is in order, and satisfying rather than maximizing[7] goals and mechanisms are developed. What is best is abandoned in favor of what will work or what can be successfully exchanged in the marketplace of constant intra- and interorganizational adjustment. Thus, in order to survive against strong and constantly shifting outside forces in an environment marked by uncertainty, the organizational system makes constant adjustments in its technical core. Open-system thinking, much like closed-system thinking, leads one to conclude that the professional subsystem of the educational organization is again subordinate to the organizational subsystem. In this case, however, subordination takes the form of being a source of fodder for organizational trade-offs and side payments as the organizational subsystem increases its ability to survive; it perhaps even gains in power and status by a strategy of appeasement at the institutional level. The decision-making theorists with roots in political and policy sciences are presently the most influential advocates of the open-system view of organizations where the environment reflects uncertainty.[8]

Going from "Bad" to "Worst"

When I proposed an alternate title earlier, I suggested that organizational thought was moving from "bad" to "worst" with regard to human values in education. The highly rational, closed view of organizations, which is the "bad" end of the continuum to which I refer, represents the foundation for early concepts of administration and organization in education. The view of organizations as open systems characterized by hopeless uncertainty, which is the "worst" to which I refer, is characteristic of present thinking among organizational theorists in education.

I take a somewhat more optimistic view and see complex organizations as being open systems faced with uncertainty *but* subject to norms of rationality and needing some certainty.[9] Norms of rationality, I think, depend upon strength of commitment of an organization's human system. Though I concede that it is unrealistic to see goals as unduly fixed and operational and to develop set plans and strategies, I believe that man, though quite complex and difficult to label, is capable of valuing, that agreements are possible, that goals can be determined, and that man as an individual and the human system of an organization as a whole are capable of intrinsic, goal-seeking behavior.

Perhaps it is time to trace the odyssey of organizational thought and its impact in education with greater deliberation. As I review the major benchmarks of this odyssey, I try to place them on this closed-rational and open, uncertain continuum, to describe their salient features with respect to organization and administration in education, to examine their impact on the schools' technical core or professional subsystems, and to elaborate on the image of man and accompanying management assumptions that underlie the school of thought in question.

Classical Management

Scientific

Any legacy in the evolution of organizational theory can be traced to scientific management. It was this movement that gave birth to the establishment of professional management in general and of educational administration in particular as a unique field of study and a distinct professional career. Frederick Winslow Taylor, seen by some as a villain and by others as a hero, is credited with being the founding father of scientific management. Taylor's impact on organization and management in education is now a matter of record.[10]

In his *Principles of Scientific Management* Taylor offered the four principles that were to become the foundation for his science of work and organization.[11] The first was to replace intuitive, or idiosyncratic, methods of doing the work of the organization with a scientific method based on observation and analysis to obtain the best cost-benefit ratio. For every task a *one best way* should be determined. The second was to select the best person for the job through the use of scientific methods and then train him thoroughly in the tasks and procedures to be followed. The third was to cooperate "heartily" with the man to ensure that the work was done according to established standards and procedures. The fourth and last of the principles required that the work of managers and workers be divided so

Organizational Theory

that managers could assume responsibility for planning and preparing work and for supervising. In Taylor's words, "The management takes over the work for which they are better fitted than the work man."[12]

Writing in education at about the same time, Franklin Bobbit stated:

> In any organization, the directive and supervisory members must clearly define the ends toward which the organization strives. They must co-ordinate the labors of all so as to attain those ends. They must find the best methods of work, and they must enforce the use of these methods on the part of the workers. They must determine the qualifications necessary for the workers and see that each rises to the standard qualifications, if it is possible; and when impossible, see that he is separated from the organization. This requires direct or indirect responsibility for the preliminary training of workers before service and for keeping them up to standard qualifications during service. Directors and supervisors must keep the workers supplied with detailed instructions as to the work to be done, the standards to be reached, the methods to be employed, and the materials and appliances to be used. They must place incentives before the worker in order to stimulate desirable effort. Whatever the nature or purpose of the organization, if it is an effective one, these are always the directive and supervisory tasks.[13]

For the next three decades the basic concepts and strategies of scientific management were applied to the broader question of organizational design by a host of European and American writers. Fayol offered a universal list of principles applicable to management and organization.[14] These included division of work, authority and responsibility, discipline, unity of command, and unity of direction. Gulick and Urwick offered the principles of unity of command, span of control, and matching people to the organizational structure.[15] Fayol advocated division of work not only by purpose, but by process, person, and place. And Mooney and Reilly offered the coordinative principle, the scalar principle, the functional principle, and the staff principle.[16] This classical management school of thought did not offer a theory of administration and organization as such but a set of principles and simple-minded injunctions for administrators to follow. Efficiency was to be maximized by defining objectives and outputs clearly, by specializing tasks through division of labor, and, once the *best way* was identified, by introducing a system of controls to ensure uniformity and reliability in workers' tasks, as well as standardization of product. These principles persevere today as strong considerations in curriculum development, in selecting educational materials, in developing instructional systems, and in other aspects of educational program administration.

Bureaucratic

Though principles of scientific management were enthusiastically adopted in both industry and education, they were not conceptualized into a full-fledged theory of organization. Not until the 1940's, with the advent of the translation into English of Max Weber's works, did classical management emerge from a set of rules and prescriptions to a model of organizational structure and functioning.[17]

Weber proposed a pure form or idealization of an organization that he called a bureaucracy. This idealization was in the form of a set of structural properties and characteristics now familiar to all of us. In the interest of efficiency the organization should have a well-defined hierarchy of authority with jobs and offices defined as to jurisdiction and location, a division of work based on functional specialization, a system of rules to spell out the rights and responsibilities of workers, a system of procedures for dealing with categories of activities within areas of responsibility and functional specialization, relationships characterized by impersonality, and a reward structure based on technical competence.

Bureaucracy was a mechanism for refining the norms of rationality and certainty so characteristic of scientific management. It was assumed that all aspects of the organization from its mission, technical requirement, and work flow to the details of its organizational structure could be defined into a permanent grand design. All that remained was to find people who could be programmed into this design and then to turn the key.

According to Weber, "The fully developed bureaucratic mechanism compares with other organizations exactly as does the machine with the nonmechanical modes of production ... precision, speed, unambiguity, continuity, discretion, unity, ... these are raised to the optimum point in a strictly bureaucratic administration."[18] Further, bureaucracy "is like a modern judge who is a vending machine into which the pleadings are inserted together with the fee and which then disgorges the judgment together with reasons mechanically derived from a code,"[19] and, finally, "The individual bureaucrat cannot squirm out of the apparatus in which he is harnessed ... in a great majority of cases, he is only a single cog in an ever moving mechanism which prescribes to him an eventually fixed route of march."[20]

In addition to assumptions of rationality within the organization and a steady state interface with the organization's institutional level, the classical schools of thought are perhaps most validly criticized for their fairly primitive rational-economic conception of man. Man is primarily motivated by economic concerns and works to maximize his economic gain. Since economic gain is under control of the organization, he becomes a passive agent to be engineered, manipulated, and controlled by the organization. The organization should be designed in a manner that neutralizes man's feelings and, therefore, his unpredictable decisions and activities. As Mason Haire suggests, "these are the implicit assumptions about man on which classical organization theories seem to be based: he is lazy, shortsighted, selfish, liable to make mistakes, has poor judgment, and may even be a little dishonest."[21] Douglas McGregor's well-known Theory X assumption perhaps best summarizes the conception of man implicit in classical management theories.[22] It is interesting to note, however, that the bureaucratic elites who stand at the helm of the organizational subsystem were spared this demeaning characterization of man. Indeed, because of advanced training and higher moral intelligence the elites were seen as trustworthy, much more broadly motivated, and therefore fit to organize and manage the masses.

Bureaucracy remains a part of the image of most educational organizations, and its advocates work diligently to introduce its principles of order and certainty. It would be unfair, I think, to assume that the extremely harsh conception of man typically associated with classical management theories characterizes the relationship that generally exists between administrators and teachers. But this conception remains ubiquitous as applied to students. As one might well predict from bureaucratic theory, the lower one is in the organizational hierarchy, the closer he will be seen as fitting the underlying assumptions of man characteristic of the model.

The Human Emphasis

Human Relations

Cries of protest and anguish were heard from the beginning of the advent of scientific management, but it was not until the 1930's that an effective, organized counterforce was to emerge. Human relations was the name given to this force, and the writings of Chester Barnard[23] and the experiment at Hawthorne[24] gave it impetus. Barnard is not typically associated with the human relations school (most schools of organizational thought claim Barnard in one way or another), but his notions of organizations as cooperative systems, of natural groups, and of participative authority were accepted as tenets by human relations advocates (though perhaps neither fully understood nor actually implemented as Barnard would have liked).

Clearly the work of the scientific management research team which operated from 1922 to 1932 at the Hawthorne plant of the Western Electric Company in Cicero, Illinois, provided the empirical basis for this movement. The research team was engaged in intensive efficiency and task analysis research, but a number of serendipitous human factors such as informal group and work restriction norms were destined to spoil their efforts. Humane leadership, which took into account the social group, satisfaction of workers' social needs, and psychological manipulation of workers through counseling, were, however, examples of management principles to be gleaned from the historic studies.[25]

Elton Mayo's work is of particular importance to the development of this movement. His extensive interview studies revealed that workers subjected to classical management suffered from acute alienation and loss of identity. As a result of his work Mayo offered a set of assumptions to characterize man that were quite different from those of classical management.[26] He suggested that man was primarily motivated by social needs and obtained his basic satisfaction from his relationship with others. Classical management had robbed work of meaning and, therefore, meaning must be provided in the social relationships on the job. Restoring meaning through social relationships represents an important distinction between human relationists and the behavioral theorists who were to follow. The later theorists belonged to what can be classified as the human resources school of thought, which, as we shall see, sought to restore meaning in work not through social relations per se but through more intrinsic factors such as upgrading the job in interest, challenge, and responsibility. On the basis of his interviews Mayo also concluded that man is more responsive to the social forces of his peer group than he is to extrinsic incentives and management controls. And, finally, man's identity and loyalty to management and organization depended upon the ability to provide for his social (interaction and acceptance) needs.

In education the steady use of departmentalization and curriculum fragmentation and specialization characteristic of the years from 1900 to 1930 began a thirty-year period of decline that bottomed out with the advent of *Sputnik*.[27] The St. Louis, Portland, Batavia, Burke, Winnetka, Dalton, and XYZ plans—all conceived on the basis of determining the most efficient way to deliver standardized educational experience to youngsters who were raw materials not yet standardized—began to give way to Cooperative Group Plans[28] and other mechanisms more suitable for a humane and "progressive" education.

The fall of human relations, as inglorious as its rise, was precipitated by excesses. The needs of man and organizations are inherently in conflict. In this battle man struggles for his freedom, and organization is repressive and intent on molding man to its images. This simplistic notion led to the artificial separation of man and his needs and the work of the organization. This was characteristic of classical management, but in this instance man was to be the victor.

Organizational elites were for the most part committed to organizational objectives, however, and they were not so completely gullible in accepting fully recommendations for management offered by the human relations theorists. At the same time that they acknowledged the importance of social needs, they stressed the importance of manipulating those needs to accommodate organizational requirements. Thus, in reality, the rational, closed-system precepts of classical management were not substantially altered as guides to school and classroom organization. Rather, they were modified to appease the social needs of teacher and students. Appeasement was necessary to keep workers happy but docile, cooperative but yielding. Democratic administration was built on the notion of letting teachers *feel* rather than *be* a part of the decision-making process.

Human relations ideas were never long in favor among organizational and management theorists, but practitioners found them attractive. They provided a softer, more genteel methodology with which to honor classical management principles and to dominate the technical core in the interests of the organizational subsystem. They were effective tension-reducing and conflict-avoiding mechanisms to maintain order and control. The teachings of this school and the assumptions upon which they are based today enjoy wide acceptance among school authorities as they relate to teachers and among teachers as they relate to students.

Human Resources

The human relations theorists were successful but short-lived challengers to the efficiency prescriptions of scientific management. But with the translation into English in the 1940's of Weber's works on bureaucracy, which had been written some two decades earlier, the human relations movement faltered.

Not to be undone and fueled by the wide popularity of bureaucracy, advocates of the human emphasis were to rise again but this time as a more sophisticated and better-trained group of theorists. The writings of Abraham Maslow, Douglas McGregor, Chris Argyris, Warren Bennis, and Rensis Likert[29] became the new tenets of the movement. Intent on winning academic respectability and longevity, this group accumulated an impressive array of research to document its beliefs. Most of the cardinals of human resources owned academic credentials in social psychology or in a new interdisciplinary field— human behavior in organizations. As academicians, they came from Yale, Michigan, the Massachusetts Institute of Technology, Harvard, Brandeis, and other equally respectable bastions, and their ideas still enjoy a large following among writers in educational administration and supervision.

The human resources theorists agreed with Mayo and other earlier writers about the dehumanizing aspects of classical management theories, particularly with reference to loss of meaning in work. But this loss was not attributed to man's social needs as much as his inability to use his talents fully. Certainly lower-order needs were not to be denied, but man's capacity for growth and challenge were the needs that received the greatest attention.[30]

The nature of interaction between personality and organization became the key focus of study.[31] Human relations theorists, much like many contemporary radical romanticists, viewed personality and organization as being hopelessly in conflict and sided with personality.[32] Classical management theorists shared this view, but sided with organization. Those interested in human resources recognized personality and organization conflict, but did not view it as inherent. According to those who advocated this view, the two forces were to

Organizational Theory

be integrated with man receiving maximum satisfaction and enrichment from achievement at work and work in turn reaching new levels of effectiveness because of man's commitment.[33] Shared decision making, joint planning, common goals, increased responsibility, and more autonomy were the sorts of power-equalizing strategies to be developed. Motivation was to be intrinsic because jobs were to be interesting and challenging. Job enrichment was advocated as a means of building into the jobs of workers (students and teachers) increased opportunities for experiencing achievement, recognition, advancement, opportunities for growth, and increased competence.[34]

Human resources represented more than a renewed interest in man at work; it represented a new regard for his potential. The differences between human relations and human resources were most telling when one examined the fundamental assumptions of each movement, particularly with regard to conceptions of man, views on participation, and performance expectations.[35]

Human Relations Assumptions	*Human Resources Assumptions*
\multicolumn{2}{c}{*With Regard to People*}	
1. People in our culture, teachers and students among them, share a common set of needs—to belong, to be liked, to be respected.	1. In addition to sharing common needs for belonging and respect, most people in our culture, teachers and students among them, desire to contribute effectively and creatively to the accomplishment of worthwhile objectives.
2. While teachers and students desire individual recognition, they more importantly want to *feel* useful.	2. The majority of teachers and students are capable of exercising far more initiative, responsibility, and creativity than their present jobs or work circumstances require or allow.
3. They tend to cooperate willingly and comply with school and classroom goals if these important needs are fulfilled.	3. These capabilities represent untapped resources that are presently being wasted.

With Regard to Participation

1. Management's basic task is to make each teacher and student *believe* that he is a useful and important part of the classroom or school.

2. Superordinates (administrators or teachers as the case may be) are willing to explain decisions and to discuss objections to plans. On routine matters, subordinates (teachers or students) are encouraged to participate in planning and decision making.

3. Within *narrow* limits, teachers or students should be allowed to exercise self-direction and self-control in carrying out plans.

1. Management's basic task is to create an environment in which teachers and students can contribute their full range of talents to the accomplishment of school goals.

2. Superordinates allow and encourage subordinates to participate in important as well as routine decisions. In fact, the more important a decision is to the school, the greater are the efforts to tap all resources.

3. Superordinates work to continually expand the areas over which subordinates exercise self-direction and self-control as they develop and demonstrate greater insight and ability.

With Regard to Expectations

1. Sharing information with subordinates (teachers or students) and involving them in school decision making will help satisfy their basic needs for *belonging* and for individual recognition.

2. Satisfying these needs will improve teacher morale and student morale and will *reduce* resistance to formal authority.

1. The overall quality of decision making and performance will improve as management makes use of the full range of experience, insight, and creative ability.

2. Teachers and students will exercise responsible self-direction and self-control in the accomplishment of worthwhile objectives that they understand and have helped establish.

Human resources theorists argued that man's capacities and potentials were great though often latent. These qualities were to be evoked by supportive management systems[36] and by a healthy, growth-stimulating organizational climate.[37] These important human organization[38] conditions were the mediating variables[39] from which organizational effectiveness could be predicted. The mediating variables were in turn affected by such organizational and structural characteristics as the distribution of power and authority, management assumptions, decision-making modes, and the nature of goal development. Further, the extent to which an organization was mechanistically and organically structured[40] had a telling effect on these organizationally crucial mediating variables. In mechanistic organizations man felt like a pawn, and in organic organizations, like an organ.[41]

In education, such organizational concepts as team teaching, family grouping, open space, school within a school, open corridor, integrated day, and multiunit are often based on human resources concepts. With regard to curriculum development and classroom practices, such concepts as intrinsic satisfaction, heuristic learning, personal meanings in learning, serendipitous and expressive objectives, and "being" behavior also reflect human resources views.

Patterns of student and teacher influence are key determinants of the overall quality of life that exists in classrooms. Several patterns, each associated with a particular view of management and organization, are illustrated in quadrant form in Figure 5.1. The curriculum-centered quadrant, considered by humanists as being least satisfactory, is based on classical management thinking. Here teacher and student influence with respect to goals, curriculum content and arrangement, sequence, instructional strategies, scheduling and classroom organization is low as a result of a highly programmed, impersonal instructional system. The student-centered quadrant is based upon the thinking of human relations theorists. Here the social needs of the student are considered most important, and teacher and organization assume passive roles to escape stifling student development. The teacher-centered quadrant represents the curious acceptance of human resources concepts as applied to teachers but *not to students*. Here the student assumes a passive role and exerts little influence, but the teacher is quite active in diagnosing his needs and in providing appropriate instruction. The integrated quadrant characterized by high teacher *and* student influence results from human resources principles applied to both groups. It is here, for example, that being

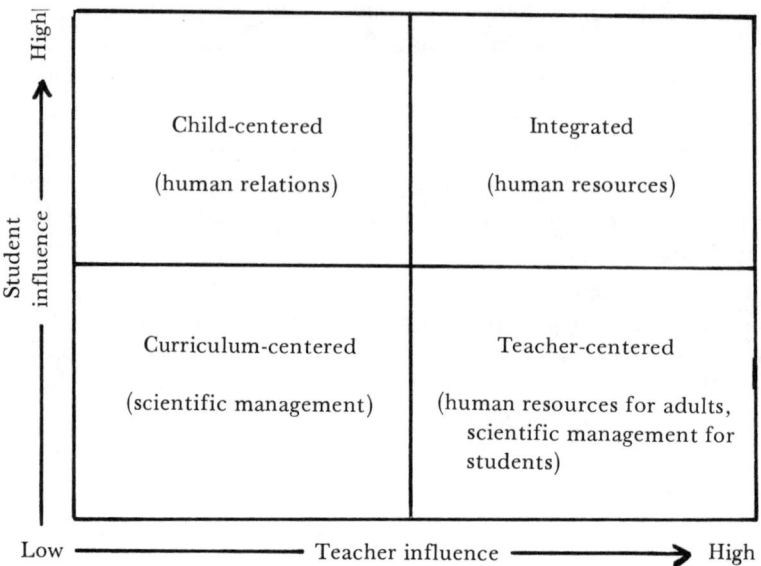

FIGURE 5.1
Quadrant showing patterns of student and teacher influence
(for detail, see Thomas J. Sergiovanni and David Elliott,
Educational and Organizational Leadership in Elementary Schools
[Englewood Cliffs, N. J.: Prentice-Hall, 1975], p. 51)

and becoming behavior[42] as well as personal *and* culturally defined meanings[43] are integrated.

Clearly the human resources school is the one to which most contemporary humanists subscribe. But this school shares with others problems of dogmatic adherence and universal application. Most human resources writers, myself included, have been quick to apply human resources concepts indiscriminately. One result has been to build unrealistic expectations among potential users and an inability to explain failures—both of which dampen credibility.

With regard to the influence of human resources thinking on education, a review of the literature reveals wide acceptance, but an examination of the practices suggests lethargic and uneven acceptance. Where they are found operational, the ideas seem reserved for teachers and other adults but not for students. Further, much confusion still exists between operationalized human resources thinking and that of human relations.

Neoscientific Management

Like old soldiers who never die, scientific management has weathered ups and downs for three-quarters of a century and today enjoys a resurgence in education brought on by demands for accountability, economic recession, a new political conservatism, and advancements in management techniques, such as hardware and software linear programming (operation research, system analysis, and computer system). Earlier scientific management has, however, evolved into a new, more sophisticated form. In education this neoscientific management offers such "new" ideas as performance contracting, behavioral objectives, state and national assessment, cost-benefit analysis, MBO, PPBS, MIS, and other elixirs, each prescribed to maximize educational reliability and productivity at decreased costs. Neoscientific management shares with its predecessors heavy management reliance on norms of rationality and closed-systems thinking as it pursues accountability, control, and efficiency.

Traditional classical management control mechanisms, such as face-to-face supervision are, however, replaced by more impersonal, technical, or rational control mechanisms.[44] It is assumed, for example, that, if visible standards of performance, objectives, or competencies can be identified and measured, then the work of teachers and that of students can be controlled by holding them accountable to these standards, thus ensuring organizational reliability and effectiveness.

A prominent neoscientific management spokesman, Leon Lessinger, for example, views accountability as a movement which "promises a major and long overdue redevelopment of the management of the present educational system, including an overhaul of its cottage-industry form of organization. Many believe this can be accomplished by making use of modern techniques currently employed in business and industry.... If education is going to be able to manage its budget properly, it must devise measurable relationships between dollars spent and results obtained."[45]

An important difference between this third type of classical management and its two predecessors is the impersonal nature of the control system associated with neoscientific management principles that permit it to be quite compatible with human relations teachings. Organizational elites can devote attention to the social needs of workers and other aspects of job *context* satisfaction, relying on the impersonal system to program behavior and ensure predetermined and standardized results. Teachers as classroom elites can function in a similar way in their relationship with students. Neoscientific management, however, violates human resources ideas because of the importance that those latter theorists place on the intrinsic value of work itself. Teachers and students are not likely to find the challenge, interest, ownership, and commitment needed for them to function at the peak of their effectiveness in highly programmed-deterministic environments, no matter how pleasant, in a human relations sense, the environments might be.[46]

This marriage between neoscientific management and human relations has often masked organizational implications. But the movement has generally provided renewed legitimacy and reinforcement to work standardization, centralization, task specialization, and formalization, not only in the educational program format but in classrooms and school organizational patterns.

The Mechanistic-Organic Dichotomy

For seventy-five years the forces on behalf of classical management in one or another of its forms seemed to line up on one side, and those who identified with the behavioral theories of management and organization on the other. Organizational structure implications of the controversy can be conveniently summarized using the perspectives of Tom Burns and G. M. Stalker.[47] Their research suggested two distinct organizational models that they labeled "mechanistic" and "organic."

Organic organizations were found to emphasize the contributive nature of knowledge, a continued redefinition of tasks and functions through interaction, ability authority, responsibility removed from the rights of office, commitment to purposes, and fluid communications between individuals at different ranks. Mechanistic organizations, on the other hand, remained true to the bureaucratic characteristics expressed by Weber.[48]

Jerald Hage described the properties and internal dynamics underlying mechanistic and organic models of organization in his Axiomatic Theory of Organizations.[49] He identified four ends or output concerns common to organization: concern for *production* effectiveness, concern for *efficiency* in costs; concern for development and *satisfaction* of organizational members, and concern for *adaptiveness* in response to internal and external needs and conditions. Though the concerns were considered universal, the emphasis placed upon each varied according to the organization or, if it was the same organization, according to the time. Variation in emphasis is important, but it has often been overlooked by true believers from both classical management and behavioral schools of thought.

Hage also identified four universal structural means used by organizations to emphasize each of the output functions and concerns.[50] The four are *complexity* defined as the extent to which emphasis is placed on person specialization or the authority vested in one's ability as opposed to task specialization—or the authority invested in programmed work; *centralization* defined as the extent to which the focus of decision making is high or low in the organization; *formalization* defined as the extent to which jobs are standardized and codified by rules or work flow; and *stratification* defined as the extent to which station and rank are emphasized.

Hage noted that the means and ends variables were related in predictable ways. As formalization increased, for example, one could expect a corresponding increase in centralization and stratification but a decrease in complexity. Further, this pattern tended to facilitate the organization's production and efficiency capabilities but to decrease its response to adaptability and satisfaction.[51] Hage used these variables to describe more fully Burns and Stalker's mechanistic and organic models of organization.

Organic organizations, he noted, placed the emphasis on adaptability and satisfaction and were characterized by:

        high complexity   high adaptiveness
        low centralization   high satisfaction
        low formalization   low production
        low stratification   low efficiency

Mechanistic organizations, with their emphasis on production and efficiency, were characterized by

        low complexity   low adaptiveness

high centralization   low satisfaction
high formalization   high production
high stratification   high efficiency

Neither Burns and Stalker nor Hage viewed one or another of these organizational models as inherently better; rather, they assumed that each could be appropriate given differences in values, environmental press, and output requirements. This "contingency" approach to viewing organization and management is discussed later. At this point in the odyssey, the classical management advocates and their behavioral theory counterparts chose sides, and neither would compromise.

The Decision-Theory School

Sociologists, social psychologists, and psychologists were not the only scholars concerned with the phenomenon of organization and management. In the second half of the 1950's this uncertain arena was invaded by a group of decision-making analysts who worked from a combined political science, game theory, and economics perspective.[52] The work of this group gained strong acceptance among those interested in business organizations during the 1960's and has been embraced by those new Brahmins interested in organization and management in education—the political scientists. The new teachings of orthodoxy can be found in the writings of Herbert Simon, John March, and Richard Cyert.[53]

The decision-theory school accepted neither the tenets of classical management nor those of behavioral theory. Organizations were neither mechanistic nor organic; they were "satisficing." Further, organizational incumbents were neither suited to rational-programmed management systems nor to systems that assumed man's ability to grow, develop, and value, for man, too, was essentially satisficing.

With reference to classical management's closed, rational view of man and organization, the decision-making school felt that man's "cognitive limits on rationality"[54] in intelligence, reasoning, ability to control future events, and availability of time denied him the possibility of seeking "optimizing" solutions or gains. Further, this "satisficing" tendency precluded the clear ordering of goals and the specification of best procedures. One does not seek the best needle in a haystack, but accepts the first he finds. In the words of the founding father of the decision-theory school, Herbert Simon:

The limits of rationality have been seen to derive from the inability of the human mind to bring to bear upon a single decision all the aspects of value, knowledge, and behavior that would be relevant. The pattern of human choice is often more nearly a stimulus-response pattern than a choice among alternatives. Human rationality operates, then, within the limits of a psychological environment. This environment imposes on the individual as "givens" a selection of factors upon which he must base his decisions. However, the stimuli of decision can themselves be controlled so as to serve broader ends, and a sequence of individual decisions can be integrated into a well conceived plan.

The deliberate control of the environment of decision permits not only the integration of choice, but its socialization as well. Social institutions may be viewed as regularizations of the behavior of individuals through subjection of their behavior to stimulus-patterns socially imposed on them. It is in these patterns that an understanding of the meaning and function of organization is to be found.[55]

Both human relations and human resources were criticized by the decision-theorists. Human resources, for example, was viewed as possessing a sort of naive rationality based on the potential of man and organization to value, to seek collective goals, and to build identity and commitment to those goals. This view was hardly realistic if man was indeed satisficing by nature. Further, the notions that man had vision, could idealize, and would naturally be predisposed to seek intrinsic satisfaction from work seem also to have been rejected on the same "satisficing" grounds. And finally, human resources advocates were "fuzzy" thinkers because of their tendency to view the study and practice of organization and management as an ethical science and because of their predisposition to mix "is" and "ought" considerations.[56]

The orthodoxy of the decision-theory school teaches that management and organization are strictly objective sciences. In summarizing his classic analysis of a science of administration,[57] Simon notes: "In the first place, an administrative science, like any science, is concerned purely with factual statements. There is no place for ethical assertion in the body of a science. Whenever ethical statements do occur, they can be separated into two parts, one factual and one ethical; and only the former has any relevance to science."[58]

This satisficing view of man and organization and this seemingly cavalier concern for man's intrinsic and valuing capabilities has interesting implications for management practices, particularly with reference to direction and control of subordinates. Managers were not to give direct orders to workers (teachers or students in our case), for workers did not like to be treated as idiots. Managers were not, however, to depend upon man's intrinsic capacities either. One controlled subordinates by controlling the premises upon which they made decisions. Left to themselves, with the premises established, subordinates would decide and function in predictable ways. The manager, thus, could maintain the status quo by maintaining the decision-making premises and could introduce change by altering the decision-making premises of subordinates.[59] A variety of devices were proposed for altering the decision-making premises of subordinates,[60] including legitimizing an organizational vocabulary and manipulating verbal symbols (academic departments with elitist verbal symbols have faculty who are likely to engage in elite activities), controlling the reward system (when faculty in department A are rewarded for pursuing a particular kind of activity, faculty in department B are likely to adopt the same behaviors), creating organizational myths, and so on. While the disciples of neoscientific management would advocate accountability systems based on measurable objectives and incentives for reaching objectives (rational-economic man), disciples of decision-theory would advocate such educational reforms as vouchers. A voucher system would change the decision-making premises of schools as they felt the need to survive (satisficing man).

The decision-making school and the classical management schools share a number of features with regard to images of man. Both assume some sort of organizational elite who by higher calling are likely to be exempt from assumptions applicable to those lower in the organization. Human resources theorists, on the other hand, recognize differences in behavior and commitment of individuals at different organizational levels, but view this as a function of more job enrichment for those at the top. Indeed, they argue that, as jobs at the bottom become more like jobs at the top, workers (teacher and students) will respond with increased commitment and more organizationally productive behavior.[61]

Secondly, both decision-theory and classical management advocates view man as a victim-spectator to be manipulated by organizational elites in accord with their vision of what is good. In classical management man is carefully programmed by systematic organization of the work usually through clearly defined objectives and stepwise activities. In decision-theory man is carefully programmed by artful manipulation of the premises upon which he makes satisficing decisions. Both deny to man origin characteristics.[62]

Decision-making theorists feel most comfortable in middle-range organizational settings that permit the greatest latitude in the management of premises. Premise management is difficult in organizations with strong mechanistic characteristics because premises there are determined by the programmed nature of the technical and organizational subsystem. In organizations with strong organic characteristics workers enjoy greater control over the premises, which somewhat restricts premise management by organizational elites.

According to decision-making teachings,[63] the organization itself is considered satisficing and reacts predictably as its premises for decision making are altered. Ideal goals and best solutions based on the demands of the organization's technology are not considered feasible. Organizations satisfice with the primary goal being an accommodation between and among their institutional levels on the one hand and their organizational and technical subsystems on the other.

In organizations with a weak technical core, such as the previous comparison of the professional subsystem of an educational organization with that of a medical organization, the organizational elites seek accommodation by adjusting the technical core to institutional demands. Best practice, for example, is not defined according to some professional standard or client need but according to that which satisfies or appeases institutional demands. (As I have earlier suggested, these observations apply as well to suborganizations within the larger organization such as departments in a high school or university and, to a lesser extent, an elementary school teaching team.) Survival of the organization becomes paramount in this unequal contest, and technical (or professional) decisions regarding classroom organization and educational programs are made on this basis.

Organizational theorists in education who identify with this view, and today most do, are likely to portray the successful educational administrator as almost exclusively a politician and organizational engineer and to separate him in tradition, training, and orientation from the organizations' professional subsystem. One need only review the list of UCEA activities and publications since its inception in 1958, the array of textbooks and publications written by others since 1958, and the content and orientation of training programs for administrators, particularly at the most prestigious universities, for evidence of this trend. As a result, educational administrators are often illiterate with regard to the schools' professional subsystem and too quick to trade off technical considerations as they seek accommodation with broader and stronger institutional social systems. Thus, this satisficing view of man and organization too often leads to an artificing management system and organizational structure and to the disenfranchisement of the school's professional subsystem.

The curvilinear relationship, as illustrated in Figure 5.2, seems best suited to comparing theories of management and organization on the basis of closed- and open-system tendencies. At both ends of the continuum organizations are viewed as closed, rational systems that enjoy a relatively steady state relationship with their environments. Those to the right combine this closed-system feature with mechanistic characteristics in organizational purpose structure and function. The human relations school to the left of the curve shares the closed-system view, but adopts a more organic orientation to organization. The middle position characterizes the open, uncertain system view of organizations and is occupied by the decision-theory school with its satisficing tenets. The human resources school is located on the organic side and occupies a position somewhere between the open, uncertain and closed, rational continuum. Its advocates accept some of the satisficing tenets and the fluid nature of interaction that exists between the institutional level and the organization and technical subsystems, but believe that man and organization can exercise control (albeit never complete) over their destinies by valuing, establishing collective goals, developing norms, building commitments, and increasing their own potential through qualitative growth and development.

Toward a Contingency Theory

The Sociotechnical School

Hardly noticed by those interested in management and organization in education and indeed only now becoming established in the

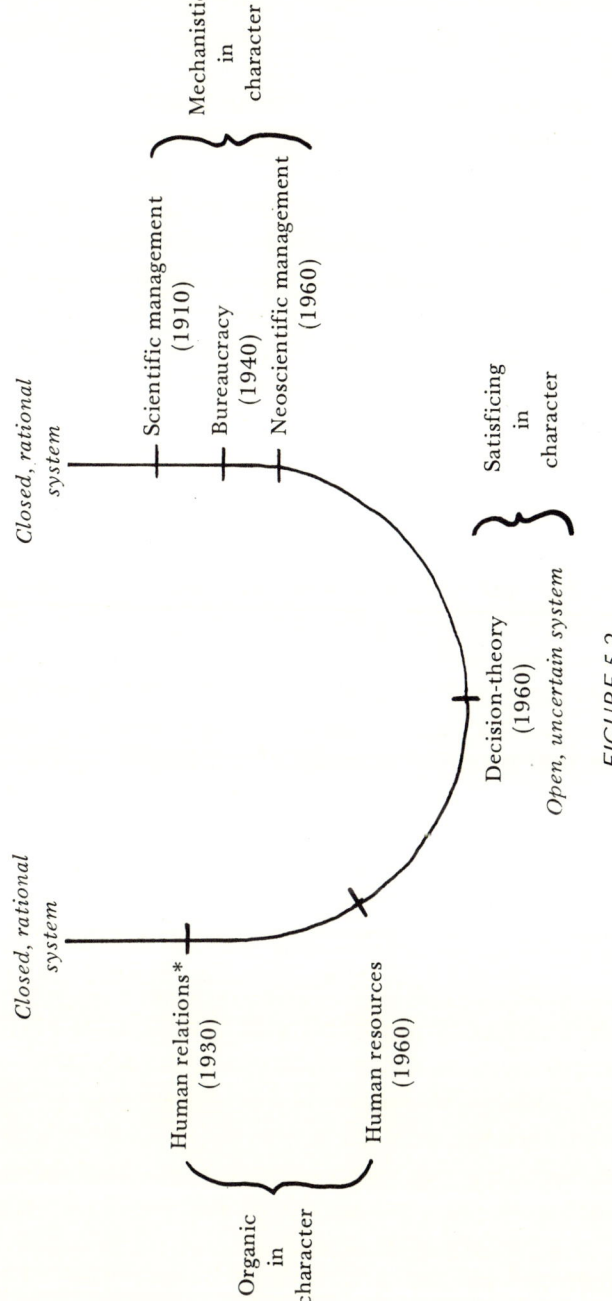

FIGURE 5.2

Management and organization theories in education (Dates are approximate, related to their impact in education. Also, human relations is difficult to place. Its teachings seem properly located, but its articulation in practice [soft theory x] locates it on the mechanistic side.)

organizational literature of business and industry were a group of theorists in England and the United States who sought to make sense of the existing balkanization of thought. *This group captured the wisdom of each of the dominant schools of thought but avoided the error of assuming universal application of any.*

First to come under fire was the notion that organizations were to be characterized universally as closed, rational or open, uncertain systems. The case studies of British industrial organizations by F. E. Emery and E. L. Trist,[64] for example, revealed at least four types of external environments which they labeled as placid randomized, placid clustered, disturbed reactive, and turbulent field, each requiring different organizational and management systems. The interview studies of key people in twenty British industrial firms by Burns and Stalker[65] suggested that "mechanistic" organizational structures were effective for organizations with a relatively stable and predictable environment and "organic" structures for organizations with "different rates of technical or market changes. By change we mean the appearance of novelties: i.e., new scientific discoveries of technical inventions, and requirements for products of a new kind not previously available or demanded."[66]

In the United States, Paul Lawrence and Jay Lorsch[67] were not only interested in management and organizational systems as they related to environmental press (for example, the demand for production and efficiency versus the demand for adaptability and satisfaction); they were also interested in the response of subsystems, such as units and departments within the organization. They found that the more certain the demands on the suborganization and the more programmed the work, the more appropriate were mechanistic management designs. Diverse demands and uncertain work required organic management systems. Further, as demands and work characteristics changed, so should management systems. Richard Hall's work on structural differences between departments within an organization reveals similar results.[68] Appropriate organization and management, according to the views of these theorists, was dependent upon stability and uncertainty in environmental press. Mechanistic concepts were found to be appropriate under stable conditions and organic under changing conditions.

Joan Woodward arrived at a similar conclusion by examining characteristics of the organization's technical subsystem.[69] Her studies, which began in 1953 and involved a hundred diverse industrial firms in South Essex, England, revealed that effective organizational and management systems were dependent upon characteristics of the organization's production or technical subsystem. This revelation resulted in the founding of the sociotechnical theory of organizations.

Researchers were able to divide the organizations under study into three distinct groups. One group was comprised of unit and small-batch organizations involved in production according to customer requirements. Organizations of this type custom-tailored products to client specification and possessed craftlike characteristics. Another group consisted of large-batch and mass production organizations that were concerned with producing large quantities of standard products. The third group contained long-run, complex, process-oriented organizations that required highly specialized technical functions.

The organizational types could be conceived as being on a continuum of technical sophistication, with the small-batch and custom product organizations at the one end being more craft than technical, then the mass production organizations requiring a moderate amount of technical sophistication, and finally the complex process organizations requiring a sophisticated technology at the other. Woodward observed that *successful* organizations *at either end of this continuum* (craft-like and complex process) displayed the characteristics of the organic model, and *successful* organizations in the middle range (mass production) displayed the characteristics of the mechanistic model. Woodward noted that, though the small batch and the complex process organizations differed in technical sophistication, they were similar in the need to be adaptive and in the importance placed upon ability (in a craft or technical sense) and authority. Further, both were geared toward problem solving while, in contrast, the mass production organizations were geared toward production.

In examining the interface between technology and organizational structure, James Thompson proposed a slightly different typology. His categories included long-linked technology, mediating technology, and intensive technology. An organization with a long-linked technology is characterized by fixed demands in product, certainty in goals, and programmed activities, or, in Thompson's words, "serial interdependence in the sense that act Z can be performed only after successful completion of act Y, which in turn rests on X, and so on."[70] Scientific management in one or another of its forms seems compatible with organizations of this type.

An organization with a mediating technology has as its primary function "the linking of clients or customers who are or wish to be interdependent." Banks, post offices, insurance companies, and telephone utilities are examples of organizations with mediating technologies. In each case the organization is faced with the challenge of handling diverse inputs in standard ways. Borrowers' needs may vary, but standard rules govern the loan. Organizations of this type find needed comfort within the bureaucratic model.

Organizations with intensive technologies bring to bear a variety of resources in order to bring about a change in a particular object. The selection, combination, and order of application of these resources, however, are determined on the basis of interaction with this object. When the object in question is human, according to Thompson, intensive technology is regarded as therapeutic, as occurs in a general hospital. In Thompson's words, "the intensive technology is a custom technology. Its successful employment rests in part on the availability of all the capacities potentially needed, but equally on the appropriate custom combination of selected capacities as required by the individual case or project."[71] The organic model of organization, particularly as articulated by human resources theorists, seems most suited to intensive technologies.

Sociotechnical Theory and the School

The sociotechnical and other contingency theorists differ from the classical management and behavioral theorists in that they deny a universal image of effective management and organization. The effectiveness question depends, instead, upon institutional-level demands for adaptiveness and performance on the one hand and unique properties that fit the organization's professional subsystem on the other.

The sociotechnical view as applied to educational organizations such as the school represents both good and bad news for the humanist. The bad news is that, if one is a true believer in the universal application of human resource concepts, he will have to concede important ground in seeking an accommodation with sociotechnical thinking. But the good news is that the sociotechnical view elevates the importance of the school's professional subsystem and accords it the position of key determiner of organizational structure and equal partner in the mediation between the organization and its institutional level.

What are the patterns of institutional-level demands for the school and what technical properties does it possess? Schools are complex organizations in that they pursue a variety of goals and are subjected to multiple expectations. There is variation from school to school with regard to which expectations are emphasized, but all schools feel some press for performance and adaptability. Performance-oriented expectations are, for example, concerned with "becoming" intents and behavior[72] and culturally defined meanings.[73] Schools and communities vary in the extent to which they define and standardize the core of knowledge that they consider worth knowing, but some core exists nevertheless. Adaptive-oriented expectations are concerned, for example, with "being" intents and behavior[74] and personal meanings.[75] Again variability exists in the extent to which adaptive expectations are emphasized, but recognition is given, nonetheless, to the notion that students vary greatly in ability, motivation, values, and interests.

Humanists are correct, I think, in their view that a serious imbalance presently exists in most schools in favor of emphasis on performance expectations. To the extent that this imbalance exists, however, the professional subsystem of the school is likely to approximate the long-linked technology, and scientific management principles are likely to be appropriate. In some quarters the adaptive qualities of youngsters are seen as a problem to be dealt with and somehow weakened. Here the school works to take varied input in terms of dispositions and mediate them in standardized ways. The professional subsystem of the school is likely to take on mediating technology characteristics, and bureaucratic principles are seen as appropriate.

But schools who take on long-linked or mediating qualities in the organization of their professional subsystems still need to deal with the human factor. Willard Waller describes this dilemma as the plight of the teacher who must work in an impersonal, bureaucratic structure but who needs the cooperation of students in order to be effective.[76] Work concerns are therefore separated from human concerns and are dealt with sequentially rather than simultaneously to avoid conflict. Counseling is institutionalized as a special function. Homeroom is the time scheduled for personal concerns. Personal interests are pursued through extracurricular activities or during free time. Recess is the time for fun, school is the time for work, and so on. These are human relations devices intended to appease man's social needs so that he will be more likely to accept controls related to the work of the organization.

Not as common but seen as desirable by many humanists is a school characterized by a clear imbalance in favor of adaptive goals and expectations. Given this imbalance, the school would take on the characteristics of a *simple* intensive technology (or perhaps a technology similar to that described by Joan Woodward as small-batch, custom-tailored) characterized by client feedback and custom tailoring of client services. Clearly this would be a client-centered organization whose survival would depend upon client satisfaction in order to meet its specifications, preferences, and needs. Further, since client preferences and needs can be expected to vary, the school would engage in craftlike activities to ensure particularistic products. Some combination of human relations and human resources management, perhaps with human relations dominating, might be appropriate for this simple intensive technology.

But none of these, in my opinion, are desirable as exclusive images of schools. I prefer to view the school as a *complex*-intensive organization characterized by a moderately open system, one with fairly steady input as to community expectations, clients, and financial resources, but able to effectively interact with and affect this input. The degree of impact depends upon the technical strength of the school's professional subsystem and upon articulate advocates in the organizational subsystem.

Since, in my view, demands for both performance and adaptability are reasonable, if balanced, then an important function of this professional subsystem and institutional-level interaction is to define the balance. (It is at this point that I think the decision-theory school fails because it tends to appease the institutional level at significant cost to professional subsystem needs and values.)

If both performance and adaptability are to be honored, then an organizational structure capable of integrating the two must be sought. Such a structure should possess the capacity to shift its form and focus in accord with a variety of technical-level demands. A school or classroom, for example, would have the capacity to function, either simultaneously or sequentially, in a long-linked fashion for certain kinds of activities and in a custom-tailored fashion for others.

Consider, for example, one important property of the school's professional subsystem—the nature of goals and objectives. To the extent that it is appropriate for objectives to be predetermined and stated precisely, then the instructional systems, together with organizational features, should take on long-linked characteristics in accord with scientific management principles. In instances where it is desirable to leave the discovery of objectives entirely to students, then a more laissez-faire instructional system more in tune with human relations principles might be suitable. And, where it is desirable for teachers and students to interact together to establish or discover objectives, then human resources concepts would likely be suitable. Additional properties, as suggested in Table 5.1, could receive similar consideration.

Much value exists, I think, in viewing the school within the rubrics of sociotechnical thinking as an intensive complex organization that adjusts its organizational form and educational program structure according to technical demands. Such an organization would be organic in character because of its adaptive capacities. Further, such adjustments require a distribution of authority and talent throughout the organization that would preclude relying, as a matter of policy, on standardization, formalization, stratification, centralization, and other traditional bureaucratic characteristics. The danger in adapting this line of reasoning, in my opinion, is that it could also lead to a classical management orientation that features "built-in" adaptability, much like branching features in a programmed text, to account for technical demands of an intensive nature.

An additional professional subsystem property particularly important to human industries such as schools is the question of values. Schools are normative organizations, as are hospitals, psychology clinics, and social work agencies. Practitioners in normative organizations are concerned with the question of most appropriate as well as most efficient or effective and, indeed, it is not uncommon for the former concern to take precedence over the latter.

In this sense, then, organization and management in education is a normative science concerned with the consequences of choice in terms of preferred values.[77] Each of the views of management and organization has much to contribute to good practice in education,

TABLE 5.1
Professional subsystem properties and corresponding organization and management features

Professional properties	Organization and management features			
	Scientific management	Combination[a]	Human relations	Human resources
Distribution of authority	Long-linked	Mediating?	Simple intensive	Complex intensive
Nature of objectives	Curriculum high	Teacher high	Student high	Teacher and student high
	Predetermined[b]	Nonexistent or teacher established	Nonexistent or student established	Teacher[c] and student established
Role of teacher and student	Both passive	Teacher active	Student active	Both active
Emphasis on meanings	Culturally defined	Culturally defined	Personal meanings	Both interdependent
Curriculum and materials	Predetermined and structured	Predetermined but teacher structured	Student choice	Teacher-student planned
Nature of motivation	Extrinsic becoming	Extrinsic becoming	Intrinsic being	Combination integration

[a] Combination refers to human resources applied to teachers but scientific management to students.
[b] Usually precise behavioral objectives.
[c] Might include behavioral objectives as per a student contract but more likely expressive and middle range objectives as advocated by Elliot Eisner in "Emerging Models for Educational Evaluation," *School Review*, 80 (No. 4, 1972).

but only human resources theory, in my view, possesses the value richness required to satisfy the umbrella image of management and organization needed by the school. The extent to which sociotechnical thinking can be applied humanistically in education will, I think, depend upon the extent to which its principles are articulated within a broad commitment to the values of human resources theory.

Discussion

Participants (in order of speaking): *Ralph Mosher, Thomas J. Sergiovanni, Walter Feinberg, Flora Nell Roebuck, Nancy R. King, James B. Macdonald, David E. Purpel,* and *Robert M. O'Kane*

Mosher: You have given us an extraordinary kind of Cook's tour. Lots of bad guys and maybe some good guys . . . .
Sergiovanni: There are lots of good guys, too!
Mosher: Maybe. I have a little more difficulty with the idea of good ones. My experience with the managers of educational institutions is that many are bumblers. Why don't you really let them have it with both barrels? You said earlier: "We've gone from bad to worst." You are obviously in the possession of facts to document that statement in a fair and balanced way. You spent pages and pages doing what you say social scientists like to do: elaborating categories and doing a careful parsing of the positions. Why don't you say *why* we've gone from bad to worst?
Sergiovanni: I have some notions about what I stated in the beginning of my presentation. One is the separateness that exists between people like you and people like me—specialization in education. One of the consequences of specialization is the blindness phenomenon. For example, when we are concerned with developing a particular approach to instructional strategy, that approach is equally influenced by the school's general curricular system, management system, organizational structure, and the whole host of other factors that exist in schools. These are actually interdependent subsystems—each affecting the other. I haven't seen enough cooperation among scholars interested in each of these subsystems.
Mosher: I can agree with that.
Sergiovanni: And I don't think we train people to do this.
Mosher: That doesn't explain the statement that we've gone from bad to worst.
Sergiovanni: Okay. Let's start with classical management. There were no secrets. You were told what your role was, and you were expected to fulfill it. The rules of the organization were reliable and predictable; they did not require participation. You could be alienated from the work and still perform adequately, even though you

might have to seek alternate sources of satisfaction. By the way, I don't think that's very natural. I think work is to an adult what play is to a child.

Mosher: Or theoretically it could be.

Sergiovanni: That's so. With the decision-theory school, however, things seem to be much more manipulative, secretive, demeaning. Somebody may assume, "Well, Sergiovanni is a satisficing sort of guy." (By satisficing, I mean that he's not going to make decisions that are best for the organization or for any higher purpose; instead, he is going to make ones that can tolerate some of his views in a compromise way so that he can exist.) If you want me to behave in a certain way in a school, you don't tell me what the school needs or what I ought to do. What you do is manage the premises, so that I eventually make the decision you want me to make. There are indications that some organizations are drifting toward this type of decision making. One sign of this trend is the reliance on treating people individually when making decisions, as opposed to group decision making.

Scholars closely associated with the decision-theory school have contributed important insights to understanding how organizations actually operate. We get in trouble, however, when disciples of these scholars confuse descriptions of reality with prescriptions for management and organization. That man has "satisficing" tendencies, for example, may be a fact. That organizations are not as rational as the literature suggests is certainly true. But that these insights should lead to pessimistic images of man or to the development of manipulative management strategies is another matter. I don't believe they necessarily follow.

Mosher: This is incredible to me! Bob Anderson once said, "The problem with school principals and administrators is that they got separated from the role of a curriculum and instructional leader of the school." It's incredible to me that administrators cannot convey notions of simple democracy and simple justice to people working in institutions, which can then serve as premises on which to build the future of the institution.

Roebuck: You have to remember that scientific management schools operate in a whole climate of psychological and scientific thought in which genetically programmed events have taken place. They operate basically in a predetermined universe that is Newtonian rather than probabilistic. What I'm saying is that looking at justice and at collective kinds of things is not really a viable alternative for people whose zeitgeist is that the universe is determined, not probabilistic. Or am I wrong?

Sergiovanni: You've got me! I really don't know.

Roebuck: I wanted to follow up your reference to Woodward. You were stating that mechanistic organizations were better during relatively stable and predictable times, and that organic structures were better for organizations with differential rates of technical and market changes and for creative kinds of things. That just blows my mind. We've learned that there is an optimal level for interpersonal skills in different situations. We seem to be finding data showing that, when students are engaged in highly concrete memory-type processes, they can have too much interpersonal skill. But when they're getting into creative kinds of things, the more facilitation they're given, the better it is. Evidently Woodward's work is a reflection of this, only at a different level.

Feinberg: I see a problem in the Woodward approach. In it you determine the kind of organization and the kind of function-tasks-product it is commissioned for; then you decide the best way to organize the human element. If an organization is designed to turn out as many motor cars as possible, well, then scientific management is appropriate. If, on the other hand, the organization happens to be a school, it may be less appropriate. I'd want to push that. It seems to me that, if I understood what you said, "Work is to adults as play is to children." Then work is as much a developmental or stultifying part of the adult life as play is to the child. We ought to consider that thought when we're deciding what the function of the organization is to be. Rather than just considering what its product is and how many products it ought to turn out, we should also look at the capacities of the people within those organizations.

Sergiovanni: I think you hit on the danger in all of the contingency approaches, of which Joan Woodward's work is just one. That is, they permit a school to simply ask, "Well, our objective is to take a bunch of diverse products and mediate them somehow so that they all come out looking the same." This, as you know, is not a minority view of what high school ought to be, for example. This obviously gives legitimacy to operating a highly bureaucratic kind of organization. But what the sociotechnical theory *could* do is to encourage us not to be borrowers, not simply to assume that organization and management principles come from elsewhere. Rather, organization and management principles have a lot to do with what the technical, or in our case the professional, subsystem *is*. Sociotechnical thinking, then, could focus attention on developing new criteria or a new rationale for how we organize the way we work together, how we make decisions, and what our structures would be, among other things.

King: If work is to become something different in the life of an adult, you must see Taylor as much more than just an anachronism; he must be seen as fundamentally incorrect. To reconstruct our workplaces, then, will require a tremendous leap of imagination.

Macdonald: This presentation constitutes a very real and interesting challenge. Let's look at some different data and compare it. For instance, if Kohlberg is right, and it's my observation that he is, the Russians go about organizing and managing their schools in much the same ways that we do. In other words, when they run a school or when they run a factory, they use the same kind of organization that we do. Now, we've been talking about the interpersonal relationships and moral development. But what's the big social frame? Please note that we did not say organizational frame. We asked, "Does this reflect the kind of lousy society we live in, the injustices, and so forth?" But now we've raised another question that has not yet been introduced: "Do organizations have a life of their *own* because of the way human nature operates when you have to do some kind of organized work or task where people have to interact in a limited kind of social structure such as an organization?" And this, I think, is a complicated and very challenging question.

Mosher: I agree that organizations have survival processes and needs of their own, at least as I've experienced and observed them. And, they certainly are realities that operate on our aspirations. I guess if I had one question it would be, "What do you say to people who come to you and plead with you to organize an institution that would permit human beings to actualize or to enhance themselves? Would you say "That's hopelessly romantic"? That isn't an adequate answer! I really want to *know* if such is possible.

Sergiovanni: I think you're dealing with two things. One is what I would call management system or climate; the other is organizational structure. The management climate has to do with assumptions and predispositions of organizational elites. And structure isn't always that important; it's those incumbent in the elite positions that make a difference. Now I can argue on the other side of that, too. I don't want to ignore that, because the truth of the matter is that there are a host of studies showing that when incumbent A occupies a role and incumbent B occupies the same role, one adopts the same manifestations as the other. And that's the regularity, the kind of notion that suggests that organizations do tend to develop personalities and cultures in and of themselves that may be greater than any one person. A modest literature also exists on organizational memory, intelligence, and reproductive capacity—further evidence that organizational personalities exist. So, what people do when they occupy various roles is to act as a carrier of that organizational culture or personality.

Mosher: So, I want to substitute cultures.

Sergiovanni: I want to go back now and say that you have to look at it in two ways. One view is concerned with the basic assumptions and predispositions of the organizational elites: the people who control decision making. For example, they might see power expanding as it's given away. Much of the literature in some schools of political science suggests that, as power is distributed throughout the organization, elites gain *more* control over organizational goals and there is *more* power accorded to the organization as a whole.

Feinberg: You see this so often in universities!

Sergiovanni: The total amount of power in the organization tends to increase. It's neither a fixed sum nor any form of mathematical phenomenon; it's a psychological phenomenon.

Mosher: It's a democratic premise!

Sergiovanni: That might very well be. I hadn't thought about it in exactly that way. Democratic administration has a negative aspect. That's a label for some management practices that just didn't work out very well in a human relations context. That's why I'm rejecting that word within the context of this conversation. I think management assumptions are important: whether an administrator thinks that people have some potential, that they are growing, that they can be trusted, that they have talent, that they should be developed as a goal of the organization, or that human development objectives of the organization should increase along with all of the other things implied by that point of view. These are what I would characterize as the management system. Now the organizational structure is a little bit more difficult. I subscribe generally to the organic, as described in my presentation, as an umbrella. But I think the secret is not to be dogmatic, not to be afraid of adopting some of the long-linked technology aspects for certain kinds of purposes on an ad hoc basis, making sure they don't become institutionalized.

Mosher: What if the assumptions that you've just enumerated as leading to a different kind of institution, don't happen to be there? What if there are already incumbents who do not believe in decentralizing the power or their authority? The implication, of course, is that they're *not* there in most institutions. . . .

Sergiovanni: The consequences then escalate throughout the organization. If the organization elites want to maintain control, they have to control what teachers do in the classroom. Because schools are "flat" organizations that do not permit close supervision, the only way you can control what teachers do in the classroom is to control the work flow. How do you control that? You develop a sequenced and standard curriculum, along with mechanisms to ensure that the workers, or in this case teachers, are meeting certain performance standards. Whether control is in the hands of the organizational elites or elsewhere in the organization has enormous implications for educational program administration.

Roebuck: What you just said about setting up the exact curriculum with so much of this and that to be done is what we got into four or five years ago with performance contracting in schools. The business people came in and ran a school and promised so much gain for so many dollars.

Sergiovanni: That's the neoscientific idea. "Paying for it" is part of the "economic man" rationale: that a man is going to be motivated by getting $200 more a year.

King: That resembles token systems in classrooms for children.

Purpel: Could I ask you [Sergiovanni] to react to a dilemma? My concern is for what industries call "worker satisfaction," which is related to the question of teachers being satisfied with their work and having a sense of involvement and participation. This seems to be complicated in the school or in a profession where we are talking about clients. It is easy to say that what is really more important than satisfaction of teachers is the quality of the experience of the students. I've always found it difficult to worry a great deal about the teacher's sense of welfare. At the same time, having humanistic notions, I have some concern about the well-being of other people. In a school setting, particularly where kids are vulnerable, powerless, and subject to manipulation and control by people, maybe we've overconcerned ourselves with the welfare of teachers.

Sergiovanni: Are you saying that, if we wanted to bring to the classroom greater decision-making prerogatives with regard to instructional system materials, objectives, formats, schedules, and other related matters, rather than having all of these things standardized, that some teachers would not be interested because it would require too much responsibility?

Purpel: No. Let me put it in clearer terms. . . .

Sergiovanni: Because some wouldn't! That's a point I would concede. I thought that was what you were getting at.

Purpel: No, I'm getting at something else, something we don't usually say in polite company. Kids are in school under difficult conditions. A lot of them don't want to be there, and for many it is a bad experience. There are incompetent teachers, many more than we really want to admit, mostly because we expect such enormous skills and capacities from so many people. Because students have little or no choice, those getting a bad deal are really being punished, and here we are spending a lot of time worrying about teachers!

Sergiovanni: Well, while I'm critical of the excesses of the human resources people, that's where I end up myself. I think that one of the problems with the articulation of that view by well-meaning management organization people is that the view is articulated for adults. There are classrooms where teachers do enjoy a great deal of decision-making prerogatives, where the curriculum isn't at all standard, where teachers can work together in teams, where teachers can work in family groups. There's real tremendous progress. Their job is enriched, they do a variety of things, they are making decisions, they have a sense of power—all of which, in my opinion, are important significant human resources principles. By increasing the person's ownership of the organization, his commitment, and his motivation, he works harder, and he learns and grows and develops. Thus, the ideology is carried to its conclusion. *But,* it is not carried to the next step. The students are not involved. The teacher does all these things in conjunction with a passive agent. The teacher still assumes he knows what's good for the student. As a teacher, I diagnose student needs and I give him this and that. The next step, it seems to me, is to adopt the same principles to enrich the job for the student. How do we apply the human resources principles to the student?

Purpel: Is that totally lacking in the organizational literature for administration?

Sergiovanni: No, I don't think it is lacking. I think it's there, in the literature, but it gets lost.

O'Kane: I think what is lacking is *antecedent* statements. People often approach the study of theory by jumping at a particular or simplistic notion without understanding the antecedents. I wish we could declare a moratorium on talk of structures of organizations while we talk about the antecedents. People have been organizing since time immemorial because they had *purpose*. We don't know what the hell we are doing in schools, and no one wants to talk about it. The faculty never wants to talk about *purpose*; neither does the university. When I was a dean, I attended a meeting of deans every Wednesday. These were the least rewarding experiences I had in seven years—zilch, nothing, garbage. Every time somebody would ask, "What are the antecedents? What is the purpose?" we'd hear, "Let's get on with it. We've been over that before."

Sergiovanni: That's *exactly* the observation I made about the decision-theory people we were talking about just a moment ago. They use that thought to reinforce their *own* perspective: that man is incapable of dealing with organizational purposes. And I think that there is some truth to it. It depends on how you define purposes. I think that one could have collective values. Or are you asking if we are going to detail a master plan . . . ?

O'Kane: No, I don't mean that. I would distinguish between management and administration. Management is the management of capital to produce capital. Administration is concerned with administering something for the social good. We confuse the two things because we don't stop and talk about purpose. We don't talk about intellectual purposes of schools; instead, we talk about the mechanics of operations and organization or some other facet of schooling that is quantifiable.

Sergiovanni: I agree. But I'm not sure how we would do otherwise or what the school would look like.

O'Kane: I don't, either, but if I live long enough I want to work in one that is sort of a voluntary-intersect organization called school! One that has enough substance built on purpose that it can sway like big buildings do in high winds. We're damned if we ever build a school to sway in high winds.

King: Are you saying one should talk about what the purposes of schools should be?

O'Kane: Yes, education and schooling, in that order. Anyway, I get angry about it, because—and I share with you knowledge of the anxieties of being an administrator—we don't talk enough to people who have varied specialties such as are present in this group. We need to talk more with people like Kenneth Boulding, J. Bronowski, and A. Huxley. Huxley made it clear: organizations have no soul, and nothing measures people. We don't stop to talk about it anymore. There's an urgency about everything. I'm using your [Sergiovanni's] textbook with a given group. I ask them to analyze each section critically, and, almost without exception, they say: "This is great, I love that Maslow eupsychian management, but it won't work." They dismiss it, and they want to get on with the "tell me how to do it" stuff.

Purpel: I'll tell you what's worse than that. When they reach stuff like humanistic education in my course, they say: "That's terrific and I *do* it!" They all say they do it! That's even worse.

Macdonald: Let's open up another dimension here. We are talking mostly about management. I'm coming away with the impression there is no such thing as leadership. You implied that if you had a different person in there it wouldn't make any difference. This goes against my own experience. For example, if you've got a good elementary principal, by my definition, within two or three years you can tell, you can almost *smell* the difference. He's doing something!

Sergiovanni: The elementary school happens to be a rather unique kind of educational organization. It's smaller, tends to be an informal, primarily a face-to-face group. There is a division of functions, but it still has self-contained dimensions. It also has better support from the parents who have greater interest in it. Incumbents tend to be mostly women who tend to be better satisfied with their jobs than many male teachers. All of which, I think, makes it easier for a principal to go in and have the kind of effect that you are talking about. He could take advantage of the informal propensity that exists and turn the organization from a formal to a rather informal organization with lots of shared decision making and similar qualities. Now, put that same principal in a high school of three thousand students, and it may be just a bit more difficult.

O'Kane: I think the difference, Jim, is that we treat the two as synonymous: leader and administrator. To me they are almost opposite, working for different things. We need both. If I were a superintendent of schools again and I had carte blanche, I'd organize with four types of people functioning as they did in basic tribal or hunting arrangements. And I'd go back to William Thompson in *At the Edge of History,* and I'd get a clown, a shaman (wise man), a hunter, and a leader, and I'd say "Let's start there—there's something essential and compelling about this grouping." My point is we need to get back to essences and antecedents of this current set of problems. More and more I'm convinced that to counteract the current explosion we need an implosion toward the purpose: "Why schools?"

Sergiovanni: I think you are hitting at another problem that is really manageable: the training and preparation of educational administrators. Right now, it seems to me, they are prepared very separately. One of the results of this separate training is that administrators often adopt a new value system. The problem with professionalizing a role is that the role has to be distinctly different from other roles; otherwise, what's the difference? How do you become a professional administrator? So there's an ethos that gets developed about what professional administration is. Second, it seems to me that the professionalization of administration provides a hierarchical constraint: not only do you have to be uniquely different, but superordinate-subordinate kinds of mechanisms are reinforced. Third, what is professional about administration? If you are going to be a professional, you have to have distinct duties, not the same duties as everybody else. Otherwise, who needs you? So now, you see, one is interested in management, organization, and politics, rather than interested in the professional subsystem by design and by intent. After all, that's what makes the administrator a distinct kind of animal! Interestingly, we have not by tradition taken administrators from elsewhere; they have come from the professional subsystem. You would think that in our kind of setting a more natural link would exist. But there's been a desertion of the previous role and the adoption of new values. For example, a fairly new university in Illinois has adopted a College of Administration concept. They prepare four different kinds of administrators, including educational administrators, together. Only modest supportive programs in education exist. This is an example of breaking clean the professional management of educational organizations from the professional subsystem. It's a big problem.

Feinberg: It's amazing how many administrators avoid talking about goals and purposes of the institutions that they are administering. I think the result is the satisficing stance: the idea of maintaining some kind of balance, keeping something surviving and moving. But this has proved a very mindless kind of thing. And it seems to me that it is becoming ever more so. Very personally, we have a dean with whom I often disagree ideologically, yet I can respect him because he is still willing to engage in discussions about what the purpose of education is. So many other administrators just want to keep the books.

Mosher: I'm sorry to say this because I respect the tour de force you [Sergiovanni] gave us, but that corpus of knowledge is mind numbing, and I'm really not very impressed by its intellectual substance. If I sound like Jerry Brown, I apologize. He was recently reported as reading something submitted from some center for an organizational development study in California and he said, "What a lot of garbage! The emperor hasn't got any clothes." My point remains: that stuff's pretty mind numbing. If that's the intellectual substance and fare of administrators, from my perspective, wow!

Sergiovanni: Let me make a couple of suggestions about that. What I tried to do was to identify the origins of administrative thought.

Mosher: I understand that, and you've done a remarkable piece of work.

Sergiovanni: You find divisions in various camps. Not all administrators are one camp or another. There are few elementary and secondary school administrators in the decision-theory camp, but the new professors of educational administration tend to be there, and it will be a while before their products will graduate and go out.

Mosher: That does not make me happy.

Sergiovanni: I know that, but the hottest commodity for a professor of educational administration today is a person with a political science background. We haven't had that type in large numbers before. We are now concerned with policy, and the political scientists appear to know the most about it. They're the ones that the departments are now buying. They're the ones that are bringing decision-theory notions with them.

Mosher: As I read those course outlines on administration, that's what they sound like.

Macdonald: I share your [Mosher's] concern. I'm not sure that the message isn't even more horrifying than you just gave it. Not only does it lack substance, but I've also a sneaking suspicion that administrative decisions have a life of their own and that they aren't usually rational. Many of these things are rationalizations that people have created to justify how they function, and, when you put the rationalizations together in organization format, the result is limiting, very dehumanizing, and almost inescapable.

Mosher: That's even more depressing, but what's built into it is not only what I would call a lack of substantive theory—it's almost amorality. You said we've gone from bad to worst, but one of the things about the bad was that at least they were "up front." They acknowledged their ideology to the people. One of the characteristics of the "worst" is that they're cynical and manipulative and devious. That's not amoral; it's immoral. I can understand why Jerry Brown got a standing ovation at the California Teacher's Association when he stood up and said: "Administrators should not be paid a penny more than teachers in school systems."

Sergiovanni: But I think there are some bright spots if you read my presentation, particularly in my elaboration at the end about the sociotechnical and the human resources umbrella. I think there are ways out. A lot of people are becoming influenced by sociotechnical thinking in a way in which it's not a dogma. It really destroys the dogma. It's a contingency kind of thing. Then, it adds legitimacy for us to think about what the purposes of the educational organization are, what the appropriate work flow is, and how to build management systems and organizational structures based on that. So I see that as a bit of optimism, too. It just seems to me that there are enough here and there in critical places interested in the sociotechnical idea and how it might fit us that we might see a turnaround.

King: One thing disturbs me. We're talking about building more humane and more responsive management systems. When we do that, we have accepted Taylor's first notion that leadership and mind work belong to one set of people and manual work belongs to another set of people. Now we'll do that as humanely and as gently and with as much tenderness as we can muster. But we must realize that we will neither confront nor evaluate those basic premises that Taylor first brought into work places.

Sergiovanni: I agree, and that's why I tried to emphasize that the crucial starting point is management assumptions, the assumptions of the principals and administrators and others.

King: Their first assumption is that management problems belong to a distinct group of people and that these people and their work roles should exist.

Sergiovanni: Well, they should exist, and they should share, according to my biases, the values that you are expressing. If you'll make note as you read, I don't hide where I am on that.

Purpel: It occurs to me that one important thing needs to be said in fairness to you and your profession and your world. That is, I think the curriculum types, like myself and others that I know, have stressed the self-isolation of administrators. We have not gone out of our way to become more informed about organizational issues or to live and talk and work with people in administrative fields. One of the reasons for this is readily apparent. It has seemed mutually beneficial to maintain separate worlds.

Sergiovanni: Not only that. We have, it seems to me, a responsibility to articulate and understand better what the school is about. To the extent that schools are open systems and are influenced by institutional forces, the organization of the school must seek its accommodation with those institutional forces. If it has a strong technical system, then it can interact on an equal basis. Medicine is an example. Certainly the institutional level affects medical organizations and medical practice. But, the medical profession in turn interacts with these forces as a stronger than equal partner.

O'Kane: One problem I'd have if I were to become an administrator again would be accepting a comfortable and bureaucratic mid-management attitude that says: "I'm responsible to a superordinate—board, or trustees, or whatever." I would think there'd be a lot of advantages if the administrator were thought to be responsible to those with whom he worked other than superordinates. He represents and acts as his faculty's agent; he is not (should not be) the agent of the trustees.

Sergiovanni: I think that is a value statement that I agree with. But the extent to which any administrator can be responsive to the inside or the outside, it seems to me, depends on the organization and the strength of the institutional system. For example, the dean of a college of education experiences a legislature and other forces interacting very strongly and forcibly on his college. If you were the dean there, you would have to recognize and deal with those external forces.

O'Kane: You would deal with them, but I might suggest that you could make it clear that the faculty (professionals) chose you.

Sergiovanni: You can only do that to the extent to which that professional subsystem is strong. If nobody knows what they are doing and if no set of values or educational platform for the college exists, you haven't got a chance. Even given a sense of purpose and an educational platform, an uninformed or inarticulate administrator with respect for these values would have difficulty.

Feinberg: I think you are right. When finances are tight, there is a tendency to centralize. But, you could think of a group of people that somehow shared information and understanding and appointed someone to speak for them, to represent their interests. I mean, those kinds of feedback and accountability systems are not unknown.

King: Are you talking about advocacy patterns?

Feinberg: Even for somebody with authority; you vest somebody with certain authority.

Sixth
   Presentation

                              Walter Feinberg

A Critical Analysis of the Social and Economic Limits to the Humanizing of Education

It is supposedly a truism that educational institutions and practices cannot be understood in isolation from the societies in which they are found. Throughout much of the history of Western educational thought, deliberations about the role and limit of education have been guided by an awareness of this essential relationship. Educational theorists spanning the centuries from Plato to Dewey have recognized the importance of the values projected and manifested in the day-to-day activities of the people in the society. The perennial debate about whether school can change the values of the society or whether it must simply follow changes initiated in other quarters cannot, of course, be answered in any absolute way, but the debate nonetheless reflects a recognition of the relationship.

However important the relationship may have been in guiding the thought of educators in the past, it has been ignored by many in the present. Three recent examples illustrate this oversight. Arthur Jensen believes that the limits of reform are to be found in the intellectual capacities of children in school. In his view, some children are unable to learn how to read and write or to do arithmetic primarily because they have intellectual deficiencies that are genetic in nature, and the deficiencies are indicated by a score on an IQ examination.

For Jensen, the deficiencies can also be explained by the dysfunctionality between certain teaching and learning styles. Edward Banfield rejects the idea that IQ scores indicate any significant limit to schooling. He argues that educational reform is limited by the class level of the children in school, and he goes on to argue that these characteristics are transmitted from generation to generation by various child-rearing practices of different families. In a further elaboration of his point, he argues that the most important characteristic of class is not social or economic status; rather, it is a person's ability to project himself into a future time and place, to delay the gratification of present impulses in order to achieve other more satisfying and worthwhile goals. Finally, Charles Silberman, on what appears to be a more promising note, makes a case for the informal, open classroom and locates the limits of schooling in the mindless practices of teachers and administrators who foster needless routine and impose harsh, external discipline upon the child.

While many differences exist among these three points of view, it is important to see how each has circumscribed the factors of schooling so as to allow the relationship between school and society to be ignored. Jensen does this by locating the major limiting factor within the child. Perhaps it is the electrical charges that carry sensory impulses to the brain, perhaps it is the structure and complexity of the brain itself, or perhaps it takes some other physiological form that is indicated by a score on an IQ examination. Banfield locates the limiting factor in the transaction between parent and child, defining class in such a way that psychological characteristics are highlighted and the social and economic conditions that might influence those characteristics are deemphasized. And Silberman does the same thing by isolating and emphasizing the exchange between teacher and child. Here the term "mindlessness" is used to dismiss social forces and values that influence the practices he finds objectionable.

In order to see the similarities between most contemporary theories of educational reform we need only to look at Table 6.1, where the two primary variables are divided into three subsections, making a nine-box matrix. The first primary variable simply indicates where a person locates the major limit to educational reform. Here the limit can be located either in something about the individuals themselves (personality structure or IQ), in their culture (Banfield's idea that the limit is transmitted presumably through child-rearing practices from

TABLE 6.1
Types of theories of educational reform according to two variables

	Location of limit		
Extent to which limit can be changed	Individual	Family-cultural	Institution of school
Impossible	1 IQ—genetically determined capacity to learn.	2 Every society has a top and a bottom or culture of poverty that is transmitted from generation to generation.	3 Every society has an agency for sorting the top from bottom group; ours is the school.
Possible, but too costly	4 To try and improve the education of the bottom will eventually take away resources from most talented members of society.	5 To attempt to eliminate culture of poverty could only be done by denying the right of parents to govern their children or by taking away opportunities from top and destroying initiative.	6 If schools try directly to bring up bottom at expense of top, there is a backlash, and everyone loses.
Possible and desirable	7 IQ is environmentally determined and can be altered through enrichment.	8 The major defects attributed to culture, such as restricted language code, deficient conceptualization, low motivation, etc., can be improved through government programs, community action, etc.	9 The problem with schools is the attitude of teachers and their poor preparation, or of school boards, etc.

generation to generation), or in the institution of schooling (Silberman's attribution of mindlessness or the poor training of teachers). Once the limit is identified, then the extent to which a particular viewpoint is associated with change depends largely upon the extent to which it is believed that the limit can be overcome.

Out of the various categories presented in the table, we could probably generate most recent positions on educational reform and the limits of schooling. It is more important to see how these factors circumscribe and limit the examination of educational reform. No matter which category or group of categories is chosen, it will circumscribe the problem as resulting from the transmission between school and child. Then the only thing that remains to be explained is whether the interference in transmission comes from the child or from the school. With the problem circumscribed in this way, the truism that the school cannot be understood in isolation from the society has been forgotten.

My purpose here is to recall that truism, to take it seriously, and to see what light it can shed on the question of educational reform. Let me begin by saying something about the nature of a limit in order to show that there is a conceptual error in speaking of schooling as if it just involved transmission between teacher and child. Then I shall relate this discussion to questions about the goals of schooling in general, after which I shall specify what I take to be the essential relationship between schooling and society and show how this relationship determines both the goals and limits of schooling. Finally, I shall conclude by saying a few words about how the more prominent educational theories serve this relationship.

One of the characteristics of existing educational theories is the failure to analyze the goals of the educational system. Rather, one or another ideal is simply postulated as being the proper one, and then the limits of schooling are addressed in light of that projection. In such an approach there is a failure to recognize that the very concept of a limit takes on meaning only in the context of some particular goal. If, for example, my goal is to run a mile in less than four minutes, then the limiting factors are such things as the length of my legs and the capacity of my lungs. For a well-trained athlete who actually has the capacity to run a mile in four minutes, the limiting factors become, perhaps, the state of the track or the quality of the competition. If, instead, my goal were to be the typing of this paper at fifty words a minute, then the limiting factors would also be different. Or, to return to the field of education, if one characterizes the goal of education as allowing each person to achieve according to his or her maximum potential, then IQ scores, even if they do indicate intelligence, cannot serve as a limiting factor because the development of a person's intelligence characterizes a goal, not the limited means to achieve it. What might constitute a limit in this case is the availability of financial resources, motivational techniques, or adequate teaching strategies. If the goal is to fill a certain number of positions in the labor market as quickly as possible, then, depending upon the nature of the positions, IQ scores could indicate the presence of certain limitations. The point of this discussion has been to show some of the problems that result when there is a failure to adequately characterize and evaluate the goal of education. It is the goal that determines what can be appropriately spoken of as a limit. Without such an evaluation, seemingly conflicting educational theories will probably continue to speak past one another, which, more often than not, allows simplistic theories to guide educational reform. And by simplistic I mean either ones that project easy changes, such as Silberman's idea that the only important goal is to get teachers to think about what they are doing, or ones that can be used to justify any social order no matter how discriminating or oppressive, which characterizes the ideas of Jensen and Banfield.

One other preliminary point needs to be made. In addition to understanding the goal that is being stipulated before we can make a judgment about the appropriateness of the limit that is being projected, there is also a need to make explicit the context of the goal. That is, we need to decide for whom or what the goal is intended. In the case of running a four-minute mile, it makes a difference, in terms of what is identified as a limit, whether the goal belongs to a well-trained athlete or to someone else. If, for example, someone were to say that what limited my running the mile in four minutes was the quality of the track and the pace of the competition, we would find this puzzling. In my case lack of natural endowments and the effect of sedentary habits would be much more likely determinants of realistic limits, and the quality of the track and the nature of the competition would be almost irrelevant. It would be quite different in the case of the well-trained runner. Now to return to the question of schooling.

When we speak of schooling, we are not just talking about a single building with classrooms, teachers, and students, where the essential transaction is indeed the one that occurs between a teacher and the students. We are also speaking of a system that is defined in terms of a series of internal and continuing relationships of the different parts to each other and to the whole. We speak, for example, of the congruence that exists between grade school and high school, and between those schools and the university. We speak, too, of selection procedures, both formal and informal, by which an individual moves from one part of the system to another. We speak of curriculum, teaching strategies, materials used (textbooks, the *Weekly Reader,* and other materials published commercially and health brochures printed and distributed by candy manufacturers, for example), and a host of other characteristics that mark the system as a whole. We can summarize the school system by saying that it consists of those procedures used to transmit a selected portion of the cultural tradition from one generation to the next in a more or less formal manner that is sanctioned by some official governmental body for the purpose of establishing ideological congruence and reproducing skills and labor. This definition is somewhat open and leaves a number of questions unanswered. For example, are private or parochial schools part of the system since they are sanctioned by the government in a very different way from public schools? The definition is, nevertheless, adequate for our purposes because it highlights the fact that, when we speak about the goals of schooling, we need to distinguish whether we are speaking about the goals of the system as a whole, or about the goals of a particular part of the system. Once this distinction is made, it becomes easier to see why some particular part of the system might be unsuccessful in achieving its goal while the system as a whole is reasonably successful in affecting its end. Think, for example, of different clubs in a professional baseball league. Each club has the goal of winning the pennant, but only one can achieve that goal. The failure of all but one of the clubs to achieve the ultimate goal does not mean, however, the league is unsuccessful in its goal, which is to keep public interest and gate receipts high. While I am sure that this analogy would break down if carried too far, the point is a rather simple one, and it can help us to see some things often overlooked in discussions of educational reform. The failure to distinguish between the goals of schooling, as it relates to a particular transaction be-

Social and Economic Limits

tween a teacher and a child in an individual school, and the general goals of the school system conceals the interrelationship between school and society. Yet it is important to realize that the goals that are established by individual members of the school system, are done so in terms of their congruence with some aspect of the goals of the system as a whole. Whether this could in fact be otherwise is a difficult question to answer, but it is recognition of the attempt to establish congruence that should lead to an examination and evaluation of the systemic goal of schooling.

In order to understand the goals of the American system of schooling we need to return to the definition offered above. While the definition itself does not spell out what the goals are, it does indicate where to look. The definition tells us that the procedures used in schools are designed to reproduce labor, skills, and ideology. And, in order to understand the nature of schooling, we must be able to characterize, at least in a general way, the kinds of skills and ideologies that are being reproduced.

The system of schooling as we know it today, with its age-specific classrooms, compulsory attendance laws, and emphasis on mass testing had its roots in the developing urban life of American society and in new processes of production which, as Lawrence Cremin reports, seemed to render apprenticeship programs obsolete and to disrupt traditional modes of socialization, such as could be found in the family and the rural community. It is to these roots that we must return in order to understand the direction and function of the American school system today. A brief word of caution needs to be voiced here. There are many scholars who would object to the attempt to characterize the goal of schooling in any general way; many others would object to looking for that goal in the origins of the school system. Both groups have a point. It may be said that people, not systems, have goals, and, further, that different people have different goals. And, whatever the goals of the past, they are clearly not the same as those of people who exist in the present. These observations seem to have the weight of common sense behind them. After all, goals do belong to persons, and systems are simply the impersonal ties that bind people together in institutions. Moreover, the difference between, say, the 1850's or 1860's and the 1970's is so obvious that no comment need be made. However much these comments may be supported by common sense, however, they are somewhat beside the point. To say that an individual has such and such a goal is to say that his behavior can be understood as a series of acts designed, even if not necessarily consciously, to bring about a certain end. Identification of the goal tells us what to count as relevant behavior and what to identify as important. Personal behavior is multifaceted. People wake up in the morning, brush their teeth, eat breakfast, rush to work, and so on. Many of these behaviors are identified as functions rather than goals because they are so common to so many people that they indicate nothing that is distinctive. There are other instances, as, for example, when a person is recovering from a nervous breakdown, where we do identify these as goals because they are intermediate stages needed to resume normal functioning.

Once we understand that a goal is identified in terms of something that is reasonably distinctive and that establishes relevance by lending continuity to otherwise discrete acts, then we can see that goals may belong to individuals, but they may also belong to individuals as they come together to act, as they do in institutions. When, for example, people moved westward, they did so for many different reasons. Some went to escape debt, others, to make a fortune; some went to farm, others, to pan gold or to sell merchandise; some went as soldiers, others, as trappers and hunters. While it is perfectly proper to speak about the continuity of any series of acts performed by an individual in terms of a goal, it seems equally appropriate to speak of a whole series of acts by different individuals, along with the acts of the government that supported homesteading and the building of railroads, in terms of the general goal of settling the West. It is this manner of speaking that allows us to make sense out of all of the acts and to see them as forming some kind of continuous, meaningful event. It is equally appropriate to speak of the goal as beginning with the first movement West, even though the people involved may have had no idea about the overall historical significance of their act. In the very same way it is appropriate to speak of the goal of the school system as a whole. To begin to characterize that goal by looking back to the origins of the system itself is not necessarily to claim that the goal was fully understood at the beginning. It is simply to say that, in light of the goal, we can understand some of the major lines of continuity between the activity of the past and the activity of the present as they involve the establishment and development of schools. With this word of caution, it is now appropriate to look briefly at the origins of schooling.

The initial link between education and industrialization was not only that schools were to assume many functions previously assigned to the family, but also that schools were expected to be a major source of manpower. The latter expectation primarily meant that schools were to provide the low-level skills and socialization needed to make the transition from farm to factory. In the beginning many professional skills, such as law and medicine, did not require university training, and most of the knowledge needed for managerial assignments was transmitted through work in family enterprises or some other form of on-the-job training. Eventually the training for these jobs was restricted to the higher units in the school system. Schools, at least on the higher levels, came to be judged more and more on their ability to match the prerequisites needed for market demands in specific fields. On the lower level and in a less formal way they were judged by the congruence between their curriculum and the occupational possibilities for a given child or group of children. The impulse behind this development came as part of a more general desire on the part of many people to control the contingencies of human life, a desire which, while it was not unique to modern times, was strengthened by the hope that people placed in the development of new technology. The impulse guiding the development of schooling at both the higher and the lower levels was the impulse to control an ever-widening sphere of activity by controlling the knowledge that those who practice the activity would be able to possess. For those at the highest levels, part of this knowledge includes an understanding of the kinds of skills needed for performing a task at the lower levels of employment, and the way to assure this knowledge is by constantly rendering those lower-level skills less complex and increasingly interchangeable with other skills. For those at the lowest levels, it requires a degree of passivity that enables them to become tractable members of the labor market. As early as the late 1800's a United States commissioner of education warned that the children of common laborers must be educated to protect property from the threat of communism and that, without a highly developed public education system, the nation's industrial development would fall behind that of other countries.[1]

While the mechanisms for matching the program of a child to his or her future possibilities are much more informal on the lower levels of education than they are on the higher ones, they are no less important, and it is this very informality that makes the mechanisms more difficult to change. For example, even though many poorer parents look upon the schools as a possible vehicle of upward mobility for their children, they also look upon them as an insurance policy which, if everything else fails, at least allows their youngsters to assume the kind of work routine that parents themselves are used to. If a parent's job is dull and routine, if it demands passivity rather than initiative, if it requires that orders be followed rather than discussed and evaluated, then it is unlikely that parents will demand anything else from their children's schools. Nor can it be unambiguously argued, given the present division of labor, that teachers should try to subvert the parents' inclinations. Yet acceptance of such a system means abandoning the educator's essential role of introducing youngsters to the elements of rational thinking, of opening their mind to different alternatives, and of developing their aesthetic and humanistic sensitivities. Given research showing strong correlation between lower-working-class status and conformity, given, too, other research suggesting that the percentage of working-class mothers who prepare their youngsters for a passive role in school is significantly higher than that of middle-class mothers, and given other studies showing that the direction of work on many different levels has been toward more routine and less discretionary roles, it is surprising how little attention has been given to the relationship between the work required of the parents and the education desired for the child.[2] The way that schools handle this dilemma may differ according to the overall composition of the student body. One observational study has shown that teachers assign children to different groups on the basis of nonintellectual criteria, such as appearance, and then encourage active behavior from the higher-status group and passive behavior from the lower-status one.[3] Details of the ways in which the structure of work is reflected in the structure of pedagogy have yet to be sufficiently examined.

If we are to understand the limits of educational reform, it must be apparent by now that we cannot focus attention solely on the transaction between student and teacher; nor can we examine just the intellectual and cultural interference that is said to distort the transaction. For what is seen as interference from the point of view of an individual school may be reasonably compatible with the demand that the system as a whole service the division of labor. It seems perfectly reasonable to suggest that, if there is to be a significant, lasting, and positive change in the school system, this can only be accomplished in the light of a projected and concomitant change in the division of labor. Moreover, in a society such as ours, which judges progress by the size of the Gross National Product and strives thereby to maximize production, it is unlikely that desired changes will take place by substituting the labor of machines for the labor of people. Machines designed to eliminate backbreaking toil are also intended to reduce complex human operations to simpler mechanical ones that can be performed by less skilled human beings. At the same time that machines have helped to ease physical labor, they have also made reasonably interesting jobs more routine. While I am not so pessimistic as to believe that machines must be used in this way, it is not too difficult to see why they have been so developed. Given the impulse to control production and to minimize costs, the more routine the labor, the more people who can perform it. The more skill required to perform a human activity and the greater the manager's dependence on the individual operator, the smaller the area of control. This observation does not seem to be mitigated by the so-called growth in skilled labor and the reported decline in the unskilled sector. As Harry Braverman points out, much of this classification relates to white- and blue-collar jobs, but the trend has been toward routinization of much white-collar work, as well as blue-collar work. A more accurate way to measure the routine of a job might be the length of time needed for training.[4]

Given the pressure that the division of labor exerts on the schools, it is not difficult to see how the education system as a whole can be reasonably successful in meeting its purpose while at the same time many parts of that system are struggling, perhaps unsuccessfully, to avoid failure. The division of labor sets limits to what the schools can do, but it does so in a way that is different for the system as a whole than for any of its particular parts. For any particular school, or group of children, the division of labor determines the goal that it is reasonable to strive for, given the likely prospects for its students. If, for example, the school is in a poorer area, perhaps populated by children from minority groups, it will seem perfectly reasonable to direct the instructional process in such a way that each student will acquire the habits needed for work in an industrial complex. If the school is located in a largely middle-class, professional area, such habits would not be sufficient since the school would be judged by its ability to prepare students for high-ranking colleges. Even if many schools happened to be unsuccessful in achieving a selected goal, this does not necessarily mean that the failure would be reflected in the school system as a whole. The success or failure of a system is not judged by the success or failure of the parts alone since the division of labor relates to the school system in a way that is different from the way that it relates to any of its parts. The division of labor, together with the specific characteristics of a group of children, determines reasonable limits for a given school. As for the system as a whole, division of labor stands not as a guide, indicating reasonable limits. Rather, it stands as an essential part of the overall goal—to reproduce labor. It fails if too many people are prepared for high-level professions; it fails if too few people are prepared.

The school is not the only institution that serves to reproduce labor. The family and other institutions serve the same function through their role as socializers, and, as more families become adjusted to the industrial age, the school's lower-level socializing roles may decrease in importance. Some of the functions that the school system performs in serving the industrial division of labor could possibly be assumed by other agencies as society completes the transition from a preindustrial to an industrial era. Many of the functions are general in nature and were first assumed by the school simply to balance and counter the socializing influence of the preindustrial family. For example, in industrial settings individuals learn to distinguish between the agent who performs an activity and the people ultimately responsible for that activity. Prices are set by an enterprise, not by the person who sells the item. The number of hours one works is determined by a contract between union and management, not by the individual performing the task. And rules, rather than sentiment, guide the conduct of welfare workers, no matter how pressing the concerns of the client may be.[5] Schools are especially important where families are organized around preindustrial personalistic norms when a transitional society requires impersonal bureaucratic and contractual ones. Once the transition has been made, however, schools may be less important in this regard. It is quite understandable to find more conservative scholars, such as Banfield, joining with some of the more radical critics of schooling in calling for a reduction of the age when students could leave school.

While the time may come when schools will no longer be expected to perform many of their present socializing functions, there is another way in which the school system has served the division of labor, and to challenge this function would require a much more radical examination of American schools and institutions. It seems that the drive to expand the human capacity to control nature has led not only to new techniques for directing people and machines, but it has also generated institutions which, within the limits of existing resources, are designed to maximize the growth of technological knowledge. The school system has been the central institution in this development.

Maximizing the growth of technological knowledge is not the only goal of the school system, but it is one of the few goals that did not arise from assuming the responsibilities of other institutions, such as the family and the community. It is, therefore, reasonable to speak of this goal as being an essential aspect of school systems in the advanced technological societies of the Western world. In order to understand the school's role in maximizing technological knowledge, schooling must be considered in terms of a longitudinal structure starting at kindergarten and ending at the university. Technological knowledge must be thought of as a generalized scheme that outlines various routes to a given goal, together with all of the possible contingencies that could arise to direct that one route rather than another be chosen as the most effective and least costly way to achieve a stipulated goal. Thus, the totality of technological knowledge can be defined in terms of an ideal scheme revealing all possible routes and all possible contingencies.[6]

The ideal of maximizing technological knowledge directs society to invest its educational resources in such a way as to provide, at some future point in time, the most detailed and comprehensive scheme possible of routes and contingencies. The idea is to invest existing knowledge in a way that will maximize the store of future knowledge. Given whatever minimum amount of education is deemed appropriate for the general student population, the most effective way to proceed is to use the initial years of education to select for subsequent training those individuals who, because of intelligence, cultural background, or the appropriate value structure, are able to absorb existing knowledge at an accelerated pace and then to exercise that knowledge in existing bureaucratic structures. The financial resources of the society and the ability of its material base to release individuals from immediately productive activity, and then to reabsorb them later at a higher level serve as limiting factors.

One important point about the goal of maximizing technological knowledge is that the goal is largely indifferent to the distribution of knowledge among members of society. In other words, if the growth of knowledge can best be served by selecting out a few individuals for extra training, the gap that develops between those individuals and the remaining members of society is not a matter of major concern. That the development of a large gap under the principle has normally been the case is strongly suggested by a recent study conducted for UNESCO by Johan Galtung and his associates. They found that the greatest educational disparity existed in countries with the highest educational growth.[7]

When we speak here of the distribution of technological knowledge, we are addressing ourselves to the way in which institutions are ordered and the purposes they serve. The distribution of knowledge, for example, is to be distinguished from the distribution of income in the sense that there is no single unified measure, such as dollars per year, that can be used to determine different allocations. There are, however, looser measures that can be used, such as the number of years of schooling, the kind of education available to different people, selection criteria determining entrance into higher-level programs, the kind of socializing influence that can be attributed to curriculum knowledge, and the extent to which different people benefit from the kind of knowledge developed. Undoubtedly some of these measures are more closely tied to the concept of growth and distribution of knowledge; others, to the likely consequences of a given system of distribution. The general impact, however, is to focus attention on areas of educational research that have often been neglected.

Given the goal of maximizing the growth of technological knowledge, it is fairly easy to see that another, related kind of discrepancy is likely to develop. It involves the question of how much different classes are likely to benefit from the growth in technological knowledge that does occur. A commitment to a high rate of technological growth is generally indifferent to questions of moral priority. Whether food research concentrates on developing potato chips of uniform size and shape, allowing them to be stacked in a can, or on making basic grain and protein sources more palatable in order to reduce the amount of protein loss that occurs when grain is fed to cattle is unimportant. These concerns are settled largely by market considerations, and there is little doubt that the race goes to the swift, to those individuals who are the repositories of existing technological knowledge.

Medical research in the United States is another case in point. Given present success in maximizing medical knowledge, a goal that can be traced back to the Flexner report in the early decades of the twentieth century, it is not surprising that there are a number of internationally known medical centers in the United States where the elite from many countries can go to receive treatment and care unavailable in their own country. Nor, given the capital resources of the United States, is it surprising that many of the advances in medical research are available to citizens of relatively average income. However, given also the general indifference to the gap that develops between the most and the least advantaged members of society, our relatively poor performance in areas of basic medical care, areas where knowledge of procedures is well established, should not be surprising. Thus, rates of infant mortality are generally high in the United States when compared to other developed societies, and the chances for survival in certain groups and areas in the country are not much higher than they are in a number of Third World countries. Infant mortality in the United States is largely a problem for the slum dweller and the poor—those essentially outside the system of technological knowledge.

The discrepancy is understandable once we recognize the implications of the generally accepted goal of maximizing the growth of technological knowledge. Without regard for the gap that develops, knowledge becomes the supreme commodity, and one pays for the fruits of one kind of knowledge with those of another. Moreover, the fewer those who share in a given knowledge system, the more valuable their knowledge and the greater access those few have to the fruits of other knowledge systems. Medical and other research is thereby directed to minimizing the hazards of everyday life by managing all possible contingencies for those whose position allows them to take advantage of the progress that is made. In advanced societies such as our own where the benefits of such research are relatively widespread and where the level of capital development allows a reasonably large percentage of people to take advantage of them, the threat to social stability has been minimized, even though the gap has not been narrowed. The need for doctors in many areas of the country and the large infant mortality rate among certain groups speak to the fact that the gap remains and that many people suffer as a result. In developing societies that adhere to the Western model of educational and technological growth, the gap between the least and the most educated and the lopsided development that occurs between rural and urban areas can go a long way toward explaining the revolutionary fervor experienced throughout the modern world. Perhaps it would also go far toward understanding the hostility expressed in places like West Virginia. According to figures for 1968, West Virginia was able to fill only 28 percent of its requested medical internships. That may give some reasonable indication of how much people in that state are benefiting from the general growth in medical knowledge.[8]

Given these observations, we can begin to see the way in which the maximum growth principle directs educational research. The educational research industry has directed most of its funds and energy to developing instruments that will match an individual student to the requirements of a given curriculum, just as medical boards attempt to identify those students most able to conform to the routines of medical training. Very little research has been done, however, on the extent to which the selection criteria and the curriculum itself matches the health needs of the population as a whole, or on the selection criteria needed to train competent general practitioners who could meet the health needs of large numbers of people. Rather, the ideal is otherwise. The goal is to weave an ever-tighter web of specialized competencies so that any conceivable contingency can be handled—if one is entitled even to enter the web.

Returning now to the basic question of the possible discrepancy that exists between the goals of an individual school and those of the system as a whole, we can begin to see that, under the goal of maximizing the growth of technological knowledge, what may be perceived as a problem on one level, may not be accepted as a problem at all on the higher level. If a particular school fails to train a large number of youngsters into the intellectual disciplines, neglects to develop their ethical and aesthetic sensibilities, or refuses to recognize them as rational individuals, or if the routine of the school is rigid, mechanical, and boring, this does not mean that the school system as a whole is failing to provide the conditions needed for maximizing the growth of technological knowledge. Whether this is occurring depends on another set of factors, among them the number of people who do not have sufficient skills to enter the labor force at any level. Such skills include certain behavioral patterns as well as minimal reading skills. Yet even these are problems only when the economy is unable to absorb such people or when the undesirable spin-offs such as crime and welfare go beyond the level accepted as tolerable. Another index of the success or failure of the system as a whole is its ability to produce sufficient high-level manpower when the material base is able to absorb it. As far as other matters, such as developing students with intellectual curiosity or enabling youngsters to solve problems and think abstractly, are concerned, the school system can tolerate many failures without significant concern.

Now it is time to go back and look at the implications of some seemingly competing views on the limits of educational reform. In light of the previous analysis, many disputes about the limits of educational reform simply evaporate. Since, for example, the goal of maximizing the growth of technological knowledge requires that an ever-larger number of people be able to work in bureaucratic settings and direct their energies toward accomplishing stipulated goals and since some groups adapt to such behavior more readily than others, it does not especially matter whether an IQ examination measures innate intelligence or whether it is culturally biased against some groups. In order to be functionally adequate such examinations must do two things: First, they will select out those individuals whose cultural development renders them dysfunctional for work in bureaucratic structures. Whether the dysfunctionality results because of behavior and attitude patterns that render an individual unable to cope with bureaucratic routine or whether it results from cultural styles that would conflict with those of the present members of the organization is somewhat irrelevant when functional matters alone are to be considered. After weeding out individuals whose cultural development renders them antagonistic to bureaucratic structures, the IQ examination must then rank those remaining according to their fit with the knowledge-generating structure. Both functions help to explain peculiarly normative items in IQ examinations: Why are senators good? Why is it better to pay one's bills with checks rather than cash?[9] If one believes that IQ scores are environmentally rather than genetically determined, there will be more enrichment programs proposed for the early years, but it should not be surprising that gains made here are often lost later in school. Of course, one may attempt to explain the drop as the result of genetically determined factors, but even if such an explanation were accepted, such factors should be looked upon as no more than indexes of human tendencies. What is much more revealing is the way such tendencies are treated. The increasing pressure for selection mechanisms and the resulting differential programs as the child moves through the early grades to high school are much more revealing factors than the hypothesized quality of a genetic pool.

With the above comments in mind, it should be easy to see the essential similarity between the theories put forward by scholars like Jensen, on the one hand, and Banfield, on the other. Even though each locates the limits of educational reform in a different place (Jensen in the intelligence of the child, Banfield in the culture of the parents), their proposals for change are governed by essentially the same considerations. Banfield's solution to the problems of schooling is to have the slower youngsters leave school earlier and enter the work force at low-level jobs, for he believes that, once the schools have trained these youngsters into the routine of the work force, little else can be done. The more interesting aspects of schooling are reserved largely for youngsters from the middle class and above. Jensen concluded his now famous article in the *Harvard Educational Review* by proposing that children with IQ scores in the middle and upper range of the scale be taught in a conceptual style while those at the lower end should be taught by associative methods, which is a euphemism for rote learning. His claim is that these children would learn the same things, but in different ways.

What is striking about both of these proposals is that, without additional assumptions regarding the goal and purpose of schooling, neither one follows very well from the data that are offered. To begin with Jensen, even if we were to accept all of the controversial aspects of Jensen's article, the hered500itability of IQ scores, the black-white difference, and the belief that IQ exams measure intelligence—all claims that could be challenged in their own right—it is clear that the claim that children would be learning essentially the same things under these proposals is simply not true. Among other things, one group is learning how to learn conceptually, and the other is not. In other words, one group is learning how to learn by devising categories, isolating similarities, discriminating differences, solving problems, and exercising general critical skills. The other group is learning how to follow prescribed routines. This difference is a major one, and it could, at least at first glance, be justified only if Jensen's data showed that the latter group simply could not learn in a conceptual way. His data in no way show this. His argument rests on the factoring of some examination scores, which showed him that there was little relationship between a high score on associative items and a high score on items that were taken to be more reflective of *general* intelligence. From these items he concluded that children learn in different ways and that, therefore, they should be taught in different ways. Such a conclusion is, however, unwarranted.

Before we show why this conclusion is unwarranted, another note of caution needs to be sounded. Jensen's proposal seems to have the merit of diversity. After all, are not children different and do not these differences require educating them in different ways? Yet we need to understand here that there are different kinds of diversity. One kind, the kind that is usually applauded, recognizes that different objects are meaningful to different cultural groups, and it tries to use meaningful material to develop important skills, skills that, upon careful analysis, may not be too different from culture to culture. The other kind of diversity, the one Jensen is advocating, simply projects youngsters into differential social roles and then trains them into behavior patterns and skills appropriate to those roles. The impact is obviously quite different.

Jensen's conclusion is unwarranted, simply because his data do not show that children, in any permanent sense, learn in different ways. At best what they show is that certain children tend to learn in one way rather than another. They do not show that this tendency is the result of any invariable genetic pattern, and this is true no matter what the heritability factor of IQ scores may be. Even if, to switch to an example, the heritability of one's propensity for tuberculosis is 80 percent, whether one actually contracts the disease depends also on the environment in which one is placed. Jensen's mistake is even less technical. He has confused two things that ought not to be confused. He has confused the fact that someone displays a tendency to learn in a conceptual way with someone's ability to learn how to learn in a conceptual way. If this is confusing, another example should illustrate the point. Assume that a tennis teacher finds that of two students one has a tendency to hit the forehand with a stiff wrist but that the other uses a great deal of wrist action in stroking the ball. If he had read Jensen, he might say, "Well some people learn tennis with a stiff wrist and others with a flexible one, and we will now develop a technique for each. One will learn in a stiff-wrist style and the other in a wrist-bending style." If he were to distinguish between one's tendency to learn tennis with a stiff wrist and one's ability to learn how to learn tennis with a stiff wrist, however, he would begin by asking, "Why is the wrist flexing? Is it a bad habit that needs to be broken? Or is it that the wrist is too weak and needs to be strengthened?" The point does not need belaboring. At best Jensen's data show a tendency. They speak not at all to the question of whether this tendency can be changed, and what the factors involved in changing it might be. Indeed, his case makes sense only because we read into it certain known facts about the division of labor and the role of schools in serving this division, and of course his analysis, if taken seriously, would assure that these facts never were challenged.

Banfield's analysis has different, equally difficult problems that can be treated here only briefly. Banfield believes that the most powerful limitation on reform is a person's class membership, and he defines class in terms of certain psychological traits, such as a person's future orientation. His analysis is interesting, not only because of a somewhat different definition of class but also because, in his *use* of the concept as distinguished from his *definition* of it, his indexes are fairly conventional ones such as socioeconomic status. The overall impression is that people have low incomes and status because of their psychological makeup, which is transmitted from generation to generation through such things as child-rearing practices that schools cannot affect. Again there is a certain ring of truth, but this analysis isolates family practices from all other aspects of a person's social situation and general life chances. One would suspect, for example, that an extended future orientation would be dysfunctional for many roles in this society, but this is ignored. In any event, by failing to analyze the general work roles and structure of the society, Banfield's proposals for schools could, as could Jensen's, do little more than intensify the division between classes, and they have the effect of simply servicing the existing division of labor. When trying to decide between the relative merits of Banfield and Jensen, it would be well to guide the deliberation by the pragmatic dictum: If there is no difference in practice, there is no difference at all. It should not be thought that liberal educational reforms are in any way exempt from pressures issuing from the division of labor. Although advocates of these reforms are generally less comfortable guiding their educational policies by such pressures, one need only to examine the different ways in which progressive educational reform was translated into practice for children of different classes to understand how forceful these pressures are. The difference between the middle-class progressive schools of the 1930's and the life adjustment ones of the 1940's was significant in terms of both subject matter and purpose.[10]

Given the failure to address the relationship between education and the division of labor, it is questionable how much improvement we can expect in education through research and reform. If there is a significant expansion of challenging and interesting jobs, we might expect at some point to see similar changes in the schools, but such expansion has not yet become the goal of consciously directed policy. Some research suggests the actual direction of work to be otherwise.[11] Without these changes, even if educational researchers help us to devise better and more effective ways to improve teaching and to help children learn, it is likely that the improvements will be delivered in such a way as to help most middle-class children to improve their conceptual skills and most lower-class children to improve their ability to learn by rote. Certain programs and styles of teaching, such as DISTAR, will be labeled "lower class" and kept far away from white, middle-class schools, and other programs, such as the new math, will be labeled as middle class and kept away from the lower-class schools. For those who agree with Jensen and Banfield, this is likely the best of all possible worlds. But, to use a more rustic classification scheme, one that runs implicitly through their writings, to accept a scheme where the dull get duller and the bright get brighter is surely questionable, even if it does serve to maximize the growth of technological knowledge.

Discussion

Participants (in order of speaking): *James B. Macdonald, Flora Nell Roebuck, David E. Purpel, Walter Feinberg, Thomas J. Sergiovanni,* and *Ralph Mosher*

Macdonald: When you put all of the different pieces that we've had together, we are squarely faced with the question: What is humanism? What really is it in the broadest sense as well as local situations?

Roebuck: I think one of the things to be considered in answering this question is in Feinberg's presentation. It is the sentence about the transition from the personalized norms of a preindustrial society to the impersonalized norms of a bureaucratic society. It seems to me that all of our humanistic attempts are basically an attempt to reestablish the personalized norms. And we must consider whether, if humanistic education is an attempt to reestablish those personalized norms, that is an appropriate endeavor.

Macdonald: I don't know. For instance, look at Dewey, who is really the foundation for most of our work. He is supposedly the philosopher who took us from an agrarian society and helped to move us toward an industrial one. But biographically, in his own value system and at his own gut level, he was an agrarian product. He may very well have fostered an inappropriate philosophical orientation.

Purpel: May I ask a factual question related to this? Is there any data to indicate that, in a country with a more equitable economic system, there are fewer differences among students in the capacity to learn? I wonder if you see some relationship there?

Feinberg: I don't know. Take, for example, the Soviet Union. I think the analysis is much more penetrating in terms of the knowledge structure than in terms of the income structure because income levels are somewhat lower in the Soviet Union. But from everything I've heard, they are even more stratified in terms of education.

Purpel: More competitive than selective.

Feinberg: Yes. The one place where this is probably not true is China. A part of their ideology, which I don't buy, simply denies there are any significant individual differences in ability. I think that's wrong. I think there *are* individual differences in ability. But it doesn't have to be reflected absolutely in the educational system. You could say that the educational system ought to be used to reduce those differences rather than to magnify them. Nor do I think analysis in terms of income alone is enough. You can have a reasonably equitable income distribution system and still have vast stratification in terms of education—partly because there are other ways to get rewards than simply income. If you make $30,000 a year as president of a university, which is low I suppose, you still get all of the other benefits, including travel, that the institution provides.

Purpel: It's a chicken-and-egg kind of problem. One of the things that I got from this presentation is that there's a vested interest in our society in having people with different abilities—and inabilities.

Feinberg: Yes. There is that vested interest, and we've been socialized to it, even if it's not in our own best interest.

Sergiovanni: Assuming as you say that we're socialized, this vested interest is latent in the capitalist system and in the broader social system, rather than manifest in the hands of 2,500 people somewhere.

Feinberg: I'd even go further than the capitalist system, because we can get into a bind if we just do a thing on capitalism. The Soviet Union has the same problems, and you can't call that capitalism.

Sergiovanni: Okay. That's related to another question I wanted to ask. Can the descriptions that you've presented be made in Afghanistan, Cuba, or elsewhere? That is, is it natural for societies to have some latent kinds of goals and needs, based on their economies, ideologies, or whatever, that get manifested in the schools?

Feinberg: There are two concerns here: one is whether the description that I've given can be applied to other countries; the other is whether the description is natural, in the sense that it is inevitable. My feeling is that the dominant mode of growth throughout the world today is a model that reflects our own, which is a commitment to maximizing what I call technological knowledge. A different kind of commitment—minimizing the distance between the least and the most educated members of society—is, however, possible. Given certain productive sorts of goals that are essential to continuity and survival, you could make a commitment, as a society, to minimizing the distance between the least and the most educated. I think there are ways to accomplish this, through programmatic considerations, that we haven't really ever taken seriously.

Roebuck: That's why I phrased my question in terms of preindustrial society and impersonalized norms. Can you estimate the distance between the least and the most educated members of that society versus the present one?

Feinberg: It's hard to give an estimate. What you can cite is that the principle of growth in the preindustrialized society just isn't there. So that, where there are discrepancies, they're not even programmed into the system. A student of mine did a paper on the milling industry that gets into this. Around the turn of the century mill masters, who had the most complete knowledge of how to produce and use flour, were dispersed throughout the country. Then, as milling continued to become mechanized, other skilled workers were downgraded. Master barrel builders were no longer needed because the machines required sacks. Holistic knowledge became dysfunctional. Instead, there was a need for people who could perform mechanized operations on the floor of the plant. In this sense, if you see knowledge as tied to technique, technique rendered knowledge obsolete.

Purpel: I thought you were implying in your focus on purpose that there's something better or more appealing or stronger about conceptual ability. Just for fun, I'd like to know why it is such a big deal to be able to conceptualize. What is the point of it? Is it its own reward, or is it particularly useful?

Feinberg: There's quite a bit to it being its own reward to be able to pull together complexities and see patterns and so forth. But, above and beyond that, it is liberating. I think an analogy with an animal is a very good one here because the training of animals is basically rote learning. You present a stimulus, and you get a response. And, when the stimulus is presented again, the animal responds in the same way. Most animals can't be taught to make connections, however. If the stimulus is not exactly what the animal is used to, there's a block. Rote learning in its purest form is doing what you've been taught to do by somebody previously. Conceptualization, among other things, permits you to make connections that you've never made before and have never seen made before. I think this is the powerful point of the transformational linguist. What is unique about our linguistic facility is that we can say things that we've never heard others say. We can make connections and go beyond imitation.

Purpel: That's a really different kind of response than the tone of your presentation suggested. There you made the connection between income, job, and social status and knowledge and abilities. Are you now making different kinds of links between the value of education and personal kinds of satisfaction?

Feinberg: I didn't push income too much. What I did was try to show the social relations that generate different kinds of classroom interaction. What we're doing now is saying that, on the individual level, one kind of social interaction generated is probably not as good as another kind. If you want to evaluate this interrelationship between school and society, one of the factors that has to be considered is the effect of depriving individuals of access to conceptual understanding.

Mosher: I think you're using an out-of-date psychology in talking about the epistemology of cognition. All people have to think concretely. We have been unsuccessful in learning how to stimulate formal operations with both blacks and whites. The estimates are that not more than 40 percent to 50 percent of American adolescents and adults ever achieve formal operations. If I said, on the basis of that psychology, that I have developed a technology that would permit us to move significant numbers of concrete thinkers to formal operations, would you then tell me that society would probably appropriate that technology unequally? Would it appropriate it along class lines, reserving it for the middle class?

Feinberg: I don't think that the technology is that new. I don't want to deny the value of the work, but . . . .

Mosher: I don't think we have that technology. I think we may have that technology soon.

Feinberg: People were learning how to think conceptually and abstractly a long time before we were born.

Mosher: But, not a majority of them!

Feinberg: No, not a majority. We may not have had the delivery systems, but I think we have had the understanding of how this is done.

Mosher: I disagree profoundly with that. I think we have an understanding of stages of cognition. I think we have one route.

Feinberg: I think the stages of cognition, if not overinterpreted, have made a major contribution. That I would say. But the essential answer to your question is that, if you analyze the structures of the society, you would clearly find that these things have been delivered differently to different people.

Mosher: Let me go to the page where you say it is the educator's essential role to introduce youngsters to the elements of rational thinking, opening their minds to different alternatives, developing their aesthetic, humanistic, and ethical sensibilities. I agree with that. And I suspect that this is close to the kind of ideology that this conference implicitly or explicitly is convened to assert. What is your program to realize those aims?

Feinberg: I think I can sketch it, although we have to think beyond the individual school to the school system or the educational system. We would do well to focus first on the question of the growth and distribution of knowledge instead of what happens in the building. I mentioned medicine in my presentation because I think it's a paradigm that illustrates why it's difficult to have a humane school in certain areas of this country. Let me give you figures that I find outlandish. If you look at the Gross National Product of a country like the United States and a country like China, you'll see the United States on top, while China is just beginning to creep along. There is an incredible difference between the wealth in this country and that in China. I don't urge that this country adopt China as a model because there are tremendous cultural differences, but there are some observations that emerge through comparison. Look at something like the infant mortality rate. This is a key index of a knowledge system, because there is no lack of knowledge. If you compare Shanghai with New York City in terms of infant mortality, you get astounding figures. New York City has something like slightly lower than eighteen deaths per thousand births per year. In Shanghai the figure is slightly more than twelve per thousand. If you factor that according to the white-nonwhite population, the figure goes down a bit for the whites, but, for the nonwhites, it goes up to twenty-eight deaths per thousand in New York City as opposed to twelve per thousand in Shanghai. If you then factor that according to class, it would be even higher. How do you talk about moral education to a child in Harlem whose mother has just delivered a child who died?

There is yet another interesting statistic. If you live in Shanghai and you're not yet seventy years old, you will probably live significantly longer than you would if you lived in New York City. We have much of the required technology, and we understand it, but something's gone haywire in the delivery of that knowledge. What? I don't know. I'm not a professional in medicine, but certain questions occur to me: What is this thing that we call medical knowledge? Why is it monopolized by physicians? Could any part of that knowledge be dispersed to people who might not be physicians but who could exercise discretion in their own right? To give you an example, in the Netherlands, which has the third lowest infant mortality rate in the world, a large number of deliveries are performed by midwives. In the United States they're performed not by midwives and not even by general practitioners, but by obstetricians. How much of this knowledge system could you begin to break down and distribute throughout the various segments of society?

Another factor comes into play with the question of medical knowledge. When I was growing up, the doctor was somebody who lived in the neighborhood and came to your house. Now you go to a doctor's office. Part of the reason, again, is specialization and the push toward growth of medical knowledge. But look what's been lost. Suppose that I lived in a tenement or an apartment without an elevator, and the doctor diagnosed a heart problem. Even though he were to give me the appropriate pills, he would not realize that I have to walk up six flights of stairs to get to my home. That is, he has no sense of my "local situation."

These examples suggest to me that we have removed the opportunity to perform human activities in a vocational position for many youngsters. It is no wonder to me that we have problems introducing humanizing activities into public schools. It's important to remember that schools aren't isolated institutions.

Sergiovanni: So, when you talk about the division of labor, are you suggesting that significant lasting changes in the school system depend upon concomitant changes in the division of labor?

Feinberg: Yes.

Sergiovanni: But aren't there other contributors to mortality rates besides social injustices and inequities? A fish and rice diet is better for you than the diet that is customary in the ghetto. This involves life style and ethnicity, rather than only economic circumstances. Smoking is much more predominant in this country, as is alcohol....

Feinberg: Not smoking!

Sergiovanni: And pollution. If you look at the incidence of cancer, you can find that, where there is more industry, there is greater incidence of cancer. And different family structures and interrelationships also have an effect. They might make the figures less dramatic, but I argue there still would be differences. I'm suggesting that the question, though, is still very complex.

Feinberg: Maybe the major health problem in this country is not even related to medical personnel. It may well be the automobile, in terms of the number of people killed each year on the highway, by pollution, and other considerations. That entails some sort of national policy to bring about effective ease of transportation without pollution.

Sergiovanni: But when I think that way it leads me to a dead end and back to the statement Macdonald made at the beginning of this discussion, which is really an indictment. In essence you are saying that for people like me, who have virtually no feeling as to how they affect society (apparently I'm not very good at social action!) but who are inclined to work in the school as it is related to teachers, school boards, buildings, and other institutional considerations, there are two problems. First, I am not making an impact on the right critical access to the problem. Second, my work actually reinforces the existing patterns.

Mosher: I second that feeling. You [Feinberg] say that the problem is to generate human activities in the marketplace, in our corporations. I've got enough problems as an educator trying to generate activities that support and stimulate human development and human functioning in one set of institutions—the schools. While you may have an analytic argument, it appears to me to be an exercise in futility.

Feinberg: Not necessarily.

Mosher: You offer no program. All you offer is a generalization: reform Avco Corporation and create interesting jobs that in time will constitute interesting developmental opportunities for people.

Feinberg: Let me pick it up in a different way. First of all, it seems to me nonproductive to deny the power of the analysis simply because it may not inform what you do. It may inform what somebody else does. It may be that Avco, or the union there, would be willing to take a much closer look at the direction available jobs are taking. Thus, the analysis may not speak to each of our personal situations. Nevertheless, if it's a reasonable analysis (and I recognize that it may *not* be), it ought to be considered. It seems to me that there are programmatic kinds of things that *can* be done. Sergiovanni talks about organizational structures. Well, it would be a powerful approach to look at organizational structures through terms like the distribution of knowledge and the directions of work, and relate these back to schools. To set our thinking straight is the first step in putting our institutions straight.

Sergiovanni: King takes the students in her teacher-training program and tries to show them that the hidden curriculum is a problem that has to be overcome. You [Feinberg] suggest that this is really rather futile for a variety of reasons. For one thing, it deals with the individual transaction between teachers and students, administrators and teachers. Then, the people likely to respond to that notion take progressive ideas back to the suburbs where students grow up and reinforce the present pattern. In other words, they don't deal with the redistribution of knowledge.

Feinberg: Well, I think what you're looking for is the place where you begin, and the point is that you begin everywhere. Suppose you began in the workplace, and suddenly General Motors abandoned the assembly line and, along with everybody else, created more human jobs. If the schools stayed the same, you'd be creating people who couldn't work in the new environments, even though they were developmentally sound. So it's not the point that you don't do what you can do in the schools, but you try to inform what you do there by providing a clear understanding of the relationship between schooling and society. And I think you also try to inform the people that you work with in those schools. As for the children, you try to bring the hidden curriculum into some level of awareness. It is important to let the parents know that there are lots of ways to teach reading and to let them know why one way is chosen over another. What one tries to do as an educator (and this is why I don't think my analysis is elitist at all) is to inform public decisions so that those decisions are based on the best available knowledge. Then, even if the public does not agree with you, you have done your best.

Purpel: I think there is another important question that we need to deal with. How can the kinds of analysis that you [Feinberg] and Apple have made inform educational practice? We know it's clear that if we want to have a more just society we have to work in many different dimensions. But we work with schools. That's our job! Are we talking about changing curriculum, organization, selection procedures, attendance policies, teacher training, or what? We need specifics. We already know that the schools are limited by social and economic forces.

Mosher: Right. I can't believe that the impulse that Dewey articulates is not still felt in this society.

Macdonald: In *my* values, perhaps, but I'm not sure about the rest of society.

Mosher: This analysis would say that John Dewey is an anachronism and that his aspiration and hope are anachronisms. . . .

Feinberg: I've been somewhat critical of Dewey.

Mosher: And it's the corporations that really now control and will determine the outcomes.

Feinberg: That was not antithetical to Dewey's vision.

Mosher: It was what he opposed.

Feinberg: That's questionable. I claim that what we have is at least a part of what Dewey wanted. And I think the reason Dewey is so compatible for us is because to a certain extent we want it, too, although uncritically. But we don't like certain results that we're seeing, like welfare and crime.

Macdonald: I'd like to follow up another lead that this takes. I think medicine was a good paradigm to use, but I don't think any of us would agree that education works in the same way as the medical profession. And this raises a very interesting question. You [Mosher] are trying to develop a technology for building moral development. Well, if you did, you would then possess knowledge that most people would not possess. Maybe one of the things that saves education is that we really don't know—we're ineffectual! If professors really *had* a powerful knowledge, they would also form a strong power group.

Purpel: That's exactly what the profession has been trying to do.

Mosher: Yes, very much to develop the posture of an elite group. Feinberg is saying that we would then be asked, seduced, or bought, in an effort to allocate that technology inequitably. Incidentally, I think that technology imminent in the next twenty years will in fact add to human rationality and human character. And the question of how it will be used is a fascinating one.

Purpel: There's some evidence that this is already going on in the world of special education. There are distinctions that depend on class. There's evidence in North Carolina that classes categorized as having "learning disabilities" are 95 percent white; classes categorized as being "retarded" are 95 percent black.

Sergiovanni: You're kidding!

Macdonald: No. A mentally retarded white child has learning disabilities; a black child with learning disabilities is mentally retarded.

Feinberg: I mean something precisely like that! I think this analysis sheds light on that information as an important piece of data. It is important that the public know this. It's not esoteric knowledge. Or, look at career education. I don't like it—not because I don't like careers, but because it puts people in low-level careers. But look at the power it could have. If a career educator went out and said, "This place is not educative. I can't put any students in here." Or, if he were to say, "The working conditions in this place are dangerous; I wouldn't put a student here." Just think of the power that would have if career education were a goal. And there's a real difference between a job and a career. This is one of the factors about medical education that's troublesome, and it goes back to an analysis of the knowledge structure. If somebody becomes a nurse, has twenty years of experience, and decides to become a doctor, those twenty years of experience don't count. It means going back to point one and beginning in medical school, to which the person cannot gain admittance because of age. It's a caste system in a sense. Medicine is clearly a caste system in this society.

Purpel: There's another social-class phenomenon that I would like somebody to study. I can't put a label on it, but I can give you an instance. Usually we talk about the distribution of wealth. In my classes I use the example of a boy in high school who comes from a farming family where the grandfather grows tobacco, the father grows tobacco, and the father expects the son to grow tobacco. This boy turns out to be terrific at ballet. Now when I present this as a problem to my students, who are experienced teachers and guidance counselors, almost to a person they say, "Well of course we'd encourage him to go to New York and attend ballet school because that's what he is really good at and he wants to do it." Now, I repeat that I don't have a label for this kind of phenomenon. I just know there's a kind of middle-class emphasis on creativity, on certain kinds of intellectual activity as being better than, say, family, community life, those kinds of things. Again, this is a phenomenon that is not related to income. As I see it, this is perhaps even more insidious.

Feinberg: It's insidious not to allow him to go, too.

Purpel: That's the value question!

Feinberg: The problem here is the dilemma of the way in which talent is often perceived by communities as being antithetical to their interests. And, in fact, it often is. You get the town-gown conflict. The black who comes from the north end of Champaign, goes to the university, and can't associate with his peers any more has a real conflict. Yes, he should be allowed to have his talent developed, but they have good intuitive reasons for understanding that it's often against their interest to have the talent developed, for he flies away. Going back again to the medical situation, you can look at the distribution of doctors in Chicago over a twenty-year period, and it's as if there were a creeping glacier moving from the south to the north. The doctors have just moved out of the south and into the north. So we're trying to get more minority kids into medical school. That's very good. Also more women and more rural kids—that's all fine. But they are not likely to practice in the areas they're from. I won't argue against them having the right to move. What I do argue is whether we are choosing our medical personnel wisely if we need to distribute medical talent more equally.

Mosher: This relates to the issue that Macdonald was speaking to. Let's assume that the technology I'm talking about might permit us to help a significant proportion of kids to move from concrete to formal operations who otherwise wouldn't have made the move. I don't think I should withold that, even apprised of your analysis that it will be unequally or inequitably appropriated according to social class.

Feinberg: You don't withold it; you apply it. But then you've got to say, "Look, I can teach this, but I know that there are some places where I can't seem to teach it." In those places you have to ask a more fundamental question: What are the conditions in this place that do not allow it to be taught?

Mosher: All right. What is my responsibility as an educator at that point? I'm not personalizing this; it is a generic educational issue.

Feinberg: The answer obviously goes beyond the classroom.

Mosher: It most certainly does.

Macdonald: There are at least programmatic directions that I can develop from this, and some of them have been with us a long time. The only reforms that seem to remain with us in various forms are highly personalistic ones. The others tend to collapse. We had the core curriculum, for example. Now, the core curriculum is in essence destructive of knowledge structures as we usually encounter them. I'm sure youngsters learn a great deal. It seems, in fact, to be an ideal kind of general interdisciplinary program. But it keeps collapsing; it doesn't "stick." Now, one of the reasons is because it presents knowledge in a usable but nonelitist way. It's hard to select students out of such a program because they don't all have the same courses or experiences. They encounter knowledge in a different way. Now, what the school could do is to create programs that make it either difficult or impossible for society to use us as a selection system in relation to knowledge. Whether the school, having done this, would affect the broader society or whether they would just delay the whole process so that society would do their own sorting later on in some way are other questions.

Mosher: That's the issue, and Feinberg's prediction is that social forces would inequitably appropriate that change and that technology, and even inequitably use that conceptual capacity to serve existing social ends. I can think of a lot of adolescents and young adults who for brief and poignant periods of time in their lives resist "the system," but small groups of independent thinkers, professors or others, do not a movement make.

Macdonald: It's kind of discouraging, even in going across campus, to think that most departments are highly professionally organized and producing role players. I don't see any evidence, over twenty-five years of interaction, that our colleagues as a group are allies to this kind of thing.

Feinberg: I suspect that in this kind of situation one of the things you must do is to pay the piper. By that I mean that the request to teach skills is not unreasonable per se, and sometimes even rote learning is the best way to learn something. For example, if I wanted to learn how to type and someone said, "I can teach you to type in a week by rote learning, but if you really want to understand everything about the typewriter and all its interrelationships it will take two years," I'd say, "Give me the rote lesson—that's how I want it." Schools have a responsibility for doing that. That's not only how the piper gets paid; it's also a reasonable responsibility. But there are efficient ways to do this, and you choose the most efficient one. I'm not against all these technologies. In their place they're okay. But there are other things that are also important. We must set the priorities straight.

Purpel: That's where I keep wanting you to go further—on the question of priorities. The problem I've seen throughout this whole conference (I'll use your potato chip metaphor.) is the awful thing that happens when schools are "successful" and train people to be imaginative, thoughtful, and reflective. Then the student goes out and puts his energies into devising a more standardized potato chip rather than improving the quality of grain production. Now, I think the "good guys" like us foster that, because we don't ever get to the question of priorities. Your own definition of education was to make people aware, to sensitize them, to give them the tools and the capacities, but none of us has really said, "We also think you ought to use them for these purposes and these goals." We always stop short of that point. And then we're mad when someone else takes those capacities we have developed in the schools and uses them for ends we don't like. Now, which is it?

Macdonald: It seems to me we have the personal development skills: personalized and individualized education, the so-called "Dewey positions." And then Counts and the others used to say, "No, schools should reconstruct society." But they weren't saying that the schools ought to teach youngsters what society should be like. They were saying we ought to teach the kids to question, to develop conceptual abilities, so that when they grew up they would be able to resolve problems. They'd participate in the democratic political process and change society. Now we have a third view: there's no use working on it through the schools; you'd better enter society and act. It seems to me that we should take a historical perspective and reexamine the Reconstructionist Movement.

Many of us seem to have forgotten this, and we are reinventing the wheel.

Feinberg: That's putting it too harshly. That's not *my* position. You work wherever you happen to be, and that may be the schools.

Sergiovanni: That doesn't come through.

Feinberg: Well, here I wanted to put forth the analysis of it. I can't say what every specialty might do. It seems to me that the major priority in education, if you're thinking of education not so much in terms of schooling but in terms of what it is to be educated, is to bring people to an awareness of the institutional and conceptual structures that limit the way they think about alternatives and the way they bring different aspects of human life together. Education should at least in part be a consciousness-raising experience that brings people to think about their condition rather than simply accepting the condition as it is. There is a good example of this in the *Autobiography of Malcolm X,* which I think is really a book on education. During a period of his life when he was in Harlem you can see the qualities of what IQ people would call a very intelligent person except that IQ people would disagree with the values that were present. He was just outstanding in the professions of hustling, thieving, and pimping. So you might say he was a very intelligent man, but I would not say he was an educated man at that point. Only later did he begin to ask and try to answer such questions as: What is it that placed me in this situation? What forces and interrelationships brought me to use my intelligence in this way rather than some other way? That seems to me to be a major priority for education.

Mosher: To return to Purpel's question, you obviously try to stimulate intellect by giving the individual greater cognitive capacity, and part of that clearly would mean to be able to make the distinctions that Feinberg is talking about. I think, however, you can fall into idolatry of intellect. Intellect is not sufficient. I think you clearly have to tie that stimulation to character development and to profound consideration of moral and ethical choices. If you are in the position that I'm in, which is basically one of saying that we should enhance human capability, maybe we can do it. It seems to me that this also entails the kind of social action that Newmann talked about, subject to the criteria that he applied. In order not to produce a bright manipulator and exploiter, I think you have to guarantee an intellect informed by some kind of character. The theory that I'm working from says that moral development will move toward greater considerations of majority interest and will and the application of justice in thinking about one's obligations. Is that trusting the people? I've got quite a lot of theory that argues why conventional moral reasoning is better than preconventional, and postconventional is more comprehensive and more principled, more just, more democratic than conventional. It clearly is an act of faith at that point. The evidence is far from in. I think that's one kind of scenario that's been struggling back and forth over the table here—whether you can trust that problematic and uncertain outcome of the enhancement of individual capacity.

Purpel: This is why I pressed Feinberg, because he does think that, or he feels he does. Take the medical analogy where a lot of powerful, bright, imaginative, creative people have combined tacitly in a number of ways to deprive a lot of other people in America of decent medical care.

Roebuck: Now, they haven't done it for that purpose.

Purpel: I want to talk to Feinberg mostly because he, I think, is part of a group that is closer to having a fairly well-articulated vision of society and a sense of justice. Yet I'm always frustrated by that group, for vision is not embodied in a program but embodied in an analysis and a criticism. That is, I have a sense that you have some standards of what social justice is, which puts you way ahead of most people who pretend that they don't know or are confused about it. I see that as an act of courage on your part. Most people cop out by saying, "Oh gee, it's too complicated." And yet I don't see you taking the next step and fighting for that vision in educational contexts now.

Feinberg: Again, I think there are lots of different ways people work and do things. I am almost called on to do three things at once by you: (1) say what the priorities are, (2) say what the program is, (3) say what the strategy is for achieving the program. I'm not being evasive. Part of the problem may be simply what we think of as being a program. There is no blueprint that anyone can provide. It would have to be a social program that involves education. Part of the program would entail distributing as widely as possible the various knowledge systems that we have. The area of law could serve as another example. You go to the South Side of Chicago, and the prime cause of death there is gunshot or knife wounds. Part of the problem is that in our bureaucratically organized structures there is no immediate and mutually respected source for resolving conflicts in a neighborhood other than the police, who are usually outsiders. There are no people indigenous to the community who understand the problems, who understand what it's like for five people to be living in two rooms, and so forth. In a sense this is what the old communities had. They had people who informally—not recognized by society (I think the Chinese still have it)—could serve these sorts of functions. And to do this would entail knowing something about what the larger legal structure is like, being able to make discretionary decisions, and other information. One would not necessarily have to be a lawyer, but one might then decide to go on to become a lawyer. Well, that's a program that might be useful for an institution like a law school to begin to push for.

The problem is you've got to do two things at once. You've got to prepare the ground in public schools, and you've got to see that the ground is eventually developed as you want it to be developed. If one were working in a public school in the ghetto area, one might, for example, teach a class that would be organized around the question: What are the kinds of things in this community that generate conflict? You could begin to work at a level like linguistics, for example, by beginning to see how people—black and white—create differences among themselves by how they speak. A friend of mine went into a Roxbury school, and the first question he asked was: "Am I from Boston?" They debated that because he had a funny kind of Wisconsin accent. Then he asked, "Are you from Boston?" And they got into a conflict over which ones were Bostonians and which were not, according to dialects and accents. Then they began to talk about how groups are marked off, differentiated, separated by the way they speak. In this way you can begin to bring youngsters to an understanding of some of the factors that generate conflict in a classroom, in a society, and so forth, and thus you expand their understanding of conflict. That seems to me a very important thing to do, and it can be done with a minimum knowledge of linguistics. It's a program.

Purpel: It just seems to me that kind of programmatic suggestion has a very different flavor and tone than your analysis, which is bold and daring and has vision. Your suggestion for attack seems to be quite cautious.

Feinberg: No, it's not cautious, because then those kids go into another room, and the teacher says, "We don't speak that way." The teacher presents these kids with a certain standard dialect, and the kids now know enough to ask, "Who's 'we'? Whaddya mean, 'we don't speak that way'?"

Purpel: You're *hoping* the kids will respond that way!

Feinberg: Yes, I could never guarantee it. The other thing you're asking for is impossible. You're saying, "Look, we know [maybe we do, and maybe we don't] what is morally right." And we know, let's say through Mosher's work, how to teach people conceptually to think about what's morally right. Now, how do we lead them by the hand . . . ?

Purpel: Your analysis indicates a greater degree of moral certainty than your program does.

Feinberg: Leading somebody by the hand to make them commit themselves to decisions that you support is sometimes morally justifiable, but it is rarely moral. You deny to them the freedom to decide for themselves.

Sergiovanni: I never thought about that difference.

Feinberg: The burden of proof is in the justification. The connotation of the act seems unjustified because you're denying rationality, but the reason for it may be so overwhelmingly powerful that you can justify it in moral terms.

Reactions

David E. Purpel
Flora Nell Roebuck
Michael W. Apple
Robert M. O'Kane

David E. Purpel

Reactions and Reflections

It was my great fortune to be involved with this project from the beginning, which means that I benefited from the discussion of a wide range of topics relating to humanistic education. It was (and continues to be) a stimulating experience, and I would like to share some personal views and reflections related to it. These reflections are divided into thoughts on the presentations themselves and thoughts on the central theme.

The Presentations

Each presentation is stimulating, frustrating, and tantalizing in its own way. Michael Apple and Nancy King cogently argue the point that schools may, indeed, be doing their job competently if the job is defined as maintaining social order and meeting the needs of the economic system. For them, the "hidden curriculum" is the underlying social and economic ideology of consensus that actually generates specific school practices and policies that we educationists like to think are the products of thoughtful pedagogy. I also gather that Apple and King see tinkering with curriculum and instruction at best as idle and, perhaps even worse, as counterproductive in the building of a just society.

Their analysis is a sobering and convincing one that carries with it some basic and disturbing questions for educators. Are we living under a delusion that we can significantly educate (that is, free or liberate) individuals and that we are really providing children with access to meaningful freedom? Can or should we, as educators, separate "curriculum" from social, political, and economic ideology? Are educators sophisticated technicians or social leaders? These are important questions, certainly, but they could have been even more sharply defined if the presentation had concentrated more on social and economic vision and implications for an educational program. There are hints of what they value (intellectual activity, spontaneity, individualism, social justice), but the presentation is essentially, as Macdonald has said, "descriptive." Valuable and penetrating as description, certainly, but how much more valuable if it had clarified what a truly humane education might strive for or might be.

In contrast, the positive, clear, and bold educational program set forth by Fred Newmann is designed to enable students to become significantly involved in the affairs of state. His daring and exciting ideas are carefully, precisely, and rigorously argued. One of the most interesting dimensions of his model is how it is at once both conservative and radical. It is conservative in the sense that it takes seriously the most fundamental tenet of Americanism—that an informed and educated citizenry should be actively involved in social and political decision making. It is radical in the sense that the current political system of the United States could be drastically affected if students were to have successful experiences in the Newmann curriculum and actually learn to participate actively, lawfully, and thoughtfully in the democratic process.

What to me seemed missing from Newmann's vision was some degree of passion. His presentation is cool and precise, and, although his faith in the ultimate moral and intellectual capacities of people is deep and profound, there is no sense of the anguish and suffering that underlie the concept "social problems." Where is the sense of moral outrage that must undoubtedly generate such a thoughtful and brilliant conception? What seems to be lacking in the model is some powerful spiritual urge to participate vigorously and responsibly in social processes. There has to be more than the rather egocentric need to be competent. Newmann, of course, speaks to the moral dimension of social education but only in terms of "reasoned verification of ethical choices" and building "competence to affect the environment." What is the reasoned verification for compassion? For love? For justice? For fairness? Are these concepts to be weighed, examined, and analyzed carefully before they can be applied?

I'm also much concerned with the actual substantive issues and problems students would confront. Would these be left to chance? Is it just as valid to deal with a manageable and meaningful local issue like a school bond issue as it is to deal with a massive, apparently unmanageable problem like world hunger? How do we develop criteria for what we should most care about?

David Aspy, supported by Flora Roebuck, deals much more directly with the role of feelings and emotions in education, and their programs are indeed quite intriguing and promising. They seem to indicate that there is an effective technology to improve the quality of interpersonal relations in the schools. The ability to improve the quality of everyday life in the classroom is certainly a most valuable and cherished capacity, and one hopes that such capacities can be transmitted to schools across the land.

At the same time, one wonders about the context of "good interpersonal relations" (GIR). Is it, for example, "good interpersonal relations" to give a fine meal to a condemned man? What is the value of a teacher who teaches garbage, but does so openly and warmly? Does the statistic that school attendance rose after students were subjected to GIR reflect more effective manipulation, or that students have added insight into the values of school? On the other hand, if schools (and society) are not going to change, then I suppose warm mindlessness is better than cold mindlessness. Would Marx, though, say that GIR is the opiate of the masses? Or, as the song goes: "Is that all there is?"

To an elegant and eloquent restatement of Deweyan notions, Ralph Mosher adds some creative and imaginative curriculum ideas of his own. The stress is on the simultaneous development of several dimensions—psychological, social, moral, physical, intellectual. Much is promised: a breakthrough in curriculum, a solid theoretical framework, new technologies to promote growth, an escape from the blind alleys of the disciplines. It is difficult to be indifferent to the excitement and optimism present, rare as it is in these gloomy days. It is also quite moving to see a curriculum statement that so powerfully speaks to the human and personal dimension of education. Mosher is actually talking about real people and, in particular, about the ways in which they differ. Rather than glossing over or deploring differences, he celebrates them as human, as part of the painful process of finding meaning.

I was pleased to find a magnificent quotation from Dewey on the ultimately social nature of education, "Perhaps the greatest need for a philosophy of education . . . is the urgent need that exists for making clear in idea and effective in practice that its end is social and that the criterion to be applied in estimating the value of the practices that exist in schools is also social." I hope the inclusion of these words signals an effort to put Mosher's concept of curriculum and psychology within a still larger social framework. The concept of growth as a goal by itself is troublesome to me since it begs the question of the value of a particular stage of growth. Do our responsibilities as educators end if a person is at Stage 5, has a strong ego, can deal with abstractions fluently, has a positive self-image, and plays a smooth, well-coordinated, graceful tennis game? Are we as pleased with educating a person to become an Alan Greenspan as a Ralph Nader? What purpose and what meaning does the struggle for maturity have? Can we as educators go beyond growth as a value in itself?

The strange and terrifying world that Thomas Sergiovanni describes is the one I discovered, to my dismay and chagrin, that I inhabit. It is the world of organizations, and his presentation provides a vivid and perceptive analysis of changing and varied conceptions showing how people might best manipulate others. In many ways it was a chilling and unsettling voyage to a world that turned out to be a lot closer and more real than I had realized. I was forced to see how little I (as a so-called "curriculum person") have been in touch with the organizational world and to realize that for curriculum and organizational theorists to continue to work apart serves only to widen the chasm between teachers and administrators that seems to characterize school practice.

I suppose this may sound naive, but it came as a distinct shock to me to learn of "satisficing" and the cruelly cynical and amoral qualities present in much current administrative theorizing. What was most depressing (as in the case of the CIA) was to have one's paranoia not just confirmed, but transformed into what is regarded as a salutary and beneficent theory. What Sergiovanni calls the "decision-making school" seems to embrace what I had hitherto considered to be a somewhat sensational and unfair criticism: that school administrators need not be concerned with the substantive questions of curriculum, program, or philosophy, but, rather, with devising ways of keeping others in the system in some kind of political balance. The major attributes, then, of the school administrator are not seen as wisdom, imagination, and daring; instead, they have become shrewdness, adroitness, and cleverness. Discussion of the presentation, in effect, seemed to be a plea: "Say it ain't so, Tom." But Sergiovanni made us face the folly of ignoring this harsh and perhaps insuperable obstacle to the humanizing of schools. For the concept of "satisficing," if I understand it, represents a fundamentally decadent pandering to our worst instincts and indicates the collapse of any tradition of optimistic, enlightened, humane leadership, even as an ideal. May God protect us from "decision makers"!

Walter Feinberg's presentation was also in a descriptive and unsettling mode. Feinberg sees the schools as distributing what he calls cultural capital in order to maintain the existing social and economic framework. This sobering and fascinating analysis clearly shows how schools (and families) mirror the divisions and inequalities in society. The criticism is trenchant; the analysis, rigorous; the conclusions, solid and disturbing. But what should we do? Should we put a moratorium on schools until we develop a more just framework? What constitutes a more just framework? How should we, as educators, react to the analysis beyond experiencing depression, guilt, and paralysis?

Every page rings with a subdued sense of outrage at social injustice and how schools serve as a powerful ally in perpetuating that injustice. Yet, what about Feinberg's conception of education? It is, he says, the act of "introducing youngsters to the elements of rational thinking, of opening their minds to different alternatives, and of developing their aesthetic and humanistic sensitivities." Such a gentle and eloquent statement, but clearly and sadly not the kind of education that is going to produce major social change. Is that all educators can or should do? Introduce? Open? Develop? Nelson Rockefeller and William Colby have probably been introduced to the elements of rational thinking, have had their minds opened to alternatives, and have even had some aesthetic and humanistic sensitivities developed. Isn't something still lacking? I think so, and I say that what is missing is an analysis of ways in which education can be directly related to justice and humanity.

The Themes

In reflecting on the whole project, I came away with a mixed sense of both hope and pessimism. I had approached it with a hope that at least some of my reservations about the humanistic education movement would be eased. That did happen, but I did not foresee the inevitable: other serious problems that never occurred to me emerged.

One of my continuing concerns about humanistic education has been its almost inherently vague character that at best testifies to a rejection of mechanical and rigid formulations but at worst manifests fuzziness and sloppiness. We sometimes encourage spontaneity and reject behaviorism at the expense of the obligation to be rigorous and thorough in our work. The presentations contained here, in contrast, seem to be powerful statements openly set forth and rigorously prepared. It was refreshing to encounter searching, tough-minded analysis (within an affectionate context) applied to emotionally charged and cherished notions. More specifically, the curriculum models of Mosher and Newmann are not only imaginative and bold, but they also rest on solid and carefully considered theoretical bases. The programs outlined are far more than a list of interesting activities framed in glowing rhetoric; they represent deeper, richer orientations that merit further research and more discussion.

I also came away feeling that we are closer to a new synthesis of humanistic education ideas. Right now there is no overarching theory that unites humanistic educators. There are common roots—Dewey, humanistic psychology, political liberalism—but as yet we have no common conceptual scheme that can bring order to the wide spectrum of activities and ideas classified and claimed as humanistic. I have the strong feeling that a clearer, sharper, more coherent synthesis is emerging. All of the elements—theories on personal and moral education; ideas on education for social responsibility; imaginative pedagogy; concerns for appropriate organization—seem to be there (with perhaps one major exception that I discuss later), waiting for someone to pull them together into a powerful and compelling analysis. I see that happening; it is simply a matter of time.

I am not quite so optimistic about another concern that is finding increased expression: emphasis on the individual at the expense of community and social responsibility. The "do-your-own-thing" syndrome with its stress on the individual person as the locus of all standards seems a particularly dangerous and poignant abuse of humanistic traditions. I was, therefore, pleased to see that all curriculum programs presented significantly stressed helping youngsters to go beyond themselves and their self-centeredness. Time and time again, however, I was struck by reliance on process, on ways and procedures of thinking and behaving, on means rather than ends, with both explicit and implicit assurances that substantive issues are best left to the individual for resolution. Within the framework of values that stress freedom and autonomy, that faith is commendable, but it still leaves me wondering if our vision of a just world stops with creating a world of autonomous individuals thinking and behaving within highly sophisticated structures. Is this faith an end in itself, or does it represent a lack of clarity or commitment to any particular vision beyond individual autonomy?

There was no mention of a broader framework than the social and economic ones. There was no attempt to link all of the exciting ideas to some *religious* or *spiritual* conception of humanity. If anything, there seemed to be a tacit understanding to avoid that topic as embarrassing, irrelevant, inappropriate, or even paralyzing.

It is perhaps both ironic and revealing that most of my optimism and hope derives from the presentations concerned with curriculum programs and models and most of my pessimism from those presentations that set out to describe the larger contexts of school and curriculum. Once again, I had to confront the harsh reality that many of us in curriculum are isolated intellectually from our colleagues in other fields, but it is even more serious that we may be isolating ourselves from the realities of the very world(s) we are trying so earnestly to ameliorate.

Sergiovanni's analysis is particularly worrisome even and especially if we are merely talking about the modest scope of reforming individual schools, never mind the whole culture. What I understood him to say was that real power in the schools is in the hands of those who are increasingly divorced from matters of professional substance and are, instead, primarily concerned with maintaining that power. This analysis would explain the enormous frustration and bewilderment of those who find school administrators sympathetic to humanistic ideas theoretically and even personally, but ultimately nonsupportive in practice. The tragic reality seems to be that there is no common functional language, only common rituals, and that those in power are not so much against humanistic education but, even worse, they appear to be indifferent to *any* kind of education!

And that's just one measure of the polarization that seems to be deepening in our culture. In this case we have been talking about the chasm between leadership focused on power and leadership focused on ideas. More basic, however, is the basic social polarization that reminded Sergiovanni of Spain in the 1930's. Feinberg, Apple, and King describe a society that demands conformity, uniformity, stability, and technology from schools, rather than the spontaneity, independence, and change that mark the values of humanistic education. Are we headed toward harsh, intractable confrontations between determined and powerful forces that wish to preserve the status quo and those equally determined, highly vocal, significantly influential but, so far, gentle forces that see the need for a quantum increase in social justice? The curriculum folks (Newmann, Mosher, Aspy) seem to have faith that the process of education can avert such a disaster, but the social theorists (Feinberg, Apple, King) seem to feel that curriculum changes amount to whistling in the graveyard. It is the eternal question once again, although this time we may be asked to confront it with special urgency: Can and should the schools provide social leadership, or must they perforce mirror the more basic social and political structures?

My attitude has always been that educators should consider themselves to be part of the process that provides social leadership. I think this attitude is shared by many if not most of those who accept the humanistic orientation since notions of a larger social vision are implicit in their ideas and practices. The anguishing questions I had to face again at the conference had to do with the appropriateness and potency of education in general and curriculum in particular as significant agents of social reform. In spite of the brilliance and creativity of the curriculum ideas, I could not help but feel how impotent those ideas are in the face of overwhelming forces that are, and intend to stay, in power—the forces of status quo, indifference, apathy, and know-nothingism.

It has often been said that most of the people now in education would have been in monasteries and convents had they lived in the Middle Ages. What that perhaps reveals is a wistful yearning that the work of educators is linked to some grand and glorious purpose. I believe that many educators are content with being technically oriented. They see their job as producing materials, training teachers, teaching children, developing practices in response to prevailing social policies and attitudes. In fact, many would go beyond that and claim that schools *should* generally reflect the views and aspirations of the broader community. I do not want to deal directly with that question here. I prefer to deal with a question that concerns those of us who do in fact accept the view that educators should be in the vanguard of those seeking to improve, not just to maintain, society. As I indicated before, there seems to be within the humanistic education movement a strong element of support for social and economic reform that extends far beyond the classroom.

In thinking about the subject, it strikes me that those of us in humanistic education with strong social concerns may have fallen into a trap, ironically constructed of an overreliance and an overemphasis on the value and potency of humanistic education. We seem to feel that society has many serious social injustices such as poverty, inequality, and authoritarianism; that these injustices are aggravated by a number of cultural forces, among them bureaucratic impersonalism, institutional rigidity, pressures for conformity, and the competitive "rat race"; that a more valid and worthwhile society would be one in which there was more individual freedom, more personal creativity and spontaneity, and more social justice and equality, which might be realized if people were better educated through processes geared to the humanistic values that stress liberation and community; and that, since these values celebrate individuality and uniqueness, we must at all costs avoid manipulation, dogma, and conformity and in its stead help students to learn the *processes* that will lead them individually to God knows what. The critical point is that I'm not sure how to complete that sentence except that there is some tacit, vague faith that liberated, free people will likely work for and create a more just society.

The experiences of the late 1960's and early 1970's would seem to offer bitter testimony to the validity of this paradigm. Forgetting the excesses of the Yippies and the like, I think that we all should take enormous pride in the "civil rights and Vietnam generation." Amid all the passion, controversy, and tragedy of those times, one outcome seems quite clear to me: many young people became ideologically involved, socially responsible, and intellectually sophisticated in matters of enormous significance. I doubt if any generation of young people became as involved, both intellectually and emotionally, in struggles of equal magnitude. I like to think that educators can take some pride in that accomplishment.

It is also clear, however, that there are bitter memories. Divisions still remain, major social reforms have not been made, the basic system still operates, and many of the protesters of the 1960's are bewildered and suffer from guilt and despair as they cope with the gray and harsh world of the mid-1970's. I feel that educators must take some responsibility for those conditions, also.

The question seems to come down to this: Is it possible for humanistic educators in American public schools to move beyond a process orientation so as explicitly to link their programmatic concerns to larger social and political movements? We seem to be caught in a trap that says that, as educators, we must limit ourselves to encouraging and helping individuals to think, feel, and respond in more sophisticated but still individually determined ways. I have to confess my own confusion on this question even though I am convinced that as educators *and* human beings we must stand and commit ourselves to a set of basic community, social, and moral goals. The great difficulty is in reconciling this with a basic faith in a process orientation and commitment to individual freedom.

Moreover, we must also confront the reality of power, that is, that the current social, political, and educational power structure can easily block the very advances that emerge from a humanistic program. Can we, as educators and human beings, ignore the reality that social forces and institutions will not yield to good intentions, moral imperatives, creativity, and sophisticated thinking?

If we are blocked by pedagogical principle from pursuing a social vision in the classroom, are there other ways to provide a more meaningful framework for our curriculum and programs? It was suggested several times at the conference that it was perhaps time to work in concert with other social and political groups and movements. If we are indeed a technology, then at present we are in the anomalous position of being dysfunctional to the framework (that is, the school) within which we now work. If, as educators, we cannot ourselves directly espouse broader goals, then can we not at least offer our technology to those social movements with whom we are not only compatible but to whom we are also vital?

I am really not sure, but I am convinced that we cannot have our cake and eat it. We cannot be passionately committed to a more just society and feel we can help further this without serious thought concerning what that more just society might be and how it might be approached. It seems increasingly apparent to me that humanistic educators would best serve their cause (and themselves) by accepting a more modest conception of their role, which would be to deal with the educational implications of larger, broader-based movements. It would prevent us from deluding ourselves that we are making fundamental changes and at the same time give us both realistic goals and much-needed support. It might also help to reduce the spiritual, moral, and social vacuum in which humanistic educators now work.

This was an important project for me, both in terms of product and process. What I came away feeling most strongly about is the critical importance of maintaining such dialogues. I also came away passionately convinced that the dialogues must be nourished by a deep sense of compassion for each other. I believe deeply in our ideals. At the same time, as a professional, I have found myself critical of, and disappointed in, much of our actual work. Intellectuals are prone to abuse their responsibility to be critical by being destructive and unsupportive. They thereby neglect their responsibility to sustain hope and reenergize each other. We must find a balance between commitment to cause and colleagues and the need to be tough minded. It would be a serious mistake, for example, to either undervalue or overpraise the presentations in this volume. We must be both kind and harsh to each other, for we deal with enormously complex and ambiguous issues of the greatest import. We are all searching for meaning and for ways of integrating an existence that is maddeningly fragmented and mysterious. It would be folly approaching blasphemy to expect us to resolve these issues, and it would be a tragedy of catastrophic dimension if we were to limit the search or cease trying.

The authors have provided solid evidence that they have pursued their search with rare distinction, courage, and energy. We are obliged to examine their work (as well as that of others) rigorously and carefully, to show compassion and express our gratitude, to share the pain and anguish that must have gone into their efforts. We owe them our heartfelt thanks for keeping the flame alive.

Flora Nell Roebuck

Humanistic Education from an HRD Viewpoint

Humanistic efforts in the field of education, it seems to me, are not so much pluralistic as individualistic. That is, each humanistic educator seems to have his own idea of what humanism is and how it should be implemented in the schools. The only common element seems to be the desire on the part of the humanistic innovator to improve in some fashion the quality of life lived by young people—either while in school or later as a continuing effect of schooling.

Certainly this element is common to all of the presentations, but, because of their diverse orientations, any particular reaction requires the establishment of "a place from which to view." The Human Resource Development (HRD) model proposed by Carkhuff[1] seems to offer a suitable vantage point from which an integrated reaction can be made since it is based on the assumption that the primary goal of human effort is the effective development of human resources. Implied within that concept is an improvement of the quality of life for all individuals.

In Carkhuff's model the goal is the development of effective people, that is, people who are effective physically, intellectually, and emotionally. Effectiveness is defined as the ability to consistently establish *constructive* relationships with self and others and to produce *desired* "effects" upon the world. The key to the humanism of the model is in the adjectives "desired" and "constructive." It would seem that effectiveness is measured in terms of the achievement of the goals established by constructive individuals.

The elements that contribute to effective human resource development are specified by Carkhuff as effective people, effective programs, and effective organizations. Thus, effective people are both the goal and a major part of the process in the HRD model. That is, only people who *are* effective can constructively help other persons *become* effective. Programs are defined as the actions that people undertake—the things that they do. Organizations are defined as the ways in which people and programs are brought together or allowed to interact. Together, programs and organizations make up the technology available to attack a particular problem, while the effectiveness of the people involved in designing organizations and carrying out programs determines the ultimate outcome of the effort.

Using the model defined above, it is now possible to derive a "place from which to view" the diversity represented in the approaches to humanistic education. By arranging the elements of effective HRD as column headings and by using three dimensions of personal effectiveness in achieving the goal of HRD efforts as row labels, a classification matrix for humanistic projects can be derived. This matrix can then be used to integrate the overall status of current efforts in humanistic education. If the presentations that comprise the major part of this volume are treated as a representative sample of current projects, the matrix can be filled as shown in Table R.1.

Classification Procedures

Before proceeding to a discussion of generalizations about the presentations that can be drawn from the matrix, it is perhaps appropriate to explain the procedures used in classification. The ground rules were:

1. For purposes of clarification and simplification, each presentation is represented in only one cell of the matrix. The cell to which it is assigned should represent the *major* focus, but assignment to a cell should *not* imply that other concerns that could have been represented in other cells of the matrix were not discussed.

2. Classification into a column would be determined by relationship to *potential* increases in HRD effectiveness. Thus, each presenta-

TABLE R.1

Classification matrix for humanistic projects in education (superscript letters represent levels of change process and are explained in text)

Dimensions of personal effectiveness in achieving goal of human resource development (HRD)	Elements of effective HRD		
	Effective people	Effective programs	Effective organizations
Physical	—	—	—
Intellectual	1 (Newmann)[U,A]	1 (Feinberg)[U]	—
Emotional	2 (Aspy)[U,A] (Mosher)[U,A]	1 (Apple and King)[U,E]	1 (Sergiovanni)[U]

tion would be classified according to the element (people, programs, organizations) that it was attempting to make *more effective.*

3. Row placement was based on classification of the person constructs that received major emphasis. That is, those constructs relating to people that the presentation seemed to be concerned about explaining or affecting were classified into three dimensions of personal effectiveness: physical, intellectual, or emotional. The presentation was assigned to a row representing the dimension into which a majority of those constructs could be classified.

The application of the criteria to each of the presentations is discussed below. The presentations are identified by the name of the presenter, or, in one case, the presenters, and they are in alphabetical order.

Apple and King: Because of the focus on describing what people *do* in schools and on the students' mastery of their *role* as elementary school pupils, this presentation appears in the program column. Although it was concerned with constructs in the intellectual dimension, the major emphasis (indicated by frequent use of such constructs as cultural capital, visions, meanings, power, control, values, norms) seemed to be on describing how students attained mastery of social meanings. In Carkhuff's model of personal effectiveness, most of those constructs would fall into the emotional dimension. *Classification:* effective programs; emotional dimension.

Aspy: The diversity of projects discussed in Aspy's presentation presented problems in classification that required somewhat arbitrary decisions. It was clearly concerned with the effectiveness both of programs and of people, but, despite the presentation of a process that could be used to determine or improve the effectiveness of programs in general, most of the programs actually discussed were directed at increasing the effectiveness of individuals so the presentation was assigned to the first column. Similarly, this was the only presentation clearly concerned with all three dimensions of personal effectiveness, but its major emphasis seemed to be in the interpersonal area (emotional dimension) of both teachers and students. Constructs in the intellectual dimension were discussed for both teachers and students, but seemed to receive somewhat less emphasis than those in the interpersonal dimension. Although this was the *only* instance where the physical dimension of personal effectiveness was specifically considered, physical fitness was discussed primarily in terms of its effects upon the interpersonal effectiveness of the teacher. *Classification:* effective people; emotional dimension.

Feinberg: Classification in the program column was indicated since this presentation dealt primarily with what [people in] schools *do* and the historical and social reasons why they do it the way they do. Although consideration of the school as an institution might seem to be more appropriate for the organization column, the presentation was not so much concerned with the *way* in which schools bring people and programs together as with the *effects* of schooling in relation to expectations in the broader social setting. Row classification, however, was not so simple. It was made on the basis of the goals for schools that Feinberg presented. Those goals—labor (careers), skills, and ideologies—all fall into the intellectual dimension. This distinction was supported by the extensive discussion dismissing IQ as a limiting factor in schooling. *Classification:* effective programs; intellectual dimension.

Mosher: Although his presentation was concerned with increasing the effectiveness of school programs, Mosher's primary emphasis seemed to be on the application of selected programs to the attainment of a particular goal, that is, improving the moral and ego development of individuals and enlarging their social consciences. Because of his concern with the *total* development of the individual, row classification was rather arbitrary. Most of the *means* discussed for implementation (such as rational discussion, *understanding* the thinking and feeling of others, democratic *rule* making, determining rational justice, applying moral *judgment* in role-taking situations) fall into the intellectual dimension, but the ultimate *goal* seemed to place major emphasis in the emotional dimension. In due respect to Mosher's expressly stated position on the interrelatedness of "all dimensions of human development, including cognitive, moral, social, ego, emotional, aesthetic, vocational, physical," it must be noted that making such a dichotomous distinction in order to classify the presentation into *one* dimension of personal effectiveness is clearly *not* in accord with its spirit. *Classification:* effective people; emotional dimension.

Newmann: The column classification of Newmann's presentation rested on a distinction between what people *do* and the process of gaining the skills *prerequisite* to doing. Thus, it was addressed to the problem of enhancing the student's *ability* to do ("personal competence") in the area of social action. Although it also deals with the development of a program for achieving this goal, the presentation emphasized the *application* of a program rather than the *process* of program development. In spite of its consideration of aspects of the emotional dimension such as open-committedness and personal motives in achieving an ultimate goal of social action, the program which was delineated by Newmann focused on implementation of constructs within the intellectual dimension such as rational reflection, justification according to established principles, building competence, reasoned verification, and specialty skills in the social action arena. *Classification:* effective people; intellectual dimension.

Sergiovanni: Since the subject of this presentation was organizational theory in education, columnar classification was simple; row classification was not, however, so clear-cut. It was finally assigned to the emotional dimension because of the concern expressed for the effects of the various schools of organizational theory on such factors as values, motivation, personal meanings, expectations, and behavioral norms. *Classification:* effective organizations; emotional dimension.

In addition to assigning each presentation to one cell of the matrix, each was characterized as to the level of a three-stage change process that it seemed to exemplify. The levels are indicated in the matrix by superscripts. The categories used for this characterization, drawn from the model of learning in Aspy's presentation, are:

Learning = Exploration → Understanding → Action

It is a sequential model with each preceding level of the process seen as a necessary prerequisite to the succeeding level. The final level, action, is then recycled into the first level as the consequence or consequences of the action or actions are explored for further learning. The relationship of the three processes to the initiation of change are, thus, self-evident.

Generalizations from the Matrix

Examination of the matrix yields three generalizations: the presentations are disproportionately distributed among the cells; there is a lack of attention to the physical dimensions of human effectiveness evident in the row distribution; the projects in the first column were conducted at a different level of the change process than the projects in the second and third columns. Each of these generalizations will be discussed separately below.

Disproportionate Distribution among Columns

Exactly half of the presentations deal with increasing the effectiveness of individuals, while only two of the six are primarily concerned with the things that people do (programs) and just one deals with the relationships between people and their activities. Since this trend has important implications for the assessment of humanistic endeavors, an effort was made to determine if the presentations could, in fact, be taken as a representative sample of the focus of humanistic education. The procedure consisted of applying the classification matrix to the activities, projects, curricula, or theories described or annotated in three publications concerned with humanistic education.[2] Using the same criteria specified above, each entry for which sufficient information was available in the publications was assigned to a cell in the matrix. The resulting distribution for 161 entries from the three publications is displayed in percentages in Table R.2.

In general, then, it can be concluded that there is a trend among humanists to implement projects concerned with enhancing individual effectiveness. Secondary emphasis is on increasing the effectiveness of programs, while only slight attention is given to the question of the effectiveness of organizations. Perhaps this is only to be

TABLE R.2
Application of classification matrix to brief descriptions of 161 humanistic activities

Dimensions of personal effectiveness in achieving goal of human resource development (HRD)	Elements of effective HRD (percent)		
	Effective people	Effective programs	Effective organizations
Physical	1.2	0.0	0.0
Intellectual	24.8	7.5	1.2
Emotional	46.0	16.1	3.1

expected, given the idiographic emphases of the prevailing psychological theories[3] from which many humanistic projects are drawn. Concentration upon only one element of effective Human Resource Development, however, has serious implications for the possibility of accomplishing permanent and broad-based changes in education.

Lack of Attention to the Physical Dimension

Both matrixes demonstrate a lack of attention by humanists to the physical dimension of personal effectiveness. The consequences of this failure are indicated by recent research conducted by Aspy and Roebuck[4] and Buhler and Aspy[5] linking physical fitness and interpersonal functioning. The research began when sixth-degree orthogonal polynomial curves were fitted to data across time of teacher behavior in response to students. The resulting significant ($p < .05$) trends showed that teachers typically decrease from September to December in their usage of constructive response to students, make a slight recovery in January, and then decrease again through the end of the year (see Figure R.1).

This finding led to the hypothesis that the physical fitness of the teacher was related to the ability to support constructive interaction for extensive periods. In efforts to test this and related hypotheses, the series of investigations referenced above was launched. Results from these investigations included:

1. Teacher responsiveness toward students declines within each week from Monday morning to Friday afternoon and recovers on the following Monday.

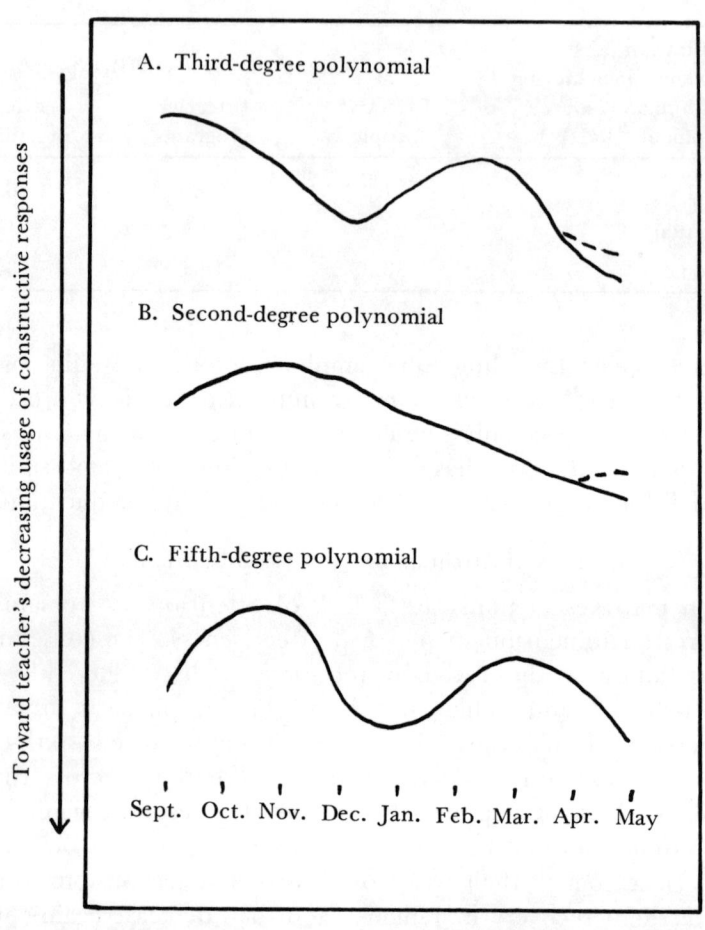

FIGURE R.1
General forms of commonly occurring significant negative trends in control group data

2. Physical fitness was a significant predictor of gain in both immediate skills learning and subsequent performance in the classroom by teachers who participated in in-service training workshops designed to increase constructive responsiveness to students.
3. When teachers are responding to students, they have significantly ($p < .02$) faster pulse rates than when they are initiating structure.
4. Physical fitness was a better predictor of practicum performance of student teachers and student nurses than grade point average.
5. When problem readers are called upon in instructional situations, they have significant and startling increases in heartbeats per minute. (A typical example is the student whose resting heartbeat was about 60 beats per minute. When his reading group was called, it rose to 70. When he was asked to perform in the group, it jumped to 140 beats per minute.)

The interrelatedness of the physical dimension to both the emotional and the intellectual dimensions demonstrated above and similar findings as to the curvilinear relationships among intellectual and emotional variables demonstrated by Roebuck and Aspy[6] serve to support the importance for humanists to consider all three dimensions when planning or implementing educational innovation. From the HRD viewpoint, failure to do so can only lead to ineffective results in attempts to enhance personal effectiveness. Integration of the three dimensions has similar implications for attempts to reach HRD goals through increasing the effectiveness of programs or of organizations.

Differential Levels of Change Process

All presentations are intimately and extensively involved with understanding the process of initiating change. That is, they represented significant endeavors in analyzing and integrating concepts or prior research in their areas of concern. In two instances understanding was the major thrust of the material presented. Three presentations also contained considerable material delineating the implementation of action projects designed to bring about specific changes, and Apple and King discussed a research project that had been conducted to explore and document the current status of an aspect of schooling. The four presentations exemplifying *two levels* of the change process carry two superscripts.

In examining the distribution of the levels of the change process in Table R.1, it is evident that the action projects were limited to attempts to increase personal effectiveness. Effective programs were the subject of efforts at both the understanding and the exploration stage, while organizations were solely approached at the understanding level.

The pattern for change levels is a direct reflection of the distribution of projects among the three columns. This leads to an intriguing hypothesis: perhaps the concentration of humanists on projects attempting change in the HRD element of effective people is a result of the state of humanistic technology (programs + organizations). In other words, it may be possible that only in the area of personal effectiveness have sufficient activities been conducted at the exploration and understanding levels to provide the basis for deriving action. A further hypothesis from the matrix would be that the phase most infrequently undertaken is that of exploration. Thus, a case for encouraging naturalistic (descriptive) research in the areas of programs and organizations would seem to be justified.

Implications for Further Research

It seems inevitable that this collection of documents ranging across a broad spectrum of humanistic endeavors should provide the basis for the initiation of much research. For example, a cursory examination of the six documents yielded thirty-five testable hypotheses. And this was from individual consideration of each presentation. Correlation and integration of the concepts in the six documents should pose many additional questions.

Two stimulating statements made by Sergiovanni were so intriguing that a pilot investigation related to them has already been conducted. Sergiovanni presented—arranged in a quadrant—four patterns of student and teacher influence, each associated with a particular view of management and organization. Subsequently, he indicated that there was a discrepancy between the acceptance of human resources thinking on education and the practices engaged in by educators. The two, together, stimulated a question as to the degree of acceptance by humanistic educators of concepts versus practices in each of the other patterns.

Accordingly, responses to two open-ended statements were obtained from a sample of two hundred middle school and junior high school teachers attending a workshop on interpersonal skills. The two statements were:

Humanistic education is . . . .

Three things that *should* be done (or *are* being done) to make a classroom more humanistic are . . . .

The information provided by Sergiovanni about influence patterns in relationship to the organizational and management features and professional subsystem properties in education for each of the four quadrants was used to code definitions and practices for quadrant membership. Coding was carried out by three graduate students in supervision and administration. Responses containing items such as "student works alone," on which the coders disagreed were eliminated from the study. Table R.3 shows the resulting distribution.

TABLE R.3

Distribution of humanistic education definitions and practices among four patterns of teacher and student influence associated with schools of organization and management theory

Patterns of influence (and associated schools of theory)	Incidence of responses	
	Definitions of humanistic education	Practices for humanizing education
Child-centered (human relations)	102	290
Integrated (human resources)	59	115
Curriculum-centered (scientific management)	8	114
Teacher-centered (combination)[a]	21	51
Total responses	190	570

[a]Human resources for adults; scientific management for students.

The data in the table make some interesting points. First, it is worth noting that educational practitioners in the sample supplied twice as many definitions related to the human relations school than to the human resources school. This is in contrast to educational academics who are currently writing primarily from the human resources viewpoint. Second, the high incidence of suggested educational practices classified as "curriculum-centered" (scientific management) is especially surprising when it is considered in view of the fact that the educators proposing them had *chosen* to attend a workshop on interpersonal skills. When asked, they classified themselves as humanistic educators. A similar point can be made in regard to the twenty-one definitions that fell in the teacher-centered (combination) quadrant.

The proposal of definitions of humanistic education associated with curriculum-centered (scientific management) patterns of influence was an unanticipated occurrence. An example of a definition coded for membership in this pattern is: "Humanistic education is putting kids into programs like cross-age groups to make sure that all humans, regardless of their abilities, get educated."

Ideally, it would be expected that there would be a one-to-one correspondence between definitions and practices. The distribution of the responses in the two columns indicates, however, that this is not the case. Chi-square analysis was conducted to determine if the discrepancy in distribution was significant. (See Table R.4.) It seems

TABLE R.4

Chi-square analysis of significance of discrepancy between distributions of definitions and practices

Associated theory	Theoretical probability (percent)	Frequency		Calculated χ^2
		Observed	Predicted	
Human relations	53.7	290	306	
Human resources	31.1	115	177	$8.77; p < .05$
Scientific management	4.2	114	24	$(\chi^2_{.05,3} = 7.82)$
Combination	11.1	51	63	
Total	100.0	570	570	

that there *is*, as anticipated, a significant discrepancy between theory and practice among humanists. Furthermore, the discrepancy exists across all four of the quadrants presented by Sergiovanni.

Significance for Humanistic Education

The above analysis of approaches to humanistic education has many implications for educators. Two of them seem to deserve major and immediate consideration. The first is the necessity for increased attention to the physical dimension of personal effectiveness, and the second is the desirability of counteracting the paucity of projects directed toward programs and organizations.

Because of the interrelatedness of the physical dimension with other dimensions of personal effectiveness, it would seem that humanistic educators need to derive or adopt a technology for dealing with the physical needs of individuals. Some technologies currently exist. For example, Ken Cooper has a well-documented program for the development of cardiovascular fitness.[7] These technologies are not, however, widely disseminated in educational settings. Cooper's program, for instance, has its greatest acceptance among business executives. Feinberg's claim that preventive medical care is not available to large groups in our society is another case in point. Since the physical dimension seems to serve as a limiting factor in personal effectiveness, the goal of the highest possible level of human resource development cannot be reached as long as physical factors such as improper prenatal nutrition and inadequate postnatal medical care are allowed to diminish the potential capabilities of a significant number of individuals.

A basic HRD premise is that the personal effectiveness of individuals is only one element of three (people, programs, organizations) necessary for bringing about increased effectiveness in developing human resources. If that premise is accepted, then humanists have a mandate to move beyond projects aimed at the enhancement of individuals. We need also to create technologies (programs and organizations) to be wielded by the effective people we are developing. As material presented earlier has demonstrated, this mandate has not yet been acknowledged. In terms of the proportionate distribution of projects undertaken, humanists are primarily engaged in many individual projects for increasing personal effectiveness.

It is possible that the humanists' preoccupation with individualism limits our endeavors. Because we have not identified immediate operational goals to which *groups* of us can subscribe, it may not be feasible to increase the effectiveness of the programs and organizations available to raise the quality of life for all. Thus, the next challenge for humanists may well be to discover a way to orchestrate our diversity.

Michael W. Apple

Humanism and the Politics of Educational Argumentation

Humanism and Its Critics

As this volume no doubt demonstrates, the controversy surrounding humanism and education has at least two sides. On the one hand, humanism is an attack on the efficiency rationality that seems to dominate so much of our thought and action in education. On the other hand, humanistic educational positions themselves are criticized as being relatively apolitical and ineffectual in confronting the problems they identify. The argument between humanists and those who might be called "technologists" and between humanists and those who are somewhat more politically and economically oriented in a critical sense is an expression of the intense social and individual crisis that confronts us all. Because of this, all of us will undoubtedly be called upon to make difficult personal choices about social and educational programs, about intellectual and political affiliation, about where we stand.

Humanism attracts adherents because its underlying and wholly meritorious goal is to bring the person, the concrete individual, into focus. Like existentialism, its impelling purpose is to "overcome the separation of thought from feeling and action."[1] Yet, as I shall argue in closing, that very separation is *not*, as some humanistic educators will argue, merely the result of a lack of personal sensitivity and expertise or a lack of concern for individualism. It is a symptom of much more pervasive problems of a collective sort. These problems cannot be dealt with only or primarily on the level of consciousness (for example, more people of humanistic beliefs). It must, instead, be confronted with a more coordinated analysis of the structural causes of these conditions in advanced industrial societies like our own. In short, they require what might best be called a "critical theory" of education, school knowledge, and society.

A critical theory of society is an attempt to understand such things as individualism, uniqueness, personal meaning (or the lack of it) on a larger scale. Individual, private, and unique sufferings are interpreted not as merely psychological phenomena, but as structural conditions arising out of the basic malfunctioning of a particular form of social collectivity. Thus, the problem of the lack of humanistic awareness is analyzed not in terms of personal adjustment or in terms of changing an individual's consciousness (though there may be a place for that), but in "categories of social transformation."[2] By analyzing this problem further, I hope to clarify the arenas in which some of our difficult choices—educational, ethical, political, and economic—may lie.

Many of my friends and colleagues of a "humanistic" bent (and I am nearly always classified among them—often to their chagrin, perhaps) may be aghast at what I shall say here. But, as the British analyst of culture Raymond Williams has noted, if you are not in a church you are not really worried about heresies. The only real interest must be in actual and well-grounded theory and practice,[3] not in whether one is "true" to the church. Thus, I do not perceive "humanism" as a church, as a set of social beliefs that are preordained. Rather, it is a *set of prior interests,* many of which I tend to share, that involve seeking ways to free concrete individuals and groups from domination, to enable the conditions for what Jürgen Habermas has called "nonrepressive communicative competence" to evolve.[4] These human interests do, however, require committed action. If one takes them seriously, they require action on a political and economic level as well as on the humanists' more familiar personal and psychological level.

Both the humanist and I see certain similar problems, to be sure. We are both disturbed by the dominance of efficiency or factory models of schooling. We are both undoubtedly less than pleased by some of the kinds of meanings schools preserve in their overt and hidden curricula. We are both aware of how difficult it is for our educational institutions to allow what Camus has called "style" to emerge. Once these, and other phenomena we may not agree on, are perceived as problems, however, the framework for interpreting them tends to be different. Whereas one (the humanist) sees these as immediate issues to be dealt with in an ameliorative fashion, the other (the critical theorist) accepts the humanistic intent but seeks to go beyond the symptoms to see *connections* between the problems of schooling and those of the dominant institutions that surround the school.

Thus, I want to argue that as long as no political and economic interpretations are attached to the problematic conditions found in so many of our schools, the conditions will remain inert. They constitute no real threat to established interests.[5]

The fact that educators today seem to see the only "real" choices as being between the traditions of technological thought or efficiency and humanism speaks less to the importance of the choice than it does to our utter inability to preserve viable alternative social and educational traditions. There is no serious attempt in the media, in schools, in teacher-training institutions, or in society's cultural apparatus in general to document the long and valuable history of what might be called socialist humanism in the United States.[6] Since this tradition is simply not preserved or readily available to both the populace at large or to professional educators, it is nearly impossible for committed individuals to affiliate with it. One has no choice but to choose between a concern for inputs and outputs or a vague romantic individualism. Thus, a perspective that offers a uniquely potent mode of analysis and an agenda for coordinated action in the economic, political, and educational sectors of a society, one that may enable us to see where ameliorative changes are realistically possible and where more major structural alterations in our institutions are necessary, cannot be turned to. I can think of no better instance of Michael Young's argument that "those in positions of power will attempt to define what is taken as [important] knowledge, how accessible to different groups any knowledge is, and what are the accepted relationships between different knowledge areas and between those who have access to them and make them available."[7]

The politics of knowledge accessibility, hence, is part and parcel of our (now very limited) range of choices for committed action. This is coupled with another problem, our commitment to a vision of individualism that totally divorces the individual from the larger social group that might give meaning to his or her life and hopes.

Our inability to think in other than individualistic terms is nicely expressed by Raymond Williams in his argument that the dominance of the bourgeois individual distorts our understanding of our real relations with others.

> I remember a miner saying to me, of someone we were discussing: "He's the sort of man who gets up in the morning and presses a switch and expects a light to come on." We are all, to some extent, in this position, in that our modes of thinking habitually suppress large areas of our real relationships, including our real dependence on others. We think of my money, my light, in these naive terms, because parts of our very idea of society are withered at root. We can hardly have any conception, in our present system, of the financing of social purposes from the social product, a method which would continually show us, in real terms, what our society is and does. In a society whose products depend almost entirely on intricate and continuous co-operation and social organization, we expect to consume as if we were isolated individuals, making our own way. We are then forced into the stupid comparison of individual consumption and social taxation—one desirable and to be extended, the other regrettably necessary and to be limited. From this kind of thinking the physical balance follows inevitably. Unless we achieve some realistic sense of community, our true standard of living will continue to be distorted.[8]

In essence, Williams is arguing that our concern for the individual can go too far, that it can act as an ideological presupposition that keeps us from establishing any genuine sense of collective commitment. Thus, the total concern for the individual is, paradoxically, ideally suited to maintaining both a rather manipulative ethic of consumption and a lack of political and economic sensitivity. It makes it very difficult for people to see and know their real relationships with others. We need to inquire quite rigorously, I think, into the latent effects of the humanists' tendency to absolutize the individual. In fact, as I shall note in the second section of this essay, such absolutizing makes it difficult to develop a potent analysis of widespread social injustice and "inhumanity."

What I am *not* asking for here is a perspective that totally reduces the individual into the social group. Rather, we must avoid the danger of all too much humanistic rhetoric that ignores the possible political and economic roots of our concerns by reducing them to "merely" individual psychological problems of, say, a person's sense of alienation because the educational institution does not respond to that person's particular set of meanings, dispositions, and desires. To leave to, say, sociology or economics the concern with abstract groups and to education an equally abstract concern for individuals is more than just a division of labor. It is a way of avoiding the complexity of reality, "a way of avoiding the reality of the interpenetration, in a final sense the unity, of the most individual and the most social forms of actual life."[9]

This complex interweaving of the personal with the social points to one of our major dilemmas in educational analysis. We do tend to reduce our problems to the psychological denominator of concrete cases so that we can "help" children. Yet, because of this "helping" ideology, we also find it hard to focus on the larger societal configurations that may actually generate the individual problems themselves.[10] This is one of my fundamental criticisms of the more romantic existential and humanistic movements in education. But in order to make it clearer, let us look more closely into a larger array of the major difficulties outlined in humanistic and romantic criticism of schools and see how the difficulties there relate to those present in other cultural and economic institutions.

Rather than talking vaguely about the varying brands of humanism in general, I shall focus on one of the latest and best statements of humanistic critiques of schooling in Charles Tesconi and Van Cleve Morris' *The Anti-Man Culture*.[11] It is an analysis, from an existential and humanistic point of view, of the dominance in schools of efficiency, bureaucratic rationality, vulgar forms of scientism, and the "inhumane" treatment of personal meanings of individuals. I shall use their analysis as a backdrop for my own arguments with humanistic educators. Thus, the position taken by Tesconi and Morris will serve as an archetype of a general educational stance that requires serious scrutiny if it is to have any lasting effect on the way our institutions, including educational ones, function. My examination of their analysis can be, I hope, generalized to apply to the larger range of humanistic versions of school problems. Therefore, the reader should go beyond the criticism of the one particular book that I offer here to examine the connections between this individual case and the larger movement of humanism and schooling. Where Tesconi and Morris are weak, so, too, are many other individuals like them.

One cautionary note is, however, in order. Because I have decided, on methodological grounds, to analyze one specific set of humanistic assertions about schools, there is a danger that the reader will assume that each and every point I make here applies to each and every member of those groups with a humanistic intent. This may not be the case, but, the general framework of criticism that will be used is applicable to all educators and critics who limit themselves to an individualistic humanism. As I shall argue, criticisms of schools as bureaucratic phenomena, as places where individual meanings are not valued enough, are not sufficient. There are other questions that are prior to these.

Depoliticization of Institutional Reform

Public analysis of social and educational ills is a risky business, not the least because its very public nature invites criticism from people who disagree or who wish that the analysis had only gone further. Having done a fair amount of public social and educational analysis myself, I can appreciate the problem that humanistic critics of schools set out to deal with and the task that Tesconi and Morris have tried to accomplish in *The Anti-Man Culture*. I must, however, also place myself among those who look at this particular style of social and educational analysis and both disagree and wish that the authors, and other humanists, had indeed gone further. Let me begin by treating their perspective as a way of talking, for it is a way of talking that I no longer feel is fruitful if we are to make serious headway toward creating institutions that are more responsive to human sentiment.

Language and Tradition

It is important, I think, to examine not merely what language says but also what it does. That is, as Wittgenstein reminds us, the meaning of language depends on its use. Now language can be used to present evidence, to describe, and so forth. It can also be used for *affiliative* purposes, as a mode of linking oneself and one's audience together with a tradition.[12] Language carries within itself a past, a way of looking that has a history of the struggles of concrete groups of people trying to comprehend and act on the world. When one employs a language, hence, one is not merely saying such and such is or is not the case; one is also affiliating with those groups who generated the linguistic system in the first place. Thus, the language we use to deal with our problems is not necessarily neutral. Because of these affiliations, language may covertly support those groups and institutions that created the problems that the users are trying to solve in the first place. This will be one of my basic points about *The Anti-Man Culture* and so much of humanistic criticism. While at first glance it offers a linguistic description that seems powerful, on second glance its perspective can do no more than confirm the existing distribution of power, ideology, economic goods and services, and even the "affective" and imaginative characteristics in this society. This is primarily because the language is divorced from any serious consideration of power and the political content of educational and bureaucratic ideologies.

In clearer terms, Tesconi and Morris and many other thoughtful humanists talk a language of commitment; they succeed in creating an affiliation, and this is certainly important. They also, however, link themselves to the wrong tradition by their continual and nearly complete depoliticization of both the problem with which they deal and the sources from which they draw. For example, they and other humanists continually speak of the "system" and of schools as reified, inhuman objects dominated by efficiency that stand above human consciousness and political and economic considerations. However, by speaking of the "system" in such a way, they preclude serious discussion of the exploitation of a large proportion of the population of advanced and underdeveloped countries by a limited class of people who control the distribution of goods and services, including educational goods and services. For schools, and the bureaucratized and technical ideology that stands behind them, *represent* the image of a larger society. Their covert yet fundamental social and economic role, in sociological terms their "function" (and in this they *are* functional), is to instill and reinforce the dispositions, propensities, and ideological presuppositions that enable the surrounding institutions to carry on,[13] institutions that generated the ideology of efficiency, what they call bureautechnocracy, in the first place.

Like most school critics today, Tesconi and Morris are linked to a long and unfortunately less than fully successful tradition of individualistic educational reform. I do not wish to debunk this tradition.

We should, however, note carefully that those who hold this position have historically shied away from the difficult question of the politics of and interrelationships among institutions. It has been assumed that increasing the "affective" or "humanistic" consciousness of individuals will guarantee more responsive institutions, yet the question of who has the power to make those changes has been ignored. In fact, in the usual current appropriation of that tradition, the position is that the lack of affectivity or, as I would like to call it, ethical responsiveness, is a result of a consciousness, the ideology of bureautechnocracy, that does not include affectivity or ethical responsiveness. In essence, teachers and others are not humanistically sensitive enough, or so the argument goes. This is somewhat of a tautology, unfortunately, for, translated into simpler terms, it merely says that the lack of "human" consciousness leads to a lack of "human" consciousness.

But ideologies, forms of social consciousness, *come* from somewhere. They may be viewed as common sense and be for their users "real" descriptions of the world, but they maintain symbolically or materially the institutions that give them their power.[14] An appreciation of this important fact transforms questions of bureautechnocracy and the lack of humanism in schools into questions of social and economic activity and control. It is not merely an issue of "being better persons," if you will, as the analysis of *The Anti-Man Culture* suggests. Without dealing with this nexus of economic and political control, educational reformers seeking curricular change or more basic institutional alterations may be condemned to repeat the past errors of humanistic models. If so, schools will continue to resemble factories. The long tradition of humanistic models has had an effect on our language, but little effect on our social and educational practice, something I do not think the vague humanism of *The Anti-Man Culture* will alter.

I find it interesting, and indicative of the apolitical nature of their arguments, that in the many quotes throughout their analysis Tesconi and Morris substitute the word "bureautechnocracy" for the original intent of the author. Perhaps the best example of this is the work of Marcuse. Tesconi and Morris, like other humanists, argue (rightly) against positivism and use Marcuse to make a case against bureaucracy. Marcuse does indeed talk about the bureaucratization of consciousness and institutions. He does describe the increasingly "quasi-scientific" frame of mind of advanced industrial society, as well.[15] But what gives his critique potency is its groundedness in the reconstructed Marxism of critical theory. If in fact positivism was and is the absolutizing of scientific facts, it was and is also the reification of an existing economic and social order.[16] That is, Marcuse cannot be used by humanists to support an argument merely against bureautechnocracy without losing the political and economic *intent* that guided his work and that gives it its generative meaning. By pulling his (Marcuse's) argument out of its critical context (let us call it Marxist humanism), Tesconi and Morris do not enable their readers to see the nature of the commitment Marcuse is actually calling upon them to make. This means that both Tesconi and Morris and their readers are spared the difficulty of analyzing whether their own tacit social, intellectual, ideological, and political commitments actually contribute to emancipation of the many oppressed people in an advanced industrial society like our own. The authors also prevent their readers from linking themselves with a critical tradition, in this case neo-Marxist analysis, that would give their humanistic critique potency.[17] Here, as in many other places, the authors go only halfway.

Science and Ideology

Let us look at another example of why many humanists do not go far enough. Tesconi and Morris are rather insightful in linking ideology with science. It is the case that the language of science and technology, especially in education, is the major mode by which the complex nexus of power that lies behind the commonsense basis of educational decisions is hidden.[18] Through its patina of supposed neutrality, it prevents educators from seeing the political and ethical nature of their acts by covering at least three things: the ideological character of educational research, the types of ideologically biased forms of knowledge distributed to children through the overt and hidden curricula within schools, and the complex relationship between schools as sorting mechanisms and a larger economic order.

Thus, it should be clear that there *is* a profound relationship between science and technology and thought, and Tesconi and Morris are correct in their assertion that our commonsense thinking and action in schools and other institutions have been strongly influenced by a technological or "one-dimensional" ideology. But quasi-scientific and technological ideologies do not exist in a vacuum. They are dialectically related to economic and social institutions that both create them, and, in turn, are supported by them. In fact, as Robert Heilbroner has recently argued, "Technology and science are not wholly independent variables in history but [are] social forces that adapt themselves to the needs and exigencies of the social milieu in which they are established."[19] They can, and do, of course, then act back upon the social milieu.

Many romantic and humanistic educational critics completely miss this dialectic. They are partially correct, though still not sufficiently political, when they see the ideology of "bureautechnocracy" as a form of control of individual action. But there is no analysis of the patterns of individual control, of the concrete *classes and groups* of people who are controlled most by other groups. This would, of course, require substantive elements of a political sensitivity, at times a radical (in terms of going to the roots of a problem, as well as political) sensitivity and one just cannot find that in *The Anti-Man Culture*.

I do not wish to totally debunk the authors' arguments about bureautechnocracy, science, efficiency, and the lack of humanism in schools. In fact, as I have argued at length elsewhere, quasi-scientific and technical thought, and the underlying rationality of certainty and control, generate the technical expertise required for policy making within institutions of social control.[20] By being relatively apolitical, however, they do not have to inquire seriously into the historical roots of the conservative ideology that permeates schooling. By not focusing on representatives of conservative epistemological and political ideologies who made and often still make a difference in schools, one does not have to illuminate the close historical connections between, on the one hand, the testing movement, race- and class-differentiated curricula, and bureaucracy in schools and, on the other hand, such things as the popular eugenics movement, conservative corporate interests, and the need to control cultural and economic dissidence in a society in an effort to achieve continued economic expansion.[21] Thus, the possible historical economic reasons for homogenization of consciousness, for the lack of individualism, are lost. It is exactly these reasons that King and I try to illuminate in analyzing the history of the hidden curriculum. Schools were often designed to do exactly what humanistic critics find so disturbing.

This realization leads to political and economic understanding, however, not apolitical discomfort.

Critical Action

With others of a similar persuasion, the authors of *The Anti-Man Culture* also show little awareness of political and economic problems, either in or out of schools, when they are proposing solutions. While the existential roots of their concerns should be applauded, Sartre has cogently argued that existential and human concerns must go hand in hand with political commitments.[22] Certainly the latter without the former is tyranny. The former (humanism, existential phenomenology, and so forth) without the latter (overt, progressively political commitment) is sterile.

The apolitical nature of Tesconi and Morris' argument is made even clearer by their suggestions for educational change, suggestions that are archetypes of the humanistic movement. What can educators do to effectively counterbalance the forces of bureautechnocracy? They can become more genuine, more affective, more "human." What is missing is the understanding that *lasting* educational reform may need to be linked with political, social, and economic reform—for instance, a change in who controls institutions—if it is to make a difference.

Ultimately, hence, the authors' emphasis is on therapy, rather than on a thorough examination of the reasons for the problems in the first place. It is possible, in fact, to interpret their position as providing the ideological foundation for a vulgar and popularized version of the affective education movement, a movement where the heart is in the right place but where the effect may well be to open student sentiment and meaning even more thoroughly to the rationalizing qualities of the school.

Given the authors' programmatic and analytic weaknesses, are there things that educators *can* do within schools? Let me note a few. Educators can engage in and strongly support student rights argumentation. They can enable students to see their own lack of rights within institutions and, even more important, they can show that the lack of "human" qualities in schools is part of a larger problem in advanced industrial societies. When women, Blacks, Latinos, workers, and others find that they have to struggle for rights and dignity within nearly all institutions, then it should be clear that the lack of dialogue and educational responsiveness within schools must be seen by students as part of a larger pattern of oppression.[23] This requires concrete work with and commitment to traditions and groups of people (students' rights advocacy groups, progressive political forces, Science for the People, and so forth), work that will enable a more fruitful understanding of the forces, both ideological and material, that provide limits on us all.

Furthermore, research models need to be developed that keep the humanistic interest so evident in the questions these school critics are asking but that do not flatten reality; that enable us to see the close connection between the ideology of control in schools, the lack of responsiveness in nearly all major institutions in our society, and who *actually* controls the distribution of educational and economic goods and services to all of us. The work of Herbert Gintis, Samuel Bowles, Clarence Karier, John S. Mann, Walter Feinberg, and others might be names worth noting here.

This is not "merely" a problem of scholarship, however. It concerns the other means by which we as educators and as individuals can come to a more complete understanding of the political, economic, and ideological roots of our problems. For me, the notion of praxis, that is, the combination of action and reflection, offers the most promise. By *reflexively inserting oneself* into the struggle against economic and educational oppression, one affiliates with those groups of people, those traditions, who have been and are engaged in changing the conditions of which the "bureautechnocracy" of Tesconi and Morris and other humanists is just a symptom.[24] But that requires a personal decision, admittedly difficult, to go beyond intellectual commitment. While humanistic criticism may sensitize us to the symptoms of our age, and thus must be continued, it does not enable us to go the next step and commit ourselves to effective action to change them.

Oddly, the very position that Professors Tesconi and Morris take is indicative of the success of what Trent Schroyer in his own excellent analysis has called a technocratic ideology[25] and points to the partial correctness of their argument. The predominant forms of rationality in our society do de-ethicize and, more importantly, do depoliticize social interaction. The fact that the latter is exactly what is missing in the humanists' position speaks to the point. After all, if something like bureaucracy or a lack of "affect" is seen as the problem, then there is no need for committed sociopolitical action. However, none of us can ignore the fact that the ideological and economic crisis now upon us requires such action. We cannot afford to wait.

Again, I do not wish to be too harsh toward humanists, especially since I share many of their concerns. As I have mentioned, of all the analyses of the lack of humanism in schools, that by Tesconi and Morris is the most serious intellectually. What I want to do is point out what to me are serious weaknesses in any position that limits itself to the existential level and does not go further to attempt to uncover the economic and political configuration surrounding the very real personal problems to which the position responds. If we are to do this, we need to begin building a conceptual framework that sees educational problems as, at least in major part, aspects of larger social issues concerning the distribution and control of work, knowledge, power, and ideology in an advanced industrial society like our own. We shall have to see that school problems, sometimes so well documented by romantic and humanistic educators, do not result from a lack of commitment on the part of liberal reformers. Nor do they necessarily result from bureaucratic exigencies and an efficiency rationality. Rather, the failure of the school "to serve individual needs for personal development" is in large measure a result of the school's tacit economic role in the selection and reproduction of the characteristics that people "require" to function in a rather unequal and stratified social order.[26] Without an understanding that this reproduction may be a "real function" of our educational system, we may be unable to find appropriate strategies for effectively dealing with the problems to which humanists often so rightly point.

Political Rationality and Educational Programs

There are, of course, other individuals like myself who are concerned with political and economic action and schooling, who, while maintaining a "humanistic" intent, see schools as centers for social action and political commitment. Walter Feinberg and Fred Newmann are among the most thoughtful of these people as their presentations and subsequent discussions document. What is also clear from the debate contained in this volume is that there are many differences between the position of Newmann and, say, those articulated by Feinberg and myself. This needs to be examined in a bit more depth.

Newmann's programmatic vision of schools as places where serious social action can go on is one of the most interesting statements currently available.[27] It points to concrete things politically minded educators can grapple with in schools. I must admit, though, that I have serious doubts about its potential for widespread success, even in terms of Newmann's commitment to participatory democracy. Given the fact that schools all too often respond to only a limited range of possible "social actions," ones that will not require too much bureaucratic restructuring, and do not want to offend any significant political constituency, Newmann's meritorious proposals, if put into practice, would probably bear little resemblance to the original. The literature on even quite well-funded educational innovations abounds with such examples.[28] This is not, though, to argue against his warranted position that students can learn to assert control over some of their affairs by engaging in social action programs. Rather, it asks us to have a clearer historical picture of past moments of educational reform.

There is, however, a more serious difference between Newmann and both Feinberg and myself. It concerns the actual ways political, social, and educational positions are developed and made internally consistent. What is behind Newmann's position is a rather traditional, and I think too limited, conception of how social, economic, and educational criticism and action are linked. One of the major difficulties is in his acceptance of an ends-means conception of rationality that is something like the following. One articulates a well-rounded social and political position, bearing in mind existing psychological and institutional constraints, and then proceeds to develop educational or other programs based on it. While this has the benefits of stability and greater ease of evaluation, it does not, and indeed must not, exhaust the limits of a conception of rationality that is in the service of developing political, economic, and educational programs and visions.

In fact, my own understanding of the problem of creating a viable program of action on a number of fronts (and here I mean this to be interpreted in its broadest sense) lies not in the rather linear ends-means projection of the last paragraph. Rather, I think it proceeds dialectically in a much more complex fashion. Here social, economic, and educational criticism goes on at the same time as an alternative program slowly evolves. It is the dialectical interplay of evolving critical power with a more clearly growing programmatic intent that provides both insight into the dilemmas that face us and illumination of the arenas *appropriate* for institutional change. In clearer terms, I would like to argue that the immediate call for alternative programs, based on a well-articulated and finished political vision that precedes it, is actually a curiously disembodied concept of reason. It does not allow for the crucial interaction between criticism and the growth of alternative political, social, and economic forms, an interaction that is evident in the work of the most creative social critics and social activists. Thus, a linear conception of programmatic rationality leaves no place for a Marx or even a Jefferson, individuals whose own programs grew slowly from the soil of continual criticism and a search for an adequate understanding of the way the world actually operated. In short, I view criticism and ultimately building and embracing a political and economic position as going hand in hand. I find much too limiting any argument that sees them as following one behind the other—crystallized political program *then* viable criticism. This is simply not an adequate description of the way alternative positions have been built in the past.[29]

That is why ongoing criticism of the humanistic position and the continued articulation of educational programs like Newmann's are so important today. It is not just that we can show humanists where "they are weak and wrong" and, hence, give them some educational and political teeth. Just as important is the fact that criticism among all of the positions enables the critic to clarify his or her own stance, to create a thoughtful position that integrates educational, political, and economic issues into a larger structural analysis and program.

This project itself has served just such a useful purpose. It goes far toward clarifying some of the basic points of contention among the various persuasions represented by the participants. Some major issues obviously remain. Yet, as committed educators and members of a larger social polity, we still must find effective ways to act. One of our most critical problems now is the identification of strategies and programs that both humanists and "critical theorists" can accept provisionally. Such a coalition might, no doubt, be relatively short-lived as further issues emerge. In the argumentation between the groups, however, lie the seeds for further progress. If humanists speak only to themselves and critical theorists disdain talking to others of a different persuasion, then no genuine movement toward a fuller understanding of educational issues can be gained. There will probably not be agreement among all of us. But only through the ongoing conflict among competing intellectual and programmatic traditions can each position grow.

Those of us whose perspective tends to be grounded in neo-Marxist and critical soil must not lose sight of the concern of existentially and humanistically inclined educators for the "real person." But I am ever more convinced that, if such a concern is to have any real meaning, it can only come from an enlarged commitment to, and action for, a more just and equal set of social and economic institutions. While the concern for an individual's personal human meanings is certainly not trivial, without a constant search for a political and economic arrangement that will enable it to be a real possibility, it may be merely one more of those many bandwagons educators so like to ride. I, for one, am tired of riding.

Robert M. O'Kane

The Fourth Face of Humanism

At Issue...

Is it conceivable that we are experiencing yet another pathway to some educational Nirvana—this time guided by that most credulous of all exhortations: "humanistic education"? There is much evidence to support this possibility. One sees increasing attention in the literature, in research activities, in school curricula, and in the religious, political, economic, and social spheres of society to something loosely called "humanistic." When one wishes to suggest that his neighbor, or friend, or employer, or teacher stands tall in one's sight, there is no more honored term than to suggest that the person is a "real human being," or that he is a "fine humanitarian."

It is too simplistic to suggest that we are all suddenly becoming concerned with the human condition because of a new awareness, or sensitivity, or feeling of remorse that perhaps we have heretofore neglected the *human* side of matters. I doubt that any of these factors has given rise to what appears to be, from many sources, our latest grand jeté on the road to that Nirvana.

Concern for the human condition is as old as mankind, and it could very well have been more seriously attended by so-called primitive man than by many of his successors. Thoughtful people have always been seriously concerned with the human condition. Or, stated another way, one might safely say that all of mankind has, at one time or another, been concerned with it. This automatically qualifies all of us as humanists, and correctly so.

One of my major concerns is that this quality, this *essence* of humanism, may become the target of specialists, whether in education, or religion, or poverty programs. In our newfound eagerness to counteract the presumed "nonhumanistic" emphases, we may embark upon the same dogmatic, specialized course pursued by other manipulators who apparently felt that the only way to examine an element, a problem, a piece of art or technology, a belief, a principle, or a behavior, was to "break it down," to fragment it, to subdivide it, and "man does not exist to be subdivided, for to subdivide him is to execute him."[1]

Are we about to try to exercise the greatest temerity of all by moving to dogmatize and specialize *humanism*? I do not restrict the possibility that this could occur to the areas of education and schooling (although that is the major focus here). It has already become evident with respect to religion and certain secular movements that might be termed areligious or antireligious.

This, then, is what I see as the major issue with which we must deal: Are some of us preparing to add "humanism" to the list of choices in the curricula, to add it as a requirement in the preparation of teachers and other educators, to use it to counter the scientific-technological drives of the society? Can humanism be comprehended, or should it be, as an option among other choices available to mankind? Or should we understand, once and for all time, that humanism is "a point of view," a "philosophy of mankind," "an ideal pattern supposed to reveal the true nature of man and the task for which he was born," and "just as humanism means that there exists a common humanity beyond all divisiveness, so humanism also means that a unitary nature unites scientist and humanist alike."[2]

If one accepts the definition that "humanism is the essence of all disciplines of the human mind," what does this description have to do with "humanistic education"? Not very much, in my opinion. And that might be listed as the second, and lesser, issue with which I am concerned here. I say lesser not because it is not significant, but rather to put the term "humanistic education" in proper perspective and perhaps cause its advocates to give attention to a larger concern—the pervasive and elusive character of humanism itself. For once in our academic and intellectual concerns, let us not react impulsively by assuming that the whole affair is really an effort to describe and prescribe a perfectly rational being.

The motivation or interest in "humanistic education" certainly is not subversive, certainly not evil or selfish; it is probably championed in good faith. But it would appear that much of what one reads or hears about "humanistic education" corroborates its major failing: it lacks description, primarily because it fails to recognize and distinguish properly that which it purports to be seeking—humanism—and replaces the complexity and wholeness of humanism with a specialized substitute—humanistic education. My general reactions to the presentations and discussions that appear in this volume are those of an observer rather than a critic, which was my role. It seems that we all share an uneasy intellectual liaison with humanism, but we are not quite prepared to move from the passion of the liaison to a full, meaningful involvement and commitment because we are, with proper humility, not sure of the condition or the implications. The search and research generated by this tentative liaison were intended, it seemed to me, to determine whether theoretical, substantive, and procedural essences might be uncovered.

The project attempted, I believe, not only that serious undertaking but also tried to focus attention on the possible alternative danger of responding with typically simplistic responses to the passion of the moment rather than to the persisting and pervasive values formed by serious reflection. The presentations demonstrate the intellectual struggle to get beyond liaison and come to grips with essences, but the problems are evident.

In one of the presentations there were several references to "human resources," "human relations," "humanizing education through organizational and structuring efforts in educational institutions," and "clearly human resources is the school to which most contemporary humanists subscribe." This shows, I think, Sergiovanni's struggle to state his case with "passion," and yet he stops short of a full declaration.

Another, entitled "A Critical Analysis of the Social and Economic Limits to the Humanizing of Education," was interesting and enlightening, but, again, it did not address itself to the essential of "humanizing education." It did, and in good form, do what Feinberg later stated was his purpose: "to recall the truism [that the school cannot be understood in isolation from the society], to take it seriously, and to see what light it can shed on the question of educational reform."

There was also emphasis on "human development, personal development, and moral development," and Mosher is persuaded that "a progressive development of human rationality, character, and social responsiveness and action *is* possible through education." I can agree, but I am curious as to the descriptions, possibilities, and limits of rationality, character, and social responsibility. Is it not part of our humanism always to be somewhat irrational and to learn how to live with it?

A further statement by Mosher helps to clarify some of my personal reactions to his presentation. He says: "That is, we have reasonable evidence now that it is feasible through education to *stimulate human development as modern psychology understands it.*" (Emphasis mine.) This again illustrates to me the absence of a description of humanism, and the further problem of proceeding to prescribe, through psychological means, how we will improve "human development" through education; perhaps the author assumes that this is humanism.

This same presentation brings out another of my concerns: we seem prone to separate our roles, or personalities, and set them up as sort of balancing, or distinct, one from the other, so that we say we are, at a particular instant, speaking as "teacher," in another instant as "psychologist," and in another instant as "humanist." It seems to me that this helps to illustrate the substance of a larger issue, namely, that we still do not see humanism as an essence in all of us and that we do not want to admit that all of us are humanists—not just those who suggest it is their specialty.

The last of the presentations I comment on also helps to illuminate what I feel to be part of our problem. It gives attention to the need for a "social action" emphasis in education and suggests that "the challenge, of course, is to distinguish between humanistic and nonhumanistic forms of social action." Humanistic is equated with "good," and nonhumanistic is equated with "bad." Newmann states the difficulty of defining humanism; instead, he stipulates three major criteria considered essential if "instruction on social action is to help humanize education." These criteria are listed as: "social action must occur in a context of rational reflection; the ends and means of social action must be justified by the students with reference to principles of representative democracy and principles of justice; the social action experience of students must contribute to their sense of personal competence."

Again, it is difficult to quarrel with the substance of the presentation as it describes the need for emphasis on social action in the curriculum, but the fact remains that we still have no clear understanding about humanism, which Newmann acknowledges by saying that "to make social action a part of the school curriculum will not necessarily 'humanize' education."

I am not taking issue with the substance of any of the presentations. I am, instead, reacting to the larger concern of "what do we mean by humanism in education?" And I feel that we are still groping with that concern. This is laudable, but there is a danger in oversimplifying, dogmatizing, and specializing something we do not fully comprehend as yet, and it is too precious to be subjected to such dangers.

Antecedents from Which . . .

I stated earlier that each of the species Homo sapiens qualifies as a humanist by the obvious fact that each of us is human and each of us, at some time, considers that condition and wonders about it. That helps to clarify the argument at a base level as to whether a humanist can only be a self-ordained or qualified specialist in the concerns of humanism. Clearly this is not so, but the response adds a further challenge: Can those who come closer to that essence, humanism, help point the way for the rest of us?

As humanists, we do not all view humanism in the same way. Nor is it wise to suggest that the form of humanism is extant in some curriculum, or constitution, or set of laws, or arrangement of dogmas. The serious problem stems from a combination of linguistic-semantic-cultural-religious-historical confusions. It is these confusions that tend to make humanism respond in so many ways to individual perceptions or motives.

The problem, so common with most of us, seems to be that we allow a term to mean what we want it to mean and we have a free substitution system that allows the terms "humane," "humanitarian," "humanists," and "humanism" to serve interchangeably when addressing ourselves to the "opposite" of the term "scientific." Further, there is a tendency to assume that the "humanities," a selected group of studies that generally includes literature, language, philosophy, and the fine and creative arts, are the academic bins out of which come the concerns of the humanist. The concerns of the scientist, ergo, come out of an academic bin labeled "the sciences." Our responses are often not visceral; they are uttered spontaneously and with attention to particular instances of human actions. We are inclined to treat humanism much as we do many other strong words or concepts—almost as a slogan, with strong moral and partisan overtones but without much careful speculation.

Howard Mumford Jones suggests that "Americans have substituted something called humanities for humanism, and make them a third part of knowledge."[3] This reaction seeks to balance the specializations of science and the social sciences (both assumed to be nonhumanistic). This has resulted in a third specialization, and readily found experts who, using the humanities, took on the proprietary rights to the areas and reserved to themselves the title of humanist. This is, of course, an untenable claim, but it illustrates the long and fruitless quarrel among scientists, social scientists, and "humanists" as to who most nearly responds to the commonweal.

The humanities are most clearly thought of as parts of the American academic curriculum, paradoxically no more and no less "humane" than science or social science ... the only "humane" aspect of the humanities is that they can be used for the purposes of humanism.

Humanistic scholarship is nothing more than the professional employment, for professional purposes in the humanities, of technical modes for the advancement of knowledge.

An archaeologist dusting off potsherds ... a student of Sartre trying to distinguish the effect on the For-itself and the In-itself of the principle of destruction .... a musicologist passing on the authenticity of a score supposedly by Orlando di Lasso .... are adding to knowledge in their several fields and are therefore practicing humanistic scholarship. They are representatives of humanistic *expertise*.

[But] ... they will not be humane because they specialize in the humanities; they will be humane only in proportion as they interpret what they do philosophically.[4]

The most significant question remains: What is humanism, the end we seek? It is *not* the practice of being humane, it is *not* the expertise of humanistic scholarship, and it does *not* reside exclusively in curriculum arrangements called the humanities. Humanism is a particular or peculiar property of any religion, movement, cult, or educational curriculum except in the sense that it is understood that humanism transcends all in that it is the essence of mankind itself.

It must be granted that "humanism," the term, is derived from mankind's concern for himself. There is common agreement as to who and what a human being is, as distinguished from other forms of life. We do not refer to animals or plants as having human characteristics. Although some animal forms share similar characteristics in a biological and physical sense with humans, the fact remains that it is not man's similarity to other forms of life that is paramount. Rather, what is most significant is man's unique difference from other forms of life. It is the uniqueness, the ability to reason, to think, to create, to leave behind evidences of cultural development, plus a deep-felt and persistent drive to *know who he is and why he is here*—a kind of transcendental curiosity—that serves to distinguish man from other forms of life.

Mankind chooses to look for answers to the question of who he is from a variety of points of view. One cannot look upon this as a negative approach, or as one that should be nullified in favor of a prescribed answer. It is useful to have many roads of inquiry to such an incomprehensible question if the purpose is to seek comprehension. There is danger if we are convinced of *the* answer by reason of our failure to be concerned as human beings, and thus vulnerable to ill-considered, less-than-thoughtful answers. It is probably wise to be suspicious of those who would try to convince us that they have exclusive answers to the question of the human condition, and to be more receptive, but still to question those who would suggest that they are prepared to help each human being seek answers to the question. In our subjective, wondering selves we have, in all ages, found someone or some ideal that seems to help us along the way to a higher humanity. It seems, in retrospect, that the leader, or the idea, was one that urged man to look to himself, to "know thyself, and so to know."

Catherine Roberts, a botanist who altered her scientific career in 1961 to devote her attention to ethical, evolutionary, and religious aspects of biological and medical advance, suggests in a paper[5] that the historical antecedents of contemporary humanism provide insight into some of the major motivating factors that have resulted in today's concerns with this problem. She characterizes the "three faces of humanism" as "divine-centered," "man-centered," and "life-centered" and proceeds to trace the antecedents of each.

Roberts reminds us that prehistoric and historic man has had "religious interests and inclinations," and, thus, one can assume that the "original face of humanism was divine-centered." This does not suggest that the "divine-centered" face was, or is, synonymous with established, organized religion. Roberts would argue that organized religions, including Christianity, "often tend to be more concerned with secular power than with ethical enlightenment."

Ancient and modern man has tended to speculate, and, as Frankfort[6] and others tell us, "its main concern is with man—his nature and his problems, his values and his destiny. For man does not quite succeed in becoming a scientific object to himself. His need of transcending chaotic experience and conflicting facts leads him to seek a metaphysical hypothesis that may clarify his urgent problems."

Different civilizations gave varying emphases to gods and man and nature. Some saw God as transcendent and different; some saw God as immanent; some saw harmony in man, nature, and the gods; some saw man as preeminent.

The Greeks, who greatly influenced modern civilizations of the West, broke away from earlier patterns of thought and philosophized that "reason is acknowledged as the highest arbiter . . . and in the systems of the Greeks the human mind recognizes its own. It may take back what is created or change or develop it." The Greeks were seeking *reasoned* thought in response to *mythopoeic thought.* Our society took that emphasis on reason, honed it in a Cartesian fashion, mixed it with good old American pragmatism, and now, like everything else, suggests that it can be packaged as "humanism."

Roberts explains that the Greeks, about 2,500 years ago, were probably responsible for the emergence of "man-centered humanism." "Although man must thus forever remain a mortal, unable to partake of divinity, his own humanness, the Greeks reasoned, was such a great and wonderful thing that he could not do better than to keep his thought centered upon himself rather than upon the divine which transcends him."

Plato, and later Christ, did not accept the narrow point of view of the Greeks, and both believed that "God, not man, provided the ethical measure." Later, the combination of the Renaissance, with its emphasis on individual freedom and the questioning of authority and dogma, together with the growing influence of science, served to turn Europeans toward a "man-centered humanism." And so, one can see something of our heritage.

But Roberts goes on to suggest that a newer "face of humanism" is emerging. It is "life-centered" and opts for an "essential Oneness of life that refuses to harbour any thoughts of human superiority . . . stressing the kinship between human and non-human life." But it is clear that *man* is the one to whom these advocates turn in their attempts to improve the world. They do not turn to plants or animals.

Each "face of humanism" turns to *man*—some to the exclusion of any authority, some to include a transcendent authority. Roberts argues strongly that the answer, among these three options, depends upon "which vision has the greatest ethical sweep." Her choice is divine-centered humanism because she feels that "ethics is not a man-made creation but man's superhuman link with the divine."

Elusive, But Worth Searching for . . .

Man's humanity and man's inhumanity—discourses about each fill books and engage all of us in discussion. There is much evidence of each; whether the balance sheet is equally weighted is sometimes hard to know. We like to think that the signs of man's humanity outdistance those that reflect his inhumanity. If we agree that "good" has infinite possibilities and "evil" has finite limitations, then we may be expressing an optimism that we are indeed most concerned with the human side of the ledger, and have a general abhorrence of the inhuman side. But we cannot just know that or be expected to know that. We have to be educated to it. Education is culture, and culture, which man creates, is education. There is no separatism; there can only be a oneness. Part of that education has to be concerned with what the reality of the human condition is—both sides of the ledger have to be known and acknowledged. To know man's humanity one must at the same time know the qualifying other side, which is man's inhumanity.

Not yet knowing with any precision what the human condition, humanism, is, or is capable of, we can badly err by encapsulating it, by building models of it to be emulated, or by being conditioned to that which some would suggest to be the model rational man—undisturbed by the fact that, being so, he has no longer to confront either his possibilities or his limitations. This is not the same as arguing for the possibility that an ideal man can exist, "for if men, who are in fact always imperfect could reach perfection, they would only be realizing all that their natural animal being might conceivably be."[7]

Education, in its broadest and most inclusive meaning, has to write its curricula around the central issue—humanism. That means finding ways to educate one to understand more fully the human condition in all of its possible attainments of rationalism, but also to understand more fully and cope more effectively with all of the vexations of man's obvious irrationality.

This calls, I think, for an emphasis on "thinking about" the human condition, in all of its complexities, through means that are more concerned with the *intrinsic* than with the *extrinsic*. Overemphasis on the extrinsic calls for one to be *accountable* or liable to the extrinsic force. The needed emphasis on the intrinsic calls for one to be *responsible* to oneself and to one's fellowman. This is an important concept in Gregory Baum's work, *Man Becoming*.[8] Baum, a professor of theology and a Catholic priest, takes the earlier work of Maurice Blondel, a theologian in France, as a starting point for his arguments that man is not merely a receiver of messages and stimuli from without. Quoting from the works of Blondel, Baum suggests that a major problem of the Catholic Church was the insistence on seeing "God [as] divine facing man from beyond history, and divine revelations is the communication of heavenly truths to men caught in their own limited earthly knowledge." This is what Blondel called "extrinsicism." He went on, as Baum tells us, to say that "the only message modern man can accept is a truth that has an intrinsic relationship to life, a truth that answers men's questions or corresponds in some way to their experience of reality."

Baum, with Blondel, is arguing that "divine revelation," or a possible transcendence, or advanced humanity, takes place *in* human life and that "truth is present in man's action.... [I]f we reflect on man's action, we find implicit in it his values, his vision of life, his view of reality.... [T]he evaluation of life and the discernment of meaning take place in human action before they become concepts in the human mind... [so] living is prior to philosophizing.... [T]he proper method for finding the truth, therefore, is to study human life, human experience, human history, and to discern the structure of reality implicit in human action." It is then that man seeks answers that suggest a transcendent relationship.

Perhaps I am now beginning to wonder if I am talking about the elusive "humanistic education." I am trying desperately to avoid the term because it still suggests to me a narrow thing, far too descriptive of extrinsic emphases, not allowing of the very subjectivity and dignity of man, his intrinsic being, his necessity to express himself, and to explain himself—that which is his essence.

This is terribly risky. Does anyone dare to make education an encounter of man seeking his reality, and, perhaps as a result, his greater humanity? Or is man too fearful an animal to be loosed upon himself, and must he, therefore, be properly constrained? Where does this all leave us? Personally, I would hope that we are left uncertain, but that our intellectual uncertainty is ever seeking a higher plane.

I see dangers in our feverish attempts to objectify something we are not yet (and may never be) certain about—that which we call humanism. I am fearful that we will assume that it can be captured, shaped, and called a course, a program, or an optional curriculum to be offered by "experts only." I do not mean that we should stop asking, by no means, but I do believe it is most important that we begin at the beginning, by asking who we are and risking all the possibilities in the world as to responses. Man is the measure of all things. Let's start there, rather than trying to make him respond to our primitive measures. These, it seems to me, are intent upon subdividing and fragmenting (to achieve a more efficient measure) the very essence with which we are concerned—man's dignity.

Is it so bad for us to admit that we just do not fully comprehend the human condition, the essence called humanism, and to go on seeking this as our major purpose in education at large? We are impulsively seeking to manufacture images of man to our own limited perceptions. Rabbi Abraham Joshua Heschel reminds us that "Doubt is an act in which the mind inspects its own ideas; wonder is an act in which the mind confronts the universe.... Wonder or radical amazement is the chief characteristic of the religious man's attitude toward history and nature.... There is thus only one way to wisdom: awe. Forfeit your sense of awe, let your conceit diminish your ability to revere, and the universe becomes a marketplace for you. The loss of awe is the great block to insight."[9]

The possibilities and the measure of man reside in man. The function of education is to draw it out, to try to see what is within. In education it would be a display of wisdom if we were to suggest that we are not ready to come to closure about the human condition, that humanism is not a fixed thing to be prearranged for us, that we are not just "human beings" but "humans becoming." To assume that we *know* sets limits to education and deters us from seeking a fourth "face"—the "ultrahuman" one Pierre Teilhard de Chardin optimistically looked to.

Epilogue

James B. Macdonald

Toward a Platform for Humanistic Education

Overview

Humanism, as a historical label, is not confined to education. There are people in scientific and technical pursuits who qualify as humanists. Further, a growing number of individuals who are theologically oriented and who have readily been identified in the past as humanists are concerned that the spiritual or moral capacity of people is being blunted, underdeveloped, or anesthetized. Nor is this concern limited to religious thinkers. It has adherents in areas related to social policy, architecture, literature, history, and the performing arts, among others. Generally such people are identified with two major ideas: first, we can and must solve human problems by exercising human capacities (among these, rationality), and, second, human endeavors should be seen in human perspective, not simply as achievements in and of themselves.

Humanistic education has, however, become part of the educational vocabulary during the past ten years in the sense of broad awareness and acceptance. Definitions differ according to proponents, but there is a general focus that appears in varied forms. This is a focus on education for human beings—in contrast to educational practices thought to be dehumanizing, to deal with limited aspects of human capability, or to focus narrowly upon role requirements designed for our present society.

Humanistic education reflects both a contemporary reaction to perceived negative school practices and the historically perceived implementation of more progressive educational practices. Movement toward behavioral objectives, instructional systems, performance contracting, test score accountability, and similar phenomena is often seen as a potential threat to the human educational process. This threat is, however, bracketed by the continuous concern for education of the "whole person," education related to the development of individuals, and education that reflects awareness of the total dimensions of humanism.

It seems apparent that humanistic education has been reinforced, at least ideologically, by major cultural phenomena such as concern for racial and general civil rights, women's liberation, ecological responsibility, the waste of war (and other violence), the rediscovery (in both religious and psychological terms) of levels of consciousness, and growing economic inequities.

There are at least three major varieties of proposals for humanistic education (not mutually exclusive, of course). For lack of better terms they can be identified as substantive, psychological, and social.

Substantive concerns focus on the balance and significance of the subject matter of the curriculum in terms of its ability to develop full human capacity. Proponents of these proposals have pointed out that the humanities have a secondary concern in determining the curriculum. Often related subjects are elective in later years, and they frequently are the last to be added or the first to be dropped in earlier years. Even when they are taught (for example, English), the focus is more often on technical and analytical approaches (grammar and syntax) than on human possibilities (semantics or literary interpretation). It is also noted that subjects such as psychology, anthropology, and sociology as directly focused studies of people are even marginal in the social studies areas. Substantive proponents argue that human survival requires that people be sensitive and alive to possibilities of human existence that can only be developed or readily encountered through training in the humanities (philosophy, history, the arts, literature, and social studies) and through the encouragement of creative vision and imagination. Most curricular proposals that stem from this perspective come under the label "General Education."

In the field of education *psychological* humanism has taken a major leaf from the book of the "third force" psychologists, and, to a lesser extent, from that of the "ego" psychologists. It represents a definite and strong rejection of behavioral psychology. There is a focus upon human growth and development (as being predominant over learning theory), placed in the context of a complex person-environment set of interactions where certain projected qualities are recognized as "good." Psychological humanism has led to a major concern for "affective education," and proposals to encourage the development of healthy self-concepts, authentic feelings, attitudinal awareness, and values, since they are seen as touchstones for reaching a full human psychological capacity, have been numerous.

Social humanists, who are somewhat fewer in number and probably related historically to the social reconstructionists, take a broader view of the potential of schooling in society. They reject both the individual and his psychological development as being the key to education. They are more prone to blame social structures within and beyond the school for the alienation and the delimitation of human possibility and potentiality, and they frequently focus upon the "hidden curriculum" implicit in cultural structures as being the source of attitudes and concepts of self. Social humanists are often concerned that school programs be clearly conceptualized in terms of the way people live together in schools (for example, students' rights or, more broadly, "shared governance"), and that the programs encourage student commitment and action in the community environment (for example, local ecological problems). Generally, social humanists would prefer a substantive emphasis upon the analysis of social structures and the interaction of human nature and institutions.

The Symposium Presentations

The presentations that appear in this volume do not deal with all three humanistic orientations. The psychological and social positions are well represented, but there are no proponents of either the substantive or theological orientations. This is most likely due to the emphasis upon research in humanistic education that guided the selection of participants in the original design of the program. It is worth noting that there apparently has not been much research even in the areas represented, although developmental and evaluative activities are mentioned frequently.

It is apparent from the presentations and from discussions among the participants that a major distinction may be made between social and psychological humanists. The dividing line is determined by the boundaries of conceptualization within which research and developmental activity takes place. David Aspy and Ralph Mosher, for example, have a straightforward psychological orientation, and they delimit their concern about schools to the development of individual behavior in any effort to promote more humane and humanistic activity.

Michael Apple, Nancy King, and Walter Feinberg, on the other hand, use social criticism as their guide, and the boundary of their analysis is the broader society, which serves as a lens through which they see the practices of schooling. These boundaries, or places where the participants began their analyses, affected the meaning and the interpretation of data concerning what is actually happening in schools.

Essentially, the question became one not of school reform but of more basic radical (root-level) social change. Social critics charge that psychologically oriented reform that focuses upon individuals and specific school settings is simply ameliorative if such efforts do not relate to broader social realms. This type of reform activity, it would appear, only provides adjustment to the status quo; it does not facilitate the kinds of changes that are truly needed. The very values for which reformers strive are subverted in the process if they do not bring about the broader social change.

Any counter to this argument rests mainly upon a "reality" factor. From their perception and experiences, psychologically oriented reformers argue that "realistically" they can only make an impact on the concrete circumstances of schooling. They believe that it is important to facilitate changes wherever, for whomever, and whenever the possibility for change arises.

Underlying this disagreement between social and psychological approaches is a philosophical question concerning human nature and change. Is change best facilitated by developing individual consciousness, or is consciousness raised by changing broader social structures?

Thomas Sergiovanni suggests a major complicating factor. As one reviews the various organizational theories, one is struck by the "fact" of organization itself. Thus, taking a leaf from Max Weber's work, it may be that it is the development of bureaucratic forms of organization in the modern industrial world that has contributed most heavily to the dehumanization of human existence. John Kenneth Galbraith, for example, has noted in a number of contexts that Russia and the United States, though economically quite different, may actually be quite similar in internal functional terms when viewed from the perspective of the monolithic bureaucracy that has grown up in each situation.[1] Bureaucracy, as rationalized and ordered procedure, seems to function similarly in either a communist or a capitalist situation.

Newmann's contribution raises an interesting problem of whether the two orientations can be satisfactorily combined in programmatic terms. Newmann believes that they can, and he argues persuasively for his position. Exciting as the possibilities are in the social studies activity he advocates, in the final analysis the attempt appears to be primarily psychological-reformist in nature. This is reflected in the individual process whereby a student selects which social concerns to address. The focus is upon democratic social process rather than upon humanistic goals for society.

Substantive Humanism

The social and psychological orientations represented in this volume deal with two of the three basic referents—persons, society, and culture—for curriculum. The importance of the cultural substance, that is, the subject matter of the school, is obvious. Schooling is a situation characterized by the dynamic interaction of persons in society with cultural substance, and any complete picture of humanistic education must come squarely to grips with substantive humanism as it focuses upon our cultural heritage.

In contemporary terms one of the most compelling advocates of classical humanism is Harry Broudy.[2] It is Broudy's contention that the foundation of humanism rests on the universal substance of the various disciplines. He goes on, however, to make a strong case for providing a general education for citizens who live in a technological society. Broudy identifies three major goals and functions—didactics, heuristics, and philetics—as being basic to education. Didactics involves the presentation of skills, basic principles, and understandings from the disciplines; heuristics refers to the personal discovery by the pupil himself of what is presented didactically. Philetics, then, concentrates upon the emotional adjustment and self-development of the pupil.

This type of curriculum essentially suggests that humanistic education must bring about an immersion in the humanities, the arts, and the sciences; thereby the universal values of human culture are transmitted to learners. It is in this way that the learner becomes a participant in the evolution of culture and develops an appreciation of how difficult the struggle for knowledge has been. This, according to Broudy and others, constitutes the only uniquely viable function of the schools.

What this amounts to prescriptively is a curriculum that begins in the early preschool years with considerable concern for discovery and the emotional well-being of students, moves into a concerted didactic effort to teach skills and ideals in the elementary grades, and increases the didactic efforts at the secondary level in an attempt to present the basic ideals and principles of the disciplines. There should be an effort to translate the basic ideals and principles into interdisciplinary form and to make them personally relevant. Strong emphasis must be placed upon those disciplines called humanistic (history, literature, philosophy, the arts, and others) if a humanizing education is to be cultivated.

Seen in the context of this volume, the substantive approach toward humanizing education becomes a commitment to developing a human consciousness of the basic knowledge and values in our culture. Those who support the substantive approach feel that it is this fundamental role of the school that justifies its existence in a humanistic orientation.

What the substantive orientation needs to round out its potential is a research and evaluation methodology appropriate to the nature of the cultural material. And it is abundantly clear that the experimental and theoretical approaches characterizing the methodology of the social and psychological orientations are incapable of addressing substantive problems.

Elliot Eisner suggests that a paradigm for examining humanistic areas of the curriculum may well be the literary criticism model.[3] It would allow an approach to research and evaluation with an aesthetic model, criteria, and methodological procedures. Classroom activity could be described in terms of aesthetic criticism.

Joseph Schwab outlined a possible methodology for dealing with the substantive approach.[4] He believes that theoretical activities have created grave difficulties in terms of both curriculum and schooling because they have led to breakdown between theory and practice. He proposes the study of curriculum from the perspective of the "practical," which he says differs in method, has different sources for its problems, and has a subject matter distinctively different from the theoretical. Inherent in Schwab's position is the contention that we possess no practical data base for much of what goes on in classrooms. We know very little about the actual problems or practical decisions that have been or can be made in the context of teaching the various disciplines. As a remedy for this situation Schwab feels that we would be much better served in developing programs or accumulating knowledge by using a methodology based on the "practical" and suggests a method of "deliberation" as opposed to the theoretical method of "induction." As he sees it, the deliberative method is not a linear, step-by-step one. Rather, it is complex, fluid, and transactional. It aims at identifying what is desirable and deciding how to achieve what is desirable—or, if necessary, how to alter the goal to make it feasible.

The first methodological step is to immerse the decision maker in the phenomena of his practical endeavors. Even though the problems that arise may not always be clear, as alternative possibilities for deliberation arise they tend to be clarified and directed. Finding solutions becomes the major focus of activity in the interplay between means and ends, problems, and data. It is in the process of finding solutions that "policy" becomes important to deliberation. Policy, in essence, is the consequence of previous deliberation. It may guide deliberation, but only to the extent that it reflects the circumstances that exist at the time of deliberation. What it is necessary to recognize is that policy can be obsolete since circumstances are constantly changing.

This deliberative process restricted to the practical can provide the data base needed for research purposes. This might be in the form of descriptive analysis of what actually occurs, of policy statements formed from deliberation, or of retrospective reflection upon the actuality of teaching. As such, it would provide considerable insight into what actually happens in schools. Out of the process could come a language of the practical that might have certain universal characteristics and possibilities for curriculum and instruction.

Another methodology that might fruitfully be utilized in research on substantive humanistic education has been presented by Paulo Freire in the context of literacy programs for adults.[5] Here the integration of theory and praxis as a dialectical relationship is the critical procedure aimed at liberating persons from social, personal, and cultural constraints. Freire proposes the use of theory as a basis for providing the individual with a lens through which to see, and each individual is to test out the theory in his own praxis, reflect upon its fruitfulness in that context, and utilize the meaningful personal insights that arise from this experience. The value of this approach rests in the reality that one probably never approaches praxis without some conceptual framework in mind, and the methodology, which creates a dialectic for gathering data and insights through a self-reflective process in the transaction between consciousness and human activity, could also be a helpful way of researching the activity of schooling.

The Problem of a Humanistic Educational "Platform"

The most fundamental problem that arises from reading and discussion in the area of humanistic education is the vagueness and ambiguity of the platform from which educators theorize, speculate, and prescribe programs. A platform, in this sense, is grounded in the assumptions and values that underlie humanistic education efforts.

These broad orientations toward humanistic education make little sense without a commitment to human liberation. The liberal arts were intended to free the individual from the bondage of ignorance and parochialism. At the same time they provide the cultural substance of humanity that increases the number of alternative possibilities available to the individual and allows individual potential to unfold. These goals are certainly no less true for the social and psychological orientations. The differences appear to lie primarily in the focus: whether one looks to social and organizational structure, individual development, or cultural substance as the point of departure.

From beginning to end the one thing that remains constant is the concern of humanistic education, which is the individual. This must be accepted carefully and thoughtfully, for there is danger that the individual may be abstractly divorced from his social situation and his cultural substance. Individual possibilities and potentialities remain within the context of a concrete human being who lives in a social world and within a cultural milieu. The heart of the matter, thus, is based upon the concept of the individual.

According to Stephen Lukes, an analysis of the history of the idea of individualism rests on four key considerations: respect for human dignity, autonomy, privacy, and self-actualization or development. Lukes points out that there is an important distinction between abstract individualism and concrete individualism. Abstract individualism treats the individual apart from the community. Many examples of this are stated in political, economic, epistemological, and methodological terms. As Lukes says:

> The crucial point about this conception [abstract individual] is that the relevant features of individuals determine the ends which social arrangements are held to fulfill, whether these features ... called instincts, faculties, needs, desires, rights, etc. are assumed or given, independently of a social context. This perspective of fixed and invariant human *psychological* features leads to an *abstract* conception of the individual who is seen as merely the bearer of those features, which determine his behavior, and specify his interests, needs, and rights.[6]

I would argue that most theories built upon developmental grounds (those of Piaget, Dewey, Erickson, Bruner, Kohlberg, and others) fall into the abstract category. As such, they are open to the criticism of the critical theorists—that to operate on this basis is simply to leave the individual at the mercy of the interests of the broader society.

Abstract individualism has historical antecedents that precede the clear expression of the "social construction of reality" and the sociohistorical determination of experience, but it is really only with Hegel that these ideas were clearly formulated. Thus, secular, concrete individualism represents a post-Hegelian (at least in time) movement. For example, from Locke to the present day there is presupposed a picture of civil society where members are independent centers of consciousness and possess interests, wants, natures, purposes, needs, and other attributes that do not depend upon their context.

Concrete individualism, on the other hand, comes from our Judeo-Christian religious traditions and arises in its ethical variety most clearly with Kierkegaard and the later existential movement. It conceives of the individual as a living person, an agent of choice, a source of intentional purposes (yet to be discovered), able to value activities and involvements (yet to be discovered), and capable of possibilities (yet to be discovered) for self-actualization.

On a common ground, then, it would appear that humanistic education has a platform that is reflected in Gibson Winter's suggestion that *liberation, participation,* and *pluralism* are critical concepts we must deal with.[7] Programs of humanistic education will vary according to local circumstances, points of application, and varied interpretation of these concepts. It would, in fact, be antithetical to the humanistic platform to standardize or systemize *a* humanistic program for general use.

The participatory aspect of humanistic education focuses upon the social situation. In so doing it implies the participation of those persons who will be involved in living with programs and activities designed to achieve programmatic goals. The critical participants will, of course, be the staff and students (who in today's school world are often the least involved). The difficulties of creating meaningful participatory situations in terms of traditional operating procedures should not deter the attempt to do this since participation, besides being an end to achieve, is critically related to all of Lukes's key considerations. Participation in making decisions that affect one's life has value *in the doing* as well as *in the outcome.*

The concept of pluralism recognizes individuality, both in terms of cultural differences in encountering substantive material and in terms of individual differences in expanding human possibility and potentiality. As Broudy is quick to point out, the public schools cannot educationally justify themselves unless they have an agreed upon purpose, which he sees as the encounter with the cultural substance of the disciplines. A monolithic and standardized format or methodology for this encounter is not, however, necessary. In fact, any hope of a liberating experience requires that such an encounter be a unique experience for each individual within a common framework. Pluralism, therefore, constitutes a plea for allowing and helping each person to see alternative possibilities and develop their own potentialities within the context of a historical, social, and cultural situation.

The platform we seek, then, must begin with granting each individual his "right" to be seen as having inherent worth and dignity. The intention is to facilitate individual liberation by providing social structures and cultural substance that open possibilities of becoming the best person one can become in a continuing process of self-actualization.

Two fundamental value questions inform and form the human condition: What is the meaning of human life? How shall we live together? These two concerns are intricately interwoven. Both are integral to humanistic education and to the moral and ethical aspects of the educational enterprise. Surely any curriculum is someone's idea of an environment that will facilitate the development or maintenance of a "good" society, with "good" people, leading to the "good" life.

It is here that one finds the "theological" orientations. The major identifiable source of values that are shared by humanistic educators in this country arise out of Judeo-Christian traditions. The dynamic impulse and desire for bringing about progressive human betterment is that core of basic spiritual value found in this and in other human religious traditions. This, at the very least, is most often the source of such values as justice, equality, fraternity, and liberty.

There is, then, a humanistic educational concern in the most general sense to examine fundamentally theological questions of meaning and living that relate to concepts of the person and social democracy. This, too, must become a recognized part of any platform.

The knowledge of "truth" gathered over the ages and found in the universals of our cultural disciplines, combined with the "knowledge of fact" as to the impact of social structures that oppress and alienate, must further be infused with what Socrates called "truths of self," or personal truths. Before one can speak a truth, one must ask whether it is a personal truth; otherwise, one must leave it to the enumeration of others. To speak another's truth is to live a life that is not one's own. In the end each individual's integrity and wholeness become the hallmark of a truly human education.

Notes

Notes

Weller: **One Perspective on Humanistic Education**
　1. Abraham Maslow, *Motivation and Personality* (2d ed., New York: Harper and Row, 1970).
　2. Joseph Grannis, "The School as a Model of Society," *Harvard Graduate School of Education Bulletin,* 21 (Fall 1967), 15-27.
　3. Ralph W. Tyler, *Basic Principles of Curriculum and Instruction* (Chicago: University of Chicago Press, 1950).
　4. Jürgen Habermas, *Knowledge and Human Interests* (Boston: Beacon Press, 1968).
　5. *Ibid.*
　6. *Science—A Process Approach* (Washington, D.C.: American Association for the Advancement of Science, Commission on Science Education, 1968; distrib. by Xerox Educational Division, Stamford, Conn.).
　7. *Science Curriculum Improvement Study* (Chicago: Rand McNally, 1970).
　8. *Elementary Science Study* (Manchester, Mo.: Webster, Division of McGraw-Hill, 1971).
　9. A. S. Neill, *Summerhill: A Radical Approach to Child Rearing* (New York: Hart Publishing Co., 1960).
　10. See, for example, Martin Buber, *Between Man and Man* (Boston: Beacon Press, 1955); Reuel Howe, *The Miracle of Dialogue* (New York: Seabury Press, 1963).
　11. See, for example, Dwayne Huebner, "The Thingness of Educational Content," paper delivered at a conference on "Reconceptualizing Curriculum Theory," Cincinnati, Ohio, 1974, and "The Tasks of the Curriculum Theorist," in *Curriculum Theorizing: The Reconceptualists,* ed. William Pinar (Berkeley, Calif.: McCutchan Publishing Corp., 1975).
　12. Charles Hampden-Turner, *Sane Asylum: Inside the Delancey Street Foundation* (New York: Simon and Schuster, 1976).
　13. See, for example, Ralph Mosher, Norman Sprinthall, *et al.,* "Psychological Education: A Means to Promote Personal Development during Adolescence," *Counseling Psychologist,* 2 (No. 4, 1971).

Apple and *King:* **What Do Schools Teach?**
　1. Charles Silberman, *Crisis in the Classroom* (New York: Random House, 1970).

2. Herbert Gintis and Samuel Bowles, "The Contradictions of Liberal Educational Reform," in *Work, Technology, and Education,* ed. Walter Feinberg and Henry Rosemont, Jr. (Urbana: University of Illinois Press, 1975), p. 109.

3. That this is not merely an "intellectual" interest, but embodies social and ideological commitments, is examined in greater depth in Michael W. Apple, "The Adequacy of Systems Management Procedures in Education," in *Regaining Educational Leadership,* ed. Ralph H. Smith (New York: John Wiley and Sons, 1975).

4. Michael F. D. Young, "Knowledge and Control," in *Knowledge and Control,* ed. *id.* (London: Collier-Macmillan, 1971).

5. John Kennett, "The Sociology of Pierre Bourdieu," *Educational Review,* 25 (June 1973), 238.

6. On the necessity of seeing institutions relationally, see Bertell Ollman, *Alienation: Marx's Conception of Man in Capitalist Society* (New York: Cambridge University Press, 1971).

7. Daniel Kallos, "Educational Phenomena and Educational Research," report from the Institute of Education, University of Lund, Lund, Sweden, p. 7.

8. Dennis Warwick, "Ideologies, Integration and Conflicts of Meaning," in *Educability, Schools and Ideology,* ed. Michael Flude and John Ahier (London: Halstead Press, 1974), p. 94. See also Michael W. Apple, "Curriculum as Ideological Selection," *Comparative Education Review,* 20 (June 1976).

9. Bill Williamson, "Continuities and Discontinuities in the Sociology of Education," in *Educability,* ed. Flude and Ahier, pp. 10-11.

10. *Ibid.*

11. Barry Franklin, "The Curriculum Field and the Problem of Social Control, 1918-1938: A Study in Critical Theory," unpublished dissertation, University of Wisconsin, Madison, 1974, pp. 2-3.

12. *Ibid.,* pp. 4-5. It should be noted here that scientific management itself was not necessarily a neutral technology for creating more efficient institutions. It was developed as a mechanism for the further division and control of labor. This is provocatively portrayed in Harry Braverman, *Labor and Monopoly Capital: The Degradation of Work in the Twentieth Century* (New York: Monthly Review Press, 1975).

13. *Ibid.*

14. *Ibid.,* p. 317.

15. Walter Feinberg, *Reason and Rhetoric: The Intellectual Foundations of Twentieth Century Liberal Educational Policy* (New York: John Wiley and Sons, 1975).

16. Philip Jackson, *Life in Classrooms* (New York: Holt, Rinehart, and Winston, 1968).

17. Elizabeth Vallance, "Hiding the Hidden Curriculum," *Curriculum Theory Network,* 4 (Fall 1973-74), 15.

18. *Ibid.*

19. *Ibid.,* pp. 18-19.

20. Gintis and Bowles, "Contradictions of Liberal Educational Reform," p. 133. These normative meanings and personality attributes are distributed un-

equally to different "types" of students, often by social class or occupational expectation as well. Not all students get the same dispositional elements; nor are the same meanings attached to them by the distributor of cultural capital. See *ibid.*, p. 136.

21. See, e.g., Michael W. Apple, "Ivan Illich and Deschooling Society: The Politics of Slogan Systems," in *Social Forces and Schooling*, ed. Nobuo Shimahara and Adam Scrupski (New York: David McKay, 1975), pp. 337-360; Michael F. D. Young, "An Approach to the Study of Curricula as Socially Organized Knowledge," in *Knowledge and Control*, ed. *id.*, pp. 19-46.

22. Nell Keddie, "Classroom Knowledge," in *Knowledge and Control*, ed. Young, pp. 133-160.

23. Michael W. Apple, "Common Sense Categories and Curriculum Thought," in *Schools in Search of Meaning*, ed. James B. Macdonald and Esther Zaret (Washington, D.C.: Association for Supervision and Curriculum Development, 1975), pp. 116-148.

24. This, of course, is a fundamental tenet of ethnomethodological studies as well. See Peter McHugh, *Defining the Situation* (Indianapolis, Ind.: Bobbs-Merrill Co., 1968); *Ethnomethodology*, ed. Roy Turner (Baltimore: Penguin Books, 1974); Aaron Cicourel, *Cognitive Sociology* (New York: Free Press, 1974).

25. For further explication of this point, see Basil Bernstein, "On the Classification and Framing of Educational Knowledge," in *Knowledge and Control*, ed. Young, pp. 47-69.

26. Robert MacKay, "Conceptions of Children and Models of Socialization," in *Recent Sociology. No. 5: Childhood and Socialization*, ed. Hans Peter Dreitzel (New York: Macmillan, 1973).

27. An excellent treatment of this "ethnographic" tradition can be found in Philip E. D. Robinson, "An Ethnography of Classrooms," *Contemporary Research in the Sociology of Education*, ed. John Eggleston (London: Methuen and Co., 1974), pp. 251-266.

28. For a more complete discussion of this research project, see Nancy R. King, "The Hidden Curriculum and the Socialization of Kindergarten Children," unpublished dissertation, University of Wisconsin, Madison, 1976.

29. Thomas R. Bates, "Gramsci and the Theory of Hegemony," *Journal of the History of Ideas*, 36 (April-June 1975), 360.

30. Michael W. Apple, "The Hidden Curriculum and the Nature of Conflict," *Interchange*, 2 (No. 4, 1971), 29-40.

31. Habermas' arguments about patterns of communicative competence in advanced industrial "orders" are quite interesting as interpretive schemata here. See, for example, Jürgen Habermas, "Towards a Theory of Communicative Competence," in *Recent Sociology. No. 2: Patterns of Communicative Behavior*, ed. Hans Peter Dreitzel (New York: Macmillan, 1970), pp. 115-148; Trent Schroyer, *The Critique of Domination* (New York: George Braziller, 1973).

32. Rachael Sharp and Anthony Green, *Education and Social Control: A Study in Progressive Primary Education* (Boston: Routledge and Kegan Paul, 1975).

33. *Ibid.*, p. 13.
34. *Ibid.*, pp. 110-112. See also the provocative analysis found in Basil Bernstein, *Class, Codes, and Control.* Vol. III: *Towards a Theory of Educational Transmissions* (Boston: Routledge and Kegan Paul, 1975).
35. Sharp and Green, *Education and Social Control*, p. 116.
36. *Ibid.*, p. x.
37. *Ibid.*, p. 221.

Newmann: **Social Action and Humanistic Education**

1. Much of this chapter is based on my book, *Education for Citizen Action: Challenge for Secondary Curriculum* (Berkeley, Calif.: McCutchan Publishing Corp., 1975), often without reference to specific page. New material appears primarily in the section "Criteria for Humanistic Social Action."
2. See National Association of Secondary School Principals, National Committee on Secondary Education, *American Youth in the Mid-Seventies* (Reston, Va.: the Association, 1972); National Association of Secondary School Principals, *25 Action Learning Schools* (Reston, Va.: the Association, 1974); National Commission on the Reform of Secondary Education, *The Reform of Secondary Education: A Report to the Public and the Profession* (New York: McGraw-Hill, 1973); Panel on Youth, Report of the President's Science Advisory Committee, *Youth: Transition to Adulthood* (Chicago: University of Chicago Press, 1974); Task Force '74 (a national task force for high school reform), *The Adolescent, Other Citizens and Their High Schools: A Report to the Public and the Profession* (New York: McGraw-Hill, 1975).
3. Action is defined as purposeful behavior in which a person attempts to exert influence in the environment (see *The Philosophy of Action*, ed. Alan R. White [Oxford, Eng.: Oxford University Press, 1968]; *The Nature of Human Action*, ed. Myles Brand [Glenview, Ill.: Scott, Foresman, 1970]). If behavior is construed as observable motions or moves, then action consists of behavior plus the conscious thought, purposes, or intentions employed to guide behavior. Clearly, much behavior cannot be classified as action, for it is nonpurposeful. Examples include behavior considered aimless, unconscious, nondeliberative, reflexive, or involuntary. There is also a wide range of purposeful behavior—reading a novel, meditation, rock climbing—that does not involve making an impact in the environment. "Action" here is reserved for behavior accompanied by a conscious intent to bring about some effect in the environment.
4. Much of the business of public affairs consists in determining which matters should be resolved through governmental channels. An unemployed person living in poverty might face a number of "personal" problems (poor diet, no recreation, or marital conflict), not recognized as public issues by the public at large. If the person were to advocate that public agencies help with these troubles, then heretofore private issues would enter the public arena. Often public policies are promoted precisely to deter government from encroachment on private life (e.g., prohibitions on electronic eavesdropping or legal protection of the confidentiality of doctor-patient relationships). The struggle in approving or opposing such policies is, of course, a public affair.

5. Robert W. White, "Motivation Reconsidered: The Concept of Competence," *Psychological Review*, 66 (1959), 297-333, "Competence and the Psychosexual Stages of Development," in *Nebraska Symposium on Motivation*, ed. M. Jones (Lincoln: University of Nebraska Press, 1960), "Ego and Reality in Psychoanalytic Theory," *Psychological Issues*, 3 (No. 3, 1963), and "The Concept of Healthy Personality: What Do We Really Mean?" *Counseling Psychologist*, 4 (No. 2, 1973).

6. *Id.*, "Ego and Reality," p. 35.

7. Jean Piaget, *The Construction of Reality in the Child* (New York: Basic Books, 1954; originally appeared in 1937).

8. John Dewey, *Democracy and Education* (New York: Macmillan, 1916), and *Experience and Education* (New York: Collier, 1938).

9. Lawrence Kohlberg, "From Is to Ought: How to Commit the Naturalistic Fallacy and Get Away with It in the Study of Moral Development," in *Cognitive and Developmental Epistemology*, ed. T. Mischel (New York: Academic Press, 1971).

10. Edrita Fried, *Active/Passive: The Crucial Psychological Dimension* (New York: Harper and Row, 1970).

11. M. Brewster Smith, "Competence and Socialization," in *Socialization and Society*, ed. John A. Clausen (Boston: Little, Brown, 1968), esp. p. 281.

12. James S. Coleman *et al.*, *Equality of Educational Opportunity* (Washington, D.C.: U.S. Government Printing Office, 1966).

13. Erik H. Erikson, "Identity and the Life Cycle," *Psychological Issues*, 1 (No. 1, 1959), and *Identity: Youth and Crisis* (New York: Norton, 1968).

14. A. H. Maslow, *Motivation and Personality* (New York: Harper, 1954).

15. John Rawls, *A Theory of Justice* (Cambridge, Mass.: Harvard University Press, 1971), p. 84.

16. This conception of moral agent depends upon the work of Stuart Hampshire, *Thought and Action* (New York: Viking, 1959); Richard M. Hare, *Freedom and Reason* (London: Oxford University Press, 1963); William K. Frankena, *Ethics* (Englewood Cliffs, N.J.: Prentice-Hall, 1963); Kurt Baier, *The Moral Point of View* (New York: Random House, 1965); and John Wilson, Norman Williams, and Barry Sugarman, *Introduction to Moral Education* (Baltimore: Penguin, 1967). None of these interpretations is, however, identical to the one presented here.

17. Hare, in *Freedom and Reason*, provides a more thorough discussion of the point that "ought" implies "can." The converse, however, does not follow. That is, the possession of specific abilities to act (e.g., the ability to swim or to type) does not imply what action, if any, ought to be taken.

18. The ability to exert influence is not simply a function of learned skills, knowledge, attitudes, etc. People can be limited by physical disabilities, economic deprivation, incarceration, and other factors. This concept of moral agent does not suggest that persons restricted by such factors are less "moral" than persons not so restricted. It does suggest, however, that, to the extent that such factors deprive a person of asking what one ought to do, they also limit one's opportunity to function as a moral agent.

19. Even with more sophisticated knowledge of techniques of exerting influence, one might still have chosen to drop the matter if one felt, for example, that it could involve too much work or self-sacrifice. The point remains that, without such knowledge, the option to pursue certain convictions was not as readily available to the student.

20. Louis E. Raths, Merrill Harmin, and Sidney B. Simon, *Values and Teaching: Working with Values in the Classroom* (Columbus, Ohio: Charles E. Merrill, 1966).

21. Lawrence Kohlberg, "Stage and Sequence: The Cognitive-Developmental Approach to Socialization," in *Handbook of Socialization Theory and Research*, ed. David A. Goslin (Chicago: Rand McNally, 1969), and "From Is to Ought." See also Lawrence Kohlberg and Rochelle Meyer, "Development as the Aim of Education," *Harvard Educational Review*, 42 (No. 4, 1972), for a critique of the inculcation or "bag of virtues" approach, and Alan Lockwood, "A Critical View of Values Clarification," *Teachers College Record*, 77 (No. 1, 1975), 35-50, for a critique of the "values clarification" approach.

22. Fred M. Newmann, "Consent of the Governed and Citizenship Education in Modern America," *School Review*, 71 (No. 4, 1963).

23. Gregory Vlastos, "Justice and Equality," in *Social Justice*, ed. Richard B. Brandt (Englewood Cliffs, N.J.: Prentice-Hall, 1962); Michael Scriven, *Primary Philosophy* (New York: McGraw-Hill, 1966); Kohlberg, "From Is to Ought"; Rawls, *Theory of Justice*.

24. Some authors recognize justice as the central principle of morality and, in turn, equality as the central principle of justice. Others will link morality and equality more directly.

25. E.g., Dewey, *Democracy and Education*; Thomas L. Thorson, *The Logic of Democracy* (New York: Holt, Rinehart, and Winston, 1962).

26. In spite of general positive regard for the consent ideal, some would balk at the prospect of every citizen armed with actual ability to make an impact in public affairs. Would this lead to such massive and continuous participation that no stable policies could be made? Would public policy be formulated more impulsively, less rationally? Fears related to predictions of "excessive" participatory democracy are discussed in my *Education for Citizen Action*, pp. 65-68.

27. The objections are discussed in detail in my *Education for Citizen Action*.

28. Fred M. Newmann and Donald W. Oliver, *Clarifying Public Controversy: An Approach to Teaching Social Studies* (Boston: Little, Brown, 1970).

29. This concept of justice is based largely upon the recent philosophical work of Kohlberg ("From Is to Ought") and Rawls (*Theory of Justice*), who rely upon the work of earlier writers, especially Kant. Note that this represents a rejection of ethical relativism or the position that there can be no universally acceptable moral principles. Relativists tend to claim that moral principles are only subjective opinions that are culturally conditioned according to different societal values, and, since societies differ, there can be no universal, objectively verifiable values. All values or moral preferences should, therefore, be considered equally valid. The relativist position has been persuasively repudiated (see, e.g.,

Henry B. Veatch, *Rational Man: A Modern Interpretation of Aristotelian Ethics* [Bloomington: Indiana University Press, 1962]; Kohlberg and Mayer, "Development as the Aim of Education").

30. This point should not be interpreted as downgrading the many "unskilled," routine tasks that must be completed for successful social action efforts. Students, like any other participants, should bear their equal share of this work. If their time is spent *exclusively* in such tasks, however, it is unlikely to contribute to increased competence.

31. Newmann, *Education for Citizen Action*.

32. Dewey, *Experience and Education*.

33. Panel on Youth, *Youth: Transition to Adulthood*.

34. National Commission on the Reform of Secondary Education, *Reform of Secondary Education*; Task Force '74, *Adolescent, Other Citizens and Their High Schools*.

35. National Association of Secondary School Principals, *American Youth in the Mid-Seventies* and *25 Action Learning Schools*.

36. National Commission on Resources for Youth, *New Roles for Youth*.

37. Lawrence Kohlberg, "Moral Education for a Society in Transition," *Educational Leadership*, 33 (No. 1, 1975).

38. Todd Clark, *Education for Participation: A Development Guide for Secondary School Programs in Law and Public Affairs* (Los Angeles: Constitutional Rights Foundation, 1974); American Bar Association, *Law Related Education in America: Guidelines for the Future* (St. Paul, Minn.: West, 1975).

39. Newmann and Oliver, *Clarifying Public Controversy*; Donald W. Oliver and James P. Shaver, *Teaching Public Issues in the High School* (Logan: Utah State University Press, 1974; originally published by Houghton Mifflin in 1966).

40. A comprehensive program of this sort is described in Fred M. Newmann, Thomas A. Bertocci, and Ruthanne M. Landsness, *Skills in Citizen Action: An English-Social Studies Program for Secondary Schools* (Madison: Citizen Participation Curriculum Project, 225 North Mills Street, University of Wisconsin, 1977).

Aspy: **An Interpersonal Approach to Humanizing Education**

1. C. R. Rogers, *On Becoming a Person* (Boston: Houghton Mifflin, 1961).

2. R. R. Carkhuff, *Helping and Human Relations: A Primer for Lay and Professional Helpers*. Vol. 1: *Selection and Training*; Vol. II: *Practice and Research* (New York: Holt, Rinehart, and Winston, 1971).

3. This model and the two that follow it were drawn from the Human Resource Development paradigms proposed by R. R. Carkhuff. See his *The Development of Human Resources* (New York: Holt, Rinehart, and Winston, 1971).

4. D. N. Aspy et al., *Maintaining Reliability in a Longitudinal Study: Interim Report No. 1; Interpersonal Skills Training for Teachers: Interim Report No. 2; Response Surface Analysis: Interim Report No. 3; Research Summary—Effects of Training in Interpersonal Skills: Interim Report No. 4* (Monroe, La.: National Consortium for Humanizing Education, Northeast Louisiana University [National Institute of Mental Health Research Grant No. 5 PO 1 MH 19871], 1974).

Reports 1, 3, and 4 are abstracted in *Resources in Education* (October 1975), ERIC: ED 106730, ED 106732, ED 106733.

5. D. N. Aspy, *Toward a Technology for Humanizing Education* (Champaign, Ill.: Research Press Company, 1972).

6. N. A. Flanders, *Teacher Influence on Pupil Attitudes and Achievement.* U.S. Department of Health, Education, and Welfare, Cooperative Research Monograph No. 12 (Washington, D.C.: U.S. Government Printing Office, 1965).

7. M. D. Englehart, E. J. Furst, W. H. Hill, and D. R. Krathwohl, *A Taxonomy of Educational Objectives.* Handbook I: *The Cognitive Domain,* ed. B. S. Bloom (New York: Longmans, Green, 1956).

8. J. H. Buhler and D. N. Aspy, *Physical Health for Educators: A Book of Readings* (Denton: North Texas State University Press, 1975).

Mosher: **Education for Human Development**

1. Ralph Mosher and Norman Sprinthall, "Psychological Education in Secondary Schools," *American Psychologist,* 25 (October 1970), 911-924.

2. *John Dewey on Education: Selected Writings,* ed. Reginald D. Archambault (New York: Random House, 1964).

3. John Dewey, "The Need for a Philosophy of Education," *ibid.*

4. I should add that Dewey's position has recently been persuasively restated by Lawrence Kohlberg and Rochelle Mayer ("Development as the Aim of Education," *Harvard Educational Review,* 42 [No. 4, 1972], 449-496): "The stream of educational ideology which is still best termed progressive following Dewey ... holds that education should nourish the child's natural interaction with a developing society or environment ... development [is] a progression through invariant ordered sequential stages. The educational goal is the eventual attainment of a higher level or stage of development in adulthood, not merely the healthy functioning of the child at a present level .... This aim requires an educational environment that actively stimulates development through the presentation of resolvable but genuine problems or conflicts. For progressives, the organizing and developing force in the child's experience is the child's active thinking and thinking is stimulated by the problematic, by cognitive conflict. Educational experience makes the child think—think in ways which organize both cognition and emotion. The acquisition of "knowledge" is an active change in patterns of thinking brought about by experiential problem-solving situations."

5. Lawrence Kohlberg, "Humanistic and Cognitive-Developmental Perspectives on Psychological Education," *Counseling Psychologist,* 2 (No. 4, 1971), 3-82.

6. Everett Dulit, "Adolescent Thinking a la Piaget," *Journal of Youth and Adolescence,* 1 (No. 4, 1972), 281-301.

7. Lawrence Kohlberg, *Collected Papers on Moral Development and Moral Education* (Cambridge, Mass.: Laboratory of Human Development, 1973).

8. Mao Tse-tung, *Five Articles* (Peking: Foreign Language Press, 1972).

9. Mosher and Sprinthall, "Psychological Education in Secondary Schools"; Victor Atkins, "High School Students Who Teach: An Approach to Personal Learning," unpublished dissertation, Graduate School of Education, Harvard University, 1972; R. C. Dowell, "Adolescents as Peer Counselors: A Program for

Psychological Growth," unpublished dissertation, Graduate School of Education, Harvard University, 1971; Albert Griffin, "Teaching Counselor Education to Black Teenagers," unpublished dissertation, Graduate School of Education, Harvard University, 1972; Theodore Katz, "The Arts as a Vehicle for the Exploration of Personal Concerns," unpublished dissertation, Harvard University, 1972; G. Mager, "Improvisation Drama as a Way to Learn about Oneself," unpublished dissertation, Harvard University, 1972; Barbara Greenspan, "Facilitating Psychological Growth in Adolescents through Child Development Curricula," unpublished dissertation, Graduate School of Education, Harvard University, 1974.

10. Kohlberg, *Collected Papers on Moral Development and Moral Education*; Moshe Blatt, "Studies on the Effects of Classroom Discussions upon Children's Moral Development," unpublished dissertation, University of Chicago, 1970; Joseph Hickey, "The Effects of Guided Moral Discussion upon Youthful Offenders' Level of Moral Judgment," unpublished dissertation, School of Education, Boston University, 1972; Peter Scharf, "Moral Atmosphere and Intervention in the Prison: The Creation of a Participatory Community in Prison," unpublished dissertation, Graduate School of Education, Harvard University, 1973.

11. Patricia Grimes, "Teaching Moral Reasoning to Eleven Year Olds and Their Mothers: A Means of Promoting Moral Development," unpublished dissertation, School of Education, Boston University, 1974; Robert Lorish, "Teaching Counseling to Disadvantaged Young Adults," unpublished dissertation, School of Education, Boston University, 1974; Peter Mackie, "Teaching Counseling Skills to Low Achieving High School Students," unpublished dissertation, School of Education, Boston University, 1974; Louise Felton, "Teaching Counseling to Adolescents and Adults," unpublished dissertation, School of Education, Boston University, 1974; Paul Sullivan, "A Curriculum for Stimulating Moral Reasoning and Ego Development in Adolescents," unpublished dissertation, School of Education, Boston University, 1975; Diana Paolitto, "Role-Taking Opportunities for Early Adolescents: A Program in Moral Education," unpublished dissertation, School of Education, Boston University, 1975; Sheila Stanley, "A Curriculum to Affect the Moral Atmosphere of the Family and the Moral Development of Adolescents," unpublished dissertation, School of Education, Boston University, 1975.

12. V. L. Erickson, "Psychological Growth for Women: A Cognitive-Developmental Curriculum Intervention," unpublished dissertation, University of Minnesota, 1973; Kenneth Rustad, "Teaching Counseling Skills to Adolescents: A Cognitive-Developmental Approach to Psychological Education," unpublished dissertation, University of Minnesota, 1974; P. A. Schaeffer, "Moral Judgment: A Cognitive-Developmental Project in Psychological Education," unpublished dissertation, University of Minnesota, 1974; B. L. Hurt and N. A. Sprinthall, "Psychological and Moral Development for Teacher Education," *Journal of Moral Education*, 4 (No. 3, 1975).

13. Clive Beck, E. Sullivan, and N. Taylor, "Stimulating Transition to Postconventional Morality: The Pickering High School Study," *Interchange*, 3 (No. 4, 1972), 28-37.

14. Lawrence Kohlberg and Carol Gilligan, "The Adolescent as a Philos-

opher: The Discovery of the Self in a Postconventional World," *Daedalus*, 100 (No. 4, 1971), pp. 1051-1086.

15. Stanley, "Curriculum to Affect the Moral Atmosphere of the Family and of Adolescents."

16. Experimental, although by no means *educationally* definitive, studies indicate that stimulating the development of formal operational thinking through systematic intervention is extremely difficult (Deana Kuhn, "Inducing Development Experimentally: Comments on a Research Paradigm," *Developmental Psychology*, 10 [No. 5, 1974], 590-600; M. Schwebel, "Logical Thinking in College Freshmen," unpublished manuscript, Rutgers University, 1972). It is interesting that similar statements were made by developmental psychologists about both moral and ego development before the intensive educational interventions reported here were undertaken.

17. Anne Colby, Betsy Speicher, and Moshe Blatt, *Hypothetical Dilemmas for Use in Moral Discussions* (Cambridge, Mass.: Center for Moral Education, Harvard University, 1973); Alan Lockwood, *Moral Reasoning—The Value of Life* (Middletown, Conn.: American Educational Publications, 1972).

18. George H. Mead, "The Philosophies of Royce, James, and Dewey in Their American Setting," *International Journal of Ethics*, 40 (1929-30), 211-231.

19. Stanley, "Curriculum to Affect the Moral Atmosphere of the Family and the Moral Development of Adolescents."

20. Ralph Mosher, "The Brookline Moral Education Project: A Report of Year 1," unpublished report, Center for Moral Education, Harvard University, 1975.

Sergiovanni: **The Odyssey of Organizational Theory and Implications for Humanizing Education**

1. Talcott Parsons, *Structure and Process in Modern Societies* (New York: Free Press of Glencoe, 1960).

2. James D. Thompson, *Organizations in Action* (New York: McGraw-Hill, 1967).

3. W. Ross Ashby, *An Introduction to Cybernetics* (London: Chapman and Hall, 1956).

4. Frederick Taylor, *The Principles of Scientific Management* (New York: Harper and Brothers, 1911; reprinted by Harper and Row in 1945); *Papers on the Science of Administration*, ed. Luther Gulick and L. Urwick (New York: Institute of Public Administration, 1937); James D. Mooney and Allen C. Reilly, *Onward Industry* (New York: Harper and Brothers, 1939); Henri Fayol, *General and Industrial Management*, tr. Constance Storrs (London: Sir Isaac Pitman and Sons, 1949); Max Weber, "Bureaucracy," in *id.*, *Essays in Sociology*, tr. and ed. H. H. Gerth and C. W. Mills (New York: Oxford University Press, 1946; reprinted in Joseph Litterer, *Organizations: Structure and Behavior*, published by John Wiley in 1969), and *The Theory of Social and Economic Organization*, tr. A. M. Henderson and T. Parsons, ed. T. Parsons (New York: Free Press of Glencoe, 1947).

5. J. D. Thompson, *Organizations in Action.*
6. Herbert Simon, *Administrative Behavior: A Study of Decision-Making Processes in Administrative Organizations* (New York: Macmillan, 1945; 2d ed., 1957).
7. John March and Herbert Simon, *Organizations* (New York: John Wiley, 1958).
8. Simon, *Administrative Behavior*; March and Simon, *Organizations*; Richard Cyert and John March, *A Behavioral Theory of the Firm* (Englewood Cliffs, N.J.: Prentice-Hall, 1963); Michael Crozier, *The Bureaucratic Phenomenon* (Chicago: University of Chicago Press, 1964).
9. J. D. Thompson, *Organizations in Action.*
10. Raymond Callahan, *Education and the Cult of Efficiency* (Chicago: University of Chicago Press, 1962).
11. Taylor, *Principles of Scientific Management.*
12. *Ibid.*, p. 37.
13. Franklin Bobbitt, "The Supervision of City Schools: Some General Principles of Management Applied to the Problems of City-School Systems," in *Twelfth Yearbook of the National Society for the Study of Education* (Bloomington, Ill.: the Society, 1913), pp. 7-8.
14. Fayol, *General and Industrial Management.*
15. Gulick and Urwick, *Papers on the Science of Administration.*
16. Mooney and Reilly, *Onward Industry.*
17. Weber was a contemporary of Taylor and Fayol and completed his major works on bureaucracy in the 1920's. He wrote, however, as an intellectual in contrast to Taylor and Fayol, whose works were written from the perspective of practicing managers. E.g., Weber, "Bureaucracy," and *Theory of Social and Economic Organization.*
18. Weber, "Bureaucracy," p. 34.
19. R. Bendix, *Max Weber: An Intellectual Portrait* (New York: Doubleday, 1960), p. 421.
20. Weber, "Bureaucracy," p. 37.
21. Mason Haire, "The Concept of Power and the Concept of Man," in *Social Science Approaches to Business Behavior,* ed. George Strother (Homewood, Ill.: Dorsey Press, 1962), p. 176.
22. Douglas McGregor, *The Human Side of Enterprise* (New York: McGraw-Hill, 1958). McGregor viewed classical management (or Theory X) as being based on the following assumption:

MANAGEMENT PROPOSITIONS—THEORY X

1. Management is responsible for organizing the elements of productive enterprise—money, materials, equipment, people—in the interest of economic [educational] ends.
2. With respect to people, this is a process of directing their efforts, motivating them, controlling their actions, modifying their behavior to fit the needs of the organization.
3. Without this active intervention by management, people would be passive—even resistant—to organizational needs. They must therefore be persuaded, rewarded, punished, controlled—their activities must be directed. This is management's task—in

managing subordinate managers or workers. We often sum it up by saying that management consists of getting things done through other people.

Behind this conventional theory are several additional beliefs—less explicit, but widespread:

4. The average man is by nature indolent—he works as little as possible.
5. He lacks ambition, dislikes responsibility, prefers to be led.
6. He is inherently self-centered, indifferent to organizational needs.
7. He is by nature resistant to change.
8. He is gullible, not very bright, the ready dupe of the charlatan and the demagogue.

23. Chester Barnard, *Functions of the Executive* (Cambridge, Mass.: Harvard University Press, 1938).

24. Fritz Roethlisberger and William Dickson, *Management and the Worker* (Cambridge, Mass.: Harvard University Press, 1939).

25. *Ibid.*

26. Elton Mayo, *The Social Problems of an Industrial Civilization* (Boston: Harvard Graduate School of Business, 1945).

27. Charles Faber and Gilbert Shearron, *Elementary School Administration Theory and Practice* (New York: Holt, Rinehart, and Winston, 1970).

28. James Hosic, "The Cooperative Group Plan of Organization," *School and Society*, 31 (January 1930).

29. Abraham Maslow, *Motivation and Personality* (New York: Harper and Row, 1954); McGregor, *Human Side of Enterprise*; Chris Argyris, *Personality and Organization* (New York: Harper and Row, 1957); Warren Bennis, *Changing Organizations* (New York: McGraw-Hill, 1966); Rensis Likert, *New Patterns of Management* (New York: McGraw-Hill, 1961), and *The Human Organization* (New York: McGraw-Hill, 1967).

30. Maslow, *Motivation and Personality*; McGregor, *Human Side of Enterprise*.

31. Argyris, *Personality and Organization*; *id.*, *Integrating the Individual and the Organization* (New York: John Wiley, 1964); *id.*, "Personality and Organization Theory Revisited," *Administrative Science Quarterly*, 18 (No. 2, 1973); Jacob Getzels and Egon Guba, "Social Behavior and Administrative Process," *School Review*, 65 (Winter 1957); Andrew Halpin, *Theory and Research in Administration* (New York: Macmillan, 1967).

32. The practices based on human relations theory, however, often tended to resemble those of classical management with the added dimension of a series of appeasement policies for workers to encourage their cooperation. Sugar-coated classical management might be an apt description of these practices.

33. Frederick Herzberg, Bernard Mausner, and Barbara Snyderman, *The Motivation to Work* (New York: John Wiley, 1959); Thomas Sergiovanni and Fred D. Carver, *The New School Executive: A Theory of Administration* (New York: Dodd, Mead, 1973).

34. Thomas J. Sergiovanni, "Human Resources Supervision," in *Professional Supervision for Professional Teachers*, ed. *id.* (Washington, D.C.: Association for Supervision and Curriculum Development, 1975).

35. Raymond E. Miles, "Human Relations or Human Resources?" *Harvard Business Review*, 43 (No. 4, 1965); Mason Haire, Edwin Ghiselli, and Lyman

Porter, *Managerial Thinking: An International Study* (New York: John Wiley, 1966).

36. Likert, *New Patterns of Management.*

37. Halpin, *Theory and Research in Administration*; Mathew Miles, "Planned Change and Organizational Health: Figure and Ground," in *Change Processes in the Public Schools* (Eugene, Ore.: Center for the Advanced Study of Educational Administration, 1965).

38. Likert, *Human Organization.*

39. Thomas Sergiovanni and Robert Starratt, *Emerging Patterns of Supervision: Human Perspectives* (New York: McGraw-Hill, 1971).

40. Tom Burns and G. M. Stalker, *The Management of Innovation* (London: Tavistock Publications, 1961).

41. Richard De Charms, *Personal Causation* (New York: Academic Press, 1968).

42. Abraham Maslow, "Some Basic Propositions of a Growth and Self-Actualizing Psychology," in *Perceiving, Behaving, Becoming,* ed. Arthur Combs (Washington, D.C.: Association for Supervision and Curriculum Development, 1962).

43. James Macdonald, "An Image of Man: The Learner Himself," in *Individualized Instruction,* ed. Ronald Doll (Washington, D.C.: Association for Supervision and Curriculum Development, 1964).

44. Thomas J. Sergiovanni, "Financial Incentives and Teacher Accountability: Are We Paying for the Wrong Thing?" *Educational Administration Quarterly,* 11 (No. 2, 1975).

45. *Accountability in Education,* ed. Leon Lessinger (Worthington, Ohio: Charles A. Jones Publishing Co., 1971). The cottage-level imagery is a popular one among advocates of neoscientific management as they criticize ideas concerning behavioral theory. Cottage industries tend to produce products that are not uniform in quality and a style of work in which the artisan or craftsman is more likely to interact with the product under development, seeking to discover and bring out its unique characteristics. Though few theorists of neoscientific management would prefer assembly line paintings, Indian jewelry, or furniture over those crafted in cottage industries, in education they seem clearly to prefer bland and standardized products.

46. Thomas J. Sergiovanni and David Elliott, *Educational and Organizational Leadership in Elementary Schools* (Englewood Cliffs, N.J.: Prentice-Hall, 1975).

47. Burns and Stalker, *Management of Innovation.*

48. Weber, *Theory of Social and Economic Organization.*

49. Jerald Hage, "An Axiomatic Theory of Organizations," *Administrative Science Quarterly,* 10 (No. 3, 1965).

50. Weber, *Theory of Social and Economic Organization*; Barnard, *Functions of the Executive*; Victor Thompson, *Modern Organizations* (New York: Knopf, 1961).

51. The eight organizational means and ends variables can be grouped into two constellations: a smaller one containing complexity, adaptability, and satisfaction; and a larger one containing stratification, formalization, centralization,

production, and efficiency. When one variable in any of the two constellations changes, each other variable in the same constellation changes similarly, but opposite changes can be expected in variables of the other constellation. By assuming interdependency in a fairly steady state and by applying the rules of syllogism, each of the variables can be related to the other. (Hage, "Axiomatic Theory of Organizations.")

52. Political science is, of course, a broad field of study, and here I refer primarily to those within this field who are behaviorally inclined (Arnold Tannenbaum, *Control in Organizations* [New York: McGraw-Hill, 1968]; and Crozier, *Bureaucratic Phenomenon,* for example). Building upon their interests in the world of politics, pressure groups, and legislative groups and borrowing heavily from game theory (M. Shubik, *Strategy and Market Structure* [New York: John Wiley, 1959]) concepts, this group turned their attention to organizations. They became ardent students of organizational legitimacy, conflicting goals, and techniques for preserving, building, and using power in organizations.

53. Simon, *Administrative Behavior*; March and Simon, *Organizations*; Cyert and March, *Behavioral Theory of the Firm.*

54. March and Simon, *Organizations.*

55. Simon, *Administrative Behavior,* pp. 108-109.

56. See, for example, Charles A. Beard, *The Nature of the Social Sciences* (New York: Charles Scribner, 1934). Beard argues that all of the social sciences are ethical sciences inescapably concerned with good and better. For a discussion of educational administration as an ethical science, see the introduction and the first chapter of Sergiovanni and Carver, *New School Executive.*

57. Contrast Simon's views with those of Broudy, who maintains: "The educator, however, deals with nothing but values—human beings who are clusters and constellations of value potentials. Nothing human is really alien to the educational enterprise and there is, therefore, something incongruous about educational administrators evading fundamental value conflicts." Harry S. Broudy, "Conflicts in Values," in *Educational Administration Philosophy in Action,* ed. Robert Ohm and William Monohan (Norman: University of Oklahoma Press, 1965), p. 52.

58. Simon, *Administrative Behavior,* p. 253.

59. *Ibid.*; Charles Perrow, *Organizational Analysis: A Sociological View* (London: Tavistock Institute, 1970).

60. March and Simon, *Organizations.*

61. M. Scott Myers, *Every Employee a Manager* (New York: McGraw-Hill, 1971).

62. De Charms, *Personal Causation.*

63. Cyert and March, *Behavioral Theory of the Firm.*

64. F. E. Emery and E. L. Trist, "The Causal Texture of Organizational Environments," *Human Relations,* 18 (No. 1, 1965).

65. Burns and Stalker, *Management of Innovation.*

66. *Ibid.,* p. 96.

67. Paul Lawrence and Jay Lorsch, "Differentiation and Integration in Complex Organizations," *Administrative Science Quarterly,* 12 (No. 1, 1967).

68. Richard Hall, "Intraorganizational Structure Variation: Application of the Bureaucratic Model," *Administrative Science Quarterly*, 7 (No. 3, 1962).
69. Joan Woodward, *Industrial Organization: Theory and Practice* (London: Oxford University Press, 1965).
70. J. D. Thompson, *Organizations in Action*, p. 16.
71. *Ibid.*, p. 18.
72. Maslow, "Some Basic Propositions of a Growth and Self-Actualizing Psychology."
73. Macdonald, "An Image of Man."
74. Maslow, "Some Basic Propositions of a Growth and Self-Actualizing Psychology."
75. Macdonald, "An Image of Man."
76. Willard Waller, *The Sociology of Teaching* (New York: John Wiley, 1932).
77. Sergiovanni and Carver, *New School Executive*.

Feinberg: **A Critical Analysis of the Social and Economic Limits to the Humanizing of Education**

1. For a more elaborate treatment of these remarks by W. T. Harris, see my *Reason and Rhetoric: The Intellectual Foundations of Twentieth Century Liberal Educational Policy* (New York: John Wiley, 1975), chapter on e.
2. For an example of the first kind of study, see Melvin L. Kohn, *Class and Conformity: A Study in Values* (Homewood, Ill.: Dorsey Press, 1969). For an example of the second study, see Walter Brandeis and Basil Bernstein, *Selection and Control Teacher Ratings of Children in the Infant School* (London: Routledge and Kegan Paul, 1974).
3. See Ray C. Rist, "Student Social Class and Teacher Expectations: The Self-Fulfilling Prophecy in Ghetto Education," *Harvard Educational Review*, 40 (August 1970), 411-451.
4. See Harry Braverman, *Labor and Monopoly Capital* (New York: Monthly Review Press, 1974).
5. For a general discussion of the role that schools play in teaching functions like these, see Robert Dreeben, *On What Is Learned in School* (Reading, Mass.: Addison-Wesley, 1968).
6. For an elaboration of this concept, see my "Educational Development under Two Conflicting Models of Equality," *Theory and Society*, 2 (Summer 1975), 183-210.
7. Johan Galtung *et al.*, *Educational Growth and Educational Disparity, Current Surveys and Research in Statistics* (Paris: UNESCO, 1974).
8. *Journal of the American Medical Association*, 210 (No. 8, 1969), 1494.
9. Both of these items are found in the Wechsler examination. For a treatment of this subject that focuses more on the early testers, see Clarence Karier, "Testing for Order and Control," in *Roots of Crisis*, ed. *id.*, P. C. Violas, and J. Spring (Chicago: Rand McNally, 1974).
10. For a more detailed look at this difference, see my *Reason and Rhetoric*, Chapter 4.

11. See Braverman, *Labor and Monopoly Capital*.

Roebuck: **Humanistic Education from an HRD Viewpoint**
  1. R. R. Carkhuff, *The Development of Human Resources* (New York: Holt, Rinehart and Winston, 1971).
  2. The publications from which entries were classified are: J. T. Canfield and M. Phillips, "Humanisticography," *Media and Methods*, 9 (September 1972), 41-56; H. C. Lyon, Jr., *Learning to Feel—Feeling to Learn* (Columbus, Ohio: Charles E. Merrill, 1971); *Activities and Exercises for Affective Education*, ed. L. Thayer and K. D. Beeler, *Annual Handbook of the Special Interest Group, Affective Aspects of Education* (Washington, D.C.: American Educational Research Association, 1975).
  3. A. W. Combs and D. Snygg, *Individual Behavior* (New York: Harper and Row, 1959); H. Ginott, *Teacher and Child* (New York: Macmillan, 1972); W. Glasser, *Schools without Failure* (New York: Harper and Row, 1969); C. Rogers, *Freedom to Learn* (Columbus, Ohio: Charles E. Merrill, 1969); A. Maslow, "Some Educational Implications of the Humanistic Psychologies," *Harvard Educational Review*, 38 (No. 4, 1968).
  4. D. N. Aspy and F. N. Roebuck, *Research Summary—Effects of Training in Interpersonal Skills: Interim Report No. 4* (Monroe, La.: National Consortium for Humanizing Education, Northeast Louisiana University [National Institute of Mental Health Research Grant No. 5 PO 1 MH 19871], 1974). Abstracted in *Resources in Education* (October 1975), ERIC: ED 106733.
  5. *Physical Health for Educators: A Book of Readings*, ed. J. H. Buhler and D. N. Aspy (Denton: North Texas State University Press, 1975).
  6. F. N. Roebuck and D. N. Aspy, *Response Surface Analysis: Interim Report No. 3* (Monroe, La.: National Consortium for Humanizing Education, Northeast Louisiana University [National Institute of Mental Health Research Grant No. 5 PO 1 MH 19871], 1974). Abstracted in *Resources in Education* (October 1975), ERIC: ED 106732.
  7. K. Cooper, "Executives on an Exercise Kick," *Business Week* (June 3, 1972), 44.

Apple: **Humanism and the Politics of Educational Argumentation**
  1. George Novack, "Introduction," in *Existentialism versus Marxism*, ed. *id.* (New York: Delta Books, 1966), p. 9.
  2. Zygmunt Bauman, "Modern Times, Modern Marxism," in *Marxism and Sociology*, ed. Peter Berger (New York: Appleton-Century-Crofts, 1969), p. 10.
  3. Raymond Williams, "Introduction," in Lucien Goldmann, *Racine* (Cambridge, Eng.: Rivers Press, 1972), p. xiv.
  4. Jürgen Habermas, *Theory and Practice* (Boston: Beacon Press, 1973), pp. 10-19.
  5. Claus Mueller, *The Politics of Communication* (New York: Oxford University Press, 1973), p. 113.
  6. For an analysis of this tradition, see Michael Harrington, *Socialism* (New York: Bantam Books, 1972), and Ludwig Kolakowski, *Toward a Marxist Humanism* (New York: Grove Press, 1968).

7. Michael F. D. Young, "An Approach to the Study of Curricula as Socially Organized Knowledge," in *Knowledge and Control*, ed. *id*. (London: Collier-Macmillan, 1971), p. 32.

8. Raymond Williams, *The Long Revolution* (London: Chatto and Windus, 1961), pp. 298-299. See also Bertell Ollman, *Alienation: Marx's Conception of Man in Capitalist Societies* (London: Cambridge University Press, 1971).

9. Williams, "Introduction," p. xxi.

10. See Michael W. Apple, "The Process and Ideology of Valuing in Educational Settings," in *Educational Evaluation: Analysis and Responsibility*, ed. Michael W. Apple, Michael J. Subkoviak, and Henry S. Lufler, Jr. (Berkeley, Calif.: McCutchan Publishing Corp., 1974).

11. Charles Tesconi and Van Cleve Morris, *The Anti-Man Culture: Bureautechnocracy and the Schools* (Urbana: University of Illinois Press, 1972).

12. Dwayne Huebner, "The Tasks of the Curricular Theorist," paper presented at the Association for Supervision and Curriculum Development, March 1968. See also the penetrating discussion in Murray Edelman, *The Symbolic Uses of Politics* (Urbana: University of Illinois Press, 1964).

13. See Samuel Bowles, "Unequal Education and the Reproduction of the Social Division of Labor," in *Schooling in a Corporate Society*, ed. Martin Carnoy (New York: David McKay, 1972), pp. 36-64.

14. See, e.g., Nigel Harris, *Beliefs in Society: The Problem of Ideology* (London: C. A. Watts, 1968), and Peter Berger and Thomas Luckmann, *The Social Construction of Reality* (New York: Doubleday, 1966).

15. I say quasi-scientific here because in-depth analyses of the logic-in-use of scientific activity of the best sort reveal many fewer of the characteristics that Tesconi and Morris ascribe to it. For cogent treatments of the complex blend of skill, aesthetic sensitivity, and personal value in science worthy of its name, see Michael Polanyi, *Personal Knowledge* (New York: Harper and Row, 1962), and Jacob Bronowski, *The Identity of Man* (New York: Natural History Press, 1966).

16. Martin Jay, *The Dialectical Imagination* (Boston: Little, Brown, 1973), p. 62.

17. This may be caused by our own unfortunate continual misinterpretation of Marx as a thoroughgoing economic determinist. We tend to forget that Marx was also a poet. See Bertell Ollman, *Alienation: Marx's Conception of Man in Capitalist Society* (London: Cambridge University Press, 1971).

18. Trent Schroyer, *The Critique of Domination* (New York: George Braziller, 1973), p. 172.

19. Robert L. Heilbroner, "Men at Work: A Review of Harry Braverman, *Labor and Monopoly Capital: The Degradation of Work in the Twentieth Century*," *New York Review of Books*, XXI (January 23, 1975), 8.

20. Cf. Michael W. Apple, "Common-Sense Categories and Curriculum Thought," in *Schools in Search of Meaning*, ed. James B. Macdonald and Esther Zaret (Washington, D.C.: Association for Supervision and Curriculum Development, 1975).

21. Clarence Karier, "Ideology and Evaluation," in *Educational Evaluation*, ed. Apple, Subkoviak, and Lufler, pp. 279-320.

22. Jean-Paul Sartre, *Search for a Method* (New York: Vintage Books, 1963).

23. For a more extensive discussion, see *Schooling and the Rights of Children*, ed. Vernon F. Haubrich and Michael W. Apple (Berkeley, Calif.: McCutchan Publishing Corp., 1975).

24. This is not just a problem for Tesconi and Morris, but also for such supposedly Marxist critics as Illich. See, e.g., Michael W. Apple, "Ivan Illich and Deschooling Society: The Politics of Slogan Systems," in *Social Forces and Schooling*, ed. Nobuo Shimahara and Adam Scrupski (New York: David McKay, 1975).

25. Trent Schroyer, "Towards a Critical Theory for Advanced Industrial Society," *Recent Sociology II*, ed. Hans Peter Dreitzel (New York: Macmillan, 1970), pp. 210-234.

26. Herbert Gintis and Samuel Bowles, "The Contradictions of Liberal Educational Reform," in *Work, Technology, and Education*, ed. Walter Feinberg and Henry Rosemont, Jr. (Urbana: University of Illinois Press, 1975), pp. 120, 133.

27. See also Newmann's provocative book, *Education for Citizen Action* (Berkeley, Calif.: McCutchan Publishing Corp., 1975).

28. See, e.g., Seymour Sarason, *The Culture of the School and the Problem of Change* (Boston: Allyn & Bacon, 1971).

29. In taking this position I am drawing upon the conception of rationality found in the chapter on "Traditional and Critical Theory," in Max Horkheimer, *Critical Theory* (New York: Herder and Herder, 1972), pp. 188-243, and Trent Schroyer, "The Dialectical Foundations of Critical Theory," *Telos*, XII (Summer 1972), pp. 93-114.

O'Kane: **The Fourth Face of Humanism**

1. Quoted from Ruth Nanda Anshen, "Perspectives in Humanism, the Future of Tradition," introductory essay to Moses Hadas, *The Living Tradition*, ed. Ruth N. Anshen (New York: New American Library, 1967), p. vii.

2. *Ibid.*, p. xii.

3. Howard Mumford Jones, *American Humanism* (New York: Harper and Brothers, 1957), p. 28.

4. *Ibid.*, pp. 94-95.

5. Catherine Roberts, "The Three Faces of Humanism," an occasional paper of the Farmington Institute, Oxford, England, and revised and abridged from an article under the same title in *Tract* (March 1975).

6. H. and H. A. Frankfort, John Wilson, Thorkild Jacobsen, *Before Philosophy* (Baltimore: Penguin Books, 1973), p. 12.

7. *The Republic of Plato*, tr. Francis Macdonald Cornford, Book V, quoted from translator's notes in introductory section to chapter xviii (London: Oxford University Press, 1971), p. 175.

8. Gregory Baum, *Man Becoming* (New York: Seabury Press, 1970).

9. Abraham J. Heschel, *God in Search of Man* (New York: Meridian Books, 1961).

Macdonald: Toward a Platform for Humanistic Education
  1. John K. Galbraith, *The New Industrial State* (2d rev. ed., Boston: Houghton Mifflin, 1972).
  2. Harry S. Broudy, *The Real World of the Public Schools* (New York: Harcourt Brace Jovanovich, 1972).
  3. Elliot Eisner, "The Curriculum Field Today: Where We Are, Where We Were, Where We Are Going," paper presented at the Milwaukee Curriculum Theory Conference, Milwaukee, Wisc., November 1976.
  4. Joseph Schwab, *The Practical: A Language for Curriculum* (Washington, D.C.: National Education Association, 1970), see esp. p. 5.
  5. Paulo Freire, *Pedagogy of the Oppressed* (New York: Herder and Herder, 1970).
  6. Stephen Lukes, *Individualism* (New York: Harper and Row, 1973), esp. p. 89.
  7. Gibson Winter, *Being Free* (London: Collier-Macmillan, Ltd., 1970).